Drug War Zone

THE WILLIAM & BETTYE NOWLIN SERIES
in Art, History, and Culture of the Western Hemisphere

Drug War Zone

Frontline Dispatches from the Streets
of El Paso and Juárez

HOWARD CAMPBELL

University of Texas Press ❧ *Austin*

Fourth paperback printing, 2011

An excerpt from *Weed: Adventures of a Dope Smuggler*, by Jerry Kamstra, is reproduced with the permission of the author.

Requests for permission to reproduce material from this work should be sent to:
Permissions
University of Texas Press
P.O. Box 7819
Austin, TX 78713-7819
www.utexas.edu/utpress/about/bpermission.html

♾ The paper used in this book meets the minimum requirements of ANSI/NISO Z39.48-1992 (R1997) (Permanence of Paper).

Library of Congress Cataloging-in-Publication Data

Campbell, Howard, 1957–
    Drug war zone : frontline dispatches from the streets of El Paso and Juárez / Howard Campbell. — 1st ed.
        p.   cm. — (The William and Bettye Nowlin series in art, history, and culture of the Western Hemisphere)
    Includes bibliographical references and index.
    ISBN 978-0-292-72126-5 (cloth : alk. paper) — ISBN 978-0-292-72179-1 (pbk. : alk. paper)
    1. Drug traffic—Mexican-American border region—Case studies. 2. Drug control—Mexican-American border region—Case studies. 3. Drug traffic—Social aspects—Texas—El Paso—Case studies. 4. Drug traffic—Social aspects—Mexico—Ciudad Juárez—Case studies. I. Title.
    HV5831.M46C36 2009
    363.450972'16—dc22
                                                            2009021911

Contents

Introduction

On July 2, 2007, Joaquín "El Chapo" Guzmán, a drug lord and the most wanted man in Mexico, reportedly married a woman from La Angostura, Durango, in a public ceremony. Though already married twice, Guzmán fell in love with eighteen-year-old Emma Coronel—described by a reporter as being white skinned and having a well-formed body—who had recently been named queen of the 2007 Coffee and Guava Fair (Dávila 2007b, 7). Emma had met Chapo at a village dance. Before he arrived at the wedding, a small army of heavily armed, masked, and black-clad bodyguards on 200 two-seater all-terrain motorcycles took over the town in what must have appeared like a scene out of a James Bond movie.

While the bodyguards protected all ten entrances to the village, a *narcocorrido* band, Los Canelos de Durango, armed with gold-handled pistols, arrived in a small plane. Six more planes touched down, from one of which El Chapo emerged, dressed in his customary jeans, vest, and baseball cap, an AK-47 *cuerno de chivo* (goat horn) rifle strapped across his chest and a pistol that matched his clothes attached to his belt. Helicopters circled overhead as other planes landed and unloaded innumerable cases of whiskey, crates of weapons (grenades, machine guns, more AK-47s, etc.), and more security guards dressed in green military fatigues and sporting bullet-proof vests with police-style radios clipped to their chests. According to the reporter who described the event, Chapo's entourage was more ostentatious than that of a Mexican president (Dávila 2007b, 6–11).

By now, such flamboyant events, as well as stories about jetliners stuffed to the gills with cocaine, narco-manifestos attacking the government, pop singers slaughtered for offending drug bosses, and safe houses packed with millions of dollars in small bills or numerous beheaded bodies, have become a regular feature of the Mexican news. Cross-border drug trafficking and the "war on drugs" are also critical U.S. foreign-policy and domestic-police issues.[1] Yet the inside stories of the people involved in the drug world remain opaque, seldom explored by journalists or social scientists. There is much word-of-mouth folklore but little reliable data about the lives of drug traffickers and their governmental adversaries on the U.S.-Mexico border.

This book attempts to break the academic silence and apply an anthropological lens to a much-neglected topic. Modeled on Studs Terkel's classic portrayal of working Americans, *Working* (1974), my study explores in detail the personal histories and careers of various people involved on both sides of the drug war.[2] Based on deep access to the drug-trafficking world, this ethnography examines border narco-trafficking through the eyes, and in the words, of firsthand participants. In-depth interviews and oral histories form the corpus of the text. These portraits put a human face on issues that are often handled sensationally by news media or shrouded in gossip, myth, and stereotype.

Ethnographic Encounters

Customs and Border Protection officers made 10 marijuana seizures at El Paso's international bridges Wednesday, or one every two to four hours, agency officials said.
EL PASO TIMES, JULY 12, 2007

I first learned about drug trafficking while living in Mexico City in the early 1980s. At that time, I read about the Alberto Sicilia Falcón and Miguel Ángel Félix Gallardo drug organizations—the first big cartels.[3] The public suddenly became aware of the heroic adventures of the flamboyant narcotics cop Florentino Ventura and the brutality and drug-related corruption of Mexico City police chief Arturo Durazo. In 1984, turncoat secret police, allied with organized crime, gunned down the highly respected journalist Manuel Buendía in broad daylight near the touristy Zona Rosa section of the city. The following year, Mexican drug traffickers sadistically tortured and murdered revered U.S. Drug Enforcement Administration (DEA) agent Kiki Camarena (Shannon 1988). The intricate webs of criminals, police, and corrupt government officials seriously unraveled during the presidency of Carlos

Salinas (1988–1994), when the Gulf, Sinaloa, Tijuana, and Juárez cartels boomed (Bowden 2002).[4]

Before I moved to El Paso from the Midwest in 1990, I devoured *Drug Lord* (1998) by Terrence Poppa, a shocking account of the heroin- and cocaine-smuggling empire built by Pablo Acosta in the Ojinaga-Presidio area close to El Paso. Fearing for his life, Poppa left the area after the book's publication. When I got to the Mexican border, I casually met a resident of Ojinaga who knew Acosta and his partner, a then-unknown Amado Carrillo Fuentes. In El Paso, I immediately heard about and met members of the Chagra family of El Paso, some of whom the government linked to a major international drug business and the killing of federal judge John Wood of San Antonio (Cartwright 1998). At that time in Ciudad Juárez, the megacartel of Carrillo Fuentes began to supplant the large narcotics organization founded by Rafael Muñoz Talavera, owner of a trendy El Paso shopping center and a lavish rural mansion, and Rafael Aguilar, a federal police commandant in Ciudad Juárez. Before he was murdered by the Carrillo Fuentes family, Muñoz Talavera had smuggled at least seventy-seven tons of cocaine through El Paso–Juárez to California (Lupsha 1991, 58).

In my first class as a professor at the University of Texas–El Paso (UTEP), I had a student who, as a U.S. immigration officer, had facilitated the passage of a large quantity of the twenty-one tons of Muñoz Talavera's cocaine that was seized in the Los Angeles area in the largest drug confiscation in American history (Bowden 2002); the student was later convicted of the crime. Subsequently, I encountered close friends of both founding families of the Juárez cartel. Each day, faster than I could fully assimilate, I became immersed in a border environment that was an ideal setting for research on drug trafficking.

I did not intend to write a book about drug trafficking, the study of which was just a hobby. The topic seemed too dangerous, strictly off-limits. Yet the longer I lived in the El Paso–Ciudad Juárez border area, the more I realized I could not avoid the issue. Regardless of where I resided—in wealthy, upper-middle-class or working-class neighborhoods—major trafficking families or stash houses were located nearby. At one point I lived so close to the border that my neighbors could hear gunshots from shootouts between *narcotraficantes* and Mexican cops. Every day the local television channels recounted a litany of drug busts and accounts of dead bodies found in stew pots or severed heads tossed onto a dance-hall floor by Mexican drug-trafficking organizations. I lectured about the drug trade in my classes, and students later came forward and privately confided in me their stories of being involved in the business, of relatives who were imprisoned, or of their parents' jobs as immigration, customs, or Border Patrol agents on the frontlines of antidrug initiatives.[5]

The vendor on the corner regaled me with tales about marijuana selling while he made me burritos. He also used and sold heroin and cocaine, as did many close and casual acquaintances. DEA agents, or narcs, lived nearby, as did gang members associated with the Cártel de Juárez. Many of my friends and even my in-laws were well connected on both sides of the drug-war divide. On the streets, in bars, or at birthday parties, cocaine and marijuana abounded, and the fancy trucks, gaudy *norteño* or *chero* clothing, and other symbols and paraphernalia of the drug business were also on display. Juárez radio stations heard all over El Paso trumpeted *narcocorridos*, melodramatic anthems celebrating drug smuggling (Campbell 2004). While walking along the avenues of Juárez, I passed enormous narco-mansions and numerous bars, restaurants, and other businesses owned by drug capos.[6] During lunch at a Mexican restaurant near my university office (from which I can see Ciudad Juárez), I could overhear conversations of DEA and FBI agents. In the parking lot, the sharp desert sunlight reflected off the shiny hoods of Border Patrol trucks.

I finally decided that I had to take advantage of this opportunity to study ethnographically an important social issue unfolding all around me. The result is this volume of oral histories of drug traffickers, antidrug officials, and others whose lives have been deeply marked by the drug trade. Lengthy, in-depth interviews with direct participants focused on two issues: their personal histories before their involvement with the drug world, and their lives in what I call the "drug war zone." I corroborated these accounts and details with other sources of information: different informants, newspaper stories, agency reports, expert opinion from knowledgeable journalists and analysts, and my own knowledge of the border drug trade, gleaned from seventeen years spent in El Paso.

The short introductions to each account contextualize the life stories within larger social, cultural, political, and economic processes. Because of the dangerous and secretive nature of the subject matter, my interview pool resulted from a snowball sampling technique rather than a random sample. To put it simply, I exploited every available opportunity to interview key players in the drug world. The issue of drug trafficking, because of the illegality and taboos associated with it, is inherently ambiguous and multilayered. As Macdonald (2007, 251) observes: "Scorpion tales [that is, stories about drugs] remind us that much of our taken for granted knowledge and understanding of drugs and drug users, as well as drug policies, is frequently flawed and based on uncertainties and unresolved paradoxes." My analytical comments, the oral histories, and the interviews take this into account: there is an endless interplay between facts and narratives, whether the issue is drug-trafficking folklore or government reports of drug busts or "victories" in the war on drugs.

Nonetheless, my approach is not primarily relativistic; that is, when I can verify to a reasonable degree my ethnographic data, I make that clear. Yet in other cases I am more skeptical. Is there really a drug epidemic ruining elements of our society, as the U.S. government has proclaimed for eighty years (see, for example, Reinarman and Levine 2004)? Does U.S. Customs actually confiscate as many tons of coke as it claims to? Are we actually "winning" the war on drugs?

Without such a critical view, one can easily fall into the trap of "seeing like a state," thus aping the perspectives of the powerful (Scott 1999). Yet, as West and Sanders (2003) have pointed out, the modern world, despite the efforts of powerful state and business interests to encourage free trade and transparency, is riddled with mystery, obscurity, and arbitrary power—a condition that lends itself to conspiracy theories. This book cannot clarify all the many opacities existing in the secretive drug-trafficking world or the equally secretive war on drugs, but it can contribute to a growing dialogue about the effects of drugs and anti-drug policies on society.

I oppose the U.S. war on drugs for reasons that will be discussed in detail below. Moreover, I have more compassion for common workers in the drug trade—who, above all, work to make a living and provide for their families—than for Washington policy wonks or well-paid drug-war bureaucrats, who are often insulated from the dirty work in the streets but whose actions and decisions may negatively affect hundreds or thousands of families, especially those whose members have been incarcerated for selling drugs.[7] One could be equally critical of everyday drug smugglers, yet one could also argue that they engage—at least in marijuana commerce—in victimless crimes.[8]

But I am also critical of the drug kingpins who routinely order the brutal murders of dozens of people, and I am well aware of the social harm caused by heroin, cocaine, and methamphetamine addiction. With these issues in mind, it is my hope that the ethnographic portraits and analytical points presented here can help us rethink and rework policies and practices concerned with drugs so as to lessen the harm already being done, whether from drug abuse, incarceration for drug crimes, or violence associated with drug-trafficking groups (Macdonald 2007).

The material that follows provides theoretical and analytical tools for conceptualizing what I call the "drug war zone." Readers who are more interested in Mexican drug-trafficking culture than in anthropological literature may want to skip this discussion and proceed directly to the section "El Paso–Juárez in the Drug War Zone," later in this chapter.

The Mexican-American Drug War Zone: Theoretical Issues

I can't even produce a metaphor for the drug world anymore. I don't even like the phrase the drug world since the phrase implies that it is a separate world.
CHARLES BOWDEN, *DOWN BY THE RIVER: DRUGS, MONEY, MURDER, AND FAMILY* (2002)

I use the term "drug war zone" to refer to the cultural world of drug traffickers ("narco-culture") and the law-enforcement agents who combat drug trafficking. It is the transnational, fluid cultural space in which contending forces battle over the meaning, value, and control of drugs. Drug war zone (henceforth DWZ) is an orienting frame that helps explain how political and cultural connections and separations are materially and discursively produced and reproduced through drug-trafficking and law-enforcement activities. This zone is especially prominent and physically observable on the U.S.-Mexico border, but the term also applies to any place or situation in which drug traffickers, drug users, and antidrug narcs confront, avoid, or attempt to subvert one another. I would argue that such battles have been a nearly permanent part of world culture since the advent of agriculture. As long as humans have gathered or harvested and consumed mind-altering, transformative substances, such substances have been endowed with deep symbolic power and enmeshed within intricate prisms of meaning, especially those related to sacred or profane properties (Douglas 1978) or to complex webs of social and economic power (Courtwright 2001; Davis 1997; Dobkin de Rios 1984; Furst 1972; Schaefer and Furst 1997).[9]

The DWZ is thus a theoretical concept that refers not only to a historically contingent, constructed geographical location (Gupta and Ferguson 1997) but also to a mental place and a symbolic domain—similar in Foucauldian terms to the dialectic between "real society" and "heterotopia" (Foucault 1967)—that connect drug producers, drug smugglers, and drug consumers to their police, military, and intelligence counterparts in a strategic, tactical, and ideological fight (Certeau 2002). The conflict is waged sometimes in the open, but more often in a clandestine, subterranean world, a social space in which the truth is elusive and relative and in which paranoia, fear, and mystery are the orders of the day. Antidrug warriors rely especially on undercover informants ("snitches"), while traffickers specialize in trickery and deception. Kafka's claustrophobic writing prefigured the secretive, duplicitous, unpredictable texture of the DWZ (Kafka 2003). The DWZ is a world where insecurity prevails and powerful forces, whose essence can never be fully known, impinge on the lives of individuals and communities.

I avoid the term "war on drugs" because I feel the U.S. government's deployment of this concept is hypocritical and misleading. A drug war pitting two tightly organized armies in a traditional military campaign, as in a World War I trench battle, simply does not exist, nor could it. War in this sense is the wrong metaphor, whether for contemporary military conflict or law-enforcement campaigns. The DWZ is more akin to the shifting terrain where military and intelligence forces pursue terrorists or guerrilla revolutionaries (Packer 2006). Drug traffickers, though they may be well organized, are generally covert, embedded in the civilian population, disappearing and eternally reemerging (if a leading drug lord is eliminated, a new one soon emerges), global, and constantly evolving and transforming. In any case, the DWZ, if in some sense involving a war, entails a cultural war that imbricates everyday life, moral values, popular culture, and political power (McCoy 1999).

Moreover, in major trafficking countries like Mexico, organized crime and official government are so tightly interwoven yet secretive that they indeed form an "underground empire," in the evocative language of journalist James Mills (Mills 1986), or a "deep politics," in the words of Kennedy assassination analyst Peter Dale Scott (1996).[10] Hence a Manichean logic that conceives of drug traffickers as evil criminals outside the clean legal system, whether in Mexico or the United States, is erroneous (Heyman and Campbell 2007). Corruption cases involving U.S. law-enforcement agents have risen dramatically in recent years (ibid.). Moreover, Mexican intellectuals now debate the *colombianización* or "Afghanistan-ization" of the country, which refers to a condition of uncontrolled, extreme violence, a terrified citizenry, and a government outgunned in certain regions by traffickers and riddled with corruption. Some even discuss the Mexican state's loss of control of its territory and sovereignty, although this may be exaggerated and may belie the state's own toleration and complicity in the drug trade (Ravelo 2007d).[11] The concept of the DWZ can help us rethink the rapidly changing, global, postmodern terrain of drug-antidrug movements.

Drugs in the World Political Economy: Issues of Globalization, Sovereignty, Resistance, and Complicity

Although the activities of drug traffickers and narcs may appear marginal and separate from mainstream society, the DWZ pervades modern life to such a degree that it has become critical for social scientists to gauge its international impact. Rather than conceptualizing the DWZ as a cultural space riven with clear ethnic-national-social dichotomies (drug-smuggling Mexicans vs. drug-busting or drug-consuming gringos, and marginal drug abusers vs. straight society), I prefer to see the DWZ as a cultural matrix with logics, practices, patterns, symbols, and worldviews that crisscross and transcend international boundaries, moral categories, social classes, and ethnic groups. The sociocultural terrain of the DWZ also possesses similar properties to the global domains and flows that Appadurai (1996) refers to as "scapes." For Appadurai, "ethnoscapes" are the mobile "landscape of persons who constitute the shifting world in which we live" (33). But my perspective differs from Appadurai's formulation of scapes to the extent that the DWZ refers to concrete, systematic, economically based, material practices (producing, selling, and consuming drugs as part of the international drug market) as well as their disjunctive, imagined dimensions or symbolic representations. That is, my approach to the DWZ is much more rooted in the mainstream political economy of Wolf (1982) and Roseberry (1989), although it still takes into account the discursive and semiotic dimensions of drug trafficking.

Other scholars (Knauft 2007; Ong 2006; Agamben 1998; Gupta and Ferguson 1997) have discussed political-economic spaces in the contemporary world similar to what I call the DWZ, but without focusing specifically on the narcotics trade. Ong (1999) uses the concept of "zones of graduated sovereignty" to refer to ways neoliberal state practices favor some areas and sideline others. This point is obviously relevant to why some regions or segments of Mexico, such as parts of urban and border areas, have benefited from free-trade policies, and why some drug-producing and drug-trafficking countries or regions prosper while others falter. Knauft (2007, 786), following Ferguson (2006), observes that "topologies of domination increasingly combine vertical impositions of organizational power with capitalist exploitations around and outside this power and, in the process, open new spaces for transnational and subnational resistance." These formulations help us understand how political-economic globalization and neoliberalism are not one-dimensional but instead create both domination and counterhegemony across international space and territory. Drug-trafficking flows clearly are strongly shaped by neoliberal globalization.

Yet it is not obvious that drug trafficking per se is resistance—at least not as that is conceived in anticapitalist political or ideological terms (see Benavides 2008).[12] Rather, it is an illegal form of capitalist accumulation. In some cases, it is an almost caricatured celebration of consumerism and wealth—narco-mansions, big trucks, expensive tasteless clothing, gaudy jewelry—facilitated by neoliberalism and collusion with elements of the state. Certainly, traffickers resist and defy U.S and Mexican law enforcement and bourgeois society; but I argue that ultimately the drug trade is part of the U.S. and Mexican economic systems (Schlosser 2003; Naim 2006; Walker 1996). Drug trafficking, thus, is similar in this respect to the way that "illegal" immigration self-supplies labor to the U.S. agricultural, industrial, and service industries, although in this case, a commodity—one used for "self-medication"—not labor, is supplied.

Yet we should be cautious about labeling drug-trafficking networks an "experiment in freedom" (Ong 2006, 4), because they are also generators of arbitrary and brutal violence as well as social inequality (Hansen and Stepputat 2005). Thus, we should not romanticize countersystemic forces such as drug cartels; instead, we must understand how drug traffickers and the social circumstances they create are complex and contradictory or how they can be resistant on one level and not resistant on another (Campbell and Heyman 2007).[13] We also need to understand how spaces such as the DWZ are the product of both state and nonstate forces, operating in the same social field (McCoy 1999; Nuijten and Anders 2007).

As Heyman and Smart (1999) and van Schendel and Abraham (2005) convincingly argue, states and illicit or illegal activities are not separate, distinct fields of social action, but are tightly intertwined in a dialectic relationship. To put it simply, a mutually parasitic relationship exists between the drug traffickers who profit from the illegal status of drugs such as cocaine and heroin, and the "drug warriors," bureaucracies, and prison-industrial complexes that justify their existence by reference to the "scourge" of drug traffickers.

As in Mintz's analysis of sugar and the commodity chains that sugar's production, distribution, and consumption create, drugs link large numbers of people across national and cultural boundaries (Mintz 1986). In this sense, sugar and drugs, as commodities and cultural icons, share many common characteristics. But unlike sugar and other legal commodities, drugs are imbued with unique conditions and marketing arrangements that derive from their illicit, clandestine status. Hence, border drug trafficking and the cultural complex I refer to as the DWZ cannot be fully understood without reference to international crime networks and global social and economic power structures.

Much academic debate discusses whether a U.S. empire dominates the world or whether (Hardt and Negri 2001) it is in decline (Knauft 2007). For my purposes, this issue is less important than the fact that drug-trafficking organizations in Mexico, Colombia, Afghanistan, and elsewhere—though at times in collusion with elements of national states—generally operate in ways that frustrate the most powerful state authorities in the United States. Yet at the same time, I argue that First World demand for drugs is the impetus for much of the world's illegal commerce (contra Courtwright 2001), and in that sense, drug markets hinge on consumer demand from within the imperial metropole.

Furthermore, less powerful countries of the world, such as Mexico, where marijuana, coca and cocaine, and opium and heroin are produced, suffer the worst consequences of the illegal drug trade, namely, the seemingly ceaseless drug-trafficking-related executions (*la narco-violencia*) of recent years. The consuming countries clearly have the most power in this context—the power to cut domestic drug demand (Burnett 2007, 1), the power to pressure the policies of drug-producing countries and otherwise meddle in their internal affairs, the power to demonize and otherwise stigmatize drug producers. Moreover, whether or not the United States is still the dominant world power, it is clearly in a superordinate relationship with Mexico and has been since taking half of the country in the Mexican War, even though this relationship is, in Knauft's terms (2007, 785), one of "dominance without [cultural] hegemony."

This, then, is the larger context within which border drug trafficking occurs: an alienated North American and Mexican populace self-medicating with illicit drugs and suffering the social costs of addiction and drug-related crimes (Daudistel 2007; Campbell 2006);[14] a hypocritical U.S. government and national culture that espouse puritanical values regarding drugs while consuming them in enormous amounts as part of the "psychoactive revolution" (Courtwright 2001, 2); a political system and economy founded and structured on U.S. dominance of Mexico (whether by U.S. government certification or decertification of Mexico's antidrug policies or coercive and unequal economic treaties such as NAFTA, etc.) and other countries;[15] and a poor drug-producing, drug-smuggling, and drug-consuming country (Mexico) that needs drug profits in order to survive economically, even though drug-related violence, corruption, and public insecurity devastate the country. My focus, however, is less on the world-scale political economy of drugs or on U.S.-Mexican political relations than on the ways in which these factors play out in local border communities and individual lives. In that sense, my project is closer to Lutz's "empire . . . in the [cultural] details" (Lutz 2006) than in the larger-scale political-economic theorizing of scholars like Wallerstein (2003). The next section discusses analytical, empirical, and moral issues that complicate the ethnographic study of the DWZ.

Creativity, Mystery, and Conspiracy in the Drug War Zone: Understanding the Cultural Space of Drug Trafficking on the Ground

The seizures, totaling 703 pounds, were made at the Paso Del Norte Bridge, the Bridge of the Americas and the Zaragoza Bridge. The drugs were found in "a wide variety of hidden compartments," according to a written release. Ten drivers from El Paso, San Elizario, Albuquerque, Juárez and Chihuahua City were arrested.
EL PASO TIMES, JULY 12, 2007

Although the international political-economic structures within which drug trafficking operates are readily identifiable, the actors and playing field of the DWZ change constantly because drug-trafficking groups continually improvise and innovate. They create new smuggling techniques and technologies, refine old ones, and go to great lengths to disguise their identities. An example from my field notes (July 10, 2007) illustrates why U.S. efforts to fully secure the southern border from drug or human smugglers is ultimately futile because of the creativity of smugglers and the ways smugglers use the system against itself:[16]

Last night while walking across the Santa Fe Bridge—which connects El Paso and Juárez in one of the most heavily fortified and guarded sections of the U.S./Mexico border—I observed an event that epitomizes for me why a border wall can't work.

The bridge was packed with cars heading from Juárez into the United States. Near the top of the bridge on the U.S. side of the pedestrian walkway to Juárez, a young man dressed as a *cholo* [barrio gangster] held a long steel chain with a hook on one end encased in thick plastic or rubber hose. He attached the hook to the steel mesh that encloses the walkway, then threw the hose over the mesh and twenty feet or so down to U.S. soil.[17] Next he boosted his partner or client onto the mesh. From there the soon-to-be *indocumentado* (and possible smuggler) crawled over the mesh like Spiderman and scaled down the hose to the ground. Last I saw he was calmly running up Santa Fe Street with no Border Patrol vehicles in sight. His accomplice then reeled in the hose and, helped by another accomplice who had been acting as a spotter on the top of the bridge, stowed the hose in a duffel bag and walked towards Juárez. I was staring so intently at the scene that the first guy asked me to please quit looking at him because he didn't want to attract attention and be filmed by the security cameras. He didn't seem too worried, though, because he paused during his work to make sexual comments to two young girls who were also heading to Juárez. This whole event took place in a matter of two minutes.

What I find interesting about all this is that the *pasamojados* [people smuggler] used the strength of the U.S. steel mesh and railing to anchor the chain, which allowed the *aspirante a indocumentado* (potential "illegal immigrant" and/or smuggler) to rappel over the bridge and into "the promised land." Drugs are transported this way on people's persons, or simply launched down to the ground where they are spirited off into the city and eventually throughout the country.

As this example demonstrates, for smugglers and drug users, the issue is avoidance, trickery, evasion, and "slantwise behavior," that is, actions that are undertaken by actors in order to achieve their own ends and that, although they do not necessarily involve intentional political resistance, frustrate state interests (Campbell and Heyman 2007). Smugglers and drug users will do whatever it takes to get a load to its destination or smoke through one's pipe. Simultaneously, for the narcotics agents, it is an endless intelligence game: decoding the signs, symbols, and movements of often faceless, nameless traffickers. It is a battle reminiscent of the tit-for-tat volleying and the absurdity of the *Spy vs. Spy* comic strip in *Mad* magazine. Anthropologists who study such phenomena face a tremendous challenge: how to sort out fact from fiction, and how to keep track of the creative legerdemain of smugglers and their adversaries. Drug ethnography is made more difficult by the pervading atmosphere of paranoia and betrayal in the drug world.

Mystery and Treachery in the DWZ

A mood of uncertainty, anxiety, fear, and treachery predominates in the DWZ—an atmosphere presciently captured by Phillip K. Dick in many brilliant novels, especially *A Scanner Darkly:* "But then, too, certain dealers, to burn their enemies or when expecting imminent busts, began narking and went that route, winding up as sort of unofficial narks. It all got murky. The drug world was a murky world for everyone anyhow" (Dick 1991, 87).

Deleuze and Guattari (1983), in their ruminations on the schizophrenic feeling of contemporary capitalism, and Taussig (1992a), on the anxiety-laden "ordered disorder" or "state of emergency" provoked by the "Nervous State," also provide insight into the DWZ. No one has all the information—neither the traffickers nor the cops, and certainly not the general public. Informants lie, cheat, and double-cross their handlers. Smugglers disappear with loads of drugs and money, and their relatives, close friends, and business partners get busted and then "flip" and snitch (or maybe they don't). Traffickers are arrested and then swallowed up by a vast prison bureaucracy. Rumors fly as to whether the drug convict snitched.

On the streets of Mexican cities, bodies without identification, but sometimes bearing cryptic, threatening notes or signs of stylized torture, turn up wrapped in blankets, stuffed in barrels of acid, or crammed into car trunks. Other individuals are simply picked up (*levantado*) by hooded commandos armed with AK-47s and sometimes wearing Mexican military or police uniforms, never to be seen or heard from again. Are they alive or dead? Who killed or "disappeared" them? Was it cops or narcotraffickers? Who is more violent and treacherous, the cops or the traffickers? Are they one and the same? This is what Taussig (1992a, 17) means by "terror as usual," a condition all too familiar for residents of Ciudad Juárez or other prominent nodes in the border DWZ.

Some know who did it or what happened in a particular incident, but they can't be found or they have been murdered or threatened into silence. The Mexican press prints a luridly detailed description of events, and then later prints a completely contradictory but equally plausible alternative account. The government denies that any incident took place. There is no reconciliation of the distinct versions. Myth, folklore, *chisme* (gossip), and unverifiable stories endlessly proliferate. Who killed Luis Donaldo Colosio? Is Amado Carrillo Fuentes alive or dead? *¿Quién sabe?* Multiply these unanswered questions by the thousands. Few crimes are solved in Mexico—it is said that crime does pay in Mexico—and only a small percentage of drugs smuggled across the U.S. border are actually intercepted.[18]

These are some of the confusing, labyrinthine facets and dimensions of the DWZ. Such conditions are fertile ground for "discourses of suspicion," the conspiracy theories discussed by West and Sanders (2003). Indeed, the border DWZ is filled with colorful conjecture about the Mexican government's complicity in drug trafficking, the commission of monstrous acts by specific drug cartels, and the hidden corruption and complicity of U.S. government agencies in the drug trade. Given such a murky environment, an ethnographer must accept that many things will be unknowable and that the best one can hope for is to get numerous accounts of, or versions about, the same event, issue, or person in order to have some sense of the range of possible partial truths.

Smuggling Techniques

The subject of drug trafficking and antidrug actions is vast, as author Joel Miller (2004) notes about drug-smuggling techniques. Miller struggled to keep his book *Bad Trip: How the War against Drugs Is Destroying America* down to a reasonable length because "smuggling is really about one of the biggest and broadest subjects any author can cover—human ingenuity." Miller quotes the legendary cocaine trafficker "Zachary Swan," who states that there are "a million ways" to smuggle cocaine, and lists the following examples:

Covertly building a submarine capable of hauling 10 tons of cocaine to carry it from Colombia to the U.S. [a tactic now being used to send cocaine from Colombia to Mexico].

Using time-released buoys and GPS trackers to sync drug shipments on the open sea.

Combining cocaine with plastic resin and producing functioning, commercial goods from which the drug can be chemically extracted once across the border.

Disguising stashes of cocaine in hollowed-out passion fruit or in plastic plantains; hiding psilocybin mushrooms in chocolates.

Digging a 1,200-foot tunnel, complete with ventilation ducts and electric lights[,] to take marijuana and cocaine from a home in Mexico to another in California.

Dropping drugs in the uninhabited desert by plane and using GPS locaters on the ground to find and bring them across the poorly manned border.

Training—no lie here, folks—*pigeons* to fly packets of dope across the border.

Miller further notes that "Swan used to buy cocaine in Colombia and then tightly compress it into wooden souvenirs—like rolling pins, carved tribal heads, and statuettes of the Madonna (who would suspect Mary?)—which he would easily smuggle into the United States. He never got busted with a load." Creative drug-trafficking strategies encountered during this research include swimming backpacks of drugs underwater through tunnels; floating loads across the Rio Grande on rafts; cleverly packing shipments of cocaine, marijuana, and heroin in hidden compartments of cars and trucks; hiding drugs in the mouth, genital, or breast areas, or in girdles and other items of clothing; etc.[19] Clever smuggling tactics have a deep history in the El Paso–Juárez area, where in the 1920s, maybe even earlier, smugglers attached loads of contraband drugs to dogs and passenger pigeons, which easily crossed the international border.[20]

Morality, Ambiguity, and What Can Be Known about the Drug War Zone

As noted, a "war" against such smuggling is not a normal war, and in any case is not winnable, in spite of the power of the U.S. military, police, and intelligence forces and their massive budgets.[21] Moreover, unlike John Wayne in a western, neither side in the drug war commands the moral high ground. Drug lords murder their enemies in unimaginably sadistic ways—the creativity applied to murder and torture techniques seems boundless. Yet various capos have argued that their actions are actually good for Mexico, at least economically. Rafael Caro Quintero once braggingly offered to pay off Mexico's foreign debt with "green" (that is, marijuana).[22] Amado Carrillo Fuentes compared himself favorably to corrupt politicians who take money from Mexico and hide it in Swiss banks: "Compadre . . . I don't sell even one gram of anything here in Mexico . . . I do bring money into Mexico, and activate the Mexican economy . . . In the same airplanes that I send out [full of cocaine] the money comes back in" (Andrade Bojorges 1999, 195). While such boasts hardly justify the massive drug violence, U.S. law enforcement can scarcely claim moral superiority either, since its policies have criminalized generations of drug users and petty traffickers.

Although an atmosphere of amorality, terror, and confusion pervades the DWZ, the zone—akin to the fictional Interzone of William Burroughs (1989), a multibordered netherworld loosely based on post–World War II Tangier—is not entirely chaotic or disorderly, nor simply in stochastic flux. Drug trafficking is above all a business that responds to market conditions. In fact, Mexican drug cartels and their counterparts, the antidrug bureaucracies, can be neatly diagrammed on organizational charts.

Yet the growth and decline of different drug organizations is not a result of either a grand unitary conspiracy or simple, single causes. Despite some arguments to the contrary, there is no cohesive structure that unites all drug cartels under a functioning umbrella-like organization (sometimes called "the Federation"), although several attempts to do so have perhaps succeeded for short periods (Blancornelas 2002, 46–52; Ravelo 2005; Payán 2006).[23] The particular configuration of drug-trafficking organizations at any given moment is the product of conflicts and alliances among and between different trafficking groups and their allies or enemies within the government. Drug-related events or developments within society or the economy, though sometimes the outcome of large-scale conspiracy, are more often the result of the interlocking general forces of powerful groups, each pursuing its own specific interests.

Nonetheless, the DWZ is also pinholed with spaces of anarchy and unpredictable realities. On one hand, it is well established that the Mexican police, judicial, and military forces are deeply marked by corruption and collusion with drug traffickers. But the exact alliances and arrangements of the moment are known to few besides the immediate actors. Many actors in the Mexican drug panorama are, in fact, double agents working with one group of traffickers or one faction within the government while fighting other drug-trafficking or political groups. On the other hand, the U.S. antidrug bureaucracy appears to be a well-planned, determined force deeply committed to its antinarcotics mission. Yet, within antidrug agencies, a swirl of rumors of alleged corruption and collusion weakens organizational solidarity, and rampant envy, uncooperativeness, and competition divide the various antidrug forces. Moreover, despite billion-dollar budgets, these agencies seem helpless to stop smugglers from operating right under their noses. Many career agents, in fact, admit that the war on drugs is an untenable policy that they carry out simply because of the need for a paycheck. Overall, the DWZ is a complex blend of order and chaos, structure and antistructure.

The preceding discussion makes clear how difficult it is to conduct research on such an elusive topic as drug trafficking. However, the Mexican cartels have become so large and successful that it is now possible to know many things about them, which is the subject of the next section.

Cultural Dimensions of Mexican Drug Cartels (*La Narcocultura*)

At 7:30 A.M., officers at the same bridge [Paso Del Norte] discovered 48.5 pounds of marijuana in the rocker panels of a 1993 Pontiac Bonneville and arrested the 41-year-old San Elizario driver.
EL PASO TIMES, JULY 12, 2007

El narcotráfico (drug trafficking) is so pervasive and firmly embedded in daily life in Mexico and in the border region that the idea of a narco-culture—that is, a cultural complex or whole way of life centered around drug trafficking—is now accepted as a given by *mexicanos, fronterizos* (border people), and many social scientists (Ovalle 2007). So common is the prefix *narco-* that it is attached to almost any noun to specify some reputed aspect of *la narcocultura*, not just in the case of the drug ballads known as *narcocorridos*, but also in reference to *narcomansiones* or *narcocastillos* (drug mansions or castles), *narcoarte* (narco-art), *narcotienditas* (narco-stores, that is, buildings or places from which drugs are sold), *narcointeligencia* (cartel intelligence operatives), *narcoabogados* (lawyers who defend traffickers), *narcotumbas* (elaborate tombs), *narcosantos* (narco-saints, especially Jesús Malverde and La Santa Muerte, literally "Saint Death," roughly equivalent to the Grim Reaper), *narcocumbres* (high-level meetings between leaders of multiple trafficking groups), *narcocerveza* (narco-beer), and even *narcomenonitas* (Mennonite farmers of Chihuahua who have delved in drug smuggling; see Quiñones 2007).[24] Additionally, drug traffickers have developed a complex vocabulary of slang and colloquial terminology to refer to all aspects of drug trafficking, including various drugs; the tools, objects, technologies, and vehicles used to produce, process, and transport them; and the various social types and roles associated with the drug-trafficking culture. Thus, *narco* has become a powerful, multivalent social identity.

In analyzing narco-culture, however, it is important not to "criminalize entire populations believed to have a common culture" (Schneider and Schneider 2005, 501); that is, the discussion of narco-culture that follows is limited to the inner workings of Mexican and border drug-trafficking organizations, not Mexican or border culture as a whole. Moreover, as Benavides (2008, 112) points out, narco-identity is a quintessential example of contemporary cultural hybridity, not an expression of an essential Mexican culture: "Mexico's northern frontier and being narco do not respond exclusively to a Mexican identity but, rather, to a wider transnational dialogue between the neocolonial U.S. empire and the postcolonial existence of Latin America."

Although there are, according to some sources, seven main Mexican cartels (Ravelo 2007b, 11), the largest ones share similar characteristics and circumstances, including dense webs of family ties, local loyalties, and long-term friendships and working relationships; an authoritarian structure; a main regional base with satellite centers and cells throughout Mexico, the United States, other parts of Latin America, and elsewhere; a style of living oscillating between extravagantly conspicuous consumption (of drugs, houses, cars and trucks, clothing, jewelry, elaborate fiestas, etc.) and seclusion; violent disputes over territory, lost or stolen loads of drugs or money, and alleged treason; close connections with and protection from police and governmental authorities, purchased through bribery; and the loss of members to violent death, incapacitation, or incarceration.

The biggest Mexican drug-trafficking organizations are composed of complex structures and strata comparable to legitimate multinational corporations. The huge Mexican cartels of Tijuana, Juárez, Sinaloa, and the Gulf are in fact multinational economic entities with hundreds or thousands of members or affiliates whose roles, functions, or titles range from capo–drug lord–*jefe* through numerous other, often hierarchically layered positions, including purchasing agent–negotiator, political liaison, financial manager–money launderer, accountant, lawyer, transportation specialist (pilot, boat captain, driver, "mule" [pedestrian transporter], etc.), intelligence agent, telecommunications specialist, arms procurer, car thief, enforcer or hit man, packager, warehouse foreman, guard, spotter, distribution agent, and street seller. Additionally, numerous other bribed operatives, politicians, policemen, military officers, customs officers, soldiers, and intelligence officers perform vital functions without which drug cartels cannot operate.

Cartels: A Critique and Reformulation

I have been careful about using the term "cartels," out of sensitivity to the loose and often misleading use of this term in the journalistic stories and chronicles of Mexican drug-trafficking organizations that constitute the main published documentation of such groups. As Astorga (2005, 154–155) has noted, the profligate use of "cartel" may sustain a number of incorrect assumptions about drug-trafficking organizations. Some faulty, essentialist assumptions about cartels consist of the following: that they are all enormous, unified, permanent, and tightly organized from top to bottom; they are isomorphic with the Mexican landscape such that each region, route, or drug market has one and only one cartel (the Juárez cartel, the Tijuana cartel, the Gulf cartel, etc.); they are absolutely vertical in structure; they are removed from the larger society and strictly separate from the other equally seamless, coherent cartels that are their rivals.

This simplistic notion of drug-trafficking organizations should be replaced by a more supple concept of cartels as shifting, contingent, temporal alliances of traffickers whose territories and memberships evolve and change because of conflicts, imprisonment, deaths, changing political circumstances, etc., and whose fortunes and strengths wax and wane or die out over time. This is henceforth how I will use the term "cartel," and this usage applies only to the largest Mexican drug-trafficking organizations. Moreover, many of the functions of a cartel are in fact carried out by cells, which are groups of outsourced growers, packagers, drivers, warehouse guards, gunmen, street sellers, etc., who have little or no connection to the larger drug organization (to, for example, the Juárez cartel) and whose services are bought and paid for with cash or drugs. This more flexible view of cartels is referred to by some observers as a "rectangular" (Ravelo 2005, 19) rather than a pyramidal structure.[25] As Astorga (2005, 154) also points out, the various drug-trafficking groups, rather than forming a single, horizontally linked entity, actually engage in "open competition" and adhere to the "business ethos of pure liberalism," although because of the governmental favoritism shown to some cartels over others, the largest drug-trafficking organizations form a quasi-monopolistic, "oligopolistic structure."

Consequently, our analytical emphasis, rather than being centered on essentialized cartels, should be more sharply focused on the ever-changing negotiated relationship between various kinds and sizes of trafficking organizations and the political, military, and law-enforcement authorities that control territories; I refer to the intersection of these two sets of forces over a given territory or trafficking route as *la plaza*.[26] The *plaza* is a more useful frame of analysis than the cartel because of the inherently unstable dimension of cartels compared to the relatively fixed physical geography in which they operate;[27] the persistently optimal features of particular drug-transportation routes; and the more stable structure of the political system and its associated military and police apparatus.[28] Furthermore, Astorga (2005, 124–125) correctly explains that drug organizations do not represent a "parallel power," completely independent of the state, but rather a form of economic activity connected with, tolerated, promoted, or protected by various sectors of the state.[29] Our analyses, thus, should not focus on cartels in isolation from the national political context that sustains and permits large-scale drug trafficking, or from the international political-economic context within which they function.

Drug Lords and the Extension of Cartels

The main Mexican drug lords (Fonseca, Félix Gallardo, Acosta, Caro Quintero, García Ábrego, the Carrillo Fuentes brothers, the Arellano Félix brothers, "Chapo" Guzmán), for the most part, have emerged from the lower socioeconomic strata of the peasantry and the working class.[30] Like the legendary guerrilla revolutionary Pancho Villa and Friedrich's princes of Naranja, the drug capos have been relatively uneducated social bandits who made up for their lack of mainstream cultural capital with their knowledge of the mountains and back roads, marijuana cultivation, the clandestine codes and norms of underworld police corruption and crime, and the informal rules of masculine combat (Katz 1998; Friedrich 1987). Drug lords generally serve a long apprenticeship in the lower echelons of the drug trade before they reach the top. Their position at the top of a cartel, often gained through a violent takeover or the death of the incumbent, is generally rooted in family and regional loyalties. Many are considered heroes in their rural hometowns.

During their reign, drug lords run their organizations dictatorially and patriarchally, surrounded by bodyguards and served by a series of close advisors, relatives, and lieutenants who administer orders to the middle-level cadres of money managers, political operatives, communications specialists, corrupted officials, logistics operators, etc. Despite the great power of drug lords vis-à-vis their subordinates, such power is tenuous because the capos are hunted by the law and their drug-lord rivals, hence they are constantly moving and in danger of being caught or killed. Every phone call or trip they take may be monitored. They rule by force and through the money they provide to cartel members, but no formal law or official social convention sustains their power, and they are always vulnerable to treachery or the jealousy of their closest associates. They are dangerous, yet always endangered.

In standard imagery, Mexican drug cartels are depicted as evil, sanguinary, and hierarchical organizations that dominate vast areas of land. Certainly, Mexican trafficking organizations have committed countless murders.[31] Yet this violence, which stems from the unregulated, illegal status of drug businesses, may cause us to forget that, ultimately, drug cartels, like normal businesses, are pragmatic firms whose bottom line is profit. Moreover, the notion that cartels are run autocratically, from top to bottom by authoritarian leaders, though partially correct, is misleading to the extent that drug-cartel activity involves intricate, loosely knit webs of individuals and organizations that stretch from peasant farmers in Latin America to consumers in U.S. towns and cities.

These networks far transcend the boundaries of one cartel or of unitary, regionally based organizations. This reflects trends in the structure of global business generally—a shift to horizontal linkages (and subcontracting) and away from vertical integration. Yet the emergence of drug cartels, in some sense, also reflects grassroots organization by local entrepreneurs rather than the structure of legitimate transnational corporations, which are procedurally protected within a formal political economy (Recio 2002; Martínez 1978). In the drug trade, numerous informal links in the commodity chain are semiautonomous, flexibly affiliated, temporary, etc.

Hence, the Cártel de Juárez does not produce the cocaine it buys from Colombian and other South American sources, and the cartel leaves much of the shipping in the hands of South Americans until the drugs reach Mexico or its contiguous territory. Cartel workers move the drugs through the interior of Mexico to the U.S.-Mexico border. Once there, however, the cocaine is transported across the border by local smuggling cells or sold in Juárez *tienditas* (small stores) or *picaderos* that are protected by bribed policemen. These smuggling and local-distribution cells include, especially, the cross-border Aztecas–Barrio

Azteca prison gang–street gang. The cells are as mobile and elusive as the guerrilla *foco* revolutionary groups of Central and South America. As a CIA report (Central Intelligence Agency 1995, 19) describes the process: "Much of the actual movement of narcotics across the border, especially in Ciudad Juarez, is subcontracted to groups that specialize in only this aspect of transshipment. The drugs are then re-collected by Juarez cartel associates who forward the narcotics to distributor centers throughout the U.S. One such route from Ciudad Juarez to Sylmar, California, was believed to have carried over 250 tons of cocaine before it was disrupted."

Another misconception about Mexican drug cartels is that because most are regionally based—as in the Gulf, Juárez, or Sinaloa cartel—everyone in the drug-trafficking area, *la plaza*, is part of the cartel or connected to it by regional, ethnic, or family ties. Some drug-trafficking organizations—most especially La Familia in Michoacán; the Herrera family's organization in Durango, which has dominated the heroin trade from Durango through El Paso–Juárez to Chicago since the 1930s (Lupsha and Schlegel 1980); the Gulf cartel, whose roots in the Gulf of Mexico region and specific families date to the 1930s; and various Sinaloa and Michoacán groups—possess elements of such a regional model. But the Gulf cartel is also trans-Mexican and indeed pan-American in addition to having dealings with groups in other hemispheres. Yet other organizations, such as the Juárez cartel of the Carrillo Fuentes family, are run by outsiders who took control from local people or have engaged in complex alliances with regional groups while maintaining a transnational, multisited global reach that far transcends the strictly local or regional. Still others, such as the Zetas (Corchado 2007), are neither strictly regional nor based on family ties.[32] Several *narcocumbres*, most notably one convened by Félix Gallardo in 1989 and another between members of the Chapo Guzmán cartel, the Gulf cartel, and the Zetas in 2007, have attempted to lessen conflicts, apportion territories, and encourage intercartel cooperation. However, such arrangements have invariably broken down relatively quickly (Ravelo 2007a, 8–9).

How Drug-Trafficking *Plazas* Operate

Given these caveats, several features of Mexican narco-culture stand out and can be amply documented. Marijuana plants and opium poppies require certain climatological and environmental conditions in order to prosper.[33] Consequently, over the last fifty years, several key states have dominated the cultivation of drug crops. And because of the cultivation of new areas, an estimated 30 percent of arable land in Mexico is now devoted to marijuana and opium cultivation (Dávila 2007a, 16). According to Mexican antidrug authorities, there are fifteen main microregions where pot is produced. These are located along the western Sierra Madre range in the states of Sinaloa, Michoacán, Guerrero, Durango, Chihuahua, Sonora, Oaxaca, Nayarit, and Jalisco. The fertility of these regions has made Mexico one of the world's leading producers of marijuana, yet sadly, and not coincidentally, the drug-producing areas are located in the zones of greatest poverty. Opium is primarily grown in eleven microregions in the states of Guerrero, Oaxaca, Durango, Chihuahua, Nayarit, Sinaloa, and Sonora. Also, not surprisingly, the largest drug cartels are located in the vicinity of these producing areas, adjacent to the United States or along the main Mexican transportation routes by which South American cocaine is shipped north (Dávila 2007a, 14–17).

Transportation routes and territories controlled by specific cartels in collusion with police, military, and government officials, as noted above, are known as *plazas*.[34] Control of a *plaza* gives the drug lord and police commander of an area the power to charge less-powerful traffickers tolls, known as *pisos*. Generally, one main cartel dominates a *plaza* at any given time, although this control is often contested or subverted by internal conflict, may be disputed among several groups, and is subject to rapid change. Attempts by rival cartels to ship drugs through a *plaza* or take over a *plaza* controlled by their enemies has led to much of the recent drug violence in Mexico. The cartel that has the most power in a particular *plaza* receives police or military protection for its drug shipments. Authorities provide official documentation for loaded airplanes, freight trucks, and cars and allow traffickers to pass freely through airports and landing strips, freeway toll roads and desert highways, and checkpoints and border crossings.

Typically, a cartel purchases the loyalty of the head of the federal police or the military commander in a particular district.[35] This official provides officers or soldiers to physically protect drug loads in transit or in storage facilities, and in some cases to serve as bodyguards for high-level cartel members. Police on the cartel payroll intimidate, kidnap, or murder opponents of the organization, although they also may pressure and extort larger payments from the cartel with which they are associated. Additionally, cartel members establish connections with state governors or mayors of major cities, high-ranking officials in federal law enforcement, military and naval officers and commanders, and other powerful politicians and bureaucrats. These national connections facilitate the use of transportation routes and control of a given *plaza*. In addition to large-scale international smuggling, cartels distribute huge quantities of drugs for domestic consumption.[36]

Local and federal law-enforcement agents and authorities, often at high levels, provide inside information to cartel leaders; this facilitates smuggling and sales operations and allows cartel members to live undetected in major cities or rural areas. Additionally, governmental insiders warn drug traffickers of imminent antidrug operations (the warning is known as *el pitazo*), which allows them to escape capture. Even when drug lords are captured, by paying large bribes they may continue to run their *plazas* from prison, and they often receive special privileges or are permitted to escape in exchange for large sums of money. In general, Mexican police agencies seldom conduct thorough investigations of drug organizations, but simply make arrests at checkpoints or as the result of information provided by snitches; there is very little follow-up directed toward tracing and dismantling the webs of cartel members and accomplices (Blancornelas 2003, 92–93, 353–357).

According to a leading authority on corruption in Mexico, Alejandro Gertz, much of the Mexican police force serves the interests of drug traffickers and the politically powerful because of the hierarchical structure established by the Partido Revolucionario Institucional (PRI), the dominant Mexican political party from 1929 to 2000 and still a major force in the country.[37] According to Gertz: "The police are a vertical structure that was made to serve power and not justice or society. As a result of this local municipal and state police exercise control, but they become accomplices, hitmen, cover-ups and partners of the drug traffickers . . . [This structure] begins at the summit of power and ends in the policemen in the barrio" (quoted in Ravelo 2007e, 8).

Narco-style: Visibility in the Narco-Culture

The quotidian life and social style of drug traffickers has been codified through the often-stereotypical motifs of *narcocorridos* (Edberg 2004; Wald 2001; Valenzuela 2002). In the drug ballads, *narcotraficantes* appear as gunslinging machos, decked out in flamboyant outfits. The classic attire consists of an expensive Tejana cowboy hat, kilos of gold necklaces, medallions, bracelets, rings, a brightly colored silk Western shirt, a *cinto piteado* (woven ixtle fiber belt), Levi's jeans, and sharp-pointed boots made of exotic animal skins. The drug kingpins are referred to less often by their given names than by their underworld nicknames (e.g., "La Barbie," "El Chacky," "El Señor de los Cielos," "El Güero," "El Cochiloco," "El Tigrillo").[38] They drive *trokotas del año* (the newest trucks), live in huge, tasteless, nouveau riche mansions or on well-stocked ranches, spend money lavishly, squire sexy overdressed women draped in a female version of the narco look, and party recklessly while ostentatiously accompanied by vicious bodyguards. Such a characterization is, in fact, a caricature, but elements of the style are definitely recognizable in border towns and northern Mexico drug hotbeds. However, the narco-look is simply a monied, conspicuous extension of a general *norteño* Mexican cowboy or ranchero style brought to the city, and it is mimicked and elaborated on by thousands of *narcocorrido-banda-norteña* bands on both sides of the border as well as by their dance-hall followers and imitators in the streets.[39] "Narco-goods," thus, represent an extreme form of commodity fetishism.

Narco-style also entails elaborate public events or "spectacles" (Debord 2006), especially potlatch-like fiestas thrown to celebrate birthdays, weddings, and other rites of passage as well as to mark the successful crossing of large drug loads, horse races, cockfights, rodeos, and other highlights of the *narco-ranchero* life; similar extravagances include wild parties in exclusive restaurants, bars, and discotheques, complete with platoons of prostitutes, piles of cocaine, and expensive alcoholic beverages.[40] These shows of wealth are a direct expression of the social inequality that drug trafficking creates at the local level (Malkin 2001; McDonald 2005). The courtship and public marriage of Chapo Guzmán, described above, was only the most sensational of many recent narco-spectacles. Such lavish spending, conspicuous consumption, and heavily guarded events, and the rituals of power they represent, are engaged in only by the wealthiest and strongest drug lords, although the rank and file of the drug world may also attend and participate. The everyday lives of the common people in the DWZ are much more mundane, and their participation in *la narcocultura* expresses itself primarily in the work they do in the drug business.

Deception, Concealment, and the Transmission of Messages: Stash Houses and Hit Men

Two significant cells, or domains of activity, within narco-culture that illustrate the simultaneous processes of occlusion and projection of cultural meaning in the DWZ are the work of stash-house guards and hit men (*sicarios*). A main task in drug-trafficking areas is the warehousing of loads of drugs or money. Houses in which drugs are stored on the U.S. side of the border are known as "stash houses," a phenomenon that is so widespread in El Paso that there is an anti-stash-house police unit. The job of successfully running a stash house is tricky and requires considerable cleverness and skill in the arts of mimesis (Taussig 1992b).[41]

One stash house that I observed for an extended period in El Paso was located in an upper-middle-class neighborhood in the extreme eastern part of town on a main thoroughfare (details in this account have been changed for safety reasons). The people who ran the stash house meticulously mowed the grass; adorned it with appropriate seasonal decorations (Halloween pumpkins, Christmas lights), the American flag, or cheesy lawn ornaments; and in other small ways made the place appear a bland, standard middle-class suburban dwelling. Yet to regular observers of the house, it was noteworthy that the venetian blinds on the windows were almost never open. It was nearly impossible to see into the house, over the rock wall into the backyard, or into the closed garage. Neighbors informed me that they could see transparent plastic sheets taped to all the windows to prevent the smell of marijuana or other drugs from escaping. It was also significant that the relatively short driveway was nearly always filled to capacity with cars parked in a line, often five in a row, though the placement of the cars periodically changed, in a kind of three-card-monte-like arrangement. Unknown vehicles came to the house at odd hours.

A keen observer could tell that the mysterious occupants of the house, who changed frequently, did not socialize with neighbors or spend much time outside the dwelling. They did not appear to leave or return to the house at times consonant with a standard nine-to-five job. In fact, many longtime neighbors had no idea who lived there or how they made a living. This nosy ethnographer was once approached by one of the stash house's occupants, however, who came within one foot of me and engaged in trivial small talk while obviously trying to gauge who I was and whether I was a threat. I also observed the occupant engaging in discreet surveillance of me at other times. I found it especially telling that the residents of the house, though maintaining an image of normality successful enough to prevent them from being arrested by antidrug authorities, neglected to water a succulent pomegranate tree, which subsequently died. The functioning of this particular stash house exemplifies the general processes of hiding and deception that are central to *la narcocultura*.

Drug hit men also engage in intricate attempts to disguise their identities and activities, although many drug killings in Mexico and on the border have been conducted brazenly—with automatic weapons in broad daylight—with no attempt at camouflage or subterfuge. Besides physically eliminating enemies, drug killings are meant to intimidate rivals, law enforcement, government officials, and the public through richly choreographed rituals of brutality with specific symbolic meanings.[42] They share some of the logic of, and affect society much like, the "sacrificial terrorism" or "suicide terrorism" of Middle Eastern insurgent groups (Pape 2005; see also Agamben 1998). These killings not only destroy human lives but also send the sociopolitical message that the state (in this case, the Mexican government) can neither completely control its national territory nor fully protect the populace. In street terms, the message is clear: "Don't fuck with us, or this will happen to you, too." Such murders are especially powerful and effective because generally few people really know who committed them or exactly why; rumors spread, fears mount. The overall effect is to heighten the dominant image of the regional cartels.

Weimann and Winn (Weimann 2008, 69), referring primarily to terrorist actions by Islamist groups, characterize such actions as a "theater of terror" that communicates meaning through "orchestrated violence." Likewise, border drug violence takes on a psychological dimension that transcends the victims and is meant to speak to a mass audience. Narco-killers know that drug murders will be broadcast on local and national television. They also make their own videos, complete with musical sound tracks, for dissemination through YouTube. The use of increasingly sophisticated electronic media by cartels demonstrates the important rhetorical dimension of narco-violence. Narco-murders as visual spectacle have become regular fare in the Mexican and border news media and on the Internet.

Narco-semiotics

A recent trend in narco-killings is the attachment of a sign or banner to the body of the victim or to public monuments, such as bridges or statues. These signs may contain lists of policemen who are threatened with death if they do not cooperate with traffickers. In Ciudad Juárez, such a list was posted in public places and on YouTube. Sometimes messages are carved or inscribed in blood on a victim's body. These signs or messages are generally written in underworld drug slang (peppered with execrable spelling, bad grammar, and crude obscenities) with semisecret references to and threats against drug lords and other cartel members.[43] They are meant to inform drug-world insiders of who is either in charge or attempting to take charge of a particular *plaza* and to explain why specific individuals have been or will be slaughtered. Members of the Zetas cartel, which controls states and regions adjacent to the Gulf of Mexico and the northeastern border of Mexico, frequently issue theatrical statements in which they substitute the letter *z* for the letter *s* to advertise their power and influence. An example of this occurred in Piedras Negras, Coahuila, at a Zetas toy giveaway on Mexico's Children's Day (April 30, 2006). Announcements for the event attributed the toy donations to the "Zindicato Anónimo Altruizta de PN" [Anonymous Altruistic Syndicate of Piedras Negras], in obvious reference to the Zetas (Páez Varela 2007, 3).

YouTube, blogs, and *narcocorridos* are constantly used as venues for the transmission of intimidating messages and manifestos by drug cartels and as general forums for discussing drug-related issues and events, although there is also a growing body of copycat cartel messages, videos, and songs.[44] Online narco-terror is especially potent because it becomes immediately available to a wide audience, which may include sympathizers, enemies, and the general public. Narco-videos and narco-blogs justify violent actions and attempt to establish the military and moral superiority of one cartel over another. Weimann (2008) explains that terrorist cyber-rhetoric seeks moral disengagement through "displacement of responsibility," "dehumanization of targets" (in the case of Mexican cartels, this entails calling members of rival cartels "pigs," "dogs," etc.), "euphemistic language," "attribution of blame," and other discursive devices. In this sense, border narco-propaganda parallels that of Islamist terrorist groups. In fact, it appears that cartels have copied many terror tactics and cyberspace techniques from al Qaeda and similar groups.

Another recent trend is the murder of *narcocorrido* singers, most notably Valentín Elizalde, "El Gallo de Oro" (the Golden Rooster), or even of entire musical groups. Opinions vary about whether the singers were killed because they knew too much, revealed too much information in their songs, had a falling out with a cartel they were associated with, or were killed by members of a rival cartel.

The style of drug killings forms a semiotic system of "inscribed" bodies subject to endless interpretation by cartel members and observers. Traitors are shot in the neck, philanderers are castrated, spies are shot in the ear, and people who talk too much are shot in the mouth. A body found with one or more fingers cut off then placed in the victim's mouth, or with the tongue cut off, is considered to be a message that the victim was a police informer (a *dedo*, or finger); the mutilation is also a threat meant to discourage others from informing on traffickers. In terms used by Katz (1988, 135–138), these stylized killings represent the "construction of dread": they generate a climate of fear and reinforce the power of the perpetrators.

Other descriptive neologisms for the disposal of murder victims include *encajuelados* (dead bodies stuffed in car trunks), *ensabanados* (bodies wrapped in sheets), *encobijados* (bodies wrapped in blankets), *entambados* (bodies stuffed in metal barrels, often along with acid or wet cement), *enteipados* (bodies wrapped in industrial tape), etc. In these expressions, attaching the preposition *en* to a participial verb converts the verb into an adjective or noun; each shift is grammatically marked by a morpheme; and the active verb implies an act of violence at the level of grammar, since *en* implies the placing or rendering of a human body inside something it would not normally be inside.

Moreover, to *hacer pozole*, make pozole (pork and chile stew) or prepare a *guiso* (a generic term for prepared food) in the *narcocultura* refers to dissolving a body in a container of acid (Blancornelas 2005, 132). Cartel hit men dehumanize their victims in other ways, including cutting off limbs, stabbing a knife into a victim's skull (and leaving it there), dressing up dead bodies in Santa Claus outfits or the rustic clothes of a stereotypical Mexican peasant (a huge floppy sombrero, red bandana, and cowboy clothes), hanging beheaded bodies from bridges, and lining up cadavers in rows or piling them in heaps. Decapitated heads have been placed in beer coolers or plastic bags and left in front of police stations or in other prominent public places, such as by a Juárez statue dedicated to journalists (an obvious effort to intimidate the mass media—soon thereafter, a famous journalist who covered narco-issues was murdered). The placement of severed heads far from the bodies conveys a gruesome announcement of the drug cartels' power to destroy.

These depraved, choreographed, even ceremonialized actions and the inventive language used to refer to them are part of an emergent culture and discourse created by outsiders and marginal members of Mexican society who, however cruelly, are remaking their cultural world.[45] Such vicious forms of violence, eerily and not surprisingly, parallel the equally ritualistic styles of torture and murder regularly committed by the Mexican police: *el tehuacanazo* (pouring mineral water, often laced with dried chile, down the nostrils), *la chicharra* (burning delicate parts of the body with electrical wires), *la ducha* (shoving the head in a toilet), etc.

Stylized drug killings, symbolically charged messages, narco-slang, videos, and songs transmitted via various media, and the parading and performance of narco-style, are genres of communication and forms of publicity that attempt to rework the public sphere of Mexican society and elevate the status of drug traffickers and cartels (Habermas 1991). As Weimann (2008, 83) points out: "The new communication technologies and especially the Internet carry a paradigm shift: They empower the individuals over states or societies." This occurs within a context of the delegitimization of the PRI-dominated postrevolutionary regime that controlled Mexico from 1929 to 2000, chaotic and unequal neoliberal economic reforms, globalization challenges (including the growing power of U.S. businesses and popular culture), and attempts by the PAN to reestablish order based on conservative, free-market policies. Efforts by the Mexican government to wipe out, or at least to lessen, the power of drug-trafficking organizations through military campaigns, bans on the radio diffusion of *narcocorridos*, anticorruption crusades, and other efforts have largely failed because of preexisting ties between traffickers and elements of the state (especially within the police and judicial branches of government and among some politicians) and because of the jobs and revenue provided by drug trafficking. The Mexican drug cartels remain powerful through the use of creative tactics involving both visibility and concealment.

El Paso–Juárez in the Drug War Zone

The previous sections established a theoretical framework for understanding the Mexican American DWZ and the drug-cartel culture that operates within it. I now turn to the local setting and people illustrated in this book. Nestled in the pass (hence the Spanish name "El Paso") that cuts through the southern end of the Rocky Mountains and traverses two nations and three states, the El Paso–Ciudad Juárez region has been a smuggler's paradise for at least a hundred years (Martínez 1978; Staudt 1998). The local landscape provides myriad spaces for imaginative traffickers. Rugged mountains, creased with sharp canyons and arroyos, overlook vast deserts. The lowland, downtown section of El Paso winds along the Rio Grande. The urban population (approximately 650,000) spills out both east to west into farming, industrial, and residential lands that stretch for about fifty miles between rural Fabens, Texas, and Sunland Park, New Mexico, and to the north of the Franklin Mountains. Pecan and cotton farms with many outbuildings straddle both sides of the shallow Rio Grande (Río Bravo). Drug traffickers can easily ford the river and disappear into the maze of rural back roads scattered across El Paso County (one of the largest counties in the United States), and from there enter Interstate Highway 10, which connects the east and west coasts of the United States.

Besides the many rural, riverine smuggling venues, drug traffickers take advantage of the many connections between the two massive, densely intertwined cities of El Paso and Juárez. These include four international bridges across the Rio Grande, several railroad crossings, and numerous tunnels and drainage canals as well as holes in the chain-link fences that divide El Paso and Juárez. The city of Juárez, with a population of approximately 1.5 million, is clearly visible across the river from El Paso except where mountains or large buildings block the view. The sprawling, diffuse cities are filled with relatively new, anonymous neighborhoods as well as large industrial and warehouse districts, all of which are ideal sites for stash houses and staging areas for smuggling operations.

Social disorganization and lax public security are especially noteworthy in Ciudad Juárez, which is roughly twice the size of El Paso. Juárez extends from Avenida Juárez, the commercial hub of the decrepit central-city area—which is connected by an international bridge to El Paso Street in the heart of El Paso's vintage late-nineteenth-century western-style central business district—around the Juárez Mountains and into the desert. To the east of downtown Juárez, new commercial and residential sections and hundreds of maquiladoras loom on the horizon, and to the south and west a boundless web of impoverished *colonias* (poor neighborhoods) has replaced farm and desert lands. Just as El Pasoans can see the factories of their sister city, Juarenses can see the skyscrapers of El Paso from many parts of their city—the two border communities are inextricably linked.

Poor, and far from the centers of political power in Washington, D.C., and Mexico City, border residents often view abstract laws as simply minor obstacles to be overcome. A local culture of silence and minding one's own business treats minor cross-border smuggling of food, clothing, medicine, and other items as a regular part of life rather than a moral crime (Dugan 1997). Drug trafficking is considered an inevitable, rather than shocking, fact of the border economy. Historical economic factors have also contributed to the growth of El Paso–Juárez as a major international drug-smuggling hub. These include cross-border differences in law (for example, the United States prohibited alcohol in the 1920s while Mexico remained alcohol friendly; currently, the United States outlaws marijuana, cocaine, and other drugs, while the Mexican government often acts with complicity in smuggling operations); the enactment of the North American Free Trade Agreement, which speeded up all manner of transnational commerce and expanded the industrial economy of Juárez; the relative wealth of Mexico's northern states, which has produced an excellent infrastructure for the transportation of drugs; and the proximity of the Sierra Madre opium and marijuana fields to the large drug-consuming cities of the United States.

Furthermore, migration to Juárez from Mexican states to the south brings a huge reserve labor army to the *colonias* and urban barrios, and local government is unable to deal with this influx. There is a virtually limitless supply of unemployed workers ready and willing to make good money by driving or walking loads of drugs across the border or by serving as a stash-house guard or a hit man. Smugglers have little difficulty adapting socially or communicating in Spanish, English, or Spanglish on either side of the bilingual, bicultural border. The enormous maquiladora industry and related El Paso long-haul trucking industry provide the heavy-duty eighteen-wheelers and every possible storage facility, tool, equipment, or supply needed to package, conceal, store, and transport contraband drugs. The binational conurbation also provides all necessary banking, currency exchange, telecommunications, legal, and other services required for an effective drug-smuggling organization. Likewise, black-market guns and stolen cars used for self-defense and smuggling are readily available. Thousands of local residents live simultaneously in both El Paso and Juárez, and families bisect the border. In essence, the border is more a resource for smugglers than a hindrance.

The Carrillo Fuentes family took control of the Juárez *plaza* in 1993. Amado Carrillo Fuentes, also known as the "Lord of the Skies" because he used Boeing 747s to bring loads of cocaine from Colombia to Juárez and then the United States, ran the Juárez cartel (or the Carrillo Fuentes cartel) until his death in 1997 (Bowden 2002). Since then, his brother Vicente has assumed control. At present, the Chapo Guzmán cartel of Sinaloa and possibly elements of the Zetas and the Beltrán family are engaged in a bloody street battle with the Juárez cartel. As of December, about 2,400 homicides were documented in Juárez during 2009. The winner of this violent struggle will command the lucrative Juárez *plaza*.

The interviews and oral histories that follow present a diversity of experiences within the border DWZ, from the perspectives of drug smugglers, law enforcement officials, and others.[46] The interviewees provide details about their personal lives before their contact with the drug world as well as stories of their careers within that world. Brief introductions to each interview situate the individual biographies within the larger history of drug trafficking and law enforcement as well as within U.S.-Mexico border culture in the DWZ. Many of my informants are people whom I have known for a long time and with whom I engage, to a degree, in a common border social environment. For this reason, and as part of general anthropological ethics, I have endeavored to not reveal anything that would cause harm to the informants or anyone else. To achieve this aim, it has occasionally been necessary to change the names of people or places or to otherwise modify details of the biographies.

The interviewees include a high-level drug kingpin, middle-level organizers of drug deals, low-level mules, and street-level drug sellers. These people are or were associated with the Juárez cartel or its precursors in the region. I have inserted discussions also with experts on the history of drug trafficking in the El Paso–Juárez area, innocent bystanders, or victims of drug-trafficker activity, and a journalist whose life was threatened by *narcotraficantes*. Additionally, I present the stories of a variety of law-enforcement officials who combat drug trafficking, including an undercover narc, a Juárez beat cop, the former head of an antinarcotics task force, an active Border Patrol agent, and a retired Border Patrol–DEA agent who now opposes the war on drugs.

Note: The Spanish-language interviews were translated by the author with the assistance of Rafael Nuñez.

PART I

SMUGGLING IN THE DRUG WAR ZONE

Introduction: Drug Trafficking—Studies and Sources Relevant to the Mexican-American Drug War Zone

At 3:11 A.M., 76.7 pounds of marijuana were taken from the fuel tank of a 1998 Chevrolet truck at the Zaragoza Bridge and the 47-year-old El Paso driver was arrested.
EL PASO TIMES, JULY 12, 2007

In general, the richest, most in-depth accounts of drug trafficking are provided by journalists (Mills 1986; Poppa 1998; Shannon 1988; Molano 2004; Ravelo 2006, 2007d; Blancornelas 2005; Gómez and Fritz 2005; Bowden 2002, 2005; Cartwright 1998; Wald 2001; Caporal 2003), not social scientists, and probably also by confidential law-enforcement sources, to which, unfortunately, I have no access. Mexican newspapers provide a running, day-to-day recounting of important events from the drug-trafficking world, but often it is difficult to verify many details of these stories. The Mexican newsmagazine *Proceso* has supplied important investigative stories for three decades, but many assertions of its drug reporting cannot be corroborated.[1]

There also have been occasional first-person memoirs by direct participants in or close observers of drug trafficking or law enforcement (Ford 2005; Kuykendall 2005; Strong 1990; Kamstra 1974; Sabbag 1998, 2002; Levine 2000; Marks 1998; Andrade Bojorges 1999; Glendinning 2005). These memoirs are rich in detail, but are often narrowly focused. Additionally, there is an emerging narco-literature, much of which, not surprisingly, emanates from or focuses on Sinaloa, Mexico, home of many of the largest drug cartels (Pérez-Reverte 2004; Alfaro 2005; Flores 2001; Aridjis 2003; Mendoza 2001).[2] Some of this literature loosely chronicles events in the DWZ, such as that of Ronquillo, who sardonically notes that "any resemblance [in his short stories] to reality is not a coincidence . . . it is a disgrace" (2006, 8). Other researchers have examined *narcocorridos* (Wald 2001; Valenzuela 2002; Edberg 2004), which function as musical commentaries on the drug business. Academic studies of drug production and trafficking (Bagley and Walker 1994; Gootenberg 1999; Morales 1990; Sanabria 1993; Nordstrom 2007, 129–137; Astorga 2005; Malkin 2001; Toro 1995; Decker and Chapman 2008), however, have paled in comparison to the rich literature on drug use and abuse (for example, Singer 2006; Bourgois 1995). Moreover, most empirical social-science research on drug selling is concerned with street-level dealing in U.S. cities, not the larger-volume, international smuggling that is the primary subject of this book. An exception is criminologists Decker and Chapman's questionnaire-based study (2008) of the perspectives of Colombian and Cuban drug smugglers imprisoned in the United States.

Ethnographic literature on international drug trafficking, because of the dangers such work entails, is sparse; some relevant studies include those by Dennis (2003), Whiteford (2002), and Geffray (2002). Anthropologists have been studying illicit drug use since at least the 1930s, and the field expanded considerably during the radical 1960s and again during the 1990s AIDS epidemic, yet few ethnographers have studied the larger illegal-drug industry, that is, the business side of illicit drugs rather than their consumption. The few key studies include those by Adler (1993), Hoffer (2006), Bourgois (1995), Richardson and Resendiz (2006, 164–189), Taussig (2004), Malkin (2001), McDonald (2005), and Molano (2004).

Adler's pioneering ethnography focuses on a California drug organization as the center of a "deviant lifestyle" in the 1970s. Hoffer's and Bourgois's fine field studies concern the street selling of heroin, cocaine, and other drugs in large American cities in the 1980s and 1990s as well as the cultural arrangements and political-economic structures that sustain the trade. Malkin and McDonald show how narco-trafficking has transformed rural Mexican economics, social structures, and ways of living. Richardson and Resendiz (with contributions by Lupe Treviño) provide a largely descriptive account of drug smuggling in the South Texas border area, emphasizing in particular the role of communities and families as barriers to or facilitators of drug-trafficking activities.

Taussig's imaginative literary-theoretical-ethnographic book (2004) on the Colombian cocaine trade sheds creative new light on the subject. However, my approach, similar to the narrative accounts presented by Molano (2004), is much more "realistic" than that of Taussig, for the simple reason that I feel that the actual events and circumstances of the Mexican drug trade are sufficiently mind boggling. The details of border drug trafficking are so impressive—need we wonder why magical realism developed in Latin America?—that there is no need to resort to literary style to amplify their significance. Whereas Taussig is concerned with upending or subverting officialist histories and erasures, my project attempts to provide a close-grained empirical account of historical and contemporary participants in the DWZ.[3]

The research questions that guided this book are as follows: Who are border drug traffickers and how do they live? How do they smuggle drugs across the border and beyond? What are their emotions and reasons for doing what they do? How does drug trafficking affect their lives? What do they think about the war on drugs? What are the cultural and gender dimensions of drug trafficking?

Additional research questions include the following: What are the main strategies pursued by drug-trafficking organizations, and how do they change over time? How are drug-trafficking organizations socially organized, and what are the internal dynamics of such organizations? What are the informal cultural rules, norms, and mores of drug-trafficking organizations? What are the social and cultural consequences for the larger society of drug-trafficking culture?

These issues are illustrated in the oral histories that follow, and they are analyzed in the mini-introductions that precede them. This section begins with four accounts ("La Nacha: The Heroin Queen of Juárez," "The Roots of Contraband Smuggling in El Paso," "Female Drug Lord," and "Community-Based Drug Use, Smuggling, and Dealing in the 1970s and 1980s") that shed light on the historical development of drug trafficking in the El Paso–Juárez DWZ. The interviews that follow ("Selling Drugs in Downtown Juárez: Juan and Jorge," "A Young Smuggler and His Family," "Blaxicans: The Life of a Chicano Smuggler and Musician on the Borderlines of African American and Mexican American Cultures," "Drug Addiction and Drug Trafficking in the Life of an Anarchist," "Drug Smuggling through Tunnels: The Tale of a Scuba-Diving Instructor," and "Witness to a Juárez Drug Killing") are concerned with contemporary aspects of drug trafficking.[4]

La Nacha: The Heroin Queen of Juárez

Robert Chessey, the son of a DEA agent, has conducted research for many years on Ignacia Jasso González, aka "La Nacha," the "Dope Queen" of the El Paso–Juárez border region from the 1920s to the 1970s. Chessey's research provides revealing details on the early stages of the Mexican-American drug trade. La Nacha was one of the first major drug dealers in Ciudad Juárez, and she eventually outmuscled or outlasted all of her rivals. La Nacha learned the nuances of the drug trade from her husband ("El Pablote") and her first boss, the largest drug trafficker in Mexico in the 1930s, Enrique Fernández, the so-called Al Capone of Ciudad Juárez. After Fernández's and Pablote's deaths, La Nacha became the major player in the Juárez drug trade.

The fact that La Nacha's enterprise survived for fifty years is a reflection of the many unusual traits that she possessed. Chessey notes that La Nacha's business, public relations, and negotiating skills were the keys to her success. La Nacha bribed or deftly manipulated local and federal politicians but never aspired to climb socially. She preferred to stay in the same working-class Juárez neighborhoods—conveniently located near the Paso del Norte International Bridge and the Chihuahuita barrio of El Paso—where she lived most of her adult life. Most of La Nacha's large American junkie clientele came directly to her to make their purchases.

La Nacha helped the poor and disenfranchised in Juárez, including the financing of an orphanage and a free breakfast program, although she was known throughout the El Paso–Juárez region and beyond as the dominant drug broker on the U.S.-Mexico border. However, La Nacha did occasionally run into trouble with the authorities, and she was in and out of jail in Juárez for relatively short periods of time. She also served an extended term at the infamous Islas Marías island prison, reminiscent of Devil's Island, the harsh penal colony featured in the movie *Papillon*. The United States, despite its enormous power over Mexico, was never able to extradite her, although La Nacha's case may have set a precedent for later extraditions of Latin American drug lords.

La Nacha's organization, which we could call a smuggling gang, and which was smaller than the later, much larger cartels, grew within a border contraband milieu that developed in response to the alcohol-smuggling opportunities created by Prohibition in the United States in the 1920s. Once alcohol was legalized in the 1930s, Enrique Fernández, La Nacha, and others mainly dealt in marijuana and heroin. Before the 1960s expansion of the U.S. counterculture, which increased the demand for marijuana, Mexican drug trafficking seldom entailed the shipment of hundreds of pounds or even tons of dope, as became commonplace from the 1960s onward.

La Nacha's death, in 1977, marked the end of an era in the history of Mexican drug trafficking in general and of Juárez trafficking in particular. La Nacha and her contemporaries in other parts of Mexico made substantial revenues from their trade, but their steady yet relatively small-scale trafficking activity, which was primarily local and regional but maintained some connections across the U.S. border, was replaced in the 1970s and 1980s by much larger, more technologically sophisticated, and truly transnational businesses, the modern drug cartels, which dominate today. Cocaine emerged as a popular consumer drug in the United States in the 1970s, but the early demand was supplied primarily by Colombian traffickers, who shipped their product to Miami and other East Coast ports. The DEA crackdown on Colombian cocaine trafficking to Florida weakened the Colombian drug bosses, led to the cocaine supply being channeled through Mexico and across the less-protected U.S.-Mexico border in the 1980s, and allowed Mexican cartels to surpass the Colombians in wealth and power by the 1990s.

The first large Mexican trafficking groups that came to be known as cartels were the Sicilia Falcón organization in Tijuana, the Ernesto Fonseca and Miguel Ángel Félix Gallardo trafficking groups in Sinaloa (and later Guadalajara), the Gulf trafficking group controlled by Juan N. Guerra (and later Juan García Ábrego), and the Juárez cartel (discussed below). Sinaloa is the historical home of marijuana and opium cultivation in Mexico. Most contemporary cartel leaders, such as the Arellano Félix family, are Sinaloans who are successors to the Fonseca-Gallardo group of the 1970s.[1]

In the 1980s, Mexican traffickers such as Pablo Acosta, Rafael Muñoz Talavera, and Amado Carrillo Fuentes in Chihuahua became the innovators of a large-scale trade in cocaine across the U.S. border, made possible by the reconditioning of Boeing 747 jets as cargo planes (by removing the passenger seats) to bring South American drugs to northern Mexico. Muñoz Talavera, a businessman, and Rafael Aguilar, a federal police commander, founded the first Juárez cartel in the 1980s. Carrillo Fuentes, nicknamed the "Lord of the Skies" because of his ingenious use of large aircraft, took over the Juárez cartel in 1993 after the murders of Acosta and Aguilar and the imprisonment of Muñoz Talavera. It appears that the Carrillo Fuentes organization murdered Aguilar and also later Muñoz Talavera (in 1998) in order to maintain control of the Juárez *plaza*. In the mid-1990s, Amado Carrillo Fuentes's Juárez cartel was the largest drug-trafficking organization in the world. After Amado's death, in 1997, his brother Vicente took the reins of the cartel, although his dominion over the Juárez *plaza* is currently disputed by the Chapo Guzmán organization of Sinaloa.

La Nacha's life takes us back to the early phases of Mexican drug-trafficking history. The account of La Nacha's life that follows is presented from the standpoint of historian Robert Chessey.

Researcher Robert Chessey on Border Life, Law Enforcement, and La Nacha

We moved to El Paso when I was six years old, when my father was transferred here. He started working for the Border Patrol in 1960. When I was a senior in high school, he joined the U.S. Customs Service, working for the antinarcotics division. He was there when, under Nixon, all the antidrug efforts were merged into one organization, the DEA [Drug Enforcement Administration]. He was in the DEA for about a year and a half, and then went back to Customs. And at that point he wasn't working drug cases unless it involved trading drugs from Mexico for guns or jewelry—in other words, if the case involved customs violations.

I attended Burges High School, from where I graduated in 1972. I remember coming home my senior year sometimes and finding my dad at home, with his car parked inside the garage. My dad would be sitting there, reading the paper. At this point he was an undercover narcotics agent: a federal narc, plainclothes, undercover. So I would say to him, "I didn't expect you to be home, and your car in the garage." And he would reply, "Well, I had fifteen kilos of pot in the trunk, and I didn't feel good leaving it out in the driveway." So I would say, "Okay, Dad, I'm going to play basketball now." All the while never realizing that in other families the dad didn't come home with fifteen kilos of drugs, or $20,000 dollars in cash, in the trunk of their car.

In those days, long hair was not an option in the house. Of course, back then a lot of us had long hair. My dad was an antidrug warrior, and to me it was just his job. I had grown up with him being in law enforcement. I remember my dad introducing me to everybody working on the international bridge, saying, "This is my son, so if you ever see him coming across the bridge, you'll know who he is."

I was very aware at the time that we were in a unique situation here on the border. Even though the drinking age was twenty-one, we could slip over to Mexico and go drinking. Besides drinking, we were going to a foreign country, and I found that exotic and exciting, and a lot of my friends did too. After I was out of high school, I remember my father saying to me, "I know you're going to Mexico. Let me give you some rules to make your life a lot easier: When people offer you drugs, you don't even say no. You just keep walking. You don't want to be observed talking to them. You don't want to even have to look at it. You're being set up, and you're going down hard." He would tell me stories; he worked on the bridge, in narcotics, and so he knew about Americans getting scammed over there. I knew someone who was walking down the street in Juárez, and someone called out to him, "¡Morfina!" So my friend said to the guy, "You don't have that," which, in hindsight, was stupid. Well, the guy brought it out. Once it came out, cops started coming out of nowhere, and my friend realized it was a setup, and so he ran all the way back to the bridge and actually made it back safely to U.S. soil. That's why my father used to tell me, "You don't talk about drugs. You don't talk to cab drivers. You just go where you're going and then come back over."

My dad and his friends and coworkers would talk about drug dealing and even joke about it. My dad would come home and talk about who he busted, about chasing people and stuff like that. Even when he was in the Border Patrol, it wasn't that unusual for him to be involved in a drug bust. Around here, I guess it's no big deal. People even joke about it. I've had lunch with people and we all sit around and try to figure out which of the businesses we know are fronts. It's so internalized in El Paso, it sometimes becomes a comical topic. I remember living in Austin at a time when all the savings and loans were going under, and it was amazing how few went down along the border.

I first heard about La Nacha back when I was a senior in high school. I remember her name came up, and someone said she was the border dope queen, and that after World War II, she controlled all of the border drug trade along the Rio Grande, from Tijuana to Matamoros. We were having dinner one night, and I asked my dad who La Nacha was. He immediately put down his silverware and was literally looking at me like I had invoked the name of Satan. "How do you know about her?" he asked me. And that was pretty much it. It was obvious that she was persona non grata, and there was no more conversation, which was kind of strange, since she was often in the newspaper.

La Nacha

So that made me even more curious about La Nacha. It was pretty well known that you wouldn't ask about La Nacha in Juárez. I guess if you were trying to score, it would've been fine, but otherwise it would not have been a good move over there to ask about her. I remember back then people in El Paso would just talk about how she was a famous drug dealer. She had been active since World War II. Ironically, that seemed to be her peak, World War II, and from that point on she had declined.

Much later, about five years ago, I had just finished reading Elijah Wald's book on *narcocorridos*. I had moved to Austin in 1982, but I came back to El Paso in 2006. I had always thought El Paso's history was very rich. I loved walking through downtown El Paso. The whole downtown area, especially San Antonio Street and El Paso Street, fascinated me. It seemed that the further south you walked on El Paso Street, as you got closer to the border, you were already in another country even before you actually got to the bridge. While I would stroll through those streets and show my wife more and more of downtown El Paso, I got to thinking about Wald's book on *narcocorridos* and drug trafficking. I had also bought and read a couple of Leon Metz's books on the history of old El Paso in the Wild West days. Then I thought, what about La Nacha? Isn't there anything on her? So I started looking for stuff on her at the downtown library in the border history section. And I would only find a paragraph about her, or a couple of sentences here and there, and that was it. The most I was able to find after I got going on this subject was in *Poso del Mundo* [by Ovid Demaris], which had two or three pages about La Nacha and talked about her being exiled to Las Islas Marías.

She had been sentenced in 1943, but she was in the Juárez prison. Then she was sent to Las Islas Marías for an indefinite period of time till the war ended. So it really appears that her being sent there had more to do with pressure from the U.S. government to get her out of the picture, because, although it was only circumstantial evidence, it looked like she was targeting GIs who were coming over to Juárez on leave. I think that it was a pretty strong case and one that was easy to make. In September 1944, she was moved from the Juárez jail to the Chihuahua City prison, and then on July 9, 1945, she was sent to Las Islas Marías.

Back then in the U.S., narcotics offenses fell under the Treasury Department, and so the U.S. Treasury was involved with her case. The U.S. State Department was involved with her also, because of the extradition process. Then you've got FBN [Federal Bureau of Narcotics], BNDD [Bureau of Narcotics and Dangerous Drugs], and DEA [Drug Enforcement Administration], because she was in business at least fifty years. I have been able to find some grand jury records, with names and dates, and some of the State Department documents they had in the University of Texas library. I have a few things from the Juárez newspapers. When I started this, I began at the UTEP library.

Then I found out about Nicole Moltier, an American from Illinois who was studying at Oxford [University] and was doing research on the drug gangs of Juárez. Next I started to track down retired law-enforcement agents, figuring they would be good sources of information. I was able to find out how to contact a couple of retired drug agents who were willing to help me, one of them being Edward Heath [the former DEA agent in charge in Mexico]. I interviewed Ed Heath. He hadn't heard much about La Nacha. She was important regionally, but not nationally.

From my research, I've been able to find out La Nacha was about fifty years old in 1942; so I guess she was born in 1892. According to newspaper accounts, she was the one that caused the start of extradition requests when she was busted in 1942. She died in 1977, at roughly eighty-five years of age. According to her grandson, she was born in the state of Durango. Apparently, both she and her husband, "El Pablote," were from Durango. The first record specifically identifying her that I was able to find was an El Paso newspaper article dated November 14, 1928. She had been arrested for the second time in two days for selling drugs. At that time, she must have been about thirty-six years old.

According to an article on the Internet titled "La Leyenda Negra" [The Black Legend], she and El Pablote, prior to that, had basically killed a lot of the Chinese opium dealers. Back in those days, the early part of the twentieth century, there was a lot of discrimination and hostility toward the Chinese. In fact, Pancho Villa, the famous Mexican revolutionary leader in the north, hated the Chinese. I tend to believe that La Nacha and El Pablote muscled out the Chinese. There was a lot of resentment about Chinese individuals running businesses. But there were still Chinese people dealing drugs in Juárez into the 1930s. And even though that Internet article implies that La Nacha and El Pablote wiped out all the Chinese drug dealers in Juárez, I would bet that was not the case. They probably took out some of them, but not all.

By 1928, La Nacha was aligned with Enrique Fernández. Pablote was working for Fernández's gang, and it is my feeling that Pablote and La Nacha were part of Fernández's gang. My suspicion is that La Nacha was very bright. Probably poorly educated, academically speaking, but she had great street smarts and was very observant. She learned that those who pay off, walk off. And historically, she was known for being good at paying people off, and she died of old age. In 1973, La Nacha had $4.4 million in Juárez safe-deposit boxes, according to an article in the *El Paso Herald Post*. She also owned properties legally, and she was known as a philanthropist.

Nowadays, Natividad, one of La Nacha's sons, owns a business in Juárez. In turn, his son, Pablo, is the manager of the business. It's my guess that a lot of the money that La Nacha made during her long stint at the top of the Juárez drug-dealing world went to *la mordida* [bribes]. After all, that's how she stayed out of jail for so long.

The mayor of Juárez during most of World War II, Antonio Bermúdez, wanted her out, and it was well known that the U.S. wanted her bad, but she didn't go, and the U.S. never got her. It's also impressive to me that the U.S. government, fifty years before the Pablo Escobar case, was trying to extradite La Nacha to the U.S. for crimes she did not commit on U.S. soil. They never busted her on U.S. soil, even when she used to be able to come over. They would search her car religiously, and never found anything on her. She actually lived in the Chihuahuita barrio, in south-central El Paso, for a few months in the late 1920s—I think 1928.

La Nacha used to go to boxing matches, and even liked to go and watch boxers work out. My research into La Nacha's story has involved a lot of poring over old newspaper articles, looking for tidbits about her. It has actually been a pretty time-consuming process. Back in the early part of the twentieth century, there were more newspapers in El Paso. There was the *Herald* and the *Post*, which later became the *Herald Post*; there was the *El Paso Times*; also *El Continental*, a Spanish-language El Paso newspaper; the *El Paso Evening World News*; and several Juárez newspapers.

In 1945, she was sent to Las Islas Marías, and released in 1946. There are still big gaps in my chronology. The next thing I have was in 1954. It's a newspaper article about the dope queen being back in the Juárez jail. She spent a fair amount of time in jail. I think she survived, and was as successful as she was, because she was willing to pay, and she would pay the policemen on the streets too, not just the higher-ups. She never left the Bellavista barrio, a working-class area located just west of the downtown international bridge, as you cross into Juárez.

She liked cars. She sponsored an orphanage. She was involved in a free breakfast program for children back in the 1930s. Also at one point she was involved in a home for unwed mothers. She survived because she stayed within her class. But Antonio Bermúdez was after her. Back in the 1930s, he was named police commissioner, and was really cracking down on drugs at that time. And that foreshadowed what was going to happen when he became mayor in the early 1940s in Juárez. He was going after the drugs and the prostitution, and he was trying to at least clean up the image of Juárez. And the newspaper articles of the time stated clearly that the El Paso city leaders, and especially the military, loved Bermúdez. He was a significant actor in promoting Juárez as a modern city, a clean city, not vice ridden. I think he was sincere in not wanting Juárez to be a seedy, drug-ridden city.

Nevertheless, La Nacha survived all this. I think her greatest accomplishment was dying of old age. You generally don't live long in that type of business. You don't have to go any further than her husband to see that. Being a woman in that time period and surviving that long says a lot about her smarts. Part of her genius was paying off not just the locals, but also the state and federal law-enforcement agencies. I've even heard that the attorney general's office in Mexico City would call and ask her for "donations."

She pretty much had reached her peak by 1942. She was doing very well then. She was targeting GIs on leave going over to Juárez. Although sometimes the bridge would get shut down and interrupt business. There was a lot of activity at that point besides just the drugs. American MPs, at times with weapons, were allowed to walk the streets in Juárez. At one point, some MPs got jumped by a crowd. There were times that the military refused to let more than 1 percent of its folks go over into Juárez because of problems.

I have read, including some accusations on the El Paso courthouse steps by federal district attorney Jamie Boyd, that La Nacha was part of an international drug gang. But I've never found any documentation to back up that claim. Even when I talked to Ed Heath, he would say that he had never heard of La Nacha actually smuggling drugs into the U.S. She would sell to people who, it appears, would bring drugs into the U.S, which I see as different than her running drugs up to the U.S. I heard things about people from Albuquerque coming down to purchase drugs from her. She probably had enough of a reputation over the decades that people would come to Juárez looking for her. But there is no proof that she actually smuggled directly into the U.S. By the 1940s, she did have one or two heroin-processing labs in Guadalajara. Of course, labs in Mexico many times were just little dives, little houses with makeshift heroin-processing devices in the kitchen. But she did have her own chemist [for making heroin].

A Federal Bureau of Narcotics agent named H. B. Westover got permission from the State Department to work an important case involving narcotic trafficking in Juárez; he was after La Nacha. That information comes from State Department records dated 1942. This agent was the one who infiltrated her gang, pretending to be a buyer of opium. He told her that he would like to see her lab. She was a little skeptical, but told him that if he bought x amount of tins of opium, she would take him to meet her chemist in Guadalajara. And he eventually got her to drive him to Guadalajara to meet her chemist. He convinced the chemist, surely under promises of a lot of money for him, to drive a load of heroin to Laredo, Texas, unbeknownst to La Nacha. Of course, they busted him. And then later, Westover was still able to bust a couple of La Nacha's runners on U.S. soil, and that resulted in her eventually being arrested in Juárez, which in turn led to the whole extradition attempt.

Her Product

La Nacha sold "papers" [small packages or envelopes] of heroin and opium tins. She was a major dealer back then, but of course the quantities were a lot smaller in comparison to the quantities that are now being trafficked. La Nacha sold heroin by the grain. Five grains equaled one dose, and it was about the size of an aspirin. The opium was grown in the state of Sinaloa. Cocaine seemed to be available on the streets of

Juárez, and occasionally even in El Paso. Then, in the late twenties and the early thirties, cocaine kind of started disappearing off the reports. My guess is the Great Depression, the economy, caused the decline in cocaine use. Interestingly, some federal and local law-enforcement officials told me that cocaine was never found here in this region until the 1970s, but if you go back to the twenties, cocaine was not unusual. It wasn't as common as marijuana and heroin, but it was not unusual.

In this region back then, what was sold was sometimes morphine, sometimes opium, and sometimes heroin. They're all a little bit different, heroin, of course, being the most common. And heroin seemed to be La Nacha's specialty. She did sell some marijuana. I found no indication that she ever used heroin. I think one of the reasons she survived for as long as she did was that she didn't use. You make too many mistakes if you do that, and you're not going to last very long in her type of business. She did not live an easy life, even though she was paid well. She was known as a woman who was fair. She didn't try to shortchange you, but you better not try to shortchange her. But she still did a fair amount of time in Mexican prisons. She was assaulted several times and had to leave town, or at least she would pretend to leave town. There were several times when the heat brought down on her was bad. It could have been political changes, and she was aligned with one side which was out of favor politically, and so she would need to leave town until she was back in favor. I think it's pretty easy to assume there was pressure from the U.S. on her at certain times too, which would cause her to leave town for a while lest she be arrested. And probably at those times, since she already had the infrastructure in place, just because she personally left town did not mean that her organization stopped dealing drugs.

There was a newspaper article written by a highly regarded journalist, Rubén Salazar, who claimed that La Nacha sold heroin right out of her house. He walked into her house pretending to be a musician looking to score. So there is some consensus that she sold heroin out of her house, but there is no evidence that she would let junkies shoot up there. In that same article, it says that La Nacha's daughter was selling the heroin, and that because she had never seen Salazar and thus didn't know who he was, La Nacha came out and just stared at him with her penetrating eyes. So through sheer survival instincts, she probably had learned how to size people up to a fair degree, and I guess that would be pretty intimidating. I read in a couple of places that she had rather piercing eyes.

When she was busted in 1942, she had a little café somewhere in

Juárez. Supposedly, she was arrested when authorities walked in and found her shooting up two teenagers. She was injecting them herself. She also owned shooting galleries in Bellavista [a Juárez neighborhood], at least two, a couple of whorehouses, a used-clothing store, and also a couple of small ranches. She moved around a lot. Her main house was on Violetas Street. It was not an elaborate house—it was actually fairly simple.

Federal attorney Jamie Boyd had a press conference in the 1960s and said he had a grand jury indictment against La Nacha, and that they wanted her. He also said that she owned fencing operations, whorehouses, and that she was linked to car-theft activities. But I have not seen any documentation specifically linking her to the heads of a car-theft gang. There are stories that La Nacha gave a ten-dollar bill every Friday to policemen who stopped by her house. In some stories, she is often portrayed like a lovable grandmother.

La Nacha's Organization

Several generations of family members were involved, most famously, her grandson "El Árabe," who reputedly was a big dealer. There are also reports of her daughter and sons selling drugs. And about how at her house there were kids running around, and the heroin bindles were on the table, and close by was the shrine of her patron saint. A retired detective said that when he was the liaison between El Paso and Juárez law enforcement, he went to her house twice, and that he saw lots of pistoleros around. She had bodyguards; she had protection.

I also have a picture of the so-called *esquina alegre* [happy corner], the street corner where she sold, located in a little *callejón* [alley] between Mariscal and Juárez Avenues. There's a little alley right next to the gym that's there now [the Josué Neri Santos gymnasium]. I think her organization was sort of like an Avon thing, a pyramid scheme. You could go directly to her to buy, or you could buy from people she sold to.

La Nacha as a Woman

I'm amazed that she stayed in business as long as she did, that she didn't really get out of the business before she died. She seemed to be a very good businesswoman. She understood her market, the overhead, how to set up an infrastructure. And even though her competition eventually overtook her, part of that was age and part of it was the changing times.

But she was able to withstand different political settings in Juárez. She was also able to withstand repeated U.S. pressure to remove her. She had to have a strong sense of self. She was not a Pablo Escobar or a Meyer Lansky or a Lucky Luciano. But she knew her region. And I think that was part of it, too, that she didn't expand beyond her abilities. She knew her limits.

She seemed to have lived a pretty comfortable existence. And she did give some back to the community. Whatever her reasons were, whether she was altruistic or it was just a matter of "I'll take care of you if you take care of me." There was probably a little bit of both.

There was no second husband, but there was a man, Zeferino García, who was her *compa* [companion]. She never remarried after El Pablote died. But Zeferino was her sweetheart. They lived together, so it was pretty obvious that he was her companion, her lover. He disappeared off the radar in the 1940s. No one seemed to know about him by the 1950s. I asked people who knew her in the fifties, and nobody seemed to remember him. He worked for the railroads and was a smuggler too. But he was the only other male I've heard associated with her. It would have been during her forties when she had him by her side.

She had a lot on her mind after that. There were a lot of periods when she was in prison. The big period was from 1942 to 1945, when she was in jail. In that time period, it was claimed that she got religion, of the evangelical variety. I don't know that that really had a significant impact on the rest of her life. But she did seem to have a certain genius for public relations. She was also in jail a fair amount in the late twenties and early thirties. But she would either quickly get an *amparo* [injunction], or witnesses would mysteriously change their testimony before sentencing, and that seemed to happen at least a couple of times.

In March of 1954, she got out of jail once again, since she had been arrested and did some months behind bars. Then in the 1960s, she had to leave town once or twice. A granddaughter was supposedly the head of a drug ring in Juárez in the early seventies.

I've also heard that she has a daughter in Denver. La Nacha's oldest son, Manuel, lived in El Paso, and worked at ASARCO [the American Smelting and Refining Company]. He didn't have anything to do with the "family business." He was eleven years old in 1930, and Natividad was three. She also had a son named Gilberto González, who died in the 1964. They said it was a suicide, but it was extremely questionable. Héctor Ruiz González, better known as "El Árabe," was her grandson. He died in November of 1973 in a car wreck. Also a grandson of La Nacha,

Eduardo Amador González was busted in 1965 in El Paso by the Santa Fe Bridge. La Nacha was interrogated after he was arrested. Apparently what happened is that two brothers had just scored, and Eduardo, who was hanging around out front, asked them if they wanted him to run that over to the U.S. side for them. Eduardo was twenty years old, and these guys didn't know he was La Nacha's grandson. So he crosses over and is waiting for these guys by the bridge, and the local detective sees him and busts him [for] holding. It was quite a scandal. La Nacha had tried to keep him out of the business. So she was infuriated that he had gotten popped. Of course, at the time it was a big deal. After all, it was La Nacha's grandson who had been busted in El Paso running drugs.

The Roots of Contraband Smuggling in El Paso

La Nacha's life story chronicles the rise of drug trafficking in Ciudad Juárez. Fred ("Freddy") Morales, a historian and longtime El Pasoan, complements her story with an account of the evolution of the El Paso drug trade, which has always been closely connected with Juárez.

When he was still a child, Freddy and his family moved to the oldest Mexican neighborhood in El Paso, the area known as *el barrio de Chihuahuita*. Chihuahuita lies west, and in the shadow, of the international bridge that crosses the Rio Grande/Río Bravo and divides downtown El Paso from downtown Ciudad Juárez. As an adult, Freddy began collecting documents and artifacts concerned with Ciudad Juárez and El Paso, including all he could find about Chihuahuita's history. His research was helped by the fact that he grew up in the neighborhood and has lived, even as an adult, in various parts of the barrio. Morales experienced firsthand the traditional role Chihuahuita has played as an unofficial (that is, illegal) gateway into the United States for smugglers and their merchandise, and undocumented immigrants.

Freddy's knowledge of El Paso barrio history, gang culture and territories, and the many *tecato* (junkie) venues and smuggling operations from the 1940s through the 1970s—and in some cases to the present—is nonpareil. Morales's narrative illustrates the rich cultural life of El Paso barrios and a dynamic smuggling economy that continues today. Although many of the gangs Morales discusses have disappeared, the Barrio Azteca–Aztecas gang has become a key smuggling and local-distribution cell of the Juárez cartel. The gang also controls much of the vast street and prison retail drug trade in the El Paso–Juárez area, although other drug gangs and independent operators also abound.

The account that follows is presented from the standpoint of historian Fred Morales.

Freddy Morales

I was born in Carlsbad, New Mexico, but when I was three weeks old, my family moved to the Chihuahuita neighborhood in south-central El Paso, at 916 South Santa Fe Street, where I grew up, as well as in different areas close to the international border. At one point I lived in the same apartment where La Nacha had lived for a couple of months. There were many people that felt uncomfortable when she was residing there, and when she left, there was a big sigh of relief.

The owner of the tenements, Mona Rivera Montestruc, who owned the building in the 1930s, told me about La Nacha. She said that she had rented apartment number five, at 901 South Chihuahua Street, to La Nacha. I remember her telling me that she would see all kinds of people entering the apartment at all hours of the night. La Nacha was running her [heroin-selling] operations from there, because at that time the Juárez police were after her. So she went to live in Chihuahuita temporarily. Later, she lived across the river in Juárez, in a house that still stands on Violetas Street, in the Bellavista neighborhood.

I went to [predominantly Chicano] Bowie High School in El Paso. My parents had a business in which they drove farmworkers to fields in Dell City, Texas. They knew all the farmers in this region. I am a latecomer to historical research. I didn't study El Paso history until the 1990s. At that time, I started collecting El Paso stuff like photos and postcards. I had a good friend, an Englishman—Mr. Dickens—who was an antique dealer, and he gave me a lot of stuff. He liked what I was doing, and he knew I wouldn't sell the things that he gave me. Prior to that, I was only interested in Juárez history and then eventually Chihuahuita history. I used to be good friends with a *cronista* [local historian] in Juárez, Ignacio Esparza Marín. I was involved with the historical society in Juárez, and I used to go to the readings there. But I stopped going because it was too much of a hassle with the international bridges, the traffic, and the congestion. I was interested in Juárez because Chihuahuita is like an extension of Juárez, and in many ways it is closer to Juárez than to the rest of El Paso. So I started collecting stuff about Juárez. There was a guy who sold postcards on Francisco Villa Street in Juárez. His name was Óscar Ponce, and he was a photo and postcard collector. I also got a lot of material from him. He had a big antique-postcard collection, and he had a lot of photographs of Marilyn Monroe.

I got interested in El Paso history because I was bored and needed a new hobby to keep me out of trouble. Growing up in Chihuahuita, I experienced a lot of peer pressure. There's a lot of drugs, and I needed to get away from all that. I never liked history in high school and college. In fact, I hated it. I graduated from UTEP in 1980 with a BA in sociology.

I used to have exhibits in Juárez. I was on the radio stations, and had exhibits at the Juárez Plaza de Armas. Nowadays I don't like to go to Juárez, because I had a bad experience with reporters from the Juárez newspaper *El Diario*. I noticed that the photographers had started taking pictures of my photos, and that angered me. They hadn't even asked permission. So we had a big argument. And then those pictures came out the next day in the newspaper. So they had stolen my pictures. Nowadays I have all my stuff in storage. I've tried everything to get my stuff displayed—grants, sponsorships, the works—but they're not interested. I feel like I have all this talent to exploit, but no one here in El Paso wants it. I've tried to work with the city, but they weren't interested either.

Early Smugglers

The Chinese that had settled in Juárez smuggled opium across the river. I don't believe there were tunnels built under the river or that some of these came out in the Sunset Heights neighborhood [as many local people believe]. I think those were mostly basements that people later mistook for tunnels. Like, for example, in Chihuahuita there are a lot of basements. They were used for storage purposes, and later, during Prohibition, booze was stored there and transported elsewhere from those Chihuahuita basements. But as far as the Chinese, the only tunnels that I know of were located on Oregon Street, between Paisano Drive and Third Street. That area was honeycombed with tunnels, and I have newspaper articles to prove it. That was the heart of Chinatown in El Paso. Those tunnels were linked from house to house. When the Chinese were raided by law-enforcement agents, the people living in the house would just go in the tunnel and go to the next house.

In the 1910s, the border wasn't patrolled much. The Border Patrol was not established until 1924. Before that, U.S. Customs had their Prohibition agents working in that area, but there was really not that much

Chinese smuggling back then. I think some smugglers in those early times of the twentieth century were brave, ruthless, courageous. Those early smugglers were primarily Mexicans from Juárez and from El Paso. They would work together, smuggling what they call *latas* [tin cans], or *latas de cuatro hojas* [four-sided tin cans], which held up to five gallons. A smuggler could carry maybe two of these tin *latas* at the most. Or they would use mules, since you could carry more *latas* on a mule, or a horse. They also used little makeshift ferryboats. They would smuggle *sotol* [a cactus-based beverage similar to tequila], tequila, rum, brandy, and liquor in general. They would strap them to their backs.

There were various means to smuggle. Women were known to wear jackets with big pockets to carry bottles. They would smuggle bottles of various types of hard liquor. And automobiles that were used to cross the international bridges had secret compartments. Some cars had one or two of their cylinders removed in order to conceal the liquor in the engine block. The local smuggler would be given two gunnysacks full of bottled whiskey, and they were draped over the back of a horse or a mule. Around 1918, smugglers were being paid about five pesos for a good night's work. These people were poor, and they couldn't get jobs, especially during the Depression. So they had to resort to this type of activity. They would even force small children to bootleg, because if they were caught, they were not prosecuted because they were juveniles. In many cases the smugglers were armed.

Old Smuggling Venues

Chihuahuita and Smeltertown, located near the Cristo Rey Mountain, from way back played a role as smuggling venues in El Paso, as well as the end of Park Street in the Segundo Barrio, also Cordova Island, and La Isla near San Elizario. They have been the major smuggling entry points in this region. But Chihuahuita always beat them out. Chihuahuita, Smeltertown, and Cordova were the top smuggling areas. More agents were killed at Cordova Island and Smeltertown, whereas none were killed in Chihuahuita. In fact, in Chihuahuita it was the other way around—it was the bootleggers that were killed.

As far as notorious smugglers, the main one was Fausto Prego. He was never caught. He lived at 466 Charles Road, right next to the river and the canal. Other famous smugglers from Chihuahuita, were, for example, Pedro Cucharena, María López, Encarnación Alegre, Lázaro Avitia, and "El Chon." They had spotters, and they also had snipers. They had a system of how to notify the smuggler when to cross and when it was too hot to cross. They had systems to warn them, like lights or whistles, or they would blow their car horns, you know, different tactics. When the Border Patrol implemented Operation Hold the Line [1993], it did effectively stop these smugglers. But it still happens, although in more isolated instances. There was once a lot of drug smuggling, a lot of crime in that area.

The Puente Negro [Black Bridge] gang operated there, as well as corrupt police officers. "El Bola de Humo" [the Cloud of Smoke] was a very well-known Juárez policeman who was a high-ranking member of the Puente Negro gang. He would charge a commission to individuals that wanted to use that area to smuggle something across into the U.S. One time I got to see him, because the coyotes ran through Chihuahuita because they didn't have their quota, you know, *la mordida* [the bribe], *la comisión* [the commission] to give to him. And they were hiding in Chihuahuita. So I asked them what was going on, and they said El Bola de Humo is chasing us. He's mad because he was waiting for his *comisión*, but we don't have it, so he chased us.

The ferryman would make good money with his rubber inner tube. Sometimes he made up to three hundred dollars a day. The people who lived in Chihuahuita, we would be caught in the crossfire between Border Patrol and the illegal aliens and the smugglers. It was frustrating because the Border Patrol often thought we were illegal aliens too. We would have to show identification. It was embarrassing because the whole barrio would be watching, and sometimes they would shout, "Hey, they're going to take Freddy to the *corralón* [an INS holding pen]." We in Chihuahuita were always fighting the Puente Negro gang because they always wanted to come in and control Chihuahuita too. There was also a gang in Chihuahuita, and they didn't put up with that. There were even shootouts and stabbings between those two gangs.

In the 1970s and 1980s, the so-called Chihuahuita gang was strong. There isn't much of a gang now; it's more like a club. They play *washas* and they drink beer. But in the old days, they were involved in smuggling. In fact, almost everybody back then was a part-time smuggler; it was like a part-time job, a way to make money. So there were guys in Chihuahuita who would help illegal aliens by giving them a ride to the downtown area. Because once they were away from Chihuahuita, they were safe. But it's very risky. Smuggling undocumented aliens is a federal offense. Several people from Chihuahuita were busted for doing that. The Chihuahuita Apartments were dens for smuggling. There used to be five tenements; now there are only four. Some of those apartments even had snipers by the doors. Once there was an incident where twelve adobe units were being demolished and the residents were forced to go back to Juárez, and from Juárez they were firing on the demolition crew.

During the Mexican Revolution, when the Battle of Juárez was going on, hundreds and hundreds of people crossed into the U.S. through Chihuahuita. You wouldn't see that in other parts along the border between El Paso and Juárez. Maybe a little bit in Smeltertown and the Segundo Barrio. But Chihuahuita is more convenient, since downtown is right there. The fence they put there ended in Chihuahuita, so smugglers didn't even have to make a hole.

In Chihuahuita there is crossing activity twenty-four hours a day. Even in the middle of the night, you can hear activity going on. Even we, the residents of Chihuahuita, could use the Puente Negro to go to Juárez and buy burritos without the hassle of using the international bridges. But crossing through the Puente Negro was like running through a gauntlet. The Puente Negro, or Black Bridge, was built in 1967 as part of the Chamizal Treaty. I call it the Ellis Island of the American West for illegal immigrants.

Usually, the smugglers would form like a human chain, and they would pass one bundle to each other. In those days, the river [Rio Grande] was wide, and so it was necessary. Sometimes when the river would have hardly any water, the smugglers would put rocks across the bed of the river, sort of like stepping-stones that were used to cross the river. I remember that the human mules were first charging twenty-five cents, then later fifty cents, then one dollar, and then three dollars. I remember I used to know this guy called "El Canguro" [the Kangaroo], and he was carrying a big fat lady, and they both fell into the river. It was quite a scene. The current took them both downriver. The lady was really pissed off after getting all wet, and so she didn't even pay the Canguro for getting her across.

The worst day of the year to go across the river was El Día de San Juan [St. John's Day]. Both from Chihuahuita and Bellavista . . . there would be rock and bottle throwing between those two barrios. Every year there was a big fight on that day. Everyone was just waiting to see who would be the first one to start it. Usually, the police on both sides of the river would show up and tell everybody to go home. But there were stabbings, and people would get badly hurt from getting hit by rocks or bottles. But it never failed; people would always show up by the river on that day. There were a lot of heroin junkies in the 1970s and 1980s in Chihuahuita. There were a lot of discarded needles on the ground in some areas of Chihuahuita back then.

Old Heroin Venues in El Paso

Some of the most notorious heroin-copping venues in El Paso were, for example, the corner of Rivera Street and San Antonio Street. They used to call that La Sana, which is an abbreviation for San Antonio. Also on the corner of Estrella and San Antonio, close to Paisano, it was a hangout, and people would sell heroin there. The Scorpions gang was there. There were also the heroin-hot apartments, on Oregon Street, near the flea market. Then they moved to a park in Sunset Heights over there on El Paso Street near Schuster Street. They moved there because they had a big fight with the T-birds in south El Paso, near the Armijo Recreation Center. Each barrio had a place to buy dope. The Segundo Barrio was a hot spot in the 1970s and 1980s. There used to be drug sellers on every corner. Also near the water-treatment plant in Chihuahuita. Also in the San Juan barrio; they used to call them *sanjuaneros*. They all did drugs, and there were gangs there also. Another hot spot for heroin was the Barrio Sobaco, near San Juan; there were about fifteen adobe houses there. Also Zavala School, where in the 1940s and 1950s there was a gang called the Beboppers. And then there was Barrio La Roca, located near Thomason Hospital. Back in the seventies and eighties there were a lot of gangs in every section of El Paso. Nowadays you don't see them around anymore.

El Greñas [Gilberto Ontiveros] controlled the drug trade in Chihuahuita, and then his son did too. One time I even saw a guy smuggling a beehive across the river to Chihuahuita.

Female Drug Lord

Freddy Morales's account traces the historical and community roots of El Paso–Juárez smuggling. The following interview deepens our understanding of border drug-trafficking history, especially the expansion from relatively small-scale operations to large-scale cocaine transportation and sales. Cristal's life also sheds light on key aspects of narcoculture and gender relations within the drug world.

Large Mexican drug-trafficking cartels or quasi-cartels have been producing, transporting, and selling valuable illicit products for about forty years. Though the membership of the cartels is constantly shifting because of deaths, imprisonment, and schisms, the hierarchies within them and the unwritten rules by which they operate are well understood by insiders. Drug lords run their organizations in an authoritarian fashion. They enforce their will through violence and intimidation.

In the popular imagination, Latin American drug lords are conceived of as hypermasculine, folklorically macho characters whose excessive, extravagant lives rival those of movie stars and pop stars. This stereotype—though generally accurate—is belied by the careers of more subtle capos, such as the consummate narco-entrepreneur Miguel Ángel Félix Gallardo, whose refined style disguised his role as the top Mexican drug lord of the 1980s. Furthermore, although the drug-trafficking world is distinctly male dominated, historically there have been women who have achieved substantial power in drug-trafficking organizations.

In Colombia and Florida, Griselda Blanco, a ruthless enforcer and clever strategist, built a highly profitable minicartel. In Durango, Mexico, Manuela Caro founded a major heroin-trafficking ring. Lola La Chata controlled the heroin business in Mexico City in the 1950s, while Ignacia Jasso (La Nacha) dominated heroin sales in Ciudad Juárez from the 1930s to the 1970s. Today, Enedina Arellano Félix may hold the top position in the Arellano Félix Cartel. Recently, the Mexican public became enraptured by the television coverage of the capture and exploits of Sandra Ávila (aka the "Queen of the Pacific"), whose ravishing beauty, elegance, and insouciance belied her high-ranking position in the Sinaloa cartel. Moreover, at the lower levels of the drug trade, women's involvement is increasing exponentially, a phenomenon that is reflected in the expansion of female-oriented *narcocorridos* and other popular representations, such as the novel *The Queen of the South* (2004) by Pérez-Reverte. (One of the few ethnographic studies of female drug traffickers is by Campbell [2008]).

Few men or women have the personality traits—including temerity, intelligence, extreme cruelty, and planning ability—needed to become a drug lord. Furthermore, a long apprenticeship in drug-trafficking organizations is usually required before one can reach the top. In most cases, the obstacles preventing the ascension of women are insurmountable. Cristal's rise to prominence is remarkable because of the way she inverted or subverted the plot of the grand narrative of Mexican popular culture—the rags-to-riches epic of the *telenovela*. In Mexican soap operas, a poor, downtrodden woman climbs the steep ladder of an oppressive class system through marriage to a wealthy man, the classic white knight on a horse.

Cristal violated this cultural script in at least two ways. First, in a rare social trajectory, Cristal chose a déclassé path. She left her upper-middle-class home in a northern Mexican town and became a *chola*, a contraband smuggler in a poor barrio of Ciudad Juárez. Second, through a two-decade career, she scaled the chauvinistic ranks of various trafficking organizations and obtained economic success not through good behavior and romantic devotion to a bourgeois prince, but through clever maneuvering and fearless struggle within a vicious, sordid underworld.

My interpretation of Cristal's life is thus diametrically opposed to that of Bowden, who depicted Cristal as sleeping her way to a high position in a drug organization (Bowden 2005, 24). In fact, Cristal, who revels in her exploits and bravado, rejects those rival men and women in the drug life who succumbed to their sexual or sentimental desires. For Cristal, drug trafficking was, above all, a way to make large amounts of money—all other considerations were irrelevant. Her relationships with men were pragmatic, about business more than pleasure. Although she protected and nurtured her children, Cristal eschewed delicate, "feminine" concerns. She considered herself a drug-trafficking boss, first and foremost. In her physical presence, demeanor, and verbal style, Cristal was every inch a dominant figure. Cristal's story thus portrays the lifestyle and behavior of drug capos as well as the gendered contours and pathways of the Mexican narco-culture.

Cristal

I was born in the 1960s in a small village in Durango, Mexico. My mother was very fond of riding horses, and I think that's why I was born prematurely. I was raised in the cities of Torreón, Coahuila, and Durango, Durango. I had two brothers, and you could say that I was born into a well-to-do family. I attended La Salle Jesuit schools as a kid. My father was a doctor by profession. My dad used to say, "Ahí está tu 'domingo'" [Here is your allowance]; I was accustomed to good treatment. My mother was very strict, and had me in a school run by nuns.

Then, at the age of fifteen, I broke away [*me despeloté*]. I initially came to Ciudad Juárez on vacation [to visit my relatives]. I had grown up in an atmosphere where everything was chandeliers, propriety, and good manners. The nuns at my school were a bunch of religious fanatics [*cagadiablos*]. I guess you could say I was *toda una señorita* [a very proper young lady].

My aunt who lived in Juárez was a whore, a drunk, a crazy woman, and considered the black sheep of the family. She worked in brothels in the Mariscal area and other parts of Juárez. I had eight cousins, my aunt's kids. They were all *hijos del mole* or *hijos de diferentes chiles* [children of different fathers]. My aunt would cross into the U.S. and leave me taking care of her kids. She lived in the barrio of La Chaveña, adjacent to old downtown Juárez, and one of the oldest residential districts in Juárez. I liked the barrio. However, one of my cousins, a female, was raped by the owner of the little grocery store by my aunt's house.

I was fascinated by the poor people of the barrio who lived in train cars. I met many humble people in the barrio of La Chaveña, including coyotes, potheads, and heroin addicts. After a fight with my mom, I decided to stay in Juárez with my aunt. While I was there, I went to high school, but also got into the smuggling business. Eventually, my mother disinherited me because of how I lived.

I started out crossing undocumented people into the U.S. by wading across the Rio Grande. It was around this time that I met "El Pelirrojo" [the Red-Haired One], who was a coyote. We also called him "El Zana-horia" [the Carrot]. I felt I needed money, so I decided to go to El Zana-horia to ask if I could work with him. He agreed. So I started working with him. We would cross undocumented people into the U.S. by way of sitting them atop truck-tire inner tubes, which the coyotes called *balsas* [rafts; many coyotes described themselves with pride as *balseros*].

It was 1978, I was fifteen years old, and we were charging between three dollars and five dollars per crossing, and making anywhere between fifteen dollars and twenty dollars a day. At that time, I was taking my daily cut of the money back to my aunt's house and using it for household needs. Some people back then were calling me "La Chola," while others called me "La Güera." My daily attire at the time consisted of khaki pants, long white T-shirts, and Converse tennis shoes. When working, I invariably wore my hair in a roll and wrapped up under my baseball cap. Eventually, we began passing liquor boxes both ways—into the U.S. and also into Mexico. We were normally paid between a hundred and a hundred and fifty dollars to pass loads of liquor into the U.S. Often we crossed the river into the U.S. under cover of darkness, and through some pretty scary, dangerous places. I was never raped, since I was always, and at all times, protected by my friends, including El Zanahoria.

First, we waded or swam across the river. Then we used a rope to pull the *balsa* full of liquor boxes from the Mexican side to the U.S. side of the river. Someone from the housing projects would pick up the boxes of liquor. This type of smuggling was often done in broad daylight, and it involved hiding, sometimes for hours, in the underbrush—carrizo and foxtails—at the edge of the river, waiting for the "changing of the guard" at the international bridge [the Paso del Norte Bridge].

First Drug-Smuggling Experiences

Around this time I met "El Pelón" [a pseudonym for one of the most famous Mexican traffickers], who was then still working for Pablo Acosta. Back then, El Pelón was not well known. I had my own nicknames for both of them. I called Pablo Acosta "El Naco," while "El Pelón" was, for me, "El Rigo Tovar" [a reference to a famous Mexican singer of the period, who sported long, curly-locked hair, made in mockery of El Pelón's baldness]. El Pelón had a box of panties under his bed from all the women he had slept with.

Then, some people who worked for El Pelón asked me once to pass a box for them. "It's just liquor," they had told me. They were paying me five hundred dollars for crossing that box, which I thought was a lot, but who the hell was I to ask questions! So I took the money, and then ended up hiding in the carrizo, waiting for the cops and their horses to clear out from around the international bridge. I waited for two or three hours in the carrizo, with my feet in the water. Then, when the coast was clear, I forded the river and left the box on the U.S. side, covering it with plants and dirt in the underbrush near the edge of the river. Then I went to get a backpack in which to carry the box. When I was putting the cardboard box in the backpack, I noticed it was wet, so fearing it would tear, I decided to check out the contents. There were four or five bottles on top and some plastic bags full of white powder underneath. I had never seen cocaine before. El Zanahoria opened one of the bags and blurted out, "It's snow!" Then I asked, "What do you mean, 'snow'?" "Let's take it!" he said. "They tricked you: they gave you the money, but didn't tell you it was drugs."

So we gave the liquor bottles to Doña Cuca, a neighbor of my aunt, and she dug a hole in her backyard and hid inside it four of the five packets of cocaine. Then she opened the remaining packet and took two ounces out of it so we could sell it in bars in El Paso. When a bar owner saw this little plastic ball of two ounces of cocaine, he asked where we had found it, and then offered us a hundred dollars for it. We refused. Then we went to a coyote, and he paid us three hundred dollars for it. A kilogram of cocaine, at that time, in El Paso was worth twenty-five thousand dollars.

Then the bar owner who had offered us a hundred dollars, and some of his people, figuring we had more of the stuff, came after us, trying to steal it from us, so we had to go into hiding again. Later I went to La Placita [the central plaza of El Paso]. As usual, there was a gaggle of whores hanging around. Then the owners of the dope came after me, found me at La Placita, chased me, and caught me at the railroad tracks by the Rio Grande. El Pelón and a Colombian guy caught me and forcibly put me into their car. They started hassling me, and they threatened to kill my aunt and cousins. I told the Colombian and El Pelón, "No soy pendeja, soy estudiada" [I am educated, I am not a fool]. But yeah, I did feel afraid.

I told them, "If you're going to kill me, then do it now! You guys don't have any balls! Why did you tell me it was just a box full of liquor bottles and try to fool me?" The Colombian, who was named Abel, said, "You are a very ballsy woman." Then he told me that if I gave him the stuff back, I could have the money they promised to pay me. Then he asked if I had a watch. When I answered no, he gave me his Rolex wristwatch so I could tell time, and told me to meet them at 5:00 P.M. with the stuff on me so I could return it to them. Then the Colombian said, "I'm trusting you to meet us at five and have the stuff on you, so don't forget, or else . . . " To which I replied, "I keep my word. If I say I'll bring back the 'shit,' you can be sure I'll bring the 'shit' back, so don't worry."

So we delivered the drugs back to them, and El Pelón and several other guys took us to a hotel in El Paso. I was ordered to get out of the car in order to talk to the *jefe* [boss], who was inside the hotel. The *jefe* turned out to be none other than Abel, the Colombian guy. Abel was called "El Mexicano" because of his affinity for Mexico. He worked for a Colombian cartel. When I came face to face with him, he asked me, "Do you want to work with me?" At that time, Zanahoria and I were mostly passing undocumented people across the river into the U.S. by means of *balsas*, through an area very close to the downtown international bridge.

"I will pay you five hundred dollars right now," said the Colombian, "and two thousand per box in the future." That would make a thousand for me and a thousand for Zanahoria, I thought. I also started to think about what this money meant. With it, I could take care of my cousins and prevent them from being humiliated. My aunt lived in an old, tiny little apartment house, part of an even older *vecindad* [enclosed complex of small apartments] that had only one shared inner courtyard for all the tenants. My cousins used to peek over the rail of the neighbors to watch their television. The neighbors got mad, and I was humiliated by this.

I recall how one day I saw my little cousin watching a kid eating a banana. When the kid finished, he threw away the banana peel, flinging it carelessly across the street, where it fell to the ground, thudding against the dirt. My poor little cousin ran as fast as he could and quickly picked it up and voraciously started eating the by now dirt-covered banana peel as if it were the most precious, delicious tidbit of food he had ever encountered. I immediately yelled out at my cousin to leave it alone, to throw it away. He did, but a neighbor had seen the whole sequence of events, and from then on insulted and poked fun at my cousin every time he saw him.

When we agreed to work for him, the *jefe* gave five hundred dollars to each of us right then and there. From that point on, we were paid two thousand dollars every time we took backpacks full of drugs across the river into the U.S. and delivered them to Sunland Park, New Mexico, to a site located along the so-called *carretera del indio* [Indian highway]. I was sixteen years old, and life was beginning to look good to me. I was on my parents' passport, and since I didn't have an ID of my own, I always crossed the border as a wetback.

Spending Drug Profits

"What do we do with all this money from crossing drugs?" I asked El Zanahoria. He just shrugged his shoulders and smiled, as if to say, "I don't know—but it's good to have that kind of dilemma to ponder on." So for starters, on my first shopping spree I bought a TV and a sewing machine—so my cousin wouldn't have to show her ass to everyone when she passed by on the street, because her old, worn-out skirts and pants were always ripped in the rump area from so much wear and tear—and a refrigerator, since we didn't have one at home, and cots and mattresses, as well as many, many rolls of cloth, and fried chicken and other prepared food to feast on together with my cousins. El Zanahoria bought himself a camper truck. Up until then, he had lived in a train car.

When I got home in a taxi from the first part of my shopping spree and started unloading all the stuff I had bought, my cousins began asking, "What's this? Who did you stick up?" After I finished unloading the first bunch of goods, my cousins and I boarded the taxi and proceeded to go to the big Soriana department store and supermarket. We filled our shopping cart with boxes of meat, cereal, watermelons, and many types of fruits, as well as bottles of shampoo and bars of soap. As we brought the food and other stuff we'd bought into the house, the bitchy women neighbors were all watching us. I told my little cousin, "Sergio, go outside and eat a mango, and take the box of cookies and eat some of them also." I wanted the neighbors to see him eating the mango and some cookies!

"Surely she must have been running around prostituting herself," they commented about me. Shortly after that, we painted our little apartment house and made some curtains with the rolls of cloth so it would look better. I also bought a tall exterior antenna for the television. Then my aunt returned home from wherever she had been, and when she saw all the stuff I'd bought, she said, "What is all this? Surely you've been out selling your body for money." So I countered, "No, I haven't been prostituting myself, so shut your mouth! I'm not a whore and drunkard, like you! I've been doing this and that, but not whoring around and getting drunk, like you!" "But they can kill you," said my aunt.

At the time, I was almost seventeen years old. I was young but tough. The *viejo* [old man] who owned the corner store beat my aunt up and got my cousin pregnant. When I confronted him, he said, "I'm going to kill you!" To which I replied, "Well, I don't have what you have [testicles] hanging from your legs, but mine are bigger and better placed than yours." "Fuck your mother!" I would always shout at guys who said flirtatious remarks to me on the street, and this made them somewhat afraid of me, so afterward they would leave me alone.

Eventually, from the money we were then making, El Zanahoria bought a car, and I bought a Renault 12. In those days, we were crossing the border walking, with backpacks full of drugs that we took to deliver to Sunland Park. We were making lots of money. Then I gave the car to my aunt and bought a truck. I told myself that I was doing what I was doing so my cousins would no longer have to go hungry. I kept working like this for two years [1979–1981], then I moved to a better house.

By then, trucks loaded with drugs were crossing the border with three hundred to four hundred kilos of cocaine. My job was just to open the gate to the parking area of a stash house when the trucks full of drugs arrived. The house, in Juárez, was used to store the loads. *Era una caleta* [It was a hiding place]. Then I would open the garage door so that the truck that had just arrived could come in. At that time, El Pelón was working by himself. I worked for Abel.

Caught

Then one day, the *federales* came to the house and caught me while I was taking a dump—normally, I didn't stick around that long, since as soon as I let the truck in, I would leave the premises. I saw as much as 1,000 to 1,500 kilos of cocaine stored there at one time. As far as crossing the stuff into the U.S., there were *arreglos* [arrangements]. People [U.S. Customs agents and immigration officers] were paid off at the international bridges. When the federales caught me, I told them that I was just the maid of the house. But they noticed I was wearing a brand new pair of Converse tennis shoes, and immediately retorted, "Oh yeah? Then why are you wearing new Converse? We're going to torture you, with electric shocks and everything else."

So they took me to jail. I was seventeen at the time. They put me in a cell, and I started screaming my head off and acting dumb, like a *ranchera* [an uneducated peasant from the countryside], and talking like a *chúntara* [a hillbilly]. They shoved drugs in my face, and I vomited. I remember thinking, "If I talk, they'll kill my aunt." Then I started taunting them, "So just kill me, already! Come on, just kill me now!" Then a lawyer came and paid a million pesos to free me. Abel had sent him. In all, I had spent only a day and a half in jail.

After being freed, I went and talked to Abel about what happened, and then continued working for him. By then I was making about six thousand dollars a month crossing loads of drugs into the U.S. and watching houses where the drugs were stored, or accompanying in a separate vehicle, in convoy fashion, loaded cars across the international bridges. I used false identification documents to cross into the U.S. In fact, I was always able to buy false identity papers both for U.S. entry and Mexico entry.

It was around this time that we started putting into practice an idea I had recently thought up: we would blow lots of pot smoke into a car, then fill it with the smell of cocaine, rubbing the tires and the dashboard with coke dust. Naturally, the drug-sniffing dogs at the international bridges were immediately attracted to this car, which, of course, didn't actually have even one speck of drugs in it. This decoy car was the one I would drive to the bridge. Immediately, the attention of the dogs was on my car, and the barking would attract other agents, who hurriedly congregated around it and began to dismantle it frantically, looking for drugs that weren't there, all the while temporarily detaining me. This allowed the other cars in our convoy, which were the ones actually loaded with drugs, to cross into the U.S. without any trouble, since all the attention of the agents at the bridge was now focused on me and my "loaded" car.

To Colombia

Then the *judiciales* [Chihuahua State Judicial Police officers] started giving Abel trouble, so he decided to leave Juárez and return to Colombia. I went with him, but I was in love with money more than with him. In fact, I'm still in love with money: it's my friend, my husband, and my lover. Without money, one is nothing. I've always been very independent because of my financial freedom from men.

Abel asked me to go with him to Colombia, and I agreed to, more for the adventure than anything else. When I got to Colombia, I raised hell [*hice un desmadre*]. But before leaving, I set up my aunt with a little corner stand so she could sell magazines to passersby. So there I was, eighteen years old and about to travel to Colombia. It was 1981. I recall that when we got to the Mexico City airport and were about to board a plane leaving for Colombia, Abel told me that I looked like a tomboy, and made me get new high-heel shoes. I had a whole collection of Converse tennis shoes, and I always wore T-shirts and jeans. I thought the high-heel shoes were very uncomfortable, since I wasn't used to wearing them, and in fact didn't want to wear them.

So it was that I went to work in the dope business in Colombia with Abel. At the time, I was still *cejona*—my eyebrows had never been plucked or trimmed—and I always wore my *trenzas* [hair braids] up, and T-shirts and jeans, and I always had my backpack with me. People in Colombia said to me that I looked like a *marimacha* [a lesbian or masculine-looking woman]. "It doesn't matter," I would reply, "since I'm not one and I know it."

I went to Bogotá and then Cali. I stayed with a sister of Abel in Cali, named Mercedes. I did anything and everything. Back then, for me everything was game, except killing someone [*me valía todo, menos matar*]. Colombians were attracted to Mexican culture. They saw me as an exotic Mexicana—loud, brassy, *macha*, and different. "¡Ay, tú vienes de México, qué bonito!" [Ay, you are from Mexico, how nice!], said Abel's sister. She wanted to fix me up at a beauty parlor because they said I looked like a lesbian. And so they did my eyebrows and bought me a blouse and skirt. I took the hair off my legs and fixed my nails. "¡Ay güey, me voy a caer de estos chingados zapatos!" [Shit, asshole, I'm going to fall off these fucking shoes!], I remarked when I started walking with the high-heel shoes they bought for me. At home, I was used to mainly boots and tennis shoes.

I met Carlos Lehder and the Rodríguez Orejuela brothers at a nightclub they took me to. Daniel, brother of Abel, took me out to dance. "No me agarres así, ¿qué me vas a coger o qué?" [Don't hold me like that, are you trying to fuck me or what?], I said when he held me too tight on the dance floor. "¡Esta mexicana bocona!" [This big-mouthed Mexican], he responded. "¡Te crees mucho, pinche pendejo!" [You think you're so great, fucking asshole], I retorted. Then I was introduced to Carlos Lehder. All the women there were after him—they crowded around him like sheep.

"Esta mexicana es una berraca" [This Mexican is hot stuff], said Lehder. "Here or in China or Rome, I do what I want," I replied. I am not afraid of death; that's why I behaved the way I did. "Are you afraid of death?" he asked me. "No, I am not afraid of death. I'm from Durango. I was born and I will die," I answered. Somebody took me aside and whispered to me, "Please calm down [and watch what you say!]. He's one of the *chingones* [powerful ones], you know!" "It doesn't matter," I told this person. "He is he, and I am I."

That night, I was left with Lehder and the other women and his bodyguards. "I want to go to sleep," I said. He was going to take me to a hotel, but then he got a phone call, and after he hung up, he said, "You have to come with me." So we all went to a *finca* [ranch house]. There was a party going on there, with policemen and prostitutes. Then this Panamanian man came on to me. I turned him down. Later, Lehder said, "Have a drink." "I don't drink," I said. "Then how about a *pericazo* [a snort of cocaine]?" he countered. "No, I don't do that either," I replied.

I was tired and sleepy. They gave me a luxurious bedroom to sleep in. So I took off all my clothes and went to sleep. Carlos came into the bedroom in the middle of the night. "Don't be frightened," he said, and joined me in bed. I wanted to leave, but he said there were no other beds. I went out of the room and saw that people were sleeping everywhere and anywhere they could. On the floor and on couches.

I came back into the room where Lehder was and asked him, "What am I going to do?" "You sleep on one side of the bed, and I'll sleep on the other. After all, this is my bedroom," he said. The next day, I woke up to find that the party had continued. That day they butchered several farm animals and grilled them. And they brought Colombian mariachis "for the Mexicana." But I still felt like all I wanted to do was leave that place. "Me caes bien porque eres una culicagada" [I like you because you're the unruly type], Lehder said. Not understanding quite what he meant by *culicagada* [roughly, "dirty ass" in Mexican Spanish], I immediately replied, "But my ass is clean!" and everyone around started laughing.

Feeling that the tension had been broken, I was able to relax a bit, and eventually had a few beers. That night I went to bed, and Lehder joined me and we had sex. But beforehand he didn't caress me, he didn't kiss me, nothing. I swear! So it was just a case of getting sexually aroused and that's all. You know, a hormonal matter, or whatever. I never went with anyone sexually, but that time it just happened. Nowadays Carlos Lehder is in Germany or Cuba. He was caught and put in jail for a while, but apparently now he's essentially free, under the witness-protection program.

I remember that Carlos Lehder seemed very handsome to me, very educated. But even back then, as young as I was, I recall thinking, "If I'm going to be a *chingona* [a boss woman] and make it, I have to make it big, all the way." So I stayed with Carlos only about eight months. Basically, I'm an ungovernable person, and he wanted to control me, he wanted me to stay at home. But I thought, "No way this guy is going to hold me down. Because, let's face it, eventually this bastard is going to leave me for another woman."

I also met Pablo Escobar and the Rodríguez Orejuela family. And the Panamanian guy was good to me. In my experience, *el que menos habla es el más chingón* [he who talks least is the most powerful]. Carlos began to use drugs. Then others around us started acting like *maricones* [faggots]. They were not *putos* [receptive homosexuals], but I caught some of them in bed with other guys. And I think they liked it. But then I think the majority of people in the drug world experiment with bisexuality.

During my stay in Colombia, I also got to travel with Manuel Noriega. At the time, we could unload our dope in Mexico City with the corrupt police chief, Arturo Durazo Moreno, also known as "El Negro" Durazo. Now, truth be told, Durazo, I didn't like. He threw centenarios [Mexican gold coins worth about nine hundred U.S. dollars each] at some whores, and even broke open a whore's forehead once. Lehder, on the other hand, was a gentleman, and he once gave me a jewelry case full of emeralds as a gift.

But after eight months, I had grown tired of Carlos because of the constant parties, and what I really wanted was to work and make more—a lot more—money. So I left Carlos and hung out with Abel, and eventually got pregnant by Abel. He was married, and wanted me to get an abortion. So I decided to return, pregnant and by myself, to Juárez. Of course, as soon as I returned, I immediately became the target of constant criticism by my family.

Nuevo Laredo

Abel came back to Juárez, and then took me back to Cúcuta, Colombia, where my baby was born. Then I returned to Juárez and began selling "stuff" I got from Abel. At that time, Pablo Acosta ran the Chihuahua cartel. I was supposed to pay a percentage to the cartel, but I didn't want to. So we decided to go to Nuevo Laredo, and started working with Juan García Abrego, boss of the Gulf cartel. In Juárez, I didn't want to pay the *cuota* [an informal tariff demanded by the dominant drug cartel], and so the cartel representatives pressured Abel. In Juárez, Abel killed six *judiciales* [judicial police] . . . so we had to leave.

So it was 1983, and there we were in Nuevo Laredo, working with García Ábrego. Now I was making the decisions and sending the money to Colombia while others carried the loads across to the U.S. Since we were in a relationship, Abel said that if he ever had to leave, I was to collect all the dope and money for myself.

One day, the *judiciales* showed up and killed Abel right there inside our house. So I grabbed the diaper bag, another bag, the baby carriage, and stuffed $700,000 in cash and fifteen kilos of cocaine, worth $400,000 in the U.S. at that time, inside them. After Abel died, I never once said, "¡Ay, pobrecita de mí!" [Oh, poor little me!], ¡Ni madres! [Fuck that!]. As far as my relationship with Abel, more than anything, it was a business relationship.

After his death, I had to continue providing for my son. In other words, I didn't spend much time lamenting his death or feeling sorry for myself. Later, when my brother-in-law Daniel—without even asking how I or my child was—asked me what happened to the money, I told him the *judiciales* took it. So I escaped and went to an old, run-down hotel in downtown Nuevo Laredo. It was horrible. Then I went to a *posada* [a cheap hotel where people waited for coyotes]. I called my aunt, who picked me up and drove me back to Juárez. I had hidden the cocaine in between the diapers, and then I had bought some grilled chicken to cover the smell.

Drug Dealing in San Antonio, Dallas, and Houston

And when that *pinche güey* [asshole] Daniel went to talk to me, I said, "Y mira, aquí en México" [And look, here in Mexico], as a kind of explanation. I said this sarcastically to indicate, of course, that in Mexico, with its longstanding tradition of corruption, the *judiciales* had stolen the money. I had hidden the money very well [*encaleté bien la feria*] in my aunt's house in Juárez. With that money, I eventually bought a house in Juárez and another one in Saltillo, Coahuila, and then I moved to San Antonio. Of the fifteen or sixteen kilos I rescued from Nuevo Laredo, ten were lost when one of my people was busted trying to cross it into the U.S. The rest I crossed myself and sold. I used that money to set up business in San Antonio.

I made a lot of money in San Antonio, because when I was there, the price of pot was twenty-five dollars per pound in Oaxaca, where I bought it; seventy-five dollars per pound on the border, where I crossed it; a hundred fifty dollars a pound in San Antonio, where I kept it; and finally, three thousand dollars a pound in Philadelphia, where I sold it. My philosophy after the death of my husband was "El vivo al gozo, el muerto al pozo" [Joy is for the living, the grave is for the dead]. In San Antonio, it was a case of *lo del agua al agua* [what is from water returns to water]. As a drug dealer, naturally I returned to drug dealing. In other words, from my perspective, "once a trafficker, always a drug trafficker." In San Antonio, I was in charge of the drug operation [*yo mandaba*]. El Negro was my right-hand man.

I made the most money in Dallas, selling marijuana and cocaine. I was busted in Dallas in 1984 and 1985. The truth is that we traffickers never completely retire from drug dealing or related activities. Before, there used to be loyalty and trust, but this all changed around 1990. Amado Carrillo Fuentes wrecked everything.

In Garland, Texas, near Dallas, I had a big house and bodyguards, and I ran my drug business from there. I had begun very young, and was used to having money, and was not a credulous person. I was tough minded. When someone asked for money, I would give them money, but first they would have to take a load to Philadelphia; they were paid six thousand dollars per load. I always bailed out my people when they got busted. I never left anyone stranded in jail. I had two lawyers in Dallas. You have to share the wealth—for *el pitazo* [the "heads up" alert given to narco-traffickers by corrupt law enforcement agents], for the lawyers, etc. About 30 percent of my drug profits went to expenses [of these and other types]. I was always loyal to my people. I had six aliases. I sold cocaine in connection with the Cali cartel in Houston in the mid-1980s. I had so much money that [in one day] I would eat lunch in Dallas and dine in New York. I'm not repentant of any of the things I've done. In fact, I would do them again.

In 1985, I worked with El Gordo. He was my worker. I once told him, "Yo no traigo lo que tú traes colgando, pero soy cabrona" [I don't have what you have hanging there, but I'm a real badass]. I also told him, "Tú no me vengas con pendejadas y machismos" [Don't come to me with sexual chicanery and machismo]. He wanted to *amachar* [be chauvinistic] and dominate me. But I told him, "No, first, because I don't want an infection [a venereal disease]; and second, because I don't love you." I wasn't used to being controlled. Once I shot El Gordo with a gun, and he shot me back, in a fight.

At one point, I moved to Corpus Christi and spent one year there without working. That's where I had my experience. I got into business with a *maricona* in Corpus Christi. We were partners in a restaurant. There was a rapport, a closeness, an attraction between us, but I didn't like it. I was just like other drug traffickers. I had the mentality "Uno quiere vivir una experiencia y no que le cuenten" [One wanted to live an experience, not be told about it]. Then I was called by a "business" person in Dallas, and got back into the drug trade.

In Dallas, in 1991, I was working for myself, with a male partner. I was selling white heroin [from Colombia], working with women as my "mules" [couriers]. In fact, I prefer working with women. They're more reliable and serious than men. I liked dealing heroin because it was a simple cash-for-drugs proposition: "Aquí está el dinero, pinche güey. Aquí está la chiva, güey" [Here is the money asshole. Here is the heroin, asshole]. And the transaction is over. We used the word *pintura* [paint] as a slang for heroin or other drugs in order to confuse narcs. Sometimes things got rough. Once I threatened an enemy with an AK-47 at a Dallas nightclub.

In 1993, I was arrested with money, not drugs. I claimed I was a prostitute when the authorities asked why I had so much money on me. El Gordo's brother had turned me in at a hotel. ¡Ni madres, güey! [Fuck it, asshole!] When the narc cop caught me, he said, "Bingo!" "Fuck you, güey!" I replied. So I was sent to Mexico.

Working for the Other Side

While I worked, my children never saw dope or my male lovers. My children had their own house on the side. I had a house here, for my kids, and a house there, for business. I told my children what I did for a living. I was imprisoned in New York. I kept my kids away because of pride, to not have them mistreated. I am now working for the U.S. government.

I have no regrets about my involvement in the drug trade. If I had it all to do over again, I'd do it again the same way. The only thing I regret is the time I spent in jail. I had a lot of trouble adapting to jail life because I was ungovernable. But in jail they humiliated me, forcing me to be strip-searched. They put me in restraints or in the hole when I caused trouble. While in jail, I had fights with one black woman and one white woman, and others.

The U.S. government brought me back from Mexico to the U.S. to work as an informant. When that happened, *me sentí chingona* [I felt important, powerful]. I served four years, approximately 1996–1999, in prison in New York and Danville, Connecticut, and later Fort Worth, Texas. I paid one million dollars to lawyers to get out of prison. Two times I was in jail for any length of time: in 1993, for eight months, and in 1996, for four years.

There are now two contracts on my life, both by Mexican traffickers. I remember how one of the dopers I set up said to me once, "¡Ninguna mujer me va a chingar!" [No woman is going to bring me down!]. There are two reasons why I joined the law: first, the organization was failing; and secondly, I was scared of prison.

A female friend, who I helped bust, got busted because she was too interested in partying and meeting men. I consider myself a negotiator. Doper men see women in the drug life as *putas* [whores]. In fact, I consider many of them *putas* also. As for me, though, I would describe myself as a cold-minded, business-oriented negotiator. In Philadelphia, a Cuban trafficker came on to me, and I replied, "I didn't come here to spread my legs, I came to do business. If I wanted to, I could spread my legs at home." When I was working in the drug business, I was serious. I didn't use drugs or go to orgies—only once. I criticize men in the drug business for their irresponsible behavior with women. Men even take women to their *caleta* [the bedroom where the dope is stashed].

I don't need sex. I'm not very sex oriented. I'm interested in business. As I said before, I loved money and I still love money. If I wanted sex, I would just use a vibrator. I never have fallen in love. As to how women are treated in the drug trade, I would say many times, men don't want the competition. I was a businessperson first and foremost. As for other women in the drug life, above all they were whores. They would go crazy over men, they would go to orgies—not me. The other women were whores—too interested in sex, not enough focused on business.

Many others in the drug business, in my opinion, were too generous or too quick to believe sob stories and requests for money. Si tú eres débil te joden, si te ven fácil te chingan, si ven a uno bien, lógico, lo tratan bien. [If you are weak, they screw you; if they see you as easy, they'll fuck you; if they think you're all right, then, logically, they will treat you well.]

Community-Based Drug Use, Smuggling, and Dealing in the 1970s and 1980s

The oral history that follows deepens the theme of community-based drug smuggling presented by historian Freddy Morales and expands on the role of drug use and drug addiction as a factor in drug trafficking. The story of David (a pseudonym) is a familiar one in El Paso and the poor neighborhoods of the U.S. Southwest. He was born in the 1950s, came from a Hispanic working-class family, and grew up on the south side of town, very close to the international border. David, like many others, participated in the drug taking and petty drug trafficking that was tightly interwoven with barrio life and that expanded during the radical 1960s and early 1970s. His father was killed when he was around five years old, and by the time he was eight, he had begun to learn about alcohol and drugs.

His introduction to the heroin-addict lifestyle occurred about this time also, through a colorful uncle. By the time he was a high-school freshman, he had tried marijuana and some psychedelics, and when a teacher asked him what he wanted to be when he grew up, he replied, "I want to be the best drug dealer I can be." By then, he had also started dealing marijuana and cocaine, drugs that he and his neighborhood friends would bring across the Rio Grande from Juárez. The people selling drugs to them were Juárez notables, among them a family associated with the horse-racing track, as well as a family that owned several nightclubs, and another that owned several gas stations. He and his friends would then sell these drugs in El Paso to soldiers stationed at Fort Bliss. Much of the border drug trafficking at the time was small scale, informal, and partly integrated into the community, unlike the operations run by the violent, mercenary drug cartels that emerged in the 1990s.

David also describes the many types of corruption related to drug trafficking in El Paso, involving bail bondsmen, judges, lawyers, et al. He and his group of a dozen friends introduced their classmates to drugs. Then they started branching out to other high schools and to bars. Thereafter, the unraveling began: several of his associates became heroin addicts, and others committed suicide or were sent to prison. This, sadly, is another common theme in old El Paso neighborhoods, especially in the almost exclusively Hispanic downtown, south side, and Lower Valley areas, where drug use has taken a heavy toll over the years.

David observes that drug dealing was commonplace but that little was done to stop it. He also provides the names and locations of the various street gangs in El Paso at the time, some of which later became important trafficking organizations in their own right. David portrays drug dealing in El Paso and Juárez in the 1970s and 1980s as a sort of cottage industry in which everyone knew one another on both sides of the border, and in which the small number of families involved were generally friendly to one another. The business was conducted in a low-key, laissez-faire manner that contrasts starkly with the paranoia that surrounds dealing today. Eventually, David describes the emergence of larger-scale organizations that led to the Aguilar–Muñoz Talavera drug-trafficking group in the 1980s, which became known as the Cártel de Juárez.

David also provides information about the *tecato* (heroin addict) way of life—insights available only to an insider. His list of tecato vocabulary, as well as his descriptions of how to hide heroin while dealing it on the street, and his list of places where heroin could be obtained in El Paso, are instructive. Most of the tecato terms and techniques for street drug dealing still exist. Thus, his account illustrates processes of continuity and change in the border narco-life.

David

I was born in 1954 in El Paso, Texas. I lived in the Clardy Fox neighborhood, between Valverde and Buena Vista streets, by Delta Drive. My father is from Derry, New Mexico, in the Hatch area. He had a farming background. He grew chile. My mother is from El Paso. My relatives have been in the Las Cruces and Hatch, New Mexico, areas since the 1840s.

My maternal grandmother was born in Smeltertown [a working-class El Paso neighborhood near the ASARCO metal refinery], but was educated in Mexico City, where the schools were superior to those in the El Paso region during the 1880s–1890s. She married a wealthy man from Jalisco who was a military-academy graduate. They were Porfiristas, on the losing side of the Mexican Revolution, who ran to El Paso in the 1930s. Both of my parents are bilingual, equally fluent in English and Spanish. So I speak both languages also.

My aunt married a Jew. My uncle married a Methodist, and there were many Catholics in our family. We had Italian friends too. A cosmopolitan group always came to our family parties. We had mixed ethnic foods at holidays. Our neighborhood, in the 1950s, was a new working-class suburb. There were many veterans from World War II and the Korean War living there. A lot of the men worked at ASARCO, while many of the women worked at J. C. Penney's or other retail stores downtown, such as La Popular, where my own mom worked. Many women also worked at the Fox Plaza shopping center.

There was more agricultural land back then, especially around Ascarate Park. The city was smaller and much nicer. Burges High School was on the eastern edge of town then. There was also the McDonalds Paint company, La Fonda Hotel, and the Del Camino Hotel, which became a federal halfway house. I attended Burges High because of enforced busing. My older sisters went to Burges ahead of me, and my younger sister went to Jefferson High School [in the barrio]. Back then, Burges was 80 percent Anglo, 20 percent Mexican American. The east side was mostly white, and most kids went on to Texas Tech or Texas A&M.

My father was a bail bondsman. In 1959, he was killed in Juárez during a fight outside a bar. He intervened in a domestic quarrel, and the man shot him. It made big news in El Paso. So I grew up without a male role model. I had three sisters, and they used to gang up on me. Then there was also my mom and my grandma. So it was five females against one male. I became the black sheep of the family. A lot of the things I learned, I had to learn by myself, by trial and error. When I was eight years old, I learned about pills and how to steal beers out of coolers at family parties. I would drink beer, cop a buzz, go to my room, and go to sleep.

My mother had a brain tumor but didn't know it at first. It gave her headaches. She would come home from work and take pills and crash. My maternal grandmother was the main parental role model for me. My mother once left for six months to have an operation in California to remove the tumor. At the time, I had an uncle on my father's side who was a heroin addict, and since the 1950s, he was always in and out of prisons. My uncle was young and flamboyant, which impressed me. At my grandma's house, he gave me some downers. They made me sleepy and sick. It was not pleasurable at all.

I smoked weed in the seventh grade, when I was twelve years old. There were not many drugs in my neighborhood then, but there were characters who were drug addicts. You had to seek them out, but you knew the drugs were there, you knew they existed. Back then, the druggies got their stuff in Juárez. At that time, all the junior high kids I knew were experimenting with Lone Star beer and weed. We were playing around and not getting caught. Then, when I was a freshman in high school [1969], I broke loose, it was all happening—drugs, rock and roll, rebelling.

Being from a neighborhood that is poverty stricken, pennies counted. We were poor working people. I have never owned a home. I have been a nomad all my life. Living with my mother, three sisters, and my grandma, we never felt poor. You know, "ay, pobrecitos" [poor little ones] and that sort of crap. We didn't say it, but our relatives said that about us. We were the poorest of the family. We believed we were going to make it. Growing up poor instilled determination in us.

I remember 1969, when I was in eighth grade at Henderson Middle School and transitioning to Burges High School, I was into the Beatles' music—*Abbey Road*, "Yellow Submarine"—and psychedelics. I was into trying to stay mellow. We wanted to stay cool, but we were influenced by the Chicano movement also. There was a political and ideological split with drug use. Our parents solidified with the Chicano Democrats. But there were generational differences. Part of it was the failure of our parents to guide us, and part of it was our failure to look to our parents. Both generations share the disaster. I remember I started letting my hair grow long and getting into truancy. I went to school only three or four days a week. I became a master at writing notes in my mom's handwriting. But my oldest sister, who was a Goody Two-Shoes at that time in her life, worked in the attendance office, and she'd snitch on me, so I ended up having to go to the principal's office anyway.

The Young Dealer

I had fun making chaos as a freshman. We'd shake down the tennis players and Anglos after games, taking their money and tennis racquets. We thought we were superior. We were not a gang, just a group of friends, but we had a reputation of not being good kids. We created the illusion.

We used to go from our homeroom through the English wing to the auditorium, then through the audiovisual room and back through the English wing out into a little cottage to hang out. We burned the cottage down at the end of the school year.

I was in trouble for fighting a lot. A female teacher once asked me what I wanted to be when I grew up. I replied, "I want to be the best drug dealer I can be." But I just said it to see the expression on her face. I was acting out, and at the same time letting her know that I was not interested in what she had to offer. My freshman year in high school, I started to deal dope—marijuana and cocaine. We would bring it across the river, from Juárez. I hung out with a group of kids on a corner about half a block from the river. Back then, the river wasn't concrete all the way through El Paso. It was a free river as you got further out from downtown.

A person connected with the Hipódromo [horse-racing track] in Juárez sold us pot. We dealt with his relative. Members of a prominent business family [that eventually became connected to the Cártel de Juárez] sold us coke. Another family, that owned a chain of businesses in Juárez, also sold us drugs. The oldest son was our neighborhood connection to the people in Juárez. Three Mexican American brothers with a lot of family in Juárez were the leaders of our group. We grew up together since kindergarten, and there was absolute trust between us. It was the three brothers who had first suggested we deal drugs. We would sell drugs to military guys. El Paso always had large shipments of soldiers coming in and out of Fort Bliss. The soldiers would go to a place called The Joint [now Ardovino's Desert Crossing] in Sunland Park, New Mexico, right next to the Mexican and Texas borders. Many Vietnam vets went to The Joint at night to drink. We supplied them with drugs. Through them, we made connections to cities all over the country.

"Can you get me a pound?" they would ask. So there we were: we were paying fifteen dollars per pound in Mexico and selling it for eighty dollars a pound in El Paso. It didn't add up to a lot of money unless you took it out of town, where prices were higher. In El Paso, lids sold for twenty dollars . . . half a lid was four fingers. Lids were big and heavy back then. And it was top-quality marijuana—Acapulco Gold and other kinds. The marijuana-sales profits were enough that I owned a 1954 Jaguar as a senior in high school. I own a 2005 Jaguar now. Our moms knew, our parents knew, our relatives knew we were dealing drugs. My mom said, "You're gonna get caught and you're gonna go to prison."

They cared, but didn't care to stop us. Punishments were not as serious then. There were some tough judges, such as John Wood, Ernest Guinn, Lucius Bunton.

Judge Wood [known as "Maximum John"] was killed because he was so tough on drug criminals. I knew the people who killed Wood: I knew the Chagras. My friends all worked at Andreas' Garage, across from a bail bond company. In fact, the downtown business people were the controllers of everything going on. They were buying off judges left and right. It was all rigged. If you had enough money and the right lawyer and judge, you could get off. Everyone knew corrupt lawyers who knew how to fix a case with certain judges. I got busted for DWI when I was eighteen, on the day before Thanksgiving. My date with justice was in a particular judge's court. We had him [name withheld] paid off.

We got everybody at Burges High School involved in using drugs, and that gave us more clients. We got even more clients from Austin High and El Paso High. We branched out to other high schools and bars. The reason we could keep the business going was that we were an informal, loose-knit group of about twelve friends, all connected from the neighborhood. We were essentially all independent brokers. We would go to a stash house that was run by three brothers. That place operated as our brokerage house. Eventually, one brother became a heroin addict and committed suicide. The other two brothers also became heroin addicts, and have been in and out of the penal system since their twenties. They are in prison today. One was sentenced to twenty-five years straight for a big drug bust. There are only two or three of us left from that old group of friends. The rest are either dead or in prison from the consequences of drug running or drug use.

Selling and Smuggling

Another center for drugs was the "El Pulgas" [not its actual name] neighborhood. A guy named —— and another called —— sold heroin at a house there. They had a relative who was a narc. The place had one way in and one way out. I was a city employee and would score heroin while on duty in a city truck at El Pulgas. A long line of heroin groups have come from that place. "La Rivera" was another center like El Pulgas, where you could buy heroin. La Rivera is near the Good Luck Café and Bowie High School, down by the canal. A well-known guy lived on the corner, one block over from Copia, and sold heroin from there.

I dealt heroin in the San Juan neighborhood. I got it from my uncle, who got it in Culiacán [in Sinaloa] and brought it by bus to Juárez. I would go to Juárez, get it, and bring it across the bridge. Smuggling heroin was different: it was easier [than marijuana] to bring across the bridge, since it was smaller and easily hid. Once, I brought heroin [all the way] from Culiacán, Mexico. I transported it in a Piper Cherokee [light plane] and flew to El Coyote, a flat landing site between Samalayuca and the Casas Grandes Highway. I unloaded it and took the *rutera* [bus] to Ciudad Juárez. When we did it this way, we would then get a clean set of clothes in Juárez and drive across the bridge into El Paso.

Marijuana back then was smuggled [by] wading across the river, until the DEA made that too difficult. The first time we encountered the DEA was in May of 1973. Before the DEA crackdown, we crossed marijuana loads on the river ourselves. Once a month we would bring drugs across the river. We had police guys in Juárez who would sell it to us. They worked for a Chihuahua state judicial policeman. This guy was the *comandante* back then, and was also one of my in-laws. His cops transported drug loads from a warehouse to the river on the Juárez side.

We crossed half-ton loads at a time. We would put the marijuana bricks [each brick weighed a pound] in black trash bags—the large type for leaves—and then cross them. A black trash bag would hold twenty to twenty-five bricks. The bags were heavy on land, but in the trash bags, marijuana floats, it does not sink, so it was relatively easy to get across. We would grab a couple of these bags and simply swim across and then put it in vehicles. One time, under cover of darkness, we crossed the river to Delta Drive and went directly down to my house. We mostly crossed it at night, or at sunset sometimes. We would cross it by the drainage ditch at Ascarate Park, by the levee located by the tennis courts. Some high-tension wires were our guideposts that told us what part of the river we were at.

The Border Patrol would show up before and after we crossed. Once we fled back across to Mexico when the Border Patrol showed up. They would shoot, but not directly at us. In fact, we outgunned them. We had guys with AK-47s on the levee. Our guys would swim across and drop off the load, and then swim back to Juárez, and then walk across the bridge into El Paso to avoid getting caught on the river back on the U.S. side. The police only caught guys from the U.S. side, so they could never connect the pot to the suppliers from Juárez. The police could never connect the smugglers with the pot drivers. The drivers picked up the dope and took it to a stash house. There would be five cars on one side of the street. They would fill up the trunks with dope. There would also be five cars on the other side of the street. Then all ten cars would drive off at the same time. We knew every back corner, every street, and every place to stash pot. It was hard for the police to catch everybody. We did this once a month, because it took about that much time to distribute what we brought across each time.

The fathers of the smuggling sons were known to all the neighbors. The neighbors knew, but didn't get involved. Everyone knew who the drug runners were and who the straight athletes were. My brother was an athlete who didn't get involved with us. This type of drug dealing was very open, but no one would talk to the police. The neighbors and our families were the voice of reason. They encouraged us to stop. The parents would call one another to find out where we were, and some attempts were made to break the whole thing up. Our parents might disband us sometimes, but then later we would get back together.

Between five of us, we put in a group order to get thirty to forty bricks, all sold wholesale to us. Each one of us had our own independent deals. It's a business, you know. At eighteen years of age, we were running a business. But we knew that if we were to go to a regular enterprise, we would immediately be told that we didn't know how to run a business. But we would reply, "What the hell are you saying?"

It was a small community on both sides of the El Paso–Juárez border that dealt in narcotics. We never had a problem getting ripped off in Juárez, like now. It was hard to get away with abuse, since everyone knew each other. There were few sources of stuff. Honest growers in Mexico viewed it like a commodity. They were not users; they were farmers. There was a different culture surrounding drug dealing back then. Vicente Carrillo Fuentes wasn't here yet. There are new cartels and people now.

Coke

Cocaine distribution came from a family that owned businesses on Juárez Avenue [in Ciudad Juárez]. It was fun dealing with them. They were flamboyant. They liked fast cars, fast women. They were hip, slick, and cool—and the hip, slick, and cool people bought from them.

Cocaine was smuggled in vehicles, not across the river, but across the bridge. The loads were smaller in size, and easier to hide in a vehicle. We used the lingo of *clavo* [literally "nail"; a secret compartment], but not as much as today. We would just ask the driver, "Where is the stash?" We knew who would be driving. We would take a vehicle to a body shop and hide coke in the panels.

Barricades put up at the Cordova International Bridge were there to stop port runners like us. We drove across the bridge from Juárez up to the vehicle-inspection booths and waited for the green light, and when they turned on the green light, we slammed on the gas. The green light, of course, meant you were supposed to go to the inspection booths or guard posts. You're not gonna fool these guys and get off [if caught with drugs], like an idiot that didn't know there were drugs stashed in the car, so it was better to make a getaway. From the inspection booths to the freeway, it was a straight shot. About a quarter mile, and we would be doing about a hundred miles an hour. Once you were on the freeway, they didn't know which way you went. You could go on I-10 east and get off at Chelsea Street, and then "jump," or alley-transfer, the coke to a van. The van leaves one way, the car goes another way. Soon, cops would be all around, but the van was already gone, and the cops couldn't figure out where the drugs were. We did this several times. Sometimes they would put flashlights in the back of the car, but they didn't shoot at us. We knew they couldn't. After a while, U.S. Customs would park vehicles on the bridge to stop port runners.

My friend's father was a customs officer. He knew us by face and told us to knock it off. But it was a small community then, and we knew he wouldn't turn in his neighbors. We were just high-school kids. We weren't hurting anyone but ourselves. The market for our cocaine was motorcycle clubs like the Bandidos—also, Anglos in the northern U.S. There was a big coke market then and now, but then there was not as much local consumption. Locals didn't want coke then; they were not interested. The locals drank alcohol and smoked pot; they got into psychedelics before coke became popular.

We bought cocaine for $125 to $175 per ounce and brought it across. It was strong Colombian cocaine. We would sell it at the same price after cutting it three times with lactose. What I mean by that is that [by] cutting it, or "stepping on it," with lactose, you could triple the amount of cocaine you had in hand. Every five years there was a reduction in the size of pot one could buy, but it was sold for the same price. Cocaine and heroin was the opposite: the price stayed the same, but the quantity went up. The heroin was really pure and strong. People were overdosing and dying on us.

Heroin Addiction

Heroin was my drug of choice, even though I hate needles. It was way later when I used coke—I must have been twenty-seven when I tried coke. I didn't use it for long, or consistently. Back in the day, all of us liked playing golf and listening to rock and roll—the Allman Brothers, southern rock, later Aerosmith, that type of stuff. There are people that like to fly high and people who like to fly low in the drug culture. *Los cocos* liked using cocaine, but my idea of fun was reading the newspaper through my shoelaces [that is, to be zonked out on heroin]. I don't get a kick out of my heart racing from using cocaine. I also used pot consistently. But there's nothing like a good nod [heroin high]. I shot heroin for the first time when I was eighteen. I didn't like smoking it. Smoking it was never enough. It was offered to me by a friend. I didn't like needles, so he shot me up. I liked the initial high and everything that accompanied it: the euphoria of heroin, the long euphoria of the high, and the chase to get it.

When you first shoot up heroin, there is a rush, and then there is a stage level of coming down. The chase is to stay alive but high. You chase it: you're chasing the high to keep up and not flop over dead. You stage down without overdosing. You are chasing life. There is a ritualism of obtaining the heroin, stealing, connecting, making the deal. The ritual starts the moment you get up and feel sick, then steal something to sell, get enough money to go to the connection, the connection makes sure you have enough money to sell you the heroin. Then you shoot up and begin the chase. It is all patterned.

A lot of it has to do with the drama: a big, long, drawn-out miniseries to get high and then stay high. It is all a contradiction from beginning to end—chasing life and confronting death through heroin use. The first time you use heroin, there is euphoria. I loved it. It is God's little joke on all of us: a lie of euphoria. You think you will get a greater euphoria. It is the beginning of addiction. You don't actually feel good once you're addicted: you feel bad, you don't feel well, you feel sickly. This is a "good state" in the drug culture. Now you're using heroin to get normal.

I was hooked heavily right off the bat, from eighteen years old onward. I had long runs of addiction on heroin, consistently shooting up every day, amazingly long runs chasing that little dragon. My last run was four and a half years. A normal, average run was nine months. When people get hooked, they make mistakes. Eventually—nine months on average—you run out of resources and you make mistakes. Then you go to jail. Jail is like home base. It is like a game of tag, and you are on base. In jail, or on base, you will kick the habit, but it is never going to fully get out of your mind. Physically, you are not addicted, but mentally you are chasing something that is not there. You get out and use immediately. I would get out and use again while thinking, "Why do I have to do this?"

In the El Paso jail, one kicks heroin cold turkey, or else you would tell them you're an addict and they would give you painkillers, but no methadone. I tried methadone at clinics in LA. I also tried "geographics," that is, moving far away to get away from the addiction. I have all kinds of stories from when I was in my addiction—from getting shot to overdosing. I OD'd in a police department parking lot in 1987 in Farmington, New Mexico. The police department was connected to city hall, where I was looking for a drafting job. I ended up in the San Juan Regional Medical Center in Farmington. That was my first introduction to a twelve-step program. I said, "Hell no, I'm not doing that. There must be a better way to kick." It didn't work for me there or in Los Angeles. I didn't want a spiritual awakening, and spent five years on another run.

The Gangs of El Paso

In 1973–1974 we were nineteen or twenty years old. It was the end of the Vietnam War, and people were beginning to experiment with heroin and cocaine. Some in our group liked heroin, some liked cocaine, some liked both [that is, doing both at the same time; also known as speedballing]. Our group of twelve mushroomed to about fifty because we extended our partnership across gangs and neighborhoods. The Second Ward gangs were the Destroyers, the Comancheros, and the Shamrocks. Los del Catorce was a Fourteenth Ward gang, near Bell School at Eucalyptus and Paisano streets, near Whataburger, by Bowie High and the projects. You have those Fourteenth Ward guys, and over by the Lincoln Community Center area you had the Lincoln gang. The Diablos and a group called the Nazis were in the projects between the coliseum and the Free Bridge. Those two gangs were in the same neighborhood, and they fought each other.

The Sherman gang was in the Sherman projects. Then one street over were the Dolan Rebels, on Dolan Street. They were one street over from the Valverde Frogs. Then there was our Clardy Fox group, which, merged with the Frogs. I was a Trojan with connections to the Valverde Frogs and also involved with the Psychos—the older generation, who oversaw the Trojans. We had jackets, nicknames, and informal leaders; we were all doing heroin and other heavy drugs. From there into Buena Vista were the Parkdale Latin Kings and the Ascarate Copperheads. South of the freeway there were Los Tanques, named for refinery tanks on Trowbridge Street, and the San Juaneros, and right across the street was the Texas Addition. These gangs went to Burges High School, the same as we, from the Clardy Fox area, did.

All these gangs dissipated with drugs. We united under commerce. All of a sudden, we were dealing with guys we used to fight with. There were truces drawn because we could make money selling drugs [and drug involvement became more important than territorial gangs]. From downtown all the way to the Ascarate area became an open business—a commercial venture, selling drugs. Gangs stopped existing.

Arabs [Arab American families] and well-to-do folks controlled downtown. There was a white Anglo kid, "Smith" [pseudonym], who grew up in our neighborhood on Alisa Street and made connections with people from the west side of El Paso: the children of the wealthy Middle Eastern families—you know, Coronado-area people. West-side Arab families were in the business; if it wasn't their children, it was cousins. Smith was an Anglo in a multitude of Hispanics. He was a smart kid, black-curly-haired, wild looking, who spoke English and Spanish. He had a strict father. We used to beat the hell out of him and his younger brother, "Frankie." Smith became an important smuggler with his well-to-do west-side connections, such as Lee Chagra, the attorney [who defended many drug traffickers and was the brother of the legendary El Paso trafficker Jimmy Chagra]. Smith was our attorney connection to Chagra. Smith had a Tennessee connection for our group to sell marijuana and coke to Nashville. Smith was gunned down by Interpol, the DEA, and federal police in Mexico City in 1977, right after Lee Chagra was murdered in his El Paso office.

The Old Gang Gets Thinned Out

We knew Anglos from football games. We would play informal football games for barrels of beer and drugs. That is how we made connections with the west side and traded drugs and money. We'd ask each other, "Hey, what you got?" That is how we met. On Sundays we would play Burges guys against Coronado guys behind Coronado High School or down at Henderson Field by the post office by Paisano Drive. We met Arabs and ran drugs for them. They made their money. The only group that was not involved in drug trafficking directly was the Jews. They bankrolled it. Back then El Paso was a very quiet smuggler's paradise, completely under the radar, until the DEA got serious.

We first noticed a heavy DEA presence in the spring of 1973. When I graduated from high school, their presence on the river was palpable. They were in jeeps, trucks, and helicopters. This made it harder to smuggle drugs across the river. So we began to bring pot across the bridge. There was a noticeable influx of federal agents, and we were losing connections in northern and southern U.S. cities: Detroit, Los Angeles, Nashville. They were getting busted. We were watching people go to prison and die.

Previously, when people came to town and looked good, we'd sell to them. But from May of 1973 onwards, it was harder. We had a need for new clients. We even started making new verbal connections through the state and federal penal system. Our people that went to prison met other connections inside. Segregation by races in the penal system was starting then. Those who were sentenced by judges John Wood, Lucius Bunton, and Ernest Guinn always wound up in federal prison like in Terre Haute, Indiana. Those sentenced were actually put in a lucrative position to make connections with new clients.

The gangs from the projects were the real heavy ones. I lived in a rental house, and by my senior year in high school was driving my 1954 Jaguar. It was an old one, but a fancy car for a high-school drug runner. I bought it at a lot on North Loop Drive. We would buy old vehicles and soup them up. So here we were in the neighborhood, driving around in cars, and even our own parents didn't have them. Of course, we had drug money, and that's why we could afford them. The standard of living of the kids was beyond what the parents were making. There was a conflict of economic opportunities. The parents were working eight to five, and the kids made more money running drugs. Parents didn't like it, because it was against the law and could lead to other problems. And it did.

As time went by, the influx of drugs moved from marijuana to coke and then to heroin, and psychedelics came in. "Trash-can junkies" emerged—taking anything they can sell for drugs. From 1969 onward, some guys started overdosing and being arrested. The federal government began putting a squeeze on us. There wasn't any talk of cartels in the seventies and eighties. It was just our group, and they were trying to shut us down. The Chagras were not the biggest dealers in town, just the best known. One of our main contacts was related to a DEA agent.

From 1973 to 1975 there was a group of three guys who sold dope at Jefferson High School. We sold dope at Coronado and Burgess high schools. Vicente Carrillo Fuentes and his Juárez cartel came into the drug business after us. He used the gateways that we had opened to gain access into the U.S. I knew Rafael Muñoz Talavera [a founder of the first Juárez cartel]. I dealt with him through my contacts with Juárez business families. Armando Nava Sr. and Armando Nava Jr. were El Paso narcotics detectives who were adversaries of ours. It was Nava Jr. and another officer by the name of Estrada who busted me. From 1975 to 1979, a lot of the guys passed away, OD'd, or went to jail. The core group of guys was being thinned out by things beyond their control.

Stealing Cars

In the summer of 1975, I began working for the City of El Paso. From 1975 to 1982, I continued working for the city. Then, from 1982 to 1985, I didn't work for anyone. I did odd jobs, such as at department stores like The Popular, in El Paso, and the May Company and Buckums. From 1973 to 1987, I was addicted to heroin. In the late seventies, while I was working for the city government, I got married and my wife became pregnant. So I worked at my eight-to-five job, then from five to eleven I worked as a draftsman in architectural work for independent builders. Then, from eleven at night until four in the morning, I would dedicate my time to stealing cars. The jobs and the stealing were to pay for dope and survive. I was strung out while this was going on. I would sometimes spend two hundred to three hundred dollars per day on my heroin habit. Sometimes only twenty dollars.

We would steal cars, with the keys in them, from the dealerships on Montana and Paisano streets. We would drive the stolen vehicle to an alley and sell it on the spot. We'd sell the cars and get high. There was a whole group hanging out at Ascarate Park, getting high. Then the police began setting up sting operations on Radford and Montana streets against car theft. One night, a guy we knew steals a car and goes to sell it and finds out the buyers are cops. There was a shoot-out between two crime partners and the cops. Afterward, one cop was shot and two crime partners lay dead.

While I was a city employee, I once rented a Thunderbird from a car rental place and used it as a "trailer" car. My partner would steal a car, and then, if anyone chased him, I'd crash into them. He stole a car and dropped me at the city-county building for work. He went back to the alley at the corner of Radford and Montana streets, on the south side of Montana. Suddenly, there's a shoot-out between the cops and my friend. Others of us did not know about the shoot-out, and another friend goes to return the rental car, which was in my name. The place was full of cops, and they see him in the rental car and shoot him. My friend escaped to Juárez with the car. The Juárez police gave it back to the rental agency. The cops then came after me. I said the car was stolen. The cops were breathing down my neck and said I was part of the theft ring using rental cars. They could not convict me, even with all this evidence in court—bullet holes, etc. They said, "You got away with it this time." This all happened in the late seventies. The car rental company sued me.

Hotel California

My mother died in 1985. She was active in the Democratic Party. Her friend was a state judge. The judge's daughter got high with us [smoking pot]. In 1985, I got busted delivering cocaine to an undercover agent at Alameda and Ascarate streets, next to a school [before there were "drug-free zones"]. I was placed in the aforementioned judge's court. It was my first and only bust, and I got a light sentence. I had gone to jail for DWIs and shoplifting. Once I went to jail twice in one day for shoplifting. I was busted in the morning, bailed out, and busted again that afternoon. I would get busted, but use my cousin's name, my uncle's address, and my sister's birthday—then get off. You could beat the system that way back then, before computers connected different jurisdictions and systems. The courts would eventually realize this guy does not exist at this address with this birth date. I would go shoplifting for cigarettes, since you could get twelve dollars for a carton. You'd go to the store and simply hide it inside your jacket, then sell it to get heroin.

I left El Paso in 1982. I went to Arcadia, California, famous for its Santa Anita Race Track, outside Pasadena, to live with my stepfather. My marriage was faltering. I got a job in a department store in Glendale, California. I was introduced to the gay community through people who worked in the store. Through them, I got connected to buyers of cocaine. I went to Silver Lake, where gays congregated. I discovered the gay community and their drug use. They loved cocaine. One of my in-laws was my cocaine connection in El Paso. There were no highway checkpoints back then.

I sold to the gay community. It was near the end of the disco era, and there was a lot of cocaine use. It was uppity California: fast cars, great clothes, high-life nonsense. Nineteen eighty-two also saw the emergence of the AIDS epidemic. The gay community was deep in cocaine use, and I was trafficking cocaine to them. Through this venue, I switched from heroin to cocaine at this time. I got a DWI in Van Nuys, California, and went to jail.

When I got out of jail, I went to a methadone clinic in South Central LA. I met Armando, who was from Pico Rivera [California], at the clinic. We ventured out and began a lifestyle that supported our habit. He used to work for an ice cream company that fired him because of his addiction. Armando knew a security guard at LA Cold Storage [a food warehouse]. We paid off the guard with thirty dollars. I filled up the back of a truck with ice cream and dry ice. Armando knew where to sell it. We went to the First Street flats, and we went to the Fourth Street [black] projects, to sell ice cream for a dollar a box [eight to twelve ice cream bars a box]. We stole it every day. We lived on Klondikes. I still can't eat them to this day! For six months we did this. From there, we'd go to sell ice cream to Bonnie Beach Street and Olympic Street [in East LA]. So I was moving from the gay community to the straight community.

In California, I had a two-hundred-to-three-hundred-dollar-a-day heroin habit. I was shooting up every four hours, day and night. I was looking for a way to get out of drugs. Armando and I ended up at the Metropolitan State Hospital, in Norwalk, California. A lesbian, Tommy, from El Paso, got me into the Met. I was there for ten days, and then walked out. I've done garage living, alley living. I was living in Armando's garage in the town of Pico Rivera. Then I lived in an alley between Broadway and Hill Street. That was the first time I encountered sleeping in an alley, with a blue LA Dodgers baseball bat knocking the mice and rats off me so I could sleep.

Gone (Back) to Texas

I returned to El Paso, living with my sisters or sleeping on lawns. Next to what was Lee Chagra's office there was a house where "El Cubano," who in fact was a Mexican, sold heroin. He would sleep, and I would sell drugs to the prostitutes and transvestites. Use and sell, use and sell. The main areas where I sold drugs were down by the Plazita [San Jacinto Plaza], the main library, and the Hollywood Café. My uncle Bobby was in and out of prison during this whole time. He was also an addict. I was involved with an older generation of *pintos* [ex-cons], then I was part of the second generation of heroin addicts. This is the addiction part of it.

This is the time when I got shot. It was the night before the *Challenger* blew up [January 1986]. A son of a customs official in Juárez was buying heroin from me. *Los aguajes* [literally, the "watering holes"] is what the shooting galleries in Juárez were called. I would go to a shooting gallery in Juárez formerly run by La Nacha and El Árabe, in order to shoot up. The dominant heroin seller in Juárez for many years was La Nacha. Two guys from Las Cruces were the connections to the New Mexico prisons.

We also had a negotiator. One of my partners from Las Cruces gave the son of the customs official shit [bad heroin]. He got angry and came back with a gun. We were selling dope through the window of the house by Chagra's office. The guy comes back and fires two shots through the window, which hit me in the hand and above the elbow. The bleeding was serious, so I went right across the street to the Hotel Dieu Hospital, to the emergency room. I was thirty-one or thirty-two. And suddenly I remembered how my father was killed when he was thirty-three years old. Then my uncles and sisters showed up. My older sister said, "You almost beat your dad [getting shot at a younger age, but by the same method]." The whole thing played on my psyche. It made me want to quit the business. I was in the hospital for one week.

I was like all junkies: you live a fluid life, and you move from group to group. That summer I got busted by detectives Estrada and Nava. They had planted a snitch. I moved from downtown to the San Juan neighborhood. I got set up and busted with about a half ounce of cocaine. The guy who shot me was busted with one pound of cocaine. He thought I was the snitch. I had one indictment for coke sales and another indictment for heroin sales. I was assigned to the aforementioned judge's court. A former friend of my mother, he immediately recognized me, and I got an eight-year probated sentence. I had already served six months in jail.

Kicking

Kicking heroin is just a psychological game with yourself. You do shake, and your bones hurt to the marrow. I kicked maybe a dozen times. The times I kicked voluntarily were [*laughing*] none. I was out of jail for only one week, and I used heroin again. I was sent to CRTC [Court Residential Treatment Center], a halfway house. I was kicked out of that halfway house. I still couldn't kick, so I ended up at my sister's house, sleeping on the couch. My life was the couch and the kitchen. The only friends I had were the tree and the dog tied to the tree. I would see the chatter outside—good, positive chatter. I had a child; I didn't see my child. I thought to myself, "How did all this get away from me?" So I called Narcotics Anonymous, NA. I borrowed my neighbor's jeans and shirts and my sister's truck. The only thing I owned was my underwear.

July 7, 1987: that's my clean date. NA is a secret society for Anglos to kick drugs. They're all gay, Anglo, and rich.

Certain things had to happen for me to quit dope:

My mother's death.

I got shot.

I got busted.

Watching people early in the morning having a full life, and I had nothing.

I went to treatment in August of 1987 at NA. It was a supportive group of people. Then I was in a halfway house called Casa Grande. I went through the twelve-step process at Thomason Hospital. Then I was sent to Big Spring, Texas, for a twenty-eight-day state rehabilitation at a state mental hospital. At first I was in the behavioral unit. They transported the addicts with the loons. I never had a better time playing baseball than in the loony bin: we played without bats, balls, or gloves—everything was imaginary.

Drug Vocabulary and Knowledge

There's a lot of code switching in the junkie world. For heroin, we used the terms *chiva*, *carga* for black tar, or Mexican brown. We also said "junk" or "dope," which are the most common English words used. We didn't use the terms "smack" or "horse" or "stuff." There isn't a lot of dialogue in the drug world, but there are, however, a lot of rituals.

a good high = *me pegó*

mainlining = *me voy a picar la vena*

la erre = the rig [needle, spoon, swab, etc.]

syringes = U-80s or U-100s

heroin addict = *tecato, hypo* (not used a lot), junkie

spoon = *la cuchara*

Near Alameda and Eucalyptus streets there was a pharmacy that would sell you a syringe for twenty-five cents. I would buy a syringe, then go to a store and buy a quart of beer, for the cap, then go to Church's Fried Chicken to get a cup of water.

matches = *mechas* or *trolas* (a cholo term)

cotton = *el algodón*

Dame los algodones = "Give me the cottons" [to shoot up the residue left in the swabs]

"take the air out" = *sacarle el aire* [of the syringe]

[Before you inject heroin with a needle and syringe,] you squeeze one drop out of the needle tip [to clear all the air out]. Then lay it on the arm and tap it in.

Heroin use is highly ritualistic and mental. Some junkies are pigs. That's why they get abscesses and needle tracks. Some are dignified junkies. I create a callus, then switch to the other arm until the first arm is healed, rather than make tracks along the same vein. Tracks can hurt and collapse a vein. The vein wants to hide, and it eventually collapses. You get hung up and shoot anywhere. You resort to leg veins, then the neck. You can "tat down," or tattoo on areas you shoot up in and want to hide. I have stuck a huge veterinary needle in my vein and did not get high. Others get abscesses by shooting coke, reds, or heroin-and-coke speedballs.

mistiaron or *erraron* = to miss a shot [to miss a vein while trying to shoot up]

needle tracks = *trackes*

tacked down = a person has needle tracks

When I shoot up heroin, I like to "double plunge," which is when you start pushing the syringe plunger, stop halfway, pull the plunger back, drawing out blood, and then push the plunger in again. It prolongs the effect.

A spoon made of stainless steel causes too much evaporation of the heroin. An aluminum cap [from a forty-ounce beer bottle] does not cause as much evaporation. You swirl the cotton around in the cap to make sure everything is dissolved and to filter impurities. The needle might clog if you don't filter with cotton. Sometimes you are in a hurry and don't suck all the heroin out of the cotton [into the needle and syringe]. The cotton eventually dries hard, but still has heroin in it. You collect the cottons up, and eventually start doing the cottons when you are out of dope. You "shoot up cottons" [by resoaking them]. You say, "Vámonos al algodón" [Let's go get the cottons].

I was a rarity in the drug culture: I was strictly a heroin user. I didn't use other drugs like weed or coke very often. Not all junkies look like bums, all skinny and scraggly. Some are fat. I sold to a nurse who did tricks for me. She felt guilty; I was elated. There are lots of exchanges like that. Heroin life is an extreme life. There is stealing cars to support a habit.

There was a police captain at central command in Juárez who was corrupt. I never saw corrupt cops on the U.S. side, only in Juárez.

Dealing is mobile now: "I'll be at Pinky's or Fox Plaza." Or you rent a room and sell out of a hotel. You [the dealer and the buyer] know each other, what each other drives. You can still get away with standing on a corner and selling. The cops want big sellers with cell phones and big loads.

Andas loco = you are high

Andas prendido = you are high [also, to be addicted]

Me pegó (or *me está pegando*) *la malilla* = to be going through withdrawal

la conecta or *la conexión* = drug dealers

¿Quién es tu conecta? = Who is your connection?

los clientes = drug customers

a balloon of heroin = *un globo* [You can carry up to twenty balloons in your mouth.]

Vienes corto = you're short of money

Vamos a hacer una vaquita = pooling money to buy heroin

cocaine = soda

a cocaine dose = *un papelito*

yayo (from the Tony Montana character in *Scarface*) = cocaine

We would say "get real" to people who used lingo like "yayo." Heroin is a culture of symbols and gestures. "Dame uno, o dos" [Give me one or two] is often all people say when buying it.

Ways of hiding heroin while selling it:

You put heroin balloons in a can, crush the can as if it's trash, and then leave it on the ground within a distance of where you are so cops can't find it on you.

Un pozo [a well]: hide it in a hole in the ground, then cover it with a rock, or paper like a McDonald's wrapper.

You can also hide it under river rocks.

When the cops may be watching, you can spit a balloon from your mouth into your hand and give it to the buyer.

Or spit it on the ground, and he gets out to talk and eventually squats to pick it up.

Places to sell:

Standing all day in and all day out on a street corner. Like, for example, in San Juan—not my neighborhood, but we held the heroin bags at the time so we could sell there—under the sign by the gym.

Sitting on a bus stop.

Selling at night through the window of a house.

Selling out of a house.

At the car wash on Delta and Ascarate—heroin sellers would pretend to wash cars, but actually they were just there to sell dope.

A bar on Alameda Street by the Naked Harem [a strip club].

Eventually, drug sellers became more mobile.

Selling Drugs in Downtown Juárez: Juan and Jorge

As is evident from the previous interview, the drug smuggling business connects El Paso and Juárez as well as other communities on each side of the U.S.-Mexico border and still others far into the interior of both countries. However, it was once commonplace to state that the United States had a major drug problem, whereas Mexico did not. According to this view, the United States consumed illegal drugs, and Mexico was simply the conduit for the spread of heroin, cocaine, and marijuana northward. This perspective was somewhat accurate at least until the 1970s.

By the late 1980s or early 1990s, Mexican cartels were replete with excess cocaine, and this scenario shifted dramatically. Throughout Mexico, *tienditas* (small drug-selling outlets, usually houses, apartments, or easily identifiable street vendors who frequent a particular spot) sprang up to distribute the extra supply to a growing domestic market. Today, such tienditas or *picaderos*, which are similar to tienditas but usually sell heroin, are pervasive on the streets of large Mexican cities, especially on the border and in Mexico City, and a semblance of this system is found in medium-sized cities and even in small towns.

Ciudad Juárez, like Tijuana, fabled in song and legend as a fleshpot and vice zone, is a city whose economy has relied on contraband smuggling and the provision of sex and drugs to a U.S. and Mexican market for approximately a hundred years (Martínez 1978). From the 1920s to the 1970s, La Nacha or her relatives controlled a major heroin-distributing network from houses located in Juárez within a hundred yards of U.S. soil. Neither American nor Mexican authorities could dismantle La Nacha's personalistic and highly effective drug ring. It declined after her death and that of several family members. In the aftermath of La

Nacha's death, an extensive *tiendita* system—supplied by the Carrillo Fuentes cartel—developed in Juárez to distribute heroin and coke to a much larger domestic market.

Today, estimates of the number of Juárez *tienditas* and *picaderos* range from 400 to 6,000. It is not an exaggeration to say that buying cocaine or heroin is almost as easy as purchasing tortillas. In some ways, it is easier: one need not enter a store, wait in long lines, or pay taxes. One simply walks to a window or a street corner and says to a man like "Jorge" or "Juan," "Dame uno" or "Dame dos" [Give me one, give me two], and hands him five dollars or less. At most, the buyer will have to specify that he wants *blanca* (cocaine) or *negra* (heroin). Even an uninitiated tourist can instantly connect with a middleman once across the Paso del Norte International Bridge, which links Juárez to El Paso. Taxi drivers, touts, and street sellers are everywhere. Bartenders, prostitutes, and others will offer to get whatever drug a person desires.

Most, perhaps all, of Juarez's hundreds of neighborhoods, barrios, and colonias have *tienditas* or some functional equivalent. The situation is similar in El Paso, although there, much of the retail sale of cocaine is done by deliverymen who take orders over cell phones and deliver the drugs to the buyer's home or another convenient location. It is essentially the same (binational) system, run in the El Paso streets by the Barrio Azteca gang and in Juárez by the sister Aztecas gang, both of which are affiliated with the Cártel de Juárez. Independent operators, freelancers, or groups associated with rival cartels also have made inroads, although in most neighborhoods of Juárez, they are required by Azteca enforcers to pay a *piso* (tax) or suffer the consequences. Recently, a bloody struggle broke out between the Carrillo Fuentes cartel and the Chapo Guzmán cartel over control of the lucrative *tiendita* trade. Dozens of drug sellers, innocent bystanders, and Juárez police died in 2008 as a result of this conflict.

Juárez policemen on the payroll of the Carrillo Fuentes cartel protect its *tienditas* and discourage theft by tiendita salesmen, who work regular hours, as in mainstream retail businesses. One of my sources, a daily eyewitness to the thriving tienditas, explained the role of the police in the retail drug trade: "When I lived in Juarez, before I started school and all, drugs were a way of life for many in the areas in which I resided. I watched the municipal police arrive daily for their payoff: if a payment wasn't made, then they started to harass and arrest the junkies and customers within the proximity of the drug dealer that didn't pay. If the payoff was prompt, then it was business as usual."

Bagmen collect profits regularly during the day, and suppliers re-stock the *tienditas*. The smooth functioning of this system, ensured by government complicity, is evidenced by the laughably small quantities of drugs confiscated by police authorities from street retailers—a mere pound of cocaine and 129 grams of heroin for the entire state of Chihuahua in 2007, according to official statistics (Borunda 2008b). During this same period, dozens or even hundreds of tons of cocaine passed through the state.[1]

As noted, Barrio Azteca–Aztecas, a classic prison gang–street gang similar to the famed Mexican Mafia, provide many of the workers for the *tienditas*. The gang developed in the mid-1980s among "Chuco" (gang slang for El Paso natives) and Juárez prisoners in Texas, New Mexico, and Ciudad Juárez penitentiaries. Today, the gang is composed of about 2,000 members (*carnales*) in the Southwest, of which about 1,000 operate in El Paso County (Borunda 2008a). According to an El Paso police investigator:

The gang, run by a set of "sacred rules," has a paramilitary order of capos, lieutenants, sergeants, soldiers, prospects and *esquinas* ["corners"], who are not members but back up the organization. . . . Separate crews, or cliques, in the gang use intimidation to collect "quotas" or taxes from street-level drug dealers, known as *tiendas* (stores). . . . The money is then sent into the accounts of imprisoned members.

Imprisoned leaders issue orders to be carried out at the street level during face-to-face visitations or in *wilas* (encoded letters) that are sent to a person or address known as a bridge. The message is then forwarded to its intended recipient. . . . For example, *aguacate* (avocado) is code for an approved hit, also known as a "green light." (Borunda 2008b)

Juan and Jorge's stories illustrate the daily work life of drug sellers on the streets. Ironically, however, Juan does not even consider himself a trafficker, but rather a kind of public servant of the streets. His job, even though it runs on hours just as predictable as those of a convenience-store clerk, could hardly be considered prosaic. He has survived several attempts on his life, and he spends his days and evenings amidst female prostitutes and male transvestites, drug-hungry street people, corrupt cops, junkies, gringo castaways, drunken bar crawlers, and petty thieves. Juan's regular haunts possess an eerie atmosphere reminiscent of the mood of Nelson Algren's classic novel *The Man with the Golden*

Arm or Bob Dylan's bohemian anthem "Just like Tom Thumb's Blues," which refers to Juárez.

Yet Juan has retained a human warmth, good humor, and a philosophical bent. He casts a critical eye on the webs of corruption and depravity that make his job possible. Juan has generously shared information with the author sporadically over a fifteen-year period. Lest one be quick to morally condemn such people, it should be recognized, as Juan states quite clearly, that he proffers services to people who willingly approach him. Like any employee of a large corporation, Juan knows that he is at the bottom rung of a rigged, exploitative, and ultimately corrupt system that he must rely on for his and his family's survival.

Juan

I'm always in the heart of the brothel and vice district in downtown Juárez. Occasionally, I'll take leisurely walks back and forth between the various bars. Every day I arrive downtown at about noon. I sit outside the front doors of almost all the bars and say hello to people passing by. When I'm downtown, everyone knows me and vice versa. In my opinion, the downtown area is crooked and rotten to the bone, to the core. And all this is due to the drug traffickers and the widespread availability of illegal drugs that have literally flooded the place.

I consider myself a "social servant" or "a servant for the good of society." One of the things I do here in the downtown area is "facilitate" or acquire things for people [especially cocaine and heroin], or do "favors" for them [such as taking them to brothels], helping them with various transactions, etc. But I don't use drugs, and I also don't connect anyone directly with drug pushers. Because of this, I've suffered though and survived two homicide attempts. The first one happened at the bar El Alemán Salvaje [The Wild German]. I was sitting at the bar, and all of a sudden Pedro Rocha [an important and well-known downtown-area drug trafficker] walked in and hit me in the back of the head, close to the nape of my neck. After repeatedly punching him in return and knocking him out, leaving him stretched out and unconscious on the floor, I reached over and grabbed the handgun he had hidden in his belt, aimed it at him, and tried to pull the trigger. But the gun had a security lock on it. I was about to take the security lock off with a simple push of my index finger, but at that very moment I thought better of it and decided that it just wasn't worth it, and so I didn't kill him.

A few days later, Rocha's hired assassins "El Chango" [the Monkey] and "El Tuerto" [the One-Eyed Man] went to look for me at what was then my job, working as a bouncer at the Beso Negro [Black Kiss]. They asked for me at the bar, and when the bartender pointed me out to them and they saw who I was, they left without saying a word. A few hours later, just before closing time, they came back. I saw through the long bar mirror that they were coming directly at me. One of them pulled out a knife and buried it three times in my side, a little above the waist. I immediately felt weak, but with all the strength I had left, I managed to punch one of them as they were fleeing. Then I shouted to my boss to help me. And you know what he was doing? He was in the backroom, smoking a marijuana joint, the asshole!

The two guys that had shanked me were riding in a black pickup that was parked across the street from the bar. I was able to walk out of the bar and hang on to the back bumper of the vehicle as they started to speed away. I hung on, thinking I could climb onto the pickup's bed. But somehow one of the sleeves of my shirt, and then my belt, got stuck on some hooks that had been welded on the bumper, and so I was dragged all the way to Chamizal Park, located next to the Free Bridge [also known as the Bridge of the Americas or the Cordova International Bridge]. I finally let go right by the place where the giant Mexican flag is. The people that were there helped me get up and walk to the sidewalk. I immediately started taking my clothes off, because the blood from the wounds was choking me, not letting me breathe. I spent the better part of a year in the hospital, because I had to have several operations. The people that helped me the most during that time were the prostitutes that I worked with in the downtown area.

The second time they tried to kill me, I was at home in the Cerro del Tigre residential sector. My wife was with my grandkids, and I had just gone into the bathroom. Suddenly, I heard someone hit the front door and force it open. My wife screamed, and then shouted, "What are you doing, you sons of bitches?" I pulled out the .350 Magnum pistol that had been given to me as a gift by an El Paso sheriff's officer so I could defend myself. I came out of the bathroom and shouted at them, "There's six bullets in here, and there's five of you, so at the very minimum I'm going to take one or two of you with me to hell." I shot a bullet into the wall, and the guys started fleeing. The men who had broken into my house were, again, El Chango and El Tuerto, together with three judicial state policemen.

My job downtown is sort of like a waiter or intermediary who's able to get women for guys, or drinks, or sometimes drugs for American tourists, but only for individuals who I know and are entirely trustworthy, or else for people that go downtown fairly often. As for the drug-dealing or drug-trafficking problem downtown, I feel that the downtown area is full of mafia types. I feel the police are responsible for most of the problems with drugs. They are the main reason that drugs grew so much downtown and continue to increase. The police ranks are full of drug traffickers. [At this moment, a police patrol car passes by the ethnographer, and Juan points his index finger at it. "Look, there goes the mafia now," he says.] I had a lot of problems with Pedro Rocha and his henchmen. I guess that's why they're on my mind so much. One time I beat up a U.S. immigration agent who was downtown doing an investigation about drug trafficking in the downtown area. After that, I had a lot of problems crossing the bridge to go to El Paso, and several times they were even looking for me here.

I consider myself a healthy person, and I know the atmosphere or ambience I work in is very difficult. But even so, I don't drink, I don't smoke, and I sure in the hell don't do drugs. I will admit, though, that I like women a lot. But I've only once, in thirty years of marriage, cheated on my wife. I sometimes brag about my talent for preparing mixed drinks. It's something I'm proud of.

Concerning downtown Juárez, I can honestly say I don't see a future for it. In my view, downtown Juárez's days are numbered. I think that with Juárez's current mayor, it's possible that everything that's now part of the downtown scene will be wiped out, because the authorities have tried to clean up all the problems the downtown area has, in order to make it a tourist zone. But I know downtown will never become a tourist zone, because there is no longer any stability here, and, therefore, there is no more tourism. I remember when downtown was a better place. But with the arrival of drugs, everything here got corrupted. That's why I think the pervasive presence of drugs is so detrimental to downtown. I know a lot of people here who live off of drug dealing, and at times that can be a means of economic survival, but I just can't justify it, because of all the destruction it has caused.

I still fear the police, but I'm older now, and that's why I don't worry too much about what might happen to me. I blame the police for a lot of downtown's problems, because in the same way that the cops sell drugs, they then turn around and take the drugs away from the consumers, along with their money, of course. I call these policemen *aprovechados* [bullies]. That's why drugs in general are a two-edged sword in the downtown area. And that gets me to the subject of the *apadrinados* [people protected by a "godfather"], who are in fact untouchable to the police. The *apadrinados* are those drug dealers that enjoy the protection of heavy, influential narco-traffickers, who pay the police for protection and silence and to whom they give part of the drug load that they sell. It's quite common to see *apadrinado* [protected] drug dealers shouting at policemen, even verbally humiliating them, right in front of their customers. When it comes to cocaine, most of it is resales of the loads that are confiscated by the authorities.

In downtown Juárez, a pusher is an individual who connects a buyer with a seller of drugs. I don't consider myself a pusher or connector, although I do occasionally get drugs for my friends and people that I trust. But on repeated occasions, I've received offers or invitations to connect or sell drugs, but I've always refused them. As I said before, I consider myself a social servant, and so my future in the downtown area is clear as long as I can "serve" and make a living doing it.

When it comes to downtown Juárez and its reputation for widespread, easily available prostitution, I'm somewhat of an optimist. I think prostitution is a necessary evil, although it's also my view that in a toxic environment such as downtown, almost all people get corrupted, thanks to drugs.

Jorge

Hi, my name is Jorge and I've lived in Ciudad Juárez for the last ten years. I know the downtown area quite well and the intricate movement of the cogs of the drug and prostitution rings that operate and flourish there. I spent my childhood in Amarillo, Texas, until I was fourteen years old, which was when my family and I moved to El Paso. I started high school in El Paso, and was soon introduced to cocaine, heroin, marijuana, etc. I started selling drugs at fourteen, when a friend of mine took me to visit his "godfather," who was a drug dealer. Eventually, I was selling drugs to everyone at my school, and that was the reason I was kicked out.

Now, twenty years later, I've established a selling point from an orange-juice stand near the municipal gym and Lola's Bar, where I also work as a security guard for fifteen dollars a day on the days I rest from selling drugs. My customers arrive by themselves—so, in reality, I don't have to do any pushing or advertising—or through a connector, to whom I pay a small fee for every customer he brings me. The connector brings the customers to the orange-juice stand, where he is the intermediary between the buyer and me. I sell every dose for five dollars. I have available for sale several types of drugs, including crack cocaine and heroin. I also have to pay the woman who owns the juice stand so that she'll allow me to hide my drug cache under her counter and, of course, so that I can sell from there. I do all right, since I make about fifty to a hundred dollars a day in profit by selling drugs. Before, there used to be quite a few gringo customers, but lately that consumer group or type has decreased dramatically, probably because the police nowadays take their money away as well as the drugs they buy. My godfather, that same guy I met when I was fourteen, is the one who supplies me with drugs, and he also pays the police so they won't bother me or ask me to pay them bribes.

My godfather is a member of a gang that operates out of the barrios of El Paso. Theirs is a tiered, hierarchical society, where every godfather has a protector, until you reach the very top of the hierarchy, where there's a guy, the leader, who is currently in jail and will probably remain there for a very long time, if not for the rest of his life. I myself have started or initiated several individuals into the world of drug selling, primarily youngsters.

The Juárez downtown area is divided into zones, territories or areas in which different groups or godfathers operate by means of pushers. Since the godfathers are all—or mostly all—members of the Aztecas prison gang, there's no problem when these zones are invaded or when they overlap. The problems are all with—and between—the smaller, zealously territorial street gangs. Close to my zone of operation, there's two of these street gangs: Los Jodidos [the Fucked-Up Ones] and Los Teipiados [the Taped Ones, a reference to drug murder victims who are often wrapped in tape by their killers]. Not too long ago, some gang-bangers forced me aboard a Ford Expedition SUV and took me to the Chamizal Park and beat me up.

I'm married to an exotic dancer that works in one of the topless bars downtown. We have two sons and another one on the way. It's for their sake that I expect to retire from this way of life in a year's time and find another way of earning a living. For now, we're living in a house located close to where my wife works, and I have some money saved for my children's future. I have a sister living in California and another one in Amarillo. The rest of my siblings all live in Juárez, and they are the only family I have left.

I was into boxing for three years when I was younger. Nowadays, for work reasons, I always have a gun with me. I was arrested and jailed in El Paso when I tried to cross into the U.S. carrying a load of drugs, using the rain drainage system to get into El Paso. The police and Border Patrol agents were already waiting for me when I came out of that manhole cover. I spent twenty-eight months in prison and lost my right to cross into the U.S., since they took away my laser visa [border crossing card]. Although I'm not supposed to cross into El Paso, I can do it, since I know many ways to cross the border illegally. When I was in the El Paso jail, I met a group or prison gang called the Polar Bears, who spend their time intimidating the inmates with threats and occasionally with beatings. When I had finished serving my time in the El Paso jail and was deported back to Juárez, the police authorities took me to Mexico City, thinking that I was the leader of the drug sellers in the downtown area. No matter, however, I've always been under the tutelage of my godfather.

The only problem I have with drug dealing, besides the usual day-to-day dangers to my freedom and physical well-being, is when there's a change or rotation of the police officers I usually deal with. Or when a new police unit or agency is created, such as the recent creation of the much-ballyhooed CIPOL [Cuerpo de Inteligencia Policial, or Police Intelligence Unit, which is a special intelligence and investigative section of the Chihuahua State Police]. This causes the godfathers of each zone to have to make new accords or agreements with the new police commanders and officers as well as with the new chief in charge of that sector or district.

Because of this, there was a time when drug dealing came to a standstill in Juárez and, in fact, virtually ceased altogether. And that, in turn, caused a lot of people [primarily prostitutes] to turn up dead. I myself sell drugs to prostitutes. In fact, now that I think about it, they're some of my best repeat customers.

A Young Smuggler and His Family

The loads were like a ticking time bomb that was being passed around, so you had to get it out of your hands as soon as possible. You got it, took it to the place, and got the fuck right out ("te salías de ahí a la chingada o te podían chingar ahí mismo con la chingadera").

COMMENTS OF A YOUNG BORDER DRUG SMUGGLER, RECORDED BY UTEP
STUDENT A.S.

Much like the "poverty draft" that sends thousands of poor African American, Hispanic, and Anglo Americans into the U.S. military and the Iraq War, the common workers in the drug trade, such as Juan and Jorge, are largely poor people with few opportunities, not the glitzy drug barons celebrated or demonized in movies or television serials like *Scarface, Traffic, Blow,* or *Kingpin.* Instead, drug smuggling is a dangerous, unpredictable career that often leads to prison, death, or ruin. Low-level smugglers and other menial workers in the narco-world also suffer from their marginality, frequently low pay, and disposability at the bottom of drug-cartel operations. Their jobs are unstable and often short-term. They may be busted, cheated, not paid, snitched on, or suspected of treachery and murdered.

The families of low-level drug traffickers both absorb the hardships and reap the benefits of a smuggling job. Families are also conduits into drug trafficking. Though his father is in prison for heroin and cocaine trafficking, the young smuggler had little interest in using drugs or any intention of becoming a trafficker. He had intelligence and academic ambitions. But when domestic and financial problems struck his family, drug smuggling provided needed revenue. The young smuggler entered the business through his mother, just as she had begun selling cocaine to please her drug-using boyfriends, one of whom was connected with the Juárez cartel.

Initially, he was frightened by the very idea of drug trafficking, but eventually the young man and his mother became accomplished smugglers. They made a lot of money very quickly. The young smuggler began to enjoy the job and the lifestyle it provided. But in a sadly predictable turn of events, the smuggler's mother was caught and sent to prison. Thus, the bottom fell out of the family's contraband business, and they returned to poverty, with the added trauma of the mother's arrest and imprisonment. In that sense, poverty was both the impetus for a drug-smuggling career and its inevitable by-product.

The young smuggler's story is valuable both for the light it sheds on personal and family motives and dynamics in the drug-smuggling world, and for the information it provides about government corruption, drug-smuggling techniques, and the functioning of drug-trafficking organizations. (In the following account, some details have been changed to protect the interviewee.)

The Young Smuggler

I was born in El Paso, and as a child lived in Oklahoma, a small town near Tulsa, until the age of seven. My mother was trying to get away from her boyfriend, who would beat her; he was the guy that came after my dad. He would hit us, and my dad did too, but not as bad. When I was four, my mother caught my stepfather screwing a woman at our apartment, so she left him and moved to Oklahoma. When she complained about the adultery, he picked up a telephone cord and began to strangle her. I could hear her struggling, so I woke up my sister and we attacked him. My stepfather hit me so hard that I was knocked to the floor unconscious. Many times, he would come home angry and would hit us.

My grandpa's brother molested all five of his children, and three of them became gay. When I became sixteen, I talked to my uncle, and he told me about the child sexual abuse. The children continued to love their parents—that is, my grandpa's brother and his wife—even though they disowned my uncle, their gay son. When my grandpa's brother, the molester, died, his children were hugging him even at the funeral; this was something I really didn't like. In my own life, my sexuality became challenging. I consider myself to be bisexual, but I prefer being with women.

As for my family, my father is from New Mexico, and my mother and grandmother are from Guadalajara, Mexico. My father's parents are from Las Cruces, but originally came from Mexico, and the rest of my father's family is from Barcelona, Spain. My family is lower middle class. My father was a store clerk, and my mother was a financial representative in an accounting department. My mother's job paid her so well that it allowed her to buy a house.

My father grew up in New Mexico, and my mother grew up in a small town near El Paso, Texas, after she moved from Guadalajara. My parents have two unique personalities. My mother is very vulgar, and my father is an uptight Republican. My father was sent to federal prison for drug trafficking. He was first busted for several ounces of marijuana and received probation, but was later caught with possession of heroin. He also loved to do "foilies," which was smoking crack on a foil pipe.

My family history had many episodes of domestic problems, such as on my mother's side. Within her family there were many alcoholics and numerous instances of domestic violence. My mother got a gradual affinity for alcohol when my grandpa on my mother's side beat my mother and his wife, and hit the children as well. My grandmother was physically abusive and would hit the kids so hard with an oak broom that it would break.

Because of the violence, my mother had a miscarriage, and my grandmother kicked her out of the house. Another example of my grandmother's violence was when she tried to force my aunt into a miscarriage by forcing my aunt to carry baskets of heavy laundry. The situation became so bad that both sides of the families hate each other to this day. I do not respect my grandmother nor law enforcement. My father's brothers and sisters were open to interracial marriages and married whites and had children. They would make fun of the other ethnic group, but not in a racist way.

When my parents divorced, they had joint custody of me, but when my father received a DWI, full custody was given to my mother. After my parents' divorce, my mother became involved with a guy named Jesús. Jesús was my mom's bitch. He was physically abusive toward us. He would hit us to feel good about himself, but at times he would be nice to us. Jesús would often tell us, "Don't speak unless I say so!" He had a mean Mexican attitude about controlling people. It was so bad that we had to move to Oklahoma and live with his sister. My father soon found out what he was doing and attacked Jesús with a Bowie knife.

My father would go to La Cima [the Hill, an open-air drug market at a three-way intersection at the top of a hill immediately across the border from the Sunset Heights neighborhood of El Paso], which is a part of Juárez where there is cocaine everywhere. He would play around with heroin, and from prolonged use of the drug, he developed a lot of acne. My dad wouldn't eat, and tried to live off of Jack Daniel's. He was able to get my gay brother into drugs, and he overdosed on LSD. My brother hasn't been the same since the overdose.

My father has been in prison for many years, and will be in for another seven years. His main conviction was for heroin and cocaine trafficking. My mother has also seen prison time for drug possession. She was busted recently for crossing to the U.S. with a little more than one hundred pounds of marijuana. We went to the bridge with some hidden luggage containing drugs, but we were busted by the agents.

My mom is currently in a federal prison. Since I was seventeen, we have crossed into the United States with drugs many times. At the time, it was so exciting. I am a prude about drugs. I have never drunk or smoked cigarettes. I have only smoked a little weed. My mother and I met a drug dealer who recruited her into smuggling. His name was Luis, and my mom married him.

Luis loved his tattoos; he had a particular one he liked, which was a phoenix on his arm. He would become verbally abusive to my mother. He would say to my mother, "Shut the fuck up and go to your room!" Luis would stay up all night playing cards—hearts—with my sister. One time I got into a fight with him, and he threw me to the floor and beat the shit out of me. Luis and my mother had two children, my stepbrother and stepsister. My stepfather and I didn't get along, so he kicked me out of the house. My mother then left him, because he was sexually abusing my sixteen-year-old sister. She had been raped for several months. Eventually, he was sent to prison. Because Luis raped my sister, she became a physical abuser. "Violence breeds violence." While attending high school, she would become angry and beat up on girls and a boy.

As a child, the problems at home were getting out of hand and were affecting me. I was a fat kid and ate a lot to feel better. I was in the seventh grade and weighed one hundred eighty pounds. We moved back to El Paso from a small town and lived there until my mother bought a house in New Mexico. As time moved on, I was able to graduate from high school, which was the highlight of my life. I was admitted to both the University of Texas at Austin and to Rice, but I couldn't afford to go to either one of them. My father never paid child support, and owes me forty thousand dollars in back support payments. My mother was into the whole subordinate-Mexican-wife thing; that's just how my mother is. I would tell her about her boyfriends, and I would say to her, "Don't bring the bitch home! Don't even have sex with him here!"

My mother was trying to compensate for the love she didn't get from her mother. She would try to impress her boyfriend by using cocaine. I said to her, "I don't care if you use drugs, but if you ever choose drugs over your kids, I'll disown you!" After my mother stopped seeing Luis, she started to see another man. She was trying to please the men, so she used and sold drugs. My mother was poor, but she had a good job. We had private health insurance that paid for my sister's psychiatric bills, and the rent was always paid. When my mother was fired, she couldn't afford my sister's psychiatric care any more, and we were left with Luis's old bills also.

Because of my mother's boyfriends, she had lost her job and began selling pot. Her main boyfriend was connected with two other guys in Juárez. We would drive a car across the border, and I would help her unload one hundred twenty pounds of pot in El Paso. She was paid about one thousand dollars, part of which she used to pay for my sister's psychiatric bills.

We would usually cross the border in the evening between seven and ten, after mom was out of work and I was out of school. The first time I crossed a load of drugs, it was like losing my virginity. It was somewhat awkward. I was shaking so bad that I thought I was going to shit my pants. I was nervous. Mom knew some agents with the Border Patrol and Customs, and they told us to go to a particular area with the inspector. My mom was so calm that she didn't get nervous. The traffickers were well organized in Juárez; they gave us a car with stickers and plates to get us over the border. Many times when we started to get the load over, the border agent would stop and question us: "What was your business in Juárez?" I would reply, "I went drinking in Juárez with my aunt." My mother had big breasts, wore a low-cut dress, and often flirted with the guards. She would say, "Oh, they almost popped out!" Her breasts would always be exposed to the areola area. We would always make sure that we got an agent who was a man or a dyke lesbian in order for my mother to flirt with them and get our load across.

U.S. politics never worked for me. I lost all faith in the system, so I sold drugs because of Luis and the problems he caused. I psyched myself out in order to cross the load. I was compensating for lost income.

We would go in our car to Juárez and exchange it for one that was already loaded, and the cartel workers would follow behind. The dope was packed right in front of my face, but I could not smell it. The packages were packed behind the air-bag compartment because it has a lot of room and is great for smuggling.

They made us see the marijuana load before we crossed it over. It was wrapped in invisible tape and doused with Pine-Sol, Ajax, or other Mexican detergents. It would also be loaded in the dashboard or under the carpet in a secret compartment. It was never exposed and never in the trunk. Silicone was used to seal up the compartment under the cut carpet area underneath the back seat. They unloaded the dope and placed it in boxes. We were paid one thousand dollars per load, and for bigger loads, fifteen hundred. Other workers for the cartel were paid only five hundred dollars. The car was loaded with the maximum of one hundred fifty pounds.

Once we went into this stash house, and in the master bedroom there were stacks of green and white bricks. They would unload the dope once it arrived in El Paso. We were not allowed to do any unloading at first, but after crossing twenty loads, they allowed us to unload the cars. When we unloaded, we would get paid three hundred dollars per car. The first time I drove, my mother was shitting her pants. The first time was at the Puente Libre [the Cordova International Bridge, or Free Bridge]. We crossed to El Paso, and then went to a convenience store; one of the clerks at the store was working for them.

They sent a guy from Juárez, who walked by and gave us his signal, and we had to get into his car. We were then dropped off by the international bridge, walked across it, were picked up on the Juárez side, and went back to get our car. My mother's boyfriend would have the money, and then we would split it: half for my mother and half for me for the load we crossed. It was such a relief, a rush of adrenaline for breaking the law, and it felt so good. But if we fucked up, we knew that they would kill us. One time, one of our twenty-year-old associates was murdered for stealing thirty thousand dollars' worth of marijuana and cocaine. Each time he would get a load, he would steal a little bit of it. Many of the cartel workers were on drugs and were not trusted by the leaders of the drug-trafficking organization.

I have no remorse, no guilt, for what I did, coming from a poor family. Over the course of a year, we did it three times a week. I had new clothes, we went out to eat every night, and I always had money in my pocket. My mother bought a brand-new SUV, and she paid fifteen thousand dollars that she owed to credit card companies. One day my mother was caught, and the U.S. law enforcement wanted me to arrange another shipment that would be busted, but I didn't. I could never put someone else in danger. My mother and I made an arrangement that whoever got caught would not narc on the other. The passenger would plead the Fifth. In my case, that was what I did, and I was released. We had gotten so good that we were not even nervous; I just wanted to get it over with. I just wanted to go home, relax, and watch TV.

Blaxicans: The Life of a Chicano Smuggler and Musician on the Borderline of African American and Mexican American Culture

As in the case of the young smuggler, the next interviewee began selling drugs out of economic need. The biography that follows sheds light on a number of dimensions of border drug trafficking, including interethnic relations, drug-oriented artistic expression, the establishment and functioning of distribution networks, the devastation and desolation traffickers feel when they are arrested, and the politics of the war on drugs. "Felipe" (a pseudonym) was born and raised in Baytown, Texas, a blue-collar, industrial city near Houston that is home to an enormous oil refinery.

Felipe lived on the poor side of town, and he describes growing up with African Americans who adopted Mexican culture as their own, and Hispanics who took up African American ways. These people, "all choloed-out black dudes," or "Blaxicans," are one of the many faces of cultural hybridity in U.S. cities with large black and Hispanic populations—most notably, Houston and Los Angeles. They also represent the cultural borderlands that drug-trafficking organizations must navigate to bring their product to market.

As described by Felipe, Mexican trafficking groups, specifically the Gulf cartel and the Juárez cartel, bring drugs into the United States and then sell them to black-controlled distribution organizations in Houston, Dallas, and elsewhere. The drug-selling lifestyle and the black-Mexican nexus (in neighborhoods, on basketball courts, in streets, in nightclubs, etc.) is then celebrated and re-created artistically by hip-hop artists such as South Park and Felipe himself. His colorful description of the intermingling of African American and Mexican American culture through hip-hop and rap music sheds light on the cutting edge of urban popular culture. Especially striking is the hip-hop song line "stack his ferry," which is an African American appropriation of the Mexican slang term *feria*, which means "money" or "coins." Concerning his growing up in Baytown surrounded by Blaxicans, he states: "Houston-area Mexicans are probably the blackest Mexicans."

Felipe says he first smoked pot when he was a teenager. By the time he was seventeen, he had started running pounds of marijuana from Baytown to "white hippies" in College Station, Texas. Baytown was mostly Matamoros-dominated turf—that is, under the control of the Gulf cartel. Because of his family roots on the border, Felipe attended college in El Paso. Shortly after arriving in El Paso, he became intrigued by Juárez. He and his friends would cross the border on Tuesdays to have a *torta* (sandwich) and an apple soft drink, and to see the lights and the people. Felipe's fascination with his Mexican roots and his growing connections on the border, as well as with dealers in the black and Mexican communities of the Houston area, opened up new business opportunities.

After attending college in El Paso and establishing a Chicano reggae career, Felipe became deeply immersed in drug trafficking. He had just gotten a divorce, and he was, in his words, "pissed off at the world." His father had recently passed away, and his mother was struggling. He wanted to buy a house for his mother, and his attitude was "Fuck this! I'm going to conquer the world." Felipe's existential frustrations, coupled with his working-class radical critique of exploitative, racist capitalism, furthered his desire to beat the system through smuggling. Felipe was a clever strategist who set up an efficient smuggling unit.

Unfortunately, however, he was busted in El Paso, and his life came crashing down. He was arrested at home, in possession of a large amount of marijuana that he and his associates were wrapping in preparation for transportation to the Greater Houston area. His house was completely surrounded by law-enforcement agents: several officers from the Narcotics Stash House Task Force, county sheriff's department agents, two detectives from the El Paso Police Department, an EPPD drug dog, and an FBI agent. After Felipe had been handcuffed, the FBI agent—noticing that Felipe's house was decorated with Rastafarian posters and other "hippielike" items—asked Felipe if he was sympathetic to Fidel Castro and his communist government. Felipe replied: "Your brain is already in a box. You're a boxed intellect. You're a Babylonian man." Thus, Felipe, a talented, angry young man, became yet another statistic of the war on drugs.

Felipe defiantly describes what he saw in jail: "There were young guys . . . with 700–1,000 pounds [of marijuana]. My case, by comparison, was peanuts. It is all about money in El Paso—if you have the money, you get off; if you have a good lawyer, you get off. It's all about your lawyer. The people without money have to get a 'public pretender.'" When asked by the author what he thinks of the drug war, Felipe answered, "I think the drug war is a tool of oppression. People with limited resources and opportunity get busted."

Felipe also points out that the rap-music industry as a whole—the dress, the talk, the relationships—is shaped by the drug war. He concludes: "It is important to be vocal in opposition to the war on drugs. In the war on drugs, you have to have an enemy: the urban minorities, the urban blacks, the urban Mexicans. Mexicans are viewed as criminals, bringing their drugs from tropical areas. It is 'the criminalizing of a generation.' . . . We are living 'the disenchantment of the world' . . . 'Reenchantment' is needed."

Felipe

I have deep roots in Ysleta, Texas, and now have more connections in El Paso, but I was born and raised in Baytown, Texas, a blue-collar, industrial city that has an Exxon plant that is one of the largest refineries in the world. [Note: Some names have been changed and personal details altered to protect the privacy of individuals discussed in this account.] The whole town is focused on business. The oil industry there goes back to the turn of the century. You see hardhats everywhere in the town. It's close to Houston, and has a port atmosphere. It's also somewhat Cajun. There are a lot of southern blacks there.

There are a lot of poor blacks in Baytown. You see more Mexicans these days, more than when I was younger. The demography of Baytown is 50 percent white, about 30 percent Hispanic, and about 10–15 percent black. Like many industrial cities, Baytown has a hard-ass mentality, with hard-working people. It's a no-nonsense kind of place. Not many professional types, like lawyers and doctors. The movie *Urban Cowboy* is about that area. There are also many very tough fishermen and, of course, oil-refinery workers. Baytown's population is 70,000, and it has the same homicide rate as El Paso (which has about ten times the population). In my freshman year of high school, there were thirteen gang-related murders in Baytown. The average is about eighteen homicides a year. Homicides in Baytown are caused by straight-up money disputes, drug wars, drug deals gone bad, and violence. There are gangs trying to control neighborhoods and crack houses.

I had a hard-working father. He worked as a process technician. He was also a hard-drinking man. My father taught me that you have to fight for everything you get. My mother has worked as a secretary in a junior high school for a long time. She is very involved in civic life, and even served once as a delegate to the state Democratic convention in Texas. She is involved in local politics and is still working. During my childhood, I did a lot of fishing. Sports were very big in Baytown, so naturally I also found myself playing sports. I played baseball. Football was like a religion in Baytown. My father grew up in El Paso; he went to high school there. His older brother has two PhDs from MIT. He became an oil engineer, and eventually was able to get a job for my father in the oil industry in Baytown. My father was just starting a family with my mom and older sister when they moved from El Paso to Baytown in 1969.

I was born in Baytown's San Jacinto Hospital. I went to James Bowie Elementary School. Now, as an adult, I'm aware that Bowie, the "Texas hero," robbed slave-trader boats and illegally sold slaves—like a pirate. He also falsified Spanish land grants. I went to Robert E. Lee High School. I grew up in a very southern, Texas atmosphere. I always identified as a Mexican, [even though] I didn't know a lick of Spanish. I looked Mexican, but didn't really know what real Mexicans were, in places like El Paso. Both of my parents were bilingual, and they spoke Spanish during arguments so us kids wouldn't understand.

There was a lot of racial tension in Baytown. It was poor blacks versus poor whites versus poor Mexicans. There was a mixed barrio, where there was even more racial tension. Tension would come out of stuff like job opportunities—say, if a black guy would get a job instead of a white guy. Growing up, some of my best friends were Jamaican, and also other black kids. My Jamaican and black friends would come to our house to eat menudo. "Pinches culeros mayates" [a derogatory reference to Blacks], my dad would say, but he [really] wasn't a hard-core racist. One of my best friends, a black kid we called "Black Midnight," loved menudo, but when being served, he would always say, "No meat, please—all *pozole* [hominy]." There was an Arab family that dressed like cholos. I had white friends, black friends, Mexican friends, whatever.

There was less racism in the poor areas and more racism in the all-white, wealthy neighborhoods of Baytown. Growing up, some blacks would cross over to Mexican culture, and vice versa. You'd see Chicanos with gold teeth talking southern black. I knew one black guy we called "Psycho" who was an all cholo-ed out black dude. The section known as Old Baytown was an old Mexican neighborhood. They built the refinery in the middle of the neighborhood. Mexican labor helped build it. Many Mexicans came to the area, especially after the Mexican Revolution. They came looking for work. There is a constant flow of new Mexican immigrants still. The Chicanos there get mad at the new arrivals. [One could write a] history of Esso, Humble, and Exxon as the companies that controlled the Baytown refinery. When my family came to Baytown, we found that there were older generations of Mexican immigrants that had settled in Baytown a long time before us.

My family and I would come to Ysleta [near El Paso] every summer. I came to visit the campus at UTEP with my mom, and liked it [so much that I even] sat in on some classes. I noticed all the pretty Mexican girls too.

When I was younger, in Baytown, break dancing was the culture; it was an art form. So were the lowriders. Then crack arrived in the late 1980s, and drugs took over. Everything became about drugs, money, and gangs. It destroyed the positive things like break dancing and art. There was no life for us left in Baytown by the nineties. We were all refugees from Baytown when we arrived in El Paso. My cousin came to UTEP, and I followed him in 1998. I came to El Paso to get my education. [As it turned out,] I learned as much on Juárez Avenue in Ciudad Juárez as I did in class. All the girls at UTEP thought I was white because of the way I talked. "What are you, a *negro*, a *cholo*, or a gringo?" they would ask me. "I'm from Baytown," I would reply. They were tripping on my accent.

Border Roots in El Paso

I learned I was Chicano, not Mexican. I learned Chicano historical consciousness in El Paso. I stopped calling myself Mexican. I also remember some guy was calling me *güey* [ox; slang reference to a male] at the computer center, and I got mad because I thought it was something bad, like "asshole." My cousin was roommates with Big Al. They met by chance when they were undergraduates. My cousin, Al, and I had a lot in common. We would just sit around playing music and partying. Al had been in a successful reggae band in California. We formed La Resistencia [a leftist anti-police-brutality group].

We would go out partying or dancing, and started meeting El Paso musicians. Border Roots [a Chicano reggae band] kicked in at The Bridge. The Bridge was downtown then. David Romo invited us to play.

Big Al was known as a guitar player; I played the bongos and congas; Benito played guitar; and Juan Ramírez, from Baytown, played bass and guitar. He has a home musical studio in the Houston area. We called ourselves the Refugees. My cousin was the leader. Also part of our group was my cousin's girlfriend and a black Mexican dude who's got an MA from UT–Austin in social work. A lot of these peoples' lives were on the edge. Seven of us came from Baytown to El Paso. Al joined the scene immediately. Also Frank DeSales, a poet. And Scott Maristeen, who, in my opinion, is the best drummer in El Paso. He's a hippie, and of French-Mexican descent. There was also [the band] Radio La Chusma, formed by the old members of Border Roots. There was Louie Sarellano, a drummer, who for two years was a member of Border Roots. He is good; he works at his trade. Louie was a member of the Native American Church and invited me up to a ceremony in New Mexico, but I never went.

We created Border Roots University; Benito named it. It became the center of our lives, and we learned a lot. Al was the leader, since he had the most stage presence and experience. He was a political leader too. He never really wanted to be a political leader, but felt he had to do it. All the people that played in our band learned from him. We had an interesting group of members—many were from Baytown. Scott Maristeen, who had an albino-looking eye, lived in a van with two dogs. Juan and I rented a slummy house with poor utilities on Florence Street, near UTEP, and that was a center for Border Roots. There was also a guy named Frank González, a poet, who was one of Al's friends but was more of an outsider, not in the group like Al. One member of our old group got busted for possession of cocaine and is now serving a long sentence.

We barely paid the rent, and had no utility services. A slumlord company owned by one of the Middle Eastern families that controls a lot of El Paso property owned our house. The house became the band's practice studio. We had parties and played for our friends. The neighbors didn't complain; they liked the band and music. We played in Juárez, and were also heard quite a bit on Juárez radio. We brought tequila and girls to the house. Al met wealthy Mexicans who set us up with gigs. One guy was a big dope dealer. He wanted to back us, but the deal fell through after an argument. Border Roots supported us for several years. It paid my way through college. We had lots of good times. Our musical success grew more than we thought it ever would, which led to growing pains and problems. Conflicts arose in Border Roots. Often, fistfights almost happened. We were constantly changing the lineup in the group. There were also clashes between Tinajero and Al for the lead-singer role. Eventually, Tinajero took off for California. But Border Roots brought a social message with it—resistance, love, unity. It was in the spirit of Bob Marley. Our music was a weapon.

La Resistencia was connected with the Revolutionary Communist Party [RCP], which had been founded by Travis Morales and Ricardo Sánchez. Travis was an activist from Houston, and would fly out to visit with Al and my cousin. Travis slept on our couches. He was very articulate and radical. He started a riot in the 1970s after a black Vietnam War protester was killed by the police in Houston.

My father met Travis once, and remembered him from some documentary film. My father was a JFK supporter and a patriot. He hated communists. He checked out Travis to see if he was a good influence on his sons. He liked Travis: they had a meeting of the minds, and my dad gave him a firm workingman's handshake. My dad was a rebel, a working-class rebel, that is. My relationship with my father was shaky—I guess like any relationship with any father. He would have supported me if he had been alive when I was busted, but he would have given me a stern lecture. For a man who didn't go to college, my dad was intelligent and well read. His older brother, my uncle, was a role model for my cousin and I. When I was going to college, I had long hair, like my dad once did. He was happy I was going to college. He supported the band too.

UTEP would not sponsor a RCP chapter, but my friends and I founded a La Resistencia chapter in El Paso. We worked with MECHA [Movimiento Estudiantil Chicano de Aztlán]. For three years, we had a protest day on October 22. Artists dressed in black to protest against police brutality. We would have about fifty people and some art, and there would be cops undercover around with walkie-talkies. MECHA and the Black Student Union were accused of totally vandalizing offices at UTEP. It became a big controversy. We had a press conference [to clear our names]. People needed to know we didn't do it. I think fraternity boys did it for fun and being goofy, but they may have wished there were no Chicanos or blacks around. It seems like underneath, they hated us. Jesús "Cimi" Alvarado, the director of MECHA, was kicked out of UTEP. He was a famous artist around UTEP; he did a painting of a Chicano puffing a big cigar that was displayed downtown.

The Border Roots musical scene involved a lot of hedonism. When we played at places like Aceitunas [a bar on the west side of El Paso], we attracted a group of fans—hippies, cholos, football players, and followers of reggae. It brought people together. After shows, partying would happen. There would be drinking beer and smoking pot. I've been around drinking and drug use forever—in my family, with my friends. Growing up, there was constant drama in my house with drinking. Some people can handle it, some can't. Things were usually peaceful and cool at the parties. Sometimes there would be fights. I'm tough, but more mellow than my cousin. He's the tougher one; he's the fighter. He didn't take shit—he kicked ass. He is a small, strong man.

Selling Pot to Aggies

I didn't smoke or drink regularly until I was seventeen. I first smoked pot when I was thirteen. My family likes partying. I was an athlete. I stopped baseball in college, but before that, I constantly played. For the first ten years of my life, we lived in the projects in Baytown. I learned about pot when I was four or five years old. I remember I was playing Hot Wheels, and suddenly I saw two "roaches"—man, that was something. My sister saw me playing with the roaches and got mad; she threw them away. That made me curious: "What kind of cigarettes are those?" I thought. From that incident on, I knew about drugs. I came to think that marijuana was a pleasurable form of rebellion.

My dad and uncles were Chicanos who had parties in which they put on War on eight-track tapes, and played bongos, and had strobe lights. Us kids would be running around. I knew my male relatives smoked pot, because at some point in the party, the men had to go to the store for ice. They'd come back with red eyes. We knew what was up; all the cousins knew. The first joint I found was my father's. I found it in the house. My father was a Chicano who listened to John Lennon, James Brown, etc. But Mexicans have more conservative views about pot than Mexican Americans.

My ex-wife is from Durango. Her family drank tequila like crazy; I wanted to smoke a joint when we visited them, but pot is taboo in Mexico. Her family came back with us to the U.S., and they'd be up in the morning drinking tequila, but no smoking pot allowed. I tripped out on that. In a way, you're socialized in drug use by your friends and family. I wasn't known for drug dealing in Baytown as a kid. I played baseball, hung out with athletes. We played baseball against teams with gang kids who smoked pot. As a kid, I'd ride my BMX bicycle to the projects, and I would see crack dealing there. I grew up with friends who became drug dealers. If all your family is doing it, you do it too.

At seventeen years of age, we started running pounds of marijuana to College Station [home of Texas A&M University]. We would sell to hippies. My white homeboy, Brian, had hippie connections. We would go down there [College Station], sell dope, go to restaurants, pay for concerts. The Mexicans controlled the drugs. It was Matamoros-dominated turf. El Paso was a far-off rival cartel. Brian also grew it next door for a couple years. One of my friends was into stealing cars in order to support his cocaine habit. He was only fifteen years old. He was our connection for pounds of pot. It was simple; there were no checkpoints between Baytown and College Station, like there was near the border towns. We could transport five pounds in a backpack. College students would show up at our apartment, or we would go to their hippie apartments and smoke their bongs. It was good times and a lot of fun. We only sold pounds, not small sacks.

We would drive from Houston to College Station. We would drive through farms, and look at the college girls. It was all gravy. I would often buy brand-new pairs of tennis shoes. We didn't want to make more money or sell more pounds than we were. It was enough money to put in your wallet and have a good time. I was too busy going to junior college and playing baseball. I played for the Baytown Sox, an American Legion team. I would make four hundred dollars for every load I took to College Station. I'd always go back home with a new pair of tennis shoes. Then I'd spend $100 on partying. The profits were spent on fun. Beside the runs to College Station, though, I wouldn't sell sacks, just smoked it. . . . I wasn't the drug dealer . . . I was very independent as a kid. I made money mowing lawns. I played pool for money. Drug dealing was not a lifetime career, but I found a way to make a few hundred dollars selling pounds—just another way to make a little money.

We rode that for three years. Then Keith [an Anglo Texan who was my partner in the College Station area] got married and left for San Diego. At that time, I was in junior college. I came to El Paso to go to college; I came here to study. I was a bookworm at first. El Paso has a conservative Mexican Catholic side, but also a liberal Mexican culture in places like the Lower Valley. I was intrigued by Juárez when I first came here. My cousin didn't party much.

Selling Pot at UTEP

My friends and I would go to Juárez on Tuesdays to have a *torta* and an apple soft drink, and to see the lights and the people. There was a lot of shit going on. Al started introducing me to the different bars and people. I was also looking for weed. I was twenty-one, meeting lots of new people in lots of different circles. I made lots of connections. I never had been into cocaine. In my Baytown neighborhood, you had respect and love. They would kick your ass if you did cocaine. I didn't do it. Older people that knew my friends sold coke, but they didn't do it. It was for "hypes."

My friends from the dorms would go buy a "twenty" [of cocaine] every now and then. I would do a "bump." I started dabbling in coke a little. In the music scene, there was more cocaine around. I started meeting cousins I never knew. I met a lot of people through Border Roots. But I never sold coke. It's a different world. Friends that sold coke told me people call up at all times. People didn't do that with the weed. Heroin is another, different kind of underworld. I couldn't get involved with heroin.

Then 9/11 changed the whole thing [drug dealing] in Juárez. They used to ask me to bring drugs across to El Paso, but I didn't. Drug smuggling and dealing are back up, but it is more risky now. Smuggling across the border raises profits. There are big profits if you don't get popped. Trafficking cocaine to Chicago can get into the millions of dollars. In Chicago, coke was $22,000 a kilo; Houston is $14,000 a kilo; El Paso is $12,000 a kilo; and Juárez is $9,000 a kilo. Good Mexican pot is $80 per pound in Casas Grandes; $150 per pound in El Paso is good, but normal price is $200 or $250–$300 per pound. In Albuquerque, it's $350 a pound; in Ohio, it's $1,000-$1,200 a pound.

I had started selling weed at and around UTEP; I got the pot from my godfather. Fine brown Mexican weed. I would pick it up from my *padrino* and sell it to athletes, jazz musicians, interesting people, and players from Chicago and LA; athletes love weed. I had realized that a lot of college kids wanted weed, that I liked weed, and my godfather had weed. That's how it started. I smoked with people and got comfortable with them. I had good connections. People you never would suspect smoked pot. I sold one ounce a week to an old hippie in Sunset Heights. He cleaned the pot meticulously with a screen. He was an old man but wanted his ounce of weed.

I was selling regular amounts in El Paso, just like in Baytown. It was a spontaneous development. My godfather sold me a quarter pound for $60. So I would buy a quarter or a half a pound, and then make and sell sacks or lids—ounces—to get an extra $20. Then I would go to dinner at nice restaurants. I sold sacks for $40 per ounce, which amounted to $160 per quarter pound. So I would make $100 profit for every quarter pound I bought from my uncle. I would also sell to maintain my pot habit. I learned to smoke blunts. I am a user and abuser of weed.

The Houston and Baytown Scenes

I also kept in touch with friends in Baytown. They had moved up in the drug world and were making more money. Some wore big diamond earrings. I had friends in Baytown who sold seventy-five pounds of pot per week, from Houston to Atlanta. They already had a network. Chicanos are the perfect drug traffickers in Baytown because they can get the drugs from Mexico and sell it to the blacks. The blacks and cholos merged in Baytown when the Chicanos let the blacks in. There were more blacks, but the Chicanos had the connections and took most of the risks. My cousin saw the blacks and Chicanos merge into black cholos and cholo blacks. There used to be the blacks in one gang called UNLV—U-Niggers-Love-Violence—who were "reds," affiliated with the Bloods, and the Chicanos were in the East Side Locos, also "reds." The Chicanos were East Side Locos since the 1950s, but they rearranged gang life in Baytown when the UNLV and East Side Locos merged. That is Baytown today.

Houston is very unique. It's close to Matamoros, where drugs come from. Houston has drug connections to Tennessee, from where it goes south, to the rednecks in Atlanta, Mississippi, even Florida, but there are different routes. Driving through Louisiana is the most dangerous drug corridor for getting busted. There is a battle for control over the I-35 route, from Laredo to Dallas to Chicago. That is a big drug corridor. Nuevo Laredo is the source of those drugs. There is also a big route from El Paso to Albuquerque to Chicago and Los Angeles.

In Houston a big hip-hop scene developed with a black and Chicano flavor, [including] black rapper artists like Chamaleonaire, who started using Spanglish and rhyming words like "ferry" [*feria*]. "Stacking ferry" (*feria*) means "stacking money." Texas has a unique but big Chicano hip-hop scene. Some blacks around Baytown and Houston speak Spanish too. It became a breeding ground for people like Emiliano Zamora, who had some friends that became big in the drug world. I visited old friends in Baytown; we spent a few thousand dollars at titty bars. They wore diamond-encrusted watches. They had become prominent. My drug friends took me to the best clubs, with valet parking. It was drug-dealer success, in with the Houston hip-hop scene connected to rappers like Baby Bash and South Park Mexican.

Houston, Dallas, and places like Chicago are different than El Paso. El Paso is smaller, with smaller suburbs. There was a lot more going on out in the open in Houston's suburbs. In Baytown, on Martin Luther King Street, there's bars and shacks. There's crack selling on the street. Competitors jump in front of cars to sell crack. The main drug dealers in El Paso are businessmen, who keep it undercover. In Baytown, it's rougher and more open, with rough, hard-core drug dealers. But in El Paso neighborhoods like San Juan, people appearing to be bums are selling heroin. When I played sports in high school, we used to run from the school to the football field. One day, the TV show *Cops* was filmed in Baytown, and so I saw drug dealers running across the football field to get away. MLK Street was hot then. Gentrification destroyed this drug scene and the rough scene on MLK Street. They tore down a lot of the bars and clubs. It is way calmer now on MLK Street. Still, on MLK Street and the Houston area, people are getting killed over a twenty-dollar crack deal.

The El Paso–Houston Connection

It was through sports that I got to know drug-dealing people in Houston. . . . I had this friend who made money in drugs. . . . I started putting one and one together. . . . I met a lot of people. . . . I realized El Paso prices were cheaper than Matamoros prices. Matamoros weed was better, but the best stuff doesn't stay in El Paso—it moves on to places for more money, like Ohio. I started doing good, started selling larger quantities. I made a deal with my friend, the one who sold seventy-five pounds of pot per week. From El Paso, I would offer him a better price than what he could get from Matamoros. He paid $270 per pound in Matamoros. I charged him $250 per pound out of El Paso. I bought the pot at $150 per pound, so I would make $100 for every pound I sold. I made [more than] $7,000 in a seventy-five pound load.

At first I was holding it for Houston people, not selling it around to my own customers. I became friends with two brothers whose father was a banker in Juárez. They were from a whole different level in the pot world. They were *fresas* [yuppies]. They had family members who had ranches where the pot was grown. Back in Houston, my friend Franco had street credibility, and he became my connection at that end. You've got to have your street representative in the Houston area.

This older dude from Mexico, in his forties, looked like a businessman. This guy was a landowner. He would arrange to bring drugs across to me. He would bring the weed to El Paso. I wanted to build my own team.

I had to build the trust with Jimmy, the *fresa*. It took a year and a half. He had a badass truck with a *clavo* [secret compartment] built into it. A great *clavo* builder had done that job. I knew I could bully Jimmy, intimidate him. This guy was nerdy. He wore Abercrombie hats, Puma shoes, and listened to Enrique Iglesias. Jimmy would organize and collect the pot from his cousin. Then the driver, Christian, was busted one month before I was busted. This guy was fucking weird, a *fresa* from Juárez.

Jimmy would normally drive a work truck, but once he came to my house in a black Cadillac Escalade. We would unload the packages in the building, but sometimes we had to use the outside door. I was getting enough money together to set up my own team. It was connected like a train. Franco, in Houston, had two truck drivers to run drugs who had done a few deals with him. So I sent five pounds, in air-sealed packages, in the mail to Houston. Three times I got eighteen-pound turkey roasters—put fifteen pounds of pot in each and sent it by UPS to Albuquerque. I would pick out a name from the phone book or use an army colonel's as a return address. Jimmy was paranoid and meticulous in preparing drug loads. He would wear gloves and put Vaseline on his hands to avoid having the scent of drugs on his body. He would double-vacuum-seal and then heavily tape the bricks of dope.

The older guy from Mexico would send a guy from the ranch in Mexico to Juárez, to a work house where a fourteen-year-old kid was wrapping the bricks of pot. They used a vacuum-sealing machine with a heated bar, then covered the bricks with tape. Later, one would use a knife to cut through the plastic and tape to open it. The loads were brought to Benito's apartment for a while, and then to my house. This is when I started dealing heavily, right after my divorce happened. I was pissed off at the world. My father had recently passed away also, and my mother was struggling. I wanted to buy my mother a house. My attitude was "Fuck this! I'm going to conquer the world." I made a lot of money with dope. I was spending three hundred dollars on a stripper. I was also doing side deals in addition to setting up my big deal. I was also trying to set up my own team and trying to put a down payment on a house for my mother. I was now selling pot to my friends. The roles had reversed: my godfather was buying pot from me instead of selling to me. I moved out of the projects when I was ten, but now I was making it big.

Blaxican Culture

My friends in Houston were moving up too. Franco [Hispanic] and Louie [black] were just ordinary dudes meeting on a basketball court to play. They are unique because of the way they made it big. They were a good team. Franco got Louie the "Mexican price," the cheapest, most wholesale, and best price you can get. There can't be too many middle-men to get this kind of price. Franco had the Mexican price through his stepfather and connections in Mexico. Franco was always in trouble; he got kicked off the basketball team and quit high school. But he was an excellent basketball player, very into street ball in Houston, the best player on the east side. Franco always mentioned the recreation center in Houston where pros played. He was good enough to play there. He could also talk politics, philosophy. He was not dumb.

Franco and Louie bonded through basketball. Louie was also an ex-cellent basketball player. Franco and Louie are both smart. [Franco's] Mexican family would say, "Pinches negros" [goddamn blacks], but blacks and Mexicans got along fine. They had organic relations—just people. Louie did good. He is a real cool character, very well spoken. Franco made it big in a small town, selling seventy-five pounds every two weeks, but Louie moved to Houston and made it really big. In Hous-ton, pot and coke and crack are sold in huge amounts. There's a whole culture that comes out of drugs and is manifested in music. In Houston, everyone wants to look big. Everyone wants to be the biggest baller. In Houston, they say, "DO IT BIG!" Franco surpassed his roots; he got in the mix with record companies. He was able to stack his "ferry" with a line of black hip-hop songs. There is a strong connection between the drug cartels, drugs, and record companies. There's a whole culture that comes out of drugs and is manifested in music.

Houston-area Mexicans are probably the blackest Mexicans as well. Los Angeles is similar; both are the biggest areas of black-Mexican mix-ing. There is cross-cultural sharing. The term "throud," which means "cool," came from blacks, but Chicanos use it too. "Yayo" also. Lowrid-ers overlap with black culture. Wearing Dickies and Chuck Taylors is done by cholos and some blacks. In Houston, Mexicans and blacks are wearing Dickies and Jordans. A Jamaican guy we called Psycho was all cholo-ed out and could speak cholo lingo. Had it down to a tee: wore a "fade," used the word "throud."

The Houston-style black-Mexican culture includes whites too. One of our crew we call "Clay Dawg" is a white guy from Baytown who is heavily influenced by black culture. He'll wear just T-shirts, jeans, and drives a big old Suburban. He looks like a redneck, but Clay could have a black girlfriend if he wanted, and nobody would care. I had a black girlfriend once—my mom was freaking out a little—but the girl was more like a white chick. One south Mexican hip-hop artist who made it big was Carlos Coy. He formed Dope House Records—he was shown on a CD with a Pyrex container used for coke. He got busted for running drugs.

People started using the term "Dirty South" for the hip-hop music spreading the drug culture [around Houston]. It influences kids with rags-to-riches life stories. Dope dealers and musicians are major themes of the lifestyle. El Paso is unique, but there is a segment of the community that tries to mimic the Dirty South style. All kinds of inner-city youths are part of the culture: Jews, blacks, Hispanics, whites, etc. . . . There are four major elements to hip-hop: the MC, the DJ, graffiti artists, and dancers called B-boys or B-girls (break-dancers). Blacks started the MC part in the 1970s, and Latinos added the graffiti and B-dancing. Money blew up the hip-hop scene and created all sorts of MCs now.

Franco met South Park, who was an artist that made it big with Dope House Records but "dropped the bone." He was a shady guy, and fucked up by getting busted for molesting a thirteen-year-old girl. He is doing twenty-five years. Other girls have said he was a pervert. He had his first felony when he was nine years old. Other black Mexican hip-hop stars include Tony Montana, a Chicano Cuban who was an upcoming rap musician with a CD who bought a studio with dope money but is currently doing twenty-five years for a cocaine conviction; Baby Bash [California-Latin hip-hop artist who made it big in Houston]; Frankie J. [Tijuana–San Diego Latino rap star]; and Chingo Bling, a tamale kingpin who made a Carlos Coy CD.

Black and Mexican musicians rap together, record together, and support each other. They have drug connections, and the flip side is hip-hop rap. It looks like blacks dominate hip-hop, but the ones doing all the hardest and riskiest drug work are the Mexicans. There are black mules, but most are Mexicans. Sometimes, the blacks make the most drug profits. There is a common understanding between blacks and Chicanos: they don't want to go to war, like in jail. In jail, it is different. Franco talked southern black in jail. He had trouble with cholos. "Why does he talk this way?" the San Antonio Mexicans asked.

Louie surpassed his Mexican connection [Franco] in the neighborhood. They [the Juárez cartel] flew him here to Ciudad Juárez. He was in Juárez for four or five days. He was very impressed by the Juárez-cartel people and their wealth. When I saw Louie in Houston weeks later, he mentioned he had been to Juárez, and said, "They've got some fucking money." "Big old property." Louie and the Juárez narcos needed to see eye-to-eye. He got kicked up. It is unusual for a black person to meet with the Juárez cartel, because it is suspicious and would likely be noticed by police or the DEA. But Louie is a black cholo, and they had it worked out—probably kept it low key and quiet by paying off some police. Louie became a legend in another city, then got out of the business seven years ago.

This whole culture of dope, it affects ethnic relationships. Young people learn how to do business [by] having a street understanding of how money is made. Where you are when you are growing up affects your life. You may be a black cholo or a white cholo. Psycho is married to a Mexican woman, and he lives *pachuco* [older Chicano] style. Arab dudes in Baytown adopted cholo style. There is a huge culture and way of life about drugs, music, ethnic relationships, and street understanding of how to make money. Drivers are paid according to the value of the loads they carry. A thousand dollars per trip is what Christian was getting. It is a business with trust between those involved. Louie would say to his dope partners and friends "It's good," "My word is gold," because there's an ethics involved in dope deals. The partners become like family. They [mules] could rip off a load and say they didn't get paid on the other end by the buyers, but you have to trust them. You have to trust people. You need to have a good reputation, need to be clean, or you won't go far, or you'll get wiped out.

There is a code of honor. Members of a famous Chicano rock group [were] buying thousands of dollars worth of heroin in the Segundo Barrio of El Paso. Christian and Jimmy knew them. They knew the people, they were family, Christian is a friend of the family. It becomes a family business. There are drug families in Houston just like there are families in the drug business in El Paso. One family controlled the network from El Paso to Denver to Chicago.

Busted

Jimmy, my business partner, was running drugs out of El Paso after they came from a ranch in Chihuahua and then to Juárez. First I was helping Jimmy, but told him I was setting up my own team. We were together when we were busted. Getting through the border was usually harder than the inland checkpoints. We sometimes used two cars and cell phones. The lead car would see if they were waving cars through at the checkpoints, and speak in code, saying something like "the weather is clear." I didn't feel guilt, but felt like I fucked up. The dope was getting wrapped up a second time at my house when the cops showed up. It was going to be a two-hour thing, wrapped and gone. I was to receive $40,000 in a leather case for my part of the deal. An extra guy was hired to help with the wrapping. I heard a knocking on the door in the front room.

I looked out the peephole and saw a badge and other people outside. I looked at my two friends and said, "It's through." My friends took off, but they got caught. The whole house was surrounded. They put a gun to my head. The officers who did the bust were from the Stash House Task Force—county cops, two detectives from the El Paso Police Department, an EPPD drug dog, and one FBI guy, a gringo dude in good physical shape—a young all-American-looking guy from Maryland. It didn't seem right how it went down. The cops took steps into my house. I didn't give them permission. The cops had guns in our faces. I told the cops not to hold guns on us, that we were no threat. "Put that gun down, there are no guns here," I said. They took off the handcuffs.

They saw I was a college student with books, music, instruments, and noticed my Che Guevara calendar. The FBI guy asked if I was a Rastafarian. He also asked if I was a communist. The FBI guy said, "Are you sympathetic to Castro and his communist government?" I took him to task and told him, "Your brain is already in a box. You're a boxed intellect. You're a Babylonian man." He just looked at me. I figure the FBI guy was there to collect information.

We got put in the paddy wagon with the handcuffs on again. One of my friends was kind of a contortionist and got his handcuffs off, but they put them back on him. A friend who used to do business with us found out we were arrested first, and the police told him to come to the substation. The cops had aerial photos of me going into my house. We thought we were under the radar, that we were nothing, that we were just peanuts. Our driver was doing two trips per week. They put the drop on him at the inland checkpoint on the way to Alamogordo, near White Sands, and that started the investigation. He was busted with 160 pounds of pot.

After the bust, I just wanted to get on with my life. I was given a forty-five-day work-release program. All of the people there were marijuana dealers or fifth-offense DWI offenders. Of 180 dudes there on work release, the majority were dope dealers. There were young guys, including a white guy from a Mexican family, with 700–1,000 pounds. My case, by comparison, was peanuts. It is all about money in El Paso: if you have the money, you get off; if you have a good lawyer, you get off.

It's all about your lawyer and the judges they know. The people without money have to get a "public pretender." Perhaps another lawyer could have done better, but I was pleased with my lawyer. It is a mistake I made being involved with a drug business.

I think the drug war is a tool of oppression. People with limited resources and opportunity get busted. Carlos Coy, the CEO of Dope House Records [for example]. Carlos said, "Be your own businessman." The [hip-hop] industry as a whole—the dress, the talk, the relationships—is shaped by the drug war. It is important to be vocal in opposition to the war on drugs. In the war on drugs, you have to have an enemy: the urban minorities, the urban blacks, the urban Mexicans. Mexicans are viewed as criminals, bringing their drugs from tropical areas. It is "the criminalizing of a generation." I learned this idea from the Revolutionary Communist Party. Where are the Chicano scholars writing on this? Blacks scholars provide the framework for the Chicanos on the justice system with their writings on the crack laws.

I read a book called *The Disenchantment of the World*, by Marcel Gauchet, about how modern society has no enchantment anymore. We just work, pay bills, consume, and it is boring. Drugs and hip-hop were a way to still find enchantment. It was an escape. The movement was in the black and Chicano communities in places like Houston, Los Angeles, Chicago, Baytown, etc. The war on drugs has put us on the road to destruction.

We are living the disenchantment of the world. We need a philosophy of scientific revolution like Francis Bacon wrote about. Reenchantment is needed. I don't have the outright answers. Drugs have hurt kids, but we need to legalize drugs or lessen drug laws. There should be better opportunities and ways of living—stuff that is fun.

Drug Addiction and Drug Trafficking in the Life of an Anarchist

Unlike many of the previous interviewees, who dealt drugs primarily out of economic necessity, the Anarchist smuggled drugs as a form of rebellion and to feed a heroin habit. Coming from an upper-middle-class upbringing on El Paso's west side, the Anarchist was introduced to marijuana when he was about eleven years old, and then to heroin at age fifteen. By then, he had also tried other illicit drugs, such as alcohol, LSD, hallucinogenic mushrooms, and cocaine. But the Anarchist feels that it was when he started using heroin, upon entering high school at age fifteen, that his long downward spiral into addiction really began. He says that "domestic problems were a gateway into heroin use" and trafficking.

Contrary to the common assumption that drug traffickers emerge exclusively from poor backgrounds, members of the middle and upper classes are well represented in the drug trade. Examples include marijuana kingpin Donald Steinberg; the narco-junior cum drug lord Arellano Félix brothers and their sister, of Tijuana; Texas rancher-turned-trafficker Don Ford; the patrician Ochoa brothers of the Medellín cartel; and the cocaine mega-entrepreneur George Jung (profiled in the movie *Blow*).

In addition to illustrating the complex social origins of border traffickers, the Anarchist's account represents the existential quest of a troubled youth seeking transcendence. His vivid account begins in an affluent but abusive household, caught "between a sea of poor, uneducated Mexicans and the intellectual university culture." The Anarchist's parents were educators: his father a professor at the University of Texas at El Paso (UTEP), and his mother a teacher at various public and private schools. Kern Place, the residential district he grew up in, is located within walking distance of the UTEP campus.

The Anarchist spoke fluent Spanish—even in its more codified slang form—from an early age; therefore, he could gain acceptance among the largely Hispanic population of the poor neighborhoods of south El Paso. This in turn allowed him to become somewhat of an insider to the south-side street gangs and their drug-dealing operations. The Anarchist's story, like that of Felipe, shows that the border drug trade is composed of much more than just the demographic-majority Mexican population. Mexican nationals run the major cartels that dominate the border drug trade as well as, currently, much of the inner-city drug trafficking in Mexico and many parts of the United States. Yet Anglo Americans, African Americans, and indeed people from many other ethnic groups or nationalities work hand in hand with the Mexican cartels in the buying, selling, transportation, and distribution of drugs.

The Anarchist describes the first time he injected heroin: "There was this whole romantic experience of sharing the needle." His vivid, lyrical description is reminiscent of the best of drug fiction, such as William Burroughs's twin drug novels *Junky* and *Queer*, as well as of popular movies depicting drug use, such as *Trainspotting, Drugstore Cowboy,* and *Pandemonium.* The tragedy of drug addiction emerges from an initially seductive and euphoric experience that eventually ends in degradation and ruin.

The Anarchist's whole life has been a series of defiant acts. Thus, for him and Felipe as well, drug trafficking, in addition to providing material benefits, took on an ideological dimension. The Anarchist views U.S. capitalism as a machine that creates inequality and oppression, to which the only proper response is resistance and sedition. As he matured and overcame his addiction, the Anarchist's constant reading and reflection led him to a full-blown anarchistic philosophy. Rock musician, scholar, and former drug trafficker, the Anarchist views the war on drugs as an unjust war on people, and drug dealing as a weapon of the weak.

The Anarchist

I was born in 1975 in El Paso, Texas, at Providence Memorial Hospital, to two teachers. [Note: Some names and details have been changed to protect the privacy of individuals mentioned in this interview.] My dad was a professor at the University of Texas at El Paso, and my mother taught at private and public schools for a long period of time. I have three older sisters, and we are of Scottish-Irish descent. As a child, I went to St. Clement's, an elite private school. Growing up, I lived mostly in El Paso, except from ages fifteen to sixteen, when I lived in Roswell, New Mexico, and then again from seventeen to eighteen years of age, when I lived in Albuquerque, New Mexico. Later, as an adult, I lived in Austin, Texas, for several years. Austin was my home base, but I also wandered around the country some, camping in my car. Then I moved back to El Paso. It was 1997 when I finally sobered up and quit drugs and alcohol for good. I relocated to Taos, New Mexico, and lived there for almost two years.

As a kid, I lived in a middle-class neighborhood, Kern Place, and went to El Paso High School. It was a comfortable childhood. Not wealthy, but not poor. My first language is actually Spanish. My dad is a linguist who specializes in the Spanish language. He took his PhD in Barcelona. My father really encouraged us to embrace and appreciate a lot of Mexican culture, and we traveled all over Mexico, from Coahuila, Chihuahua, and Sonora in northern Mexico, to Chiapas and Quintana Roo in far southern Mexico.

I started using drugs overtly as a young boy. The first time I smoked pot, I was about eleven. My aunt and uncle used to grow it. My cousins were older than I was, and they turned me on to it. I smoked a lot of pot with my cousins, and as a result, I formed a habit. It was a kind of hippie culture, but there were also some aspects of my home life that I was dealing with that were extremely difficult. The domestic problems were a gateway into heroin use, not the marijuana.

On the west side of El Paso, Middle Eastern families were involved in drugs and contraband. I would go to Middle Eastern friends' houses and notice that there were pools in their backyards. I would see adults snorting coke and smoking pot. As a boy, I saw a guy snorting coke at a neighbor's house. The guy said to me, "I'm tasting sugar." Leroy Bangs, whose house we visited, was a middle manager of a drug business. I saw wife swapping. As a kid, you don't know what's going on. Drugs and drinking—beyond fucking fun—out of control.

When I hit the age of fifteen, I started attending El Paso High. I met a group of Mexican American kids. My dad had been emphatic about teaching me *caló* [Chicano barrio Spanish, or Spanglish], because he knew that I was going to attend a predominantly Hispanic school and, as an Anglo, it would benefit me to communicate with kids from the Segundo Barrio [a large, poor Mexican neighborhood] and Chihuahuita. A lot of them grew up immersed in speaking *caló*.

One of the guys I met in high school—his nickname was Jaguar—and I used to smoke pot together at lunch. He ran with a multigenerational gang out of Segundo Barrio called the T-Birds. His dad, his grandfather, and all of his uncles were T-Birds. Jaguar showed up at school one day with a foil. He asked me if I wanted to smoke some *chiva* [black-tar heroin]. I didn't know what it was, and he said it was heroin. I had never done it before, and I was kind of curious, so I did it. We "based" it off the foil. I really liked it, but it made me sick. I threw up for about an hour. Then it felt good. I had the sensation of being completely at ease and floating: the rolling sensation was almost like being in the ocean, in warm amniotic fluid, which was very appealing to me. Throwing up felt good too.

I don't know what it is about heroin. The first few times I did it, I didn't feel addicted. By then I had gotten into the punk-rock scene here in El Paso—starting in the seventh and eighth grade—so I was aware of what heroin was. I had been around it. A lot of my friends used it. Some of them would inject it. Some of my friends got ahold of the "China white" variety of heroin and snorted it. Others smoked it. Black-tar heroin is gummier. It is easier to shoot, but you can also smoke it. At that time, pot was not the only thing I was doing. I got turned on to LSD, a lot of mushrooms, and I smoked my first rock of crack cocaine. There was a whole lot of drug use going on. It was a kind of rebellion against the mainstream. But when I was fifteen and attending El Paso High, this was the first time I had been introduced to heroin.

We smoked it. For me, it was a matter of opening up the foil, with the tar heroin on it, cooking it with a lighter, rolling up a dollar bill like a straw, and inhaling the smoke that came off of it. We would hold the foil with a bandana or handkerchief to not burn our fingers. It is really not hard to do. It was easy once you got the hang of it. I would get a real strong buzz. Smoking it like that, I experienced a three- to four-hour high. It was the first time I ever really hung out in class, and I didn't give a damn about what the teacher said or what other people were doing.

It was my first semester at El Paso High School, in 1990–1991. I was not a good student. I hated school. I despised going to class. I really resented the fact that I was placed there. I was seeking avenues to make life more interesting. I studied on my own. I did a lot of reading on my own. I had a good intellectual relationship with my parents. They turned me on to Engels, Marx, Kropotkin, Bakunin, and other anarchist literature. My parents wanted to keep me interested in learning. In high school, I was pretty bored. My parents attempted to make intellectual contact with a son who was out of hand. I was rebelling against anyone I could put in my scope.

My parents were not bohemian intellectuals. My mom was an absolute, die-hard Republican. Both my mom and dad came from abusive homes. My mother's dad was a migrant from Scotland and settled in San Antonio. He came to El Paso and worked for McKee Construction Company, doing fireproofing, drywall, and then he formed his own construction company. My dad, born in 1934, was politically independent. My dad's birth mother died in childbirth. His father died in an airplane crash while teaching a flying lesson in El Paso. My father was the son of Irish immigrants, and so his relatives adopted him. They lived in the same house I grew up in on King Street, in Kern Place. My grandparents on both sides immigrated to Central Texas before coming to El Paso.

There was domestic abuse in my household. It came from my mother. I had three older sisters. My mom used to beat the shit out of my sisters. She did drink, but blamed the violence on her allergy medicine. It was bullshit and it pissed me off. As a young boy, I was too little to hit, and so I took on a protective role with my sisters. I tried to put myself in between my mom and my sisters. My father did not intervene. When shit started in the house, Pop pulled away. He would go somewhere, and then they would get in a fight with each other about it later. Then, when I got to be old enough to hit—five or six—my mother started pulling my hair, kicking me, and backhanding me in the face. At the same time, Mom could be so loving and affectionate.

Looking back, at the time I was just really confused. I never knew what would set it off, but I knew I wanted affection. I loved her affection. Sometimes she would curl up in bed with me and read books about the Knights of the Round Table. It wasn't always bad, but when it was bad, it was really bad. By the time I was eight or nine years old, my dad really put his foot down, and mom stopped being abusive. In some ways, the abuse contributed to my desire to rebel and use drugs, but on some level, I wanted my parents to know that I used drugs. My mom was older than the hippies. She was more the age of the beatniks, but my parents were not hippies or beatniks. I wasn't rebelling along with them. My aunt's house, nearby, was a hippie-ish household, and I spent a lot of time there. My uncle was a mathematics professor at UTEP.

I felt like an oddball growing up, living between a sea of poor, uneducated Mexicans and the intellectual university culture. Here you are, and you show up at school, and these kids are talking shit about you in a language you understand, and then you look at them, and they'll say something to you in Spanish to impress their friends: "¿Qué haces aquí?" [What are you doing here?]. And I would reply, "Yo entiendo español" [I understand Spanish]. They look at you and, "Oh my God! This kid who is blue eyed and towheaded is spouting Spanish at me, and not only that, he knows *caló*." That won me friends and advocates because it was kind of a novelty to have this *güerito* [blond kid] that also spoke and understood Spanish. I was immersed in Mexican culture by my dad. We went and celebrated Día de los Muertos. We knew about *calaveras* [representations of skulls used in Day of the Dead ceremonies]. We traveled all over Mexico. When I was a young kid, we went to Baja California. When I was sixteen, my mom and dad let my buddy and I go on a camping trip from Ensenada to La Paz, Baja California. That part of my life was wonderful. I was using drugs then, but it was not a bad thing.

As I said, I was fifteen when I first used *chiva* with my good friend "El Jaguar." I made a lot of friends with him. He had a cousin who used to run with the Creeps. They were like a party crew, an offshoot of the T-birds from Segundo Barrio. Jaguar was an older kid, about two years older than me, but he wasn't one of those cats who shat on young guys. He had a macho ethic, but he was really cool. By virtue of my affiliation with Jaguar, I started scoring a lot of pot from him and his family in the Segundo Barrio, which had connections to Juárez. They got lots of pot. So I would be the contact guy for a while to get pot into the punk circle at El Paso High. There was another white kid, Bob Brown, who also had connections to Juárez.

They viewed me as a comfortable middle-class white kid, for the most part, but they didn't know where I came from and they never really asked. They never went to my house, but I did go to theirs. I guess I never invited them to my house because I was scared for Jaguar and his group to find out that I was "rich," compared to them, and I didn't want to be judged on that.

Guilt was very prevalent in my mind when I first started using drugs. Pot was acceptable to me because, as my cousin said, "It's from the earth. It's okay." But I had the American stereotypical, paranoid view that drugs would destroy me. I had already used pot and heroin, but during my first trip on LSD, I really kind of flipped out. I was afraid I was going to get stuck there and become a homeless person. I did feel that guilt, for sure. I remember being riddled with it when I came home. You go home to this "Dick and Jane" lifestyle. In retrospect, I think I was lamenting losing my innocence. At the time, I remember looking at mom and dad and my sisters and thinking, "I'll never see them in the same way again."

At that point in high school, Jaguar had met a bunch of my friends from the west side of El Paso. They all knew him. The punk scene and drug thing were interconnected. There was a big brawl between the punks and the jocks—redneck guys called the *cheros* [short for *rancheros*]. It went down in the lower parking lot. The gang kids backed us up. I get really kind of excited about it. It is one of those things you feel proud about for some weird, stupid reason. We kicked the shit out of the jocks. We cleaned them up. I remember being on top of the vice principal's car, kicking people in the face and laughing and laughing, and I was high on smack that day. That was one of the big explosions.

Dealing Drugs at Military School

My friends started to score from Jaguar. We all knew each other. We wanted to score from him, and he wanted us to score from him. At that time, Bob Brown and his dad dealt drugs. They would get acid from San Francisco, and marijuana and cocaine from south of the border. They connected people up that way too. Eventually, Bob and I decided to go to military school. He had gotten into trouble because he had got busted with a gram of coke on him. That was the tail end of this drug scene. The cops didn't arrest him—they just took him home and showed his mom what he had. She got pissed and decided to send him to military school. So I also went to the New Mexico Military Institute, which was in Roswell, in 1990. I said, "Fuck it. I'll go with you; that sounds like a new experience." My mom was happy to send me to military school. She thought I would go on to West Point. Dad was not happy with the idea. He said, "What are you doing?" I just wanted to go with my buddy and check out military school. I took up military science and learned everything that soldiers do.

We set up a drug network before we left El Paso. The first two weeks were intensive boot camp. We went through bullshit. You get your ass kicked and you get hazed. New recruits at NMMI are called "rats." My first week at military school, I broke my first sergeant's jaw because he got in my face. I had mouthed off in formation. He yelled at me, I yelled back. He hit me and I hit back. I broke his jaw and knocked him out. He was a Mexican kid from Torreón, Coahuila, and came from a high-level drug family. We had kids from Torreón, Durango, Juárez. A lot of narco-traffickers send their kids to military school. They want their kids to think strategically. They learn battlefield command, networks, ambush, etc. Anything that soldiers do, you do at NMMI. Fortunately, cadets don't rat on each other. The first sergeant said he broke his jaw playing football. I didn't get in trouble, but there were reprisals. There are internal ethics, very macho. They call it "pulling the shade and locking the door." So I got "blanket-partied" over that. They gave me the treatment.

When they blanket-party you, they tell your bunkmate, "You leave the door open tonight, or we'll come and get you." When I got blanket-partied, six or seven guys came into my room and held a blanket over me, and then beat the shit out of me with a bar of soap inside a sock. The only thing you can do is cover your balls and your face. It is an ingenious way of torturing you. The soap doesn't leave a mark. You don't see the damage or discoloration; it doesn't leave a visible bruise. You get a deep-muscle bruise, and it hurts like a motherfucker. Think what a torn muscle feels like, and you'll have a good idea of how much it hurts.

At military school, you can avoid getting hazed, make friends with older cadets, and get girls by "setting up shop"—i.e., selling drugs—so I started importing drugs from El Paso and selling them at NMMI. There were girl cadets, and some of them were really hot. I also joined the drill team, which had a lot of respect. The drill team leader was a relative of Amado Carrillo Fuentes [deceased head of the Cártel de Juárez]. He was a good guy, a good soldier, brave and disciplined. He called us his rats. He protected his rats from other troops. If anyone messed with one of his rats, we would get them back, fuck them up. There were several other troops, starting with Troop Alpha, then Troop Bravo, all the way up to Troop India.

I wasn't really a tough kid back at El Paso High School. Sure, I got into a few fights while I was there. But I really wasn't a tough guy before NMMI. Since I was really crazy as a kid, while at NMMI I got into a fight almost every day I was there. I was emotionally fucked up. It isn't normal to be laughing while kicking somebody in the face. That whole thing was a survival tactic. People thought of me "That guy's gonna beat the shit out of you" or "That guy's fuckin' crazy—don't mess with him!"

At NMMI, there is a token economy. Older kids can have cash, but they don't want younger cadets to have money to get in trouble with. You need "cadet checks" to get anything from the PX store, and also a parental tobacco permit, if you are under age and wish to smoke. I was sixteen and figured out another way to make cash. I opened up shop. During my second month at NMMI, I went into the PX and bought five cartons of cigarettes and two logs of dip [snuff, or dip, is sold in small round cans that, in stacks of ten, look like logs], since I wanted to make money by selling this stuff to other cadets. One cadet, who wasn't eighteen yet, came up to me and asked about buying some cigarettes. He couldn't have cash yet, but I told him, "I'll sell to you if you transfer funds from your cadet account into mine."

I began selling packs of cigarettes. I could sell fifteen cartons in just a few days. Kids would buy them with their cadet accounts. People came to me from across the whole NMMI compound. "Whitey's store," they called it. My inventory would be out in two or three days. I kept turning it over and over. In one and a half months, I turned $2,000 into $6,000. Then one day Bob said, "If you can make money selling tobacco, let's sell drugs." I called Jaguar, and bought drugs with that money. I would buy a money order from a gas station near NMMI for half the amount and send it to Jaguar, and he would send the drugs to me using the U.S. mail or UPS. At the time, it was an easy way to send drugs.

Bob and I were bringing into NMMI a shitload of marijuana, coke, and LSD. A boatload of coke, and people bought it like crazy. Jaguar was ingenious. He would get or steal a pair of some old shoes, ratty old fucking sneakers, and he would stuff an ounce of cocaine into the toe of the shoes, split it up into two bags. Or he would cut out the inside pages of dictionaries that he got from an abandoned monastery or some such place, and then put a pound of pot inside and seal it up in a bag and mail the package. He would wrap the packages in Saran wrap and dryer sheets, and then further cover up the smell with ammonia.

My profits shot up a whole lot. I realized that as a poor teenager, I could now make a lot of money. My family had money, but didn't give me any because they knew I'd get into trouble. So I found out how to make my own trouble. A buddy of ours worked in the constabulary, where a bunch of old guns and spare parts were kept in a basement. He patrolled the rifle range for broken .22 rifles and parts. A lightbulb went on in my brain. We went over there and made friends with the constabulary staff. We started going down into the basement, pretending to repair rifles for NMMI. We would indeed fix two or three rifles for NMMI, but we'd also build fully working range rifles, and then sell them to kids in nearby Roswell, New Mexico. We would sneak the rifles out of the compound at night. The security officers were a bunch of idiots and so was the top administrator.

One time we unloaded a rifle and some cocaine on this kid, the son of a town woman who was fucking an administrator of NMMI. The kid told us, "My mom is fucking an administrator." He was a leader of the whole school. We called him Pops. This kid got high with some buddies, and then started shooting stop signs. He got caught and fingered me. We had told the kid to remove the butt plate of the rifle that said "Property of NMMI," but, of course, he didn't. We should have done it ourselves.

So to make a long story short, I got busted. The Roswell cops let the military school handle the situation. Neither the town nor school authorities wanted a public scandal that would tarnish their reputations. Bob and I were taken into an administrator's office, supposedly to be expelled. But I threatened him with revealing publicly that he was screwing a local townswoman, so in the end all I got was probation.

Pops had begun by telling me, "Your shadow will never darken NMMI again"—blah, blah, blah. And I replied, "I wonder what your lover would think about this?" Then he said, "I think probation is in order. Don't you, mister?" "Yes, I do, sir," I answered.

In the end, I took the fall for Bob, since I never ratted him out. And I couldn't help but wonder about the fact that if I could make that much money in a controlled environment, imagine how much money I could make in El Paso. After all, we had set up a network, and we were making lots of money. Eventually, I quit NMMI and returned to El Paso. It was the 1991–1992 school year, and I enrolled back at El Paso High as a sophomore. That's when I began using needles. I had smoked *chiva* at NMMI. In time, you build up a tolerance. Certain people want to use more and more often. Eventually, you'll get hooked. Addiction, plus the frequency of use, is the key correlation.

Using and Selling in El Paso

My initial heroin usage was sporadic, and I only smoked it, and I would always stop using if it was getting out of control. I first used a needle at a party. The Ne'er Do Wells, a punk group from Boston, were playing at this house party on the east side of El Paso, since their tour had fallen through. The band was playing in the backyard of a house off of Wedgewood Drive. There were kids there from all over El Paso. Kids from Jefferson High showed up, and also Lower Valley punks. These parties happened quite often. The neighbors were usually cool and did not complain because they didn't want reprisals like, for example, their cars being vandalized. Bob Brown's sister, Wanda, and Juanita del Amor, and others were in a back room. Wanda said she had some smack, and some other kids were holding too. A couple kids from Jefferson were also holding.

I asked if they wanted to smoke it, and Wanda said no. "We need to go get needles from Walgreens or someplace," she said. I remember thinking how my friend Levi had died of an overdose the year before, while I was still at NMMI. He was a junior in high school at the time he died. Juanita had been Levi's girlfriend. I had never shot up before, and so I was a little worried. Juanita said, "You'll love it, don't worry." And I had a big, big crush on Juanita. She was a "clean" junkie, since she didn't share needles. I wanted to get high with her. I think I was in love with her. God, she was beautiful! How erotic is that, huh? A beautiful chick shoots a needle into your vein. "Fuck it, I'm gonna shoot up with this chick"—that's what I was thinking at the time.

Paul went and got a box of needles from the bedroom used by his diabetic mother. Juanita showed us all how to rig. She said, "We need some water and cotton swabs." She showed us how to cook the heroin, suck it and filter it through the cotton swab, clear the bubbles from the needle, then tie your arm in order to slap up a vein. There was a comfortable feeling, a mutual experience of getting high, a group event. Same as like the ritual of rolling a joint with your friends. Juanita shot me up first. The feeling was so intense: a warm, undulating feeling. It was unbelievable. It was like being a fly caught in Vaseline. We ended up on the bed all night. Her lips on my face felt wonderful. There was this whole romantic experience of sharing the needle. You nod off together and wake up together. It's better than sex. I wanted to have sex with Juanita before I shot up, but I couldn't after the injection. It is difficult to perform sexually when you shoot up heroin.

During that period of my life, I was somebody who had a problem with authority figures in general. What I really wanted to do was get away. Dealing drugs was earning a living on the periphery. It was liberating. I saw my family slave away for what they wanted. My sisters were working themselves to the bone to get through college.

I put myself in a lot of dangerous situations. I'm happy to say that I'm lucky to be alive. When I returned from NMMI to El Paso, we used to throw parties at clubs on the strip in Juárez. Large groups of youth would go to Juárez. We charged everyone a cover fee at the door that we would later split with the club owners. It was usually ten dollars. It was a "drink and drown" type of thing. We had parties at clubs like La Playa, Sarawak, Superior, etc. During my stay at NMMI, I made friends with guys whose families were from Juárez and were in the drug trade—people who could get lots of dope. They were the kind of people that, if you ever got in trouble in Juárez, all you had to do was just drop a name, and immediately the cops would let you go.

El Güero sold coke and pot on the street outside this burger place, near Fred's Rainbow Bar. My intention was to buy half an eight ball—you know, just a few *veintones* [twenty-dollar bags] to cut up and sell inside the bar. But he gave a deal I couldn't refuse: he sold me half an ounce of coke for $200. Normally, it would have cost $1,000 to $1,700 an ounce. So I sold some of it in Juárez, but had too much to get rid of there. So I threw the rest inside my jock and walked across [the international bridge into El Paso]. This happened in 1991–1992. I just played the part of the drunken middle-class white kid. The drug war wasn't that serious at the time. They [U.S. Customs agents working at the international bridges] didn't fuck with us. It was easy.

So I started peddling the dope to friends and schoolmates at El Paso High and kids in the neighborhood. I made a shitload of money. One week later, after buying from El Güero, I went back and got an ounce from him [January 1992]. We started to throw parties at clubs in Juárez. We brought bunches of high school kids and friends over from El Paso. This was during the school year. Güero and I became friends, and I continued to buy cocaine from him, which I sold partially at the parties in Juárez and would walk the rest back over the bridge to El Paso. I also started buying pot and LSD from a guy connected to San Francisco. Frank and I sent coke by UPS to San Francisco for LSD—sheets and vials of acid—which we sold in El Paso. The coke was pink, and of very good quality: one bump, snorted through the nose, would numb your whole face. Sometimes it smelled like ether. The guy in San Francisco wanted our blow because it was such good quality. We were helping him, and he was helping us. He was a chemist. Punks loved LSD and mushrooms. I started growing mushrooms in a closet. There was a huge market for drugs in the El Paso punk scene. A lot of us were burnouts. We sold to Coronado High School kids. Güero was turning me on to black-tar heroin. I was smoking it.

I went to a rich lady's house in Juárez to pick up a couple of fingers of smack. She smelled good. It was a shitty house on the outside, but opulent inside. The lady and a guy there taught me how to shoot up. It was the first time I held the syringe. It fucked me up. After that, I was hooked. I started buying syringes downtown at the Walgreens in order to use heroin. I would take a syringe to Juárez every time I went over there. I began using heroin two or three days a week, shooting up two to three times on the days I used.

Then I flunked out of El Paso High. I got kicked out and sent to Crestline, a school for fuckups. My parents were pissed; we got into a big fight. A daughter of one of the most powerful families of Juárez also went to Crestline. People thought she was snotty, but she was cool to me. She said her family owned a big chunk of local gas companies. She had bodyguards. I went to St. Clement's middle school with two other female scions of this family. There were a bunch of other kids from Juárez families at Crestline.

I would go partying in Juárez with the rich girls and Juan, the son of a known narco-trafficker. He had access to his dad's stash—coke and smack. We shot up coke and smack together. He was working for his dad. He was my first big heroin connection. At the time, I was also crossing pot and coke from Juárez to El Paso, hidden under the seat or in the wheel-well in the trunk of the car. A son of an INS worker got busted doing the same thing, but his dad got him off.

There were interschool rivalries between drug dealers—El Paso High versus Coronado High. There were parallel groups to us at Coronado before they got pinched. I knew them and the guy that rolled over on them. It was a crazy, groovy time. We got involved in their market. We unloaded stuff at all high schools—Austin, Jefferson, Eastwood, Parkland. We supplied Northeast Bishop gangsters with drugs. I knew some poor kids through my cousins, especially one who was in the Lee Moor home for orphans. I had dealings with the East Side Locos. And I knew the Fatherless gang of the Lower Valley. I made lots of friends. It helped to speak Spanish, and I never let on that I was a relatively rich kid. They would trade me guns, and different shit they knocked off, for drugs. I would sell some of that stuff at pawnshops.

Once, a group of friends and I went to go pick up drugs in Juárez. We went to score coke and smack. I had a wad of cash on me, about six thousand dollars. It was dry; Güero was dry and did not know where to score. Somebody had been busted. I had to drive to the east of the [wealthy] Campestre neighborhood, in the desert. It was out in the Juárez desert, in the middle of nowhere—you can disappear out there. We met a dude there nicknamed "El Prieto," who was driving a car around in a vacant lot, to make the exchange.

"Do you have the money?" he asked. "Yes," my friend Juan replied.

"¿Qué pasa con los pinches gabachos?" [What's up with these fuckin' white guys?] he asked. El Prieto was dark skinned. "No te preocupes por eso" [Don't worry about it], answered Juan.

"Let me see the money!" shouted El Prieto. So I showed him the wad of money. Then El Prieto went into the back seat. He had a satchel in his hands, and then he pulled out a gun.

"Si se mueven, se mueren, cabrones!" [If you move, you die, assholes!] he shouted. Juan said, "WHOA, WHOA, WHOA, WHOA!"

I was fucked up, but said, "You pull that trigger and you're gonna have to kill us all." Dan, a white kid, had grown up in [poor, largely African American] South Dallas and was used to having guns drawn on him. Dan got wide eyed and looked at me and said, "I'm gonna fuck this guy up." He went up to Prieto and said, "Pull the fucking trigger!" Dan was crazy that way. It was a .45 caliber semiautomatic pistol. Dan grabbed the gun, putting his finger between the hammer, and head-butted Prieto. We beat the piss out of Prieto. Then we proceeded to steal his product, which consisted of three ounces of cocaine and four to five fingers of smack. Fingers are concentrated black-tar heroin rolled in foil; one finger equals one to one and a half ounces; four fingers is six ounces. For good measure, Juan cut Prieto several times with a switch-blade. Dan was going to kill him, but Juan said NO. Then I said, "Don't kill him." After all, we just wanted to send a message. We wanted the guy to get in trouble with his organization for trying to rip us off.

Prieto had been blown away by a white kid telling him off in Spanish. Dan's father was Puerto Rican, so he knew Spanish. Prieto was alone, but cocky because he had a gun. He wanted to rip us off and keep the product, which would have made his bosses happy. I wasn't about to lose six thousand dollars. After all, there were four of us and only one of him. When I woke up the next day, I freaked the fuck out.

I was filled with booze and drugs at the time of the incident, so I didn't feel fear until later. I probably would have shot the guy. Juan told his father about the incident, and there was no reprisal on us. Juan's father was big in the drug world. I assume Juan's father put reprisals on Prieto. He deserved what he got. Juan was protected. Dan became my boy and came on a lot of purchases with me. After that, the shit got kind of hairy. A penny-ante peddler at Jefferson High School was found behind Fred's Rainbow Bar in Juárez, murdered and with his tongue cut off. He was only seventeen and had a big mouth. He had pissed somebody off.

A few days after the killing of the Jefferson student, a group of Eastwood High School kids went to Juárez. We would roll with sixty to seventy kids into Juárez, a kind of party crew across class and cultural lines. Everybody knew everybody. We backed each other up: jocks, older kids—eighteen to nineteen—punks, rap crews, dance crews. The idea was to have a good time. At the La Playa bar you could find a friend or go on the roof to smoke pot. There were always kids smoking on the roof. Someone would call out "¡Ey, narizazo!" [Snorting time!] and pass out cocaine. They had "triple drink and drown" at three bars. You could pay the cover and drink all night.

[That night,] we left the Sarawak Bar and headed to the Superior Bar. A group of us was walking down the sidewalk and another group of kids from Eastwood was crossing the street. An old Lincoln drove around the corner and almost hit the group of Eastwood kids. The guys in the Lincoln looked hard. One of the kids hit the car with his hand. I told the kid to get off the street and into the club. The Lincoln came back around, and the guy driving got out and said in Spanish, "Are you the little fucker who just hit my car?" And the Eastwood kid replied, "Yeah, so what?" Suddenly, the guy pulls out a .25 caliber pistol and shoots Alex in the eye. Alex lay on the street in agony. Willie said, "Holy shit, call an ambulance!" Junior, manager of Superior, came out, then immediately ran back inside and called an ambulance. A group of kids crowded around. The kids started chanting his name, "Alex, Alex . . . " in an effort to revive him. It was sick. I felt ill. I threw up three or four times. I walked back over the Santa Fe Bridge and waited by the car for friends. Alex lived for three days in the hospital and died with a bullet in his brain. Nobody got arrested. I never saw those guys before. That fucked me up. It scared me, and I scaled back. It was a big story in the paper.

It was 1992–1993 when this happened. It was during my junior year of high school. I said to the guys, "We need to be more careful." The club owners used to love us. The scene has changed. There used to be more drugs; now it's tamer. They cracked down. The governor in Chihuahua City ordered that the bars in Juárez be closed earlier. Cops started checking IDs and imposed a curfew that didn't work. At the time, I was trying to finish private school. Eventually, I dropped out and moved to Albuquerque.

Dealing Heroin with Walter in Albuquerque

I had lent a buddy some money to score drugs, so I had no money left. I sold two pints of blood in downtown El Paso and got on a Greyhound bus to Albuquerque. In Albuquerque, I started living with a friend, Walter, the son of a "dirty" DEA agent. Walter's dad had him running drug houses when he was fourteen years old. His dad was busted, Walter was emancipated, and he was a heavy heroin user. I originally had lived with Walter in Taos after we met in secondary treatment. We got an apartment together. He got a construction job. He relapsed after six months. I was hurting for money and sick from withdrawal, so Walter hooked me up. Withdrawal was more than mental—it hurt. A hundred times the chills. Heroin addiction also plugs you up, and when you quit, you get the shits. I didn't like who I was. I was addicted. I was seventeen. and Walter had just turned nineteen. I hit rock bottom, but I had the luxury to choose where I hit rock bottom. Walter suggested we start dealing in heroin. So I had the friend who owed me money pay me in heroin instead. We quickly had a thriving business selling heroin.

There was a heavily violent, perverse scene in Albuquerque. Girls would let me do anything I wanted for drugs, but I didn't act on it; I would sell them smack or just give it to them and say, "Get out." There were more gangs there than anywhere in the U.S. We lived on Wisconsin Avenue, in the war zone, on the border between the northeast and the south side. We were in big business: [we brought drugs] from Juárez to El Paso to Albuquerque and from there to Santa Fe. My friend hired mules to bring the drugs across the border. Everything was coming from Juárez. We made a crapload of money, then I called my connection and told him I was sending more money.

I needed to support a habit, since I was shooting up two to three times a day. We would shoot up on our way to Santa Fe to sell heroin. From there, it went to northern New Mexico and Colorado, to Boulder and further. We were selling six to twenty ounces at a time. We made thousands of dollars. I had the connection in El Paso–Juárez; Walter had the network in Albuquerque. Walter had the head for it in Albuquerque; he learned how to set up there from his dad. We never had to get violent. If buyers were short on cash, we would take cars, TVs, other drugs—pot, coke. We liked money the most. I had a hundred-fifty-to-two-hundred-dollar-a-day heroin habit, and that was my incentive for dealing. It wasn't until after I overdosed that I decided to kick heroin. When I OD'd by shooting up too much, Walter shot me up with a long needle of Narcan [naloxone, an opioid antagonist] through the breast-bone, like in *Pulp Fiction*, and resuscitated me that way. My roommate Walter had been alert: he saw me nod, and snot bubbles coming out, my respiration slowing.

I quit. I came up fighting. I sat down on the couch and I said, "I have to kick this." It was 1993–1994. I lived the high life for one year. I made a lot of money and spent a lot of money on partying, girls, titty bars, fancy restaurants, clothes, furniture. It would have been too obvious to buy homes or new cars. But I had also invested some of it. I bought stocks. I used some of the money to pay for part of my college tuition and living expenses. I kicked, with the help of a heavy dose of Valium for one and a half months, and smoking pot. I took six pills twice a day of Valium. I tried to kick cold turkey, but that was a fucking bitch. Valium weans you off heroin. Eventually, I took lower doses, four pills twice a day, then four pills a day. I would start up again after smoking a hit of smack. Walter OD'd and died while I was going through detox and getting clean. I kicked heroin successfully in Albuquerque. I used a lot of pot and Valium and lower-level opiates to get over it, and also Lomotil [an antidiarrheal]. I had kicked smoking opium several times before, but mainlining was harder. But I also had to kick coke as well, since I was shooting speedballs. It ended up being a problem.

I came back to El Paso for my middle sister's wedding. At the time, I was dating a girl in Albuquerque who flushed a half ounce of cocaine down the drain. It cost a lot of cash, but I could recover that. I was upset because I didn't have any blow. I was abusive and mean to my girlfriend, the first girl I ever loved. That was what caused me to realize I needed to kick cocaine. It bothered me that I was enslaved by cocaine and acted so badly to her. I proposed to her. I was seventeen. She and I broke up when I moved back to El Paso. She thought I was fucked up. And I was. I was not the person for that sort of thing—marriage—and it bothered me.

Back in El Paso, Using and Dealing

I moved back to El Paso in 1993 and lived there until 1995. I was still smoking lots of pot. I was bartending at Clicks Billiards and at the Boiler Room Bar. I spent a year bartending at Clicks and then at the Boiler Room for another year. I was drinking every day. Drinking at work and drinking in Juárez. I lost my job at Clicks because of constant drinking. I started going to Juárez every day. I was using drinking as a replacement for heroin. I started doing coke at the Boiler Room. I was making a lot of money in tips. In two days I could make my rent in tips, and still have plenty of money to spare. I guess you could say I was like a superstar as a bartender. Girls throw themselves at you. Girls say, "I'm dating the bartender—I can get my friends into the bar for free." It's a trade-off.

My friend, a crazy surgical tech, would drink, and we did lots of cocaine together. Then he would go back to work without sleeping, high on coke and booze. I got back into cocaine, but not heroin. It was a psychological addiction, but not physical as much. I would get depressed and itchy. I was injecting some cocaine, a great rush, freebasing [heating coke on aluminum foil with an accelerant and inhaling the smoke], and using "cocoa puffs" [smoking coke rolled into joints]. It was all very addictive. One of my friends who snorted coke would blow snot out, put it on a cigarette, and smoke it.

I was mainly using, not selling. Then I started selling drugs through my buddy from El Paso and NMMI who worked at Yellowstone Park. He had been kicked out of NMMI a year after I left. I would prepare a "care package"—a couple of eight balls, several quarter-pound bags of marijuana, a couple of ounces of hallucinogenic mushrooms grown in El Paso, and a couple of sheets of acid. He would drive twenty-four hours straight from Yellowstone to El Paso with money, get the stuff, and go right back.

This was hydroponic, good-quality homegrown pot coming through Juárez. The land growers were getting more sophisticated too. I would also cross pot and coke from Juárez into El Paso. The hydro pot was worth fifty to eighty dollars per quarter ounce. In Juárez, they were growing hydroponic plants with three buds. There was also a lot of "schwag," which is just common weed. But also "one-toke choke"— you're done after one hit. Sunland Park is a good source of pot. We had another contact who was crossing it from Juárez to Sunland Park. I worked with him at a bar and became good friends of his family. We also sold local mushrooms grown from spores. Fungus spores are legal to sell. People can buy them and grow mushrooms. They are easy to grow; clean jars are the important thing. Homegrown mushrooms are more potent than those found normally in cow pies.

I had no ugly encounters with big Juárez-cartel people, except across the river from Segundo Barrio, in the Colonia Hidalgo area of Juárez. I had driven over the Stanton Street Bridge with Alberto and another guy from work. We were high on coke. I was doing a deal that Alberto had set up with someone he knew. The guy who showed up was related to somebody that they were giving a chance to make some cash. The guy had the drugs in a satchel when he got out of his car, but it got sketchy. The guy was reaching into his pocket. He pulled out a knife and reached back to his pocket to get a gun. The Juárez guy thought we were cops.

I had lent Alberto a sharpened screwdriver, which he had tucked up his sleeve. I hit the guy in the face with my fist, with a big ring on my finger, and knocked him down. Alberto ripped him with the screwdriver until he started bleeding like a stuck pig. The guy hit the ground hard. It sounded like a bag or a sack of potatoes falling on the ground. He had blood all over his torso and several broken bones. We were near the Rio Grande, behind a *bosque* [thicket].

Alberto said, "I can't leave him here without paying for the drugs." We didn't want trouble with his people, or him rolling over on us with the cops. I stuffed money in the pants pocket of the Juárez guy laying on the ground in a coma. Then we took the satchel of drugs, which contained one kilogram of pot and six ounces of coke. Alberto had it all worked out; he had done this a million times. We were going to cross it in Alberto's pimped-out Cadillac. It had hidden compartments for smuggling. The other guy with us drove the lead car. First, we smoked out this lead car with pot in order to thwart and confuse the drug dogs. The inspectors focused all their attention on that car, and the Cadillac went through to El Paso.

After this deal went down, I was afraid to go to Juárez at night—it put me on edge. I talked about it to a friend in Austin, an old acquaintance from when we were kids, who was in a rockabilly band. Later, he called me and said, "It sounds like shit is getting really crazy out there. Why don't you come to Austin?" I felt like my life was out of control. I had a fucked-up relationship with my girlfriend. It was gross. I realized I was with her because I hated her. I didn't tell anybody, but planned to leave for Austin that Monday, but decided to go Sunday instead. I had to get away from the drug culture. Most of my friends back then drank and smoked pot. Some are still in that world. I see people from ten years ago and talk about things; some are in the same shit. Ronald went to prison, but now works for the same guy in Juárez. Alberto had a heart attack. Manuel's brother—who was a founding gang member working for the Aztecas— would have killed the guy in Juárez if he had been with us that day.

Music and Drugs in the Capital City

I left El Paso for Austin on that Sunday. I packed my car with books and clothes. That's all I wanted. My cousin was in Austin. I got to Austin and settled in with my friend Ralph in an apartment with other friends from El Paso. I started working as a line cook at Hooters. I lived in Austin from 1995 to the end of 1996. I got into crystal meth and smoking crack and doing acid and ecstasy and drinking all the time. It was a wild scene. Austin was a big fucking party. El Paso people had a reputation as hard-core partiers and fighters in Austin. Austin kids are pussycats. In El Paso, if someone nudges you at the bar, you fight, but not in Austin. Drugs and drinking are more pervasive in El Paso too. I started playing in a hard-core punk band called Grease Pan with kids I knew from El Paso. We played mostly in and around Austin. The punk scene was tight knit in Austin. There are a lot of squatter kids in Austin—drug rats, homeless junkies who live on the street and panhandle. Real tight-knit community. They would come to our shows.

I also started trafficking drugs from El Paso to Austin. I was making regular trips to El Paso every two months. It's a seven- to eight-hour drive from Austin to El Paso. If we couldn't find drugs in El Paso, we would get the stuff in Juárez as a last resort. We had to get through two checkpoints rather than one if we went to Juárez: one on the bridge back from Juárez and the other one inland. [The way we did it the] first car, which was five miles ahead, goes through the checkpoint and then calls the second car; the second car comes through later. We used special walkie-talkies or a cell phone.

We sold acid, cocaine—nearly pure; we could cut and sell it at a big profit. Cocaine was huge and expensive in Austin. Some cocaine in Austin came from Laredo, which was closer, only five to six hours from Austin. But our connections were in El Paso, so we used El Paso. A friend who started working for cartel people in Juárez with stash houses on this side of the border was also muling Greyhound shipments to Minneapolis, St. Louis, and Chicago. Omaha was big. The method involved here was using a duffle bag as a carry-on aboard the Greyhound bus. Leroy got the idea of muling from us, but we got the bus idea from him.

I would fly to El Paso from Austin, pick up the stuff, and then ride the bus back to Austin. Drug dogs would only search the outside of buses. I also smuggled LSD in books, wrapped in aluminum foil. I knew people in El Paso to score from and got great deals. I had been working with them for eight or nine years. They knew I wouldn't roll over on them. The cops would come on the bus, ask your nationality, and let you on your way. Then one nice day in April I was playing hacky sack and smoking dope with my friend Aldo at Madeline Park [in an upper-middle-class section of El Paso], and I was caught by the cops. We were sitting in Aldo's car smoking some good sinsemilla pot, and Aldo blew a big hit out just as some cops drove by. The cops came back and asked if we were holding. I was holding two ounces of pot. Aldo was from a strict Lebanese family. He had three bongs in the car, and coke powder on a razor blade in the trunk. Since it was Aldo's car, he got busted. But I took the fall for Aldo. I signed an affidavit saying it was all my stuff. I got probation for misdemeanor possession of pot—I was not convicted. I blew off probation, took off for Austin, and got it expunged from my record. I had a good lawyer.

In Austin, I lived with my cousin and worked at Hooters. I sold drugs at rave parties. I also peddled heroin. I got tar heroin from Juárez. We brought heroin and coke in duffle bags on Greyhound every two months. I never got busted nor had a load confiscated. I paid in advance with our money. It was all reinvested cash. Instead of using coke, I started using meth; it was more intense and lasted longer. It turned into a sexual orgy. Lots of girls at Hooters used speed. First, I snorted "glass" [methamphetamine], and then I started smoking it. It was beyond fun—drugs every day—too much at Hooters.

My sister moved down to Austin to be with me, and she asked me to go into business with Equinox—like Amway—selling a house water purifier. So I started taking my drug money and buying these water purifiers for $250 and selling them for $1,000 to building contractors. It was a way of laundering drug money. I made lots of money too. Contractors would buy four at a time.

One day I drank two-thirds of a liter of Tanqueray and got very sick. A nurse checked on me and she told me I got alcohol poisoning. I lost my job as a line cook at Hooters. I was also selling coke on the side at a bar where I was bartending.

A Last Binge in El Paso

I thought if I went back to El Paso, I could straighten up, but that was bullshit. In May of 1997, I was twenty-one [and back in El Paso] and about to turn twenty-two. I was okay for a while and did no coke. I would drink every night. I went on a two-month bender. At the time, I had my own office with employees in Austin, selling water purifiers. I wasn't selling drugs, just spending. July to August I blew all my money partying. Then I was hung over. I scored an ounce of blow for $1,500 [while] I was house-sitting for my parents. They were in Europe for my mother's research; she was an accomplished lay medieval scholar. I started out snorting—I was using the coke to kill myself. I started drinking, and picked up a woman at a pool hall and fucked her brains out. She left the next day. Then I did a big line, and my nose started gushing blood. So I started smoking cocaine. Things started getting sketchy, and I blacked out.

I have a flash memory of being at Walgreens, buying syringes—I told them I was diabetic—to mainline coke. I don't remember anything after that. I woke up the morning of August 6, the day my parents were due home, and the whole house was destroyed. Mirrors broken, tables turned over, all my clothing was in a water-filled tub. It had all been done by me, I think. I didn't know how I had paid for the coke, but eventually figured out I had stolen money from my dad's office in the house to get it. When my parents got home, the house was a wreck. I told them the whole story. When I was finished, I said to them, "I need help." My mom called the family doctor, who gave her a list of drug-rehabilitation clinics. First on the list was the Betty Ford Clinic, but they didn't pick up. She called Cottonwood next. I was sent to the Cottonwood Rehabilitation Center in Tucson.

Before I left for Cottonwood, Bob and I went for a last hurrah. We both did half eight balls of coke and drank like crazy. We went to every bar, starting on Cincinnati Street, and ended in the Upper Valley of El Paso. We had a shot and beer at every bar. I got into a fistfight, and then don't remember what happened. We stopped drinking at five A.M. Bob's car ended up in my parent's front yard. My mom threw Bob out and drove me to Cottonwood Rehabilitation in Tucson.

I had to be locked down to stop, but I wanted to stop. I blew a .22 [blood] alcohol level at the rehab center five hours after my last drink. From age nineteen to age twenty-one, I drank every day, all day. I was on a seventy-two-hour watch while they gave me Librium to keep me from having seizures [from alcohol withdrawal]. They did a sonogram on my liver. Dr. Nash came and told me I had the beginning stages of cirrhosis of the liver. My kidneys were also bad and about to shut down. My spleen was swollen. Intestines ruined. Ulcers about to perforate. It scared the shit out of me, but at that point I wanted to go cop to deal with it. Then I decided to finish it, to get over drugs. I didn't want to die. I can't believe I wanted to get fucked up after what they told me.

Recovering from Drug Addiction and Becoming an Anarchist

At the rehab center, I met the first people I ever knew who gave unabated mutual aid, which is an anarchistic concept. The people at rehab are always there if I need them. At Cottonwood, all the staff members had been to the AA [Alcoholics Anonymous] twelve-step program; everybody had at least ten years of sobriety. I've been clean since then, since 1997. A person needs spirituality.

When I am asked if I would do things differently in the long run, I would have to give that a staunch no! I would definitely do the same thing again. If I had to do it over, I'd do everything exactly the same. The reason behind that is because of the lessons I learned, a few of which were self-sufficiency and autonomy. It really helped, in my eyes, to have a diminished view of the importance of possessions, opening my eyes to what you call commodity fetishism in the United States, which is a consumer culture by and large. Dealing with people on the streets, I also interacted with a lot of lower-class, impoverished individuals. I, myself, became part of an impoverished class.

My parents had money; I really didn't. When I moved out, I was made to live on my own. I thought the best way of survival was to deal drugs. In retrospect, that turned out to be false. I didn't need to do those things, but it took doing them to realize it. The other aspect which came after my cessation of using drugs is that I have the opportunity to orient my life from a sober perspective, to really explore my position with regard to my family, friends, and the culture and environment that I live in.

I had to reorient myself in a more realistic fashion. On one end, early on I was exposed to conservative Christian values, my mom's Republicanism, and my dad's intellectualism. Fostering [a new consciousness] in me gave me the ability to think my way through these issues in sobriety. This has helped me to formulate my opinions about everything from class to government to how society functions. I now see the hypocrisy of vegetarians who use drugs and talk about systems of oppression from an animal-rights perspective, but they are more than willing to exploit humans who are out there working on the farms or suffering because of the nature of drug trafficking, that at the higher levels seemed like a very unrestrained capitalism. At the middle and lower levels, where I tended to function, it was a lot more autonomous.

However, I don't want to paint the picture that one has to utilize drugs and live that lifestyle in order to come to the conclusions that I have. In fact, many people come out of the drug culture being much more greedy and abhorrent than they were before. So I don't want to claim that it was the drug experience necessarily that did it. It was a number of different factors: the rebellious streak in me to begin with; there was the fostering of understanding from the family I came out of that knowledge is power—to read and take a countercultural view. This was also fueled by my interest in punk rock and the music scene in general, and the discussions [about anarchism] and social activity that took place there in that scene and with my friends.

Can a drug-trafficking unit be anarchistic? A lot of middle- or lower-level drug groups tend to operate autonomously. It is a spontaneous upheaval of autonomous mutual aid that is predicated on the need to support a habit, which is often misconstrued as a need to survive. In heroin circles, people that are pleading for it, it feels like a matter of survival. But they are autonomous; they are not anarchistic in the sense that there's no political drive behind it. They are acting politically—that's the important facet. They are unaware of it, but they are acting politically. It's like going to a potluck dinner. You have a bunch of people get together as a gift. They are not charging each other for it. There is no real exchange. They are acting anarchistically.

Can a drug-trafficking unit in an anarchistic way bypass the capitalistic market? Absolutely! It becomes a capitalist black market. Many of the cartel drug rings at the higher levels became aware of the power they have. They can be extremely dangerous to the status quo. The thing that has to be transcended is this notion of greed, which is what fuels people's rise to the top, because it is an inherently capitalistic system—it is unbridled capitalism at those high levels. If they acted as a means of mutual aid, not just for the sake of making money, but to help those around them, the people that are behind their product, [then the larger drug organizations would more closely resemble anarchist groups].

In my group, there was a definite sense of community that spread through the usage of drugs and long and durable friendships that are still salient today. The people I was directly involved with, my group, made decisions on a consensus basis. Walter and I, we had to have an understanding of what was going to happen when things went wrong. Drug trafficking breeds an amazing amount of security culture: the "hate the rat" ethic, where, if somebody is known to have "rolled over," you don't do business with them ever. If they are even rumored to have ratted on some level, you don't even deal with them. What that taught us is that we had to rely upon each other in order to survive. There was a definitive aspect of mutual aid as the cornerstone of our mutual survival. That is one thing that has not changed since I have gotten sober.

I know a lot of anarchists who use drugs, and they're unrepentant users, and that's fine—I don't judge them. But we need to be aware of what's in our pipes and how it got there. I am referring to the economic aspects of it. Capitalism is an absolutely oppressive system. The upper echelons of drug-distribution networks in the global scheme tend to be extremely capitalistic, such that they become ministates within a state. Pablo Escobar and his private army in Colombia was a prime example of that. Depending upon the kind of drug one is using, whether it's coca, heroin, or pot, if it is something coming from a Third World country, one has to ask themselves the question "Who is being exploited to bring this to me?" "Who is being harmed to bring this into my pipe?"

The question, really, is whether we are willing to put our principles before our conventions. We need to understand the commodities we are buying. Because it is all a chain; whether we are talking about nature or culture, everything is connected. With regard to pot, are you buying pot from Michoacán? If you are buying pot from Michoacán, chances are it is a local farmer. Most pot is farmed by individuals that have cornfields, that are supplementing their income by the production of marijuana. Even in Las Cruces, New Mexico, hydroponic marijuana is grown by local farmers. Or take, for instance, hashish in Afghanistan. One of the results of our so-called aid to them, after we bombed the fuck out of that country, was the upsurge of hashish and heroin production by farmers going back to a traditional way of life that had been banned by the Taliban.

We need to address the problems associated with our consumption. Drug addiction is one of the major ramifications of an individual who has been programmed to consume by his or her society. In a sane society that legalized and taxed drugs, the illicit aspect that attracts kids into drugs would be removed. One of the things that is appealing to young American kids that get involved in drugs is that Mom and Dad said not to do it. So they do it because they are curious. Margaret Mead showed in her book *Coming of Age in Samoa* that Samoan teenagers do not have such problems because, for example, sex is not an illicit construct in their culture. That is the important aspect: education and allowing a child to assume responsibility for their action.

What can anarchists do about the drug war? They can traffic drugs to use against the state, but you don't want to peddle to poor people, because they have enough trouble dealing with their own economic problems already. You are probably taking food out of a child's mouth if you're dealing with their dad. There is a definite element of being able to undermine the bourgeois and the upper classes.

Anarchists may peddle to the upper classes. They may also develop means to liberate themselves from drugs and become active in their own right. There is a wonderful model already set up: AA groups that were founded by Bill Wilson and Dr. Bob Smith. Each meeting is autonomous in its own right; [the participants] just agree on certain traditions and principles. They will help any alcoholic or drug addict that is out there on the streets for free. If you are willing to go to any length to get sober, you should not have any problem. It is helping to breed an understanding in the lower classes that addiction is preventing them from being politically active.

One of the defining characteristics of an addict is that they quickly build up a tolerance; it takes them a lot more to get high. That's a warning sign. If your mind can get you that hooked on something, you can also program your mind to get yourself off it. That is the empowering aspect of it, and that is what we don't see [in public discussions]. The message we get from the government is that these things will suck you in and there is nothing you can do about it, or you need to come to us for help or you're going to go to jail or you're going to die. In looking back at my prior drug use and where I'm at now, I guess you could say that I have politicized my drug life such that my political views have become my new addiction.

I think that creative minds in general do not have room to flourish in our society. Virtually anyone who is involved in music is exposed to drugs and alcohol. It becomes a recurrent presence in their lives because of the nature of their personalities to begin with. They are coping with diminished prestige and alienation from society. They are told that they are crazy and fucked up and that they need to get help and acclimate themselves to society, but to them this really equates to not being creative. Most creative individuals are extremely passionate people.

Is it possible to create artistic scenes that don't involve heavy, self-destructive drug addiction and alcohol abuse? There is a prime example in the early punk scene in Washington, D.C., called Positive Force. The D.C. punk scene is famous throughout North America. There is a great book called *Dance of Days* that catalogues that particular scene. I came up right in the midst of it, when it was happening. You have the emergence of what is called the Straight Edge movement. The Straight Edge movement was about not having to get fucked up to enjoy the music and go to the show. It is about the music; it is not about showing up on the scene to be seen. Positive Force is an anarchist movement. It was organized as a consensus-based punk-rock movement. Other important anarcho-punk groups include Fugazi, Minor Threat, and Crass. One criticism I have of these groups is that sometimes they become moralistic about people who use drugs. That is problematic. The whole point is to breed a community. It shouldn't matter whether this person uses or not, although anarchist groups may consider drug addicts a risk because they can be busted and rat people out.

Drug Smuggling through Tunnels:
The Tale of a Scuba-Diving Instructor

In addition to those, like the Anarchist, who deliberately chose a drug-smuggling lifestyle, there are many border residents who unintentionally became part of contraband networks. Alfonso Murat's story is the classic case of such a person. Even though Murat is a savvy Juárez businessman who has been living in that city since 1974, in the course of his normal, day-to-day business activities, he found himself deeply involved in a drug-trafficking conspiracy. His story reveals how the invisible world of drug trafficking can suddenly become visible and profoundly affect border residents.

An accountant by trade, Murat nonetheless had specialized, technical skills that were coveted by technologically unsophisticated but crafty narco-traffickers, who paid him good money to instruct them in scuba diving. Although he was suspicious, only later did Murat realize he had been duped by smugglers. In this, he is not alone. In fact, being tricked by narco-traffickers or unintentionally aiding and abetting them is a common border experience for many, as is socializing with, doing business with, or in other ways interacting with drug dealers.

Lebanese Americans and Lebanese Mexicans, such as Mr. Murat—as well as Chinese Americans and Chinese Mexicans—have a long history on the border, one that goes back more than a hundred years. In the early years, migrants entered the U.S. through subterranean passages. Along the entire U.S.-Mexico border, clandestine tunnels have been a major conduit for contraband and human smuggling. Such is the case in the Mexican cities of Tijuana, Mexicali (where Chinese immigrants dug a mazelike network of tunnels that persists to the present day), Nogales, and Agua Prieta. In these cities, narco-trafficking groups, such as the Arellano Félix cartel and the Cártel de Sinaloa, have taken advantage of existing tunnels or built long underground passageways to cross major drug loads into the United States.

Yet in El Paso, these tunnels do not have to be engineered by smugglers, since the city is crisscrossed by a network of ready-made storm drains and arroyos that flow down from the Franklin Mountains and empty into the Rio Grande. Conveniently for drug traffickers, no one, not even city officials, knows exactly how many of these drains exist under El Paso, since some were constructed at least a hundred years ago. The issue of tunnels in El Paso–Juárez is shrouded in mythology, or perhaps true tales, of nineteenth-century or early twentieth-century Chinese opium dens and smuggling routes across the border. Indeed, the complex geography of the region—steep mountains, canyons, and vast deserts—coupled with the intricate network of underground passages, provides a virtual smugglers' paradise.

To the reader, the image of a gang of swarthy thugs approaching a devoutly Christian Juárez businessman to buy scuba gear in the heart of the Chihuahua Desert, one of the largest arid land regions in the world, may seem like a scene out of slapstick comedy. Yet drug incidents as incongruous as this one occur regularly along the border. For Murat, the whole affair started when three rough-looking men walked into his store. It ended when he saw their mug shots in a local newspaper, accompanying a story about smugglers arrested as they came out of a storm drain in the heart of El Paso, wearing scuba gear and carrying satchels full of cocaine. The larger story does not end here, however, since the smugglers' superordinates were not captured, and Mexican traffickers ceaselessly employ creative means to smuggle drugs into the United States.

Alfonso Murat

Before I say anything else, I want you to know that my complete name is Alfonso Murat, and that I'm a Christian, and that, therefore, I'm not afraid of anything. But let's start from the beginning: my grandfather came to Mexico from Lebanon. He arrived in Tampico aboard a big sea-cruising ship, hiding inside a potato sack, from which he also fed himself during the trip, eating nothing but potatoes. It was 1890 when my grandfather arrived in Mexico, and he was only fifteen years of age. He left Lebanon during a time of strife. He was from a rich family, and he had left his sweetheart, his fiancée, back home. He settled in the city of Guadalajara, Jalisco, and from the start, he sought to go in business for himself, since that's the way it's always been with Lebanese people living abroad. The Lebanese are natural-born businessmen, and they just won't work for anybody else. They always seek to start their own business, to be their own boss.

My grandfather started out selling hotcakes at the various regional fairs around Jalisco and its surrounding states, an area called *el bajío* [literally, "the lowland," that is, the west-central part of Mexico], as well as at all the local festivals in the greater Guadalajara area—and, in fact, at almost any type of festive occasion, including holiday celebrations, weddings, dances, and fiestas in general. Then, with the capital he accumulated doing this, he—like most Lebanese individuals living in Mexico at the time—opened up his own business. One day his business and all his equipment burned downed completely—literally to the ground. So he laced his boots up and went around Mexico selling hotcakes again. We, the Lebanese, need capital to survive, period. That's what we always need in order to start our way of life, which is business. And that's simply what my grandfather was doing: reacquiring capital to start his own business all over again. He married a Mexican woman; they had several children, were blessedly happy, and led a very long, successful life together.

Getting to Juárez

On October 14, 1974, my wife and I arrived in Ciudad Juárez. Up until then, we had lived in and around Mexico City. We came to Juárez because a Korean friend who lived here at the time invited us to come and visit and see for ourselves what he called "the outstanding, 'booming' business climate" that prevailed then in Juárez. By profession, I'm an accountant. I was brought up in Mexico City, and studied and graduated from the Politécnico [Polytechnic University in Mexico City]. It was my wanderlust, my adventurous spirit, that brought me to Juárez. I'm addicted to adrenaline, and thus always ready for a new venture, and I think that's what really brought me to Juárez.

Then one day I discovered inside myself my Lebanese identity, my Lebanese idiosyncrasy. At the time, I was in the business of fixing refrigerators, and I realized then and there that we *Turcos* don't work for other people—we work for ourselves. Even today, I often hear people say, "Vamos a la tienda del turco" [Let's go to the Lebanese guy's store], when they're talking about coming over to my industrial-gas supply store, and I don't mind one bit. I like for people to identify me as a Lebanese person. To me, my Lebanese background and heritage is a source of pride because, in my view, Lebanese people are very spiritual, and so is Lebanese culture in general.

Then one day I read a book by Napoleon Hill titled *Piense y Llegue a Ser Rico* [*Think and Grow Rich*]. I can honestly say that that book changed my life. I came to conclude, through logical thinking and much reflection, that all the concepts explained in that book were true, and I also realized that they made more sense to me than anything I had ever read before. And so I became a convert to that book. I remember that at the time I read that book, I was working for the Fuentes family [one of the wealthiest families in Juárez] as an accountant. They ordered me around, and I didn't like it. After I got done reading that book and pondering on it, I resigned. Reading that book by Hill and reading the Bible inspired me to start my own business. I also wanted to provide something for the community, provide a needed service or product at a fair price that almost everyone could afford.

So I started by selling industrial-grade oxygen, because at that time the big companies charged too much for it and, in fact, were in cahoots, engaging in monopoly-like practices such as price-fixing, practically gouging their customers with the exorbitant prices they charged. Despite the fact that these big companies had a monopoly on the supply and selling of oxygen in Juárez, through much effort and struggle, and even some battles in the court system and in the public arena of the press, I was eventually able to obtain a permit to import oxygen from El Paso to Juárez. Needless to say, there was some bribery involved. But all in all, it turned out to be an economic boom for me. Infra and other big companies in Juárez, such as Praxair—which was a subsidiary of Union Carbide—tried to put me in jail.

But let me take a step back and explain that my involvement in the oxygen-supply business had begun quite fortuitously. At the time, I was in the business of buying scrap iron, cutting it into manageable pieces, and sending it to Mexico City. I was literally selling junk iron to Altos Hornos de México, the biggest metallurgy company in the Republic of Mexico, by train. First, I would cut the scrap iron into manageable pieces with a blowtorch powered by industrial-grade oxygen. Then I would load these pieces into railroad cars and send them on to Mexico City. Three fully loaded train cars brought me twenty thousand dollars. It would take twenty days for me to get paid. I earned a good chunk of money doing this, but believe me, it was very, very hard work. And since the price of the oxygen was so high, a thought started maturing in my mind: what if I could sell oxygen for less?

In time, after many battles with the big companies and acquiring my permit to import oxygen, I landed a sizeable contract with a big French company, Air Liquide, and thus I was the first person in Juárez, and in fact in all of Mexico, who was able to effectively break up this stranglehold, this monopoly, that the big companies had on the oxygen-supply business. But before I was able to accomplish that feat, the big companies fought me tooth and nail all the way. They tried to block me and put me out of business in every way they could. They even sent the Juárez fire department to inspect my business, then the health department, all in an effort to shut me down. Finally, I decided to talk to the Juárez chamber of commerce about all this, and they defended me against the onslaught. I also went to the press, and the whole situation was published in the Juárez newspapers. After I had won my big fight against the big companies, I founded the Juárez chamber of commerce section devoted to oxygen supply. All this happened around 1980. So I started selling industrial gases retail.

Scuba-Diving Lessons and Narco-Tunnels

One day, three guys came into my store on 16 de Septiembre Street, asking if I sold scuba-diving equipment. I really didn't sell it, but I just happened to have two scuba sets that I used when giving scuba-diving lessons to kids from Arizona. These guys had previously come into the store very quietly and discreetly, as if they were trying to avoid being seen. When I would ask them any question at all, they would immediately leave. Then they would come back a week or two later. This went on for about two months, during which time they visited the store a total of five times. I could see in their faces and their eyes, and surmise from their odd behavior, that they had a dirty conscience about what they were going to use the scuba gear for—whatever that was. For example, I would ask them, "Are you going to use the gear in a river?" Instead of answering me, they would leave immediately.

You could also tell right away by their *facha* [bearing, attire] that these fellows were mere *chalanes* [helpers, workers]. In fact, I never did get to meet their jefe, since he always stayed back in the vehicle in which they would drive up to my store. The boss man drove a top-of-the-line brand-new SUV; I think it was a Hummer. During all those visits to my store, the boss man never got out of that vehicle, not even once. But by the few, fleeting, partial glimpses I got of him inside the vehicle—when the passenger door would open so the three *chalanes* could get out and come into the store—I could tell he was a well-dressed man, with expensive brand-name clothes and a very expensive gold-and-diamond watch.

In stark contrast, the three guys that always got out of the vehicle and came into the store were dressed as *cholos*. Whenever these guys would visit the store, you could sense the tension around them and the fact that they were very nervous about being there. Finally, one day my son sold them the two scuba-diving sets at a normal price. Then, a day later, they came back to put oxygen in the scuba tanks, since when they bought them, the tanks were empty. "You are going to need scuba-diving classes," I told them. Again, without uttering a single word, they started leaving in a hurry. Then—as if to explain why they didn't need those classes, or perhaps just to see what I would answer to that—one of the three turned around and told me, "We're going to be in a mine in Durango."

"But that is dangerous," I said, and added as an explanation, "the carbon dioxide you exhale every time you breathe stays trapped inside the cave, and the person ends up dying of asphyxiation with the same carbon dioxide they breathed out, and because of the eventual complete loss of oxygen inside the cave." They left anyway, without asking any questions about what I had just said. Two or three weeks later, they came back and simply said to me, "We can't submerge; why is that?" "You need weights to submerge," I informed them. This time, to my surprise, they asked if I had any sets of weights for sale, and if so, could I sell them a couple of sets. Then, after I told them I did have weights and that indeed I would sell them a couple, they asked me if I would give them lessons. After I agreed, they said they had access to a pool on the west side of Juárez, near the foothills of the Cerro Bola. The pool was in a poor neighborhood near the barrio known as El Zopilote [The Vulture].

Every time we met at that swimming pool, the people running it charged us fifteen pesos [about $1.50] to reserve the pool for an hour. And that's how I was able to teach two of these three guys how to scuba dive. They insisted on making clear to me that they wanted me to train them in only the absolutely essential basics of scuba diving, and nothing more. Again—just like previously, during their visits to my store—while I was training these guys in that pool, their boss never once got out of his vehicle. I charged them three hundred dollars per person.

Right at the beginning of these training sessions, I quickly found out that these guys didn't even know how to swim. But that wasn't a problem, since they explained to me that all they wanted to learn was how to submerge once they got into the water; and then how to walk on the bottom without falling; and then how to get out of the water; and all this, of course, without injuring or drowning themselves. That was it. They weren't interested in anything else. They didn't want to learn anything else about scuba diving, and they repeatedly made this very clear to me. So I taught them what they asked me to, and that was that. I went back to my day-to-day existence, manning my store, and I never saw them or heard from them again.

Then, about a year and a half later, I read in the Juárez newspapers that U.S. law-enforcement agents, from the DEA or the El Paso Sheriff's Department, I think, had caught and arrested in El Paso two scuba divers with sizeable drug loads on them. They had been apprehended as they were coming out of the huge storm-drain and retaining-pond system that's located on U.S. soil in an area very close to the north shore of the Rio Grande, which doubles as the international borderline between the U.S. and Mexico. The more I read and got into the details of that news story, the more certain I became that the two apprehended individuals were the two guys I had trained in that swimming pool in Juárez.

I read that story in the newspaper a few years ago and it specified that the incident had happened a day or two before the story was published. They had been caught with a duffel bag full of cocaine. After reading the whole story, I was sure it was the guys I had trained. They had used the skills I taught them to cross into the U.S. by fording the river and then scuba diving through the big storm drains and retaining ponds on the U.S. side. The story detailed that the two guys arrested were each dressed in full scuba-diving attire, including scuba-diving belts around their waists with ten-pound lead weights—exactly what I had sold the two guys I trained!

Perhaps at this point I should explain that several times a year I give scuba-diving lessons to American kids from Tucson. These scuba classes are held near Hermosillo, Sonora, in the coastal waters between Bahía de Kino and San Carlos. I occasionally give these lessons to groups of Americans that, despite the fact that they live in desert areas of the Southwest, are very dedicated to scuba diving and to getting their kids to learn this sport as well. I guess you could say that these people are true scuba-diving enthusiasts. I've been scuba diving for many, many years, and so teaching others to scuba dive comes naturally to me.

I should also mention that I don't consider myself just a good swimmer— I consider myself the best.

Anyway, getting back to the case of the two scuba guys arrested several years ago near the border on the U.S. side: after thinking about it and everything that happened before I gave those two guys those scuba lessons, I've been able to piece together what, I think, happened. The water was deep enough to cover them completely standing up, including their heads, in some stretches of the underwater path they had to follow to cross into the U.S. and reach their destination—in all likelihood, a drop-off point or a safe house in El Paso where they were to deliver the drug loads and thus accomplish their mission. They had probably made several attempts at this, but failed because they didn't have any lead weights to hold them down underwater. That's why they came back to my store a few weeks later to tell me they couldn't submerge.

But once they had worked out all the kinks and I had trained them, I suppose they figured they were ready to go. I remember the story in the newspaper said they were apparently very well prepared for what they were trying to accomplish, since when they were arrested, they even had mining lamps with them, which they had stashed in a nylon sports bag or backpack. I suppose the lamps were used to see at least a few feet in front of them underwater, particularly in the pitch black or total darkness of night. Juárez became so dangerous that I finally had to sell my store and move back to Mexico City.

Witness to a Juárez Drug Killing

The following account does not deal with drug smuggling per se, but with the psychological impact of drug violence. The numbers alone are staggering: there were 2,500 executions in Mexico in 2007 and at least 5,300 in 2008. Drug-related killings have ravaged Ciudad Juárez since the advent of the Cártel de Juárez, in 1993. From 1993 to 2007, approximately 200 people were murdered each year in the city. As of this writing (December 2008), more than 1,600 murders have been committed in Juárez in what has been the bloodiest year on record.

In addition to those executed, countless individuals have been *levantado*, that is, captured by armed commandos in the streets or taken from their homes, never to be heard from again. Witnesses to those *levantamientos* describe a common pattern: dark-colored Suburbans, Hummers, or other vehicles habitually used by the Mexican federal judicial police or the AFI [Federal Investigations Agency] roar up to the vicinity of the victims, and then groups of armed men, often in uniform, descend from the vehicles, capture the individuals at gunpoint, and immediately vanish. To date, despite the complaints and protests of the Association of Relatives and Friends of Disappeared Persons of Ciudad Juárez, led by Jaime Hervella, few civilians or police, military, or other governmental agents have ever been convicted of these crimes.[1]

In the border DWZ, persons suspected of stealing from, snitching on, or being hostile to the interests of a given drug-trafficking organization are murdered or maimed. The murders take place at all hours of the day, often in broad daylight in populous, centrally located parts of the city. In many cases, a shootout between hit men and their intended victims results in dozens to hundreds of shots being fired from automatic weapons. In other cases, the killings occur in secluded areas or behind closed doors. Thereafter, the often burned or mutilated bodies are deliberately dumped in the street, in vacant lots, or in other public places as an intimidating message to snitches, enemies, or witnesses to crimes. Some bodies are buried in clandestine graves in the desert surrounding Ciudad Juárez or under the patios or floors of houses. There have been four major cases in which narco-cemeteries [*narcofosas*] have been discovered by authorities: clandestine mass graves were found on ranches south of Juárez in 1999, under a house in 2004, and at two more houses in 2008.

In addition to the dead, drug violence produces hundreds of casualties each year that range from minor injuries to brutal tortures to maiming. The victims include those targeted by cartel hit men as well as innocent bystanders struck by stray bullets or injured in car accidents that occur during the fighting. The famous case of the approximately 400 women killed in Ciudad Juárez since 1993 is a phenomenon that overlaps with the general phenomenon of drug killings, since some of the female victims were killed by drug traffickers. According to some accounts, many of the female killings result from drug traffickers and hit men sacrificing young women in sex rituals to celebrate successful smuggling operations (Valdez 2005).

Whatever the circumstances, drug killings invariably terrorize victims, victims' relatives, observers, bystanders, and the general public. The result is a climate of fear, anger, hysteria, and paralysis in drug-dominated areas like Juárez. Consequently, citizens feel insecure and distrustful in their daily lives, and they lose faith in the government and law-enforcement bodies that are supposed to protect them. A vicious cycle emerges in which a terrorized populace refuses to report crimes, killers and criminals are left alone, and impunity reigns. This is one of the worst effects of drug violence. It is felt in Tijuana, which is dominated by the Arellano Félix cartel; Laredo, run by the Cártel del Golfo; Culiacán, controlled by the Sinaloa cartel; and throughout Mexico in regions plagued with drug traffickers.

Sadly, the horrific occurrence recounted by a witness to a drug killing in Ciudad Juárez is an all-too-common experience for thousands of border residents and hundreds of thousands of people throughout the U.S.–Mexican DWZ.

The Witness

A. B. and I decided to bet some money on blackjack at the betting parlor across from the María Chuchena restaurant and next to the Montana

Steakhouse in Ciudad Juárez. It was around seven P.M. on May 18, 2004. It was a hot evening, so we chose to have a drink and cool off at the betting parlor. I had a couple of Sol beers, but I was getting bored. The place is about the size of one and a half or two university classrooms. The business faces Lincoln Avenue, and at the rear of it there is a back door that takes you to an alley or side street. Before I was able to order my third beer, I heard the most horrible, terrifying, and loud noise I had ever heard. Time stopped, and every millisecond felt like an eternity.

That unfamiliar and annoying sound was the explosion of AK-47s firing. From the moment the assault rifles began, everyone just panicked. There were about twenty guys inside, and maybe four of them pulled out guns and prepared to defend themselves. In the meantime, a couple of strangers already inside the betting place went to the front entrance to take a peek at what was happening. They screamed, "¡Ahí vienen para acá!" [They're coming this way!]. After those words, I felt a terror and fear I cannot compare to any threatening experiences in my previous life. My heart began pumping fast; my face flushed; I was confused. My first reaction was to run to the emergency back door. After I opened it, the rest of the people in the betting parlor noticed, and got up from under the tables or other hiding places and headed in my direction. Outside, the shots continued. I could feel the weapons being fired inches away from me. The sound was loud and could have scared anyone within a kilometer's range.

In the back alley, I saw a car, and I was going to hide under it, but then the shots felt closer. I thought, "What should I do?" I was going to run into the street or anywhere I could find away from the place where the shooter was seeking his prey. I needed shelter fast. At that point, I did not even remember my friend, who was nowhere to be seen. But the shots ceased after a minute or two, although to me it was like an hour of wanting to cry, scream, kill, hide, disappear, defend myself, or just not wanting to be there. About twenty seconds after the shooting stopped, sirens could be heard, but only about two of them. I asked myself, "Will two police cars be able to protect me and the rest of the people?"

So I stayed in alert mode, hiding and looking to see anything unusual in the street, such as cars driving, *sicarios* [hit men] running, or something that might endanger me. But the sirens came from every direction, and the people inside the betting place now seemed calm. They said to each other that it was safe to come out, because the cops were there and the shooters were gone. I walked back inside the betting parlor, and the people who seemed harmless at first, before the shooting took place, still had guns in their hands. What if one of these individuals had panicked unexpectedly and harmed one of us? It is funny that the place was already dangerous and risky, because the people were just carrying guns around as if they were Swiss Army knives. It is prohibited in Mexico for any individual other than military officials or law enforcement to conceal a gun, but I guess it does not matter in a city like Juárez, that experiences scenes like this one so frequently. Like the Mexican saying goes: "Primero mis dientes que mis parientes" [I first take care of myself, and then worry about the others]. Maybe it is just a matter of protecting oneself.

So I stepped inside, and I saw my friend and asked him if he was okay. He said yes and asked me where I had gone. He had opened a door where they kept the broom and cleaning supplies and locked himself in there. We stepped out to see what had happened, and with curiosity asked the people around us for their story, what happened, who did it, what car was driven by the killers, or simply anything they saw. One of the guys just pointed across the street at a dead body. It was à *parquero* [car parking attendant] whose life had been taken just for being at his job at the wrong time and in the wrong place. He had been standing or hiding close to where the shots were aimed, and they killed him. He was dead on the sidewalk next to a car and surrounded by his own pool of blood.

I felt bad for him and worse for his family. It was so unfair. He was innocent. I was innocent. I have the right to life and to not feel threatened or in danger. I wanted to leave the scene, but I was not sure if it was the right thing to do. What if the killers were still around and could identify me for some reason? I told my friend to wait a few more minutes before taking off. In the meantime, we checked my car to make sure it did not have broken windows or had not been hit by shots. My car was okay, but the one next to me was not. A bullet had destroyed its rear window.

Right before we left, there were many paramedics and police around a 1987 or 1990 red or blue Dodge Caravan. The men were holding a little girl who was scared and crying desperately. Her mom was the second innocent life that was taken in the fight for money, power, and territory by the Juárez drug lords and the mafia. It pissed me off and enraged me that innocent individuals have to suffer the consequences for these people's greed and violent ways of getting what they want. It is unfair, unjust, and unjustifiable.

This experience was very traumatic and changed the way I see nightlife or any time of the day in Juárez. I cannot enjoy moments to their fullest. I am always on the lookout for possible threats or ambiguous situations. I feel I am being persecuted many times. It stresses me out and makes me anxious. I act almost like a schizophrenic, and it affects my mental health. Many times it wastes my energy. I feel nervous around that area of Juárez, and if anyone approaches me and tries to intimidate me or begin a fight, I just turn my head and leave the scene. I do not let it affect me, and I am not willing to risk my life for some stupid argument or because I bumped into a stranger. God only knows what the stranger does for a living or who he works for, or maybe he simply sees life as not having any value or worth—that it is disposable.

El Paso mansion formerly owned by deceased Mexican drug lord, 2008. Courtesy of David McKenney.

Cordova International Bridge, El Paso to Juárez, 2001. Courtesy of UTEP/ University Communications.

Drug killing in Ciudad Juárez, February 2008. Courtesy of Alfredo Corchado.

Border crossing from Ciudad Juárez to El Paso, 2001. Courtesy of UTEP/University Communications.

Sign posted by drug traffickers, threatening Juárez policemen, 2008. Courtesy of Alfredo Corchado.

Narco-cemetery at Juárez house, 2008. Courtesy of Alfredo Corchado.

Nightclub in the vice zone of Ciudad Juárez, 2007. Courtesy of Robert Chessey.

Location of street drug sales, Ciudad Juárez, 2007. Courtesy of Robert Chessey.

Strip club in Ciudad Juárez, 2007. Courtesy of Robert Chessey.

Zeta cartel member allegedly murdered by the Sinaloa cartel, which videotaped the killing, 2005. Courtesy of Alfredo Corchado.

Mexican soldiers confiscate weapons from drug traffickers, Juárez, 2008. Courtesy of Alfredo Corchado.

U.S. Customs drug bust, El Paso, Texas, 1989. Courtesy of C. L. Sonnichsen Special Collections, *El Paso Herald-Post* Records, UTEP Library.

Drug-load seizure, El Paso Texas, April 1990. Courtesy of C. L. Sonnichsen Special Collections, *El Paso Herald-Post* Records, UTEP Library.

U.S. Customs agents arrest the alleged smuggler of 2,942 pounds of marijuana, 1991. Courtesy of C. L. Sonnichsen Special Collections, *El Paso Herald-Post* Records, UTEP Library.

Mexican federal judicial police arrest the smugglers of 2.3 tons of marijuana, 1990. Courtesy of C. L. Sonnichsen Special Collections, *El Paso Herald-Post* Records, UTEP Library.

Federal police in Juárez arrest five men in connection with the confiscation of 1,500 pounds of marijuana. Courtesy of C. L. Sonnichsen Special Collections, *El Paso Herald-Post* Records, UTEP Library.

Confiscated drug load in the bed of a truck, El Paso, 1989. Courtesy of C. L. Sonnichsen Special Collections, *El Paso Herald-Post* Records, UTEP Library.

Two-hundred-pound marijuana load discovered underneath the wooden floor of a cattle trailer at the Free Bridge of the Americas, El Paso, 1989. Courtesy of C. L. Sonnichsen Special Collections, *El Paso Herald-Post* Records, UTEP Library.

Mexican marijuana bud, 1989. Courtesy of C. L. Sonnichsen Special Collections, *El Paso Herald-Post* Records, UTEP Library.

Man in a marijuana field, 1985. Courtesy of C. L. Sonnichsen Special Collections, *El Paso Herald-Post* Records, UTEP Library.

Downtown El Paso, Texas, 2001. Courtesy of UTEP/University Communications.

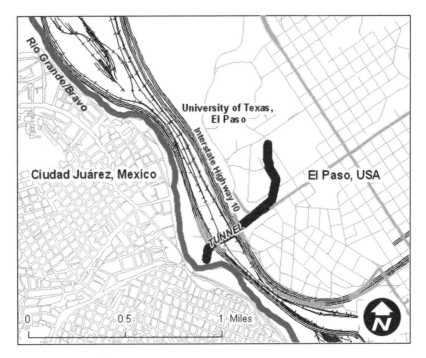

El Paso–Juárez smuggling tunnel near UTEP (mentioned in the chapter "Agent against Prohibition"). Map courtesy of Dr. Timothy Collins and David McKenney.

Mexican agents capture a drug suspect, 2008. Courtesy of Alfredo Corchado.

U.S.-Mexico international border, 2001. Courtesy of UTEP/University Communications.

A U.S. agent securing the border in El Paso after the terrorist attacks of September 11, 2001. Courtesy of UTEP/University Communications.

U.S. Customs drug dog in action, El Paso, 2001. Courtesy of UTEP/University Communications.

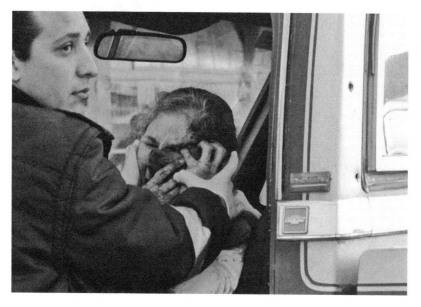

Innocent victim, 2008. Courtesy of *El Mañana*, Nuevo Laredo.

El Club Ritmo, Ciudad Juárez, 2007. Courtesy of Robert Chessey.

Juárez street scene, 2007. Courtesy of Robert Chessey.

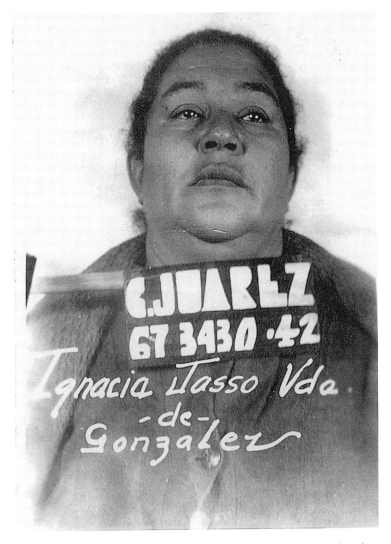

La Nacha's mug shot, 1942. Courtesy of Robert Chessey. From National Archives and Records Administration, College Park, Maryland, RG59, General Records of the Department of State, Box 6.

PART II

LAW ENFORCEMENT IN THE DRUG WAR ZONE

Introduction: Ethnographic Dimensions of Law Enforcement in the Drug War Zone

Narcs and drug merchants have a lot in common.
CHARLES BOWDEN, *DOWN BY THE RIVER: DRUGS,*
MONEY, MURDER, AND FAMILY

Journalist James Mills wrote a 1,200-page tome that remains one of the richest treatments of the international drug trade and government antidrug efforts. According to Mills, "In the five years it had taken to produce that book I had been often in the company of federal agents or international drug traffickers commenting on President Reagan's so-called War on Drugs. I never encountered anyone who thought it anything other than a joke" (1986, 119). Though this is overstated, there have been other equally scathing academic and journalistic indictments of U.S. antidrug policy (for example, Webb 1998; Agar 2006; Baum 1996; Bertram, Blachman, Sharpe, and Andreas 1996; Marez 2004; Nevins 2002; Eddy, Sabogal, and Walden 1988; Andreas 2000; Andreas and Nadelmann 2006), though the policy also has many defenders (for example, Wilson 2001). The main criticisms of the U.S. drug-war policy may be summarized as follows:

1. It is wasteful and ineffective. Billions of dollars are spent each year, and the flow of illegal drugs seems to never cease. Interdiction efforts have little effect on overall supply in the United States.
2. It demonizes behaviors and substances that are either mild or innocuous, or that involve victimless crimes or individuals' choices to consume narcotics. Legal drugs actually kill more people than do illegal ones.
3. It is unfair to producing and trafficking countries, like Mexico,

which suffer the most violence and damage from drugs that are consumed by Americans. If the U.S. drug consumer market did not exist, then international production and distribution would disappear.

4. It is racist. Latinos, African Americans, and other ethnic-minority populations are stigmatized as users and traffickers and bear an unequal weight of the enforcement of punitive drug and immigration laws and practices (Díaz-Cotto 2006; Lugo 2000).

5. It criminalizes and militarizes what is primarily a health or social issue.

6. It is counterproductive because prohibition actually creates a profitable market for illegal substances. Legalization would take the violent criminal element out of drug commerce.

7. It is misdirected. Money and resources should be channeled into drug-addiction and drug-abuse treatment, which is more effective than attempts at interdiction.

Criticism of the war on drugs persists, and I have contributed to such critiques (Campbell 2005); however, attacks on public policy do not necessarily tell us much about the lives of law enforcers in the DWZ. Moreover, in between high-level discussions of what American drug policy should be and on-the-ground realities, there is a middle-level issue concerning what we actually do (operationally) at present. This policy involves complex tactical and organizational processes.

U.S. drug-war policy employs an interdiction model (designed to stop the existing flow of drugs from getting to consumers) and, to a lesser degree, a deterrence model (designed to stop the production of drugs at the source). The interdiction approach attempts to remove drugs from the market and to make drugs scarce or prohibitively expensive in American communities. This is a monumental task because it simultaneously involves meeting two contradictory goals: stopping illegal commerce while not impeding the flow of legal commerce and people. This is the case because most illegal drugs from Mexico and elsewhere come into the United States via commercial and noncommercial shipping through ports of entry. The forces of NAFTA, global free trade, and the increased transnational movement of people and products enormously complicate the work of antidrug agents, who must systematically separate from this vast movement those substances and people deemed illegal or engaged in illegal activities. In Heyman's terms, this effort is Sisyphean in scope, because it attempts to "impose hierarchical order and control on a scenario of agency, flux and uncertainty" (2004, 323).

On one level, however, the drug war, as pursued by thousands of U.S. agents and officials in dozens of different agencies, may be viewed as simpler than the equally significant effort to stop illegal immigration. Although many antidrug agents experience tremendous moral ambiguities in the course of their work, in general the war on drugs is viewed with greater moral certainty by its participants than is the even more ethically fraught work of rounding up undocumented people along the U.S.-Mexico border and within the United States, most of whom are simply seeking a job or a better life (Joe Heyman, personal communication, December 2007). Other important distinctions can be made as well. Within the large number of agencies tasked with anti-drug-trafficking efforts (including ICE [Immigration and Customs Enforcement], the Border Patrol, the DEA, the FBI, EPIC [El Paso Intelligence Center], police forces at all levels, and various task forces), a major division exists between those officials engaged in tactical-level interdiction (involving front-line physical detection of drugs) and those concerned with organizational investigation (tracing the larger patterns of the world drug trade and the movement and composition of cartels and smaller smuggling organizations).

These two functions are usually distributed within one law-enforcement agency or between agencies. The participants in these activities also can be roughly divided into the more blue-collar-oriented tactical-level operatives and the more white-collar-oriented officials engaged in organizational activities. Antidrug law-enforcement work can also be divided between efforts that occur directly at ports of entry, where most human and drug traffic across borders also occurs, and those that occur elsewhere: in the deserts and mountains, in cities, on rural roads, etc.

With these points as a backdrop I would like to suggest the following propositions: U.S. border law enforcement in the DWZ, like Mexican narco-culture, generates a kind of cultural economy of its own. Like narco-culture, key features of border antidrug law enforcement include processes of seclusion and public presentation, although in the case of law enforcement detection of the occulted narco-culture is more important than hiding per se; that is, law-enforcement operations are designed to reveal hidden drug-trafficking operations, whether or not this entails going undercover. Public presentations by law enforcement—parallel in a sense to the performance of narco-style discussed above—include press conferences in which drug confiscations are displayed, statistics indicating successes in the drug war (or the grave threat posed by trafficking) are unveiled, and new antitrafficking technologies and equipment are touted. Other aspects of the cultural economy of border antidrug efforts include processes of symbolic classification of the civilian population into categories of criminal versus noncriminal, legal versus illegal, etc.; the performance of culturally stylized roles, such as undercover agent or narc, Border Patrol or ICE agent, drug-trafficking expert or analyst, etc.; and the development of a law-enforcement subculture with its own lingo, rituals, style, and uniforms.

The cultural dynamics of border law enforcement operate in relation to both Mexican narco-culture and the larger structures of the Mexican state and civil society (and their U.S. counterparts). Border law-enforcement culture thus must be understood as embedded in an overarching political economy, one that reinforces global inequalities and enforces U.S. political and cultural power in relation to Mexico, but that also confronts opposition, resistance, and counterhegemony. Border law enforcement accumulates and mobilizes complex technologies of surveillance and control (both real and virtual), yet these systems are never totally effective, and can be subverted from within and without, although at great risk and cost to drug-trafficking subversives (on the militarization of the border, see the study by Dunn [1996]).

In that sense, law enforcement and drug traffickers engage in a ceaseless point-counterpoint tactical struggle in a context of social proximity, cultural overlap, and even interdigitation. Border settings create a blending or confusion between "Americans" and "Mexicans" and even between criminal "outlaws" and legal "heroes." Paradoxically, drug traffickers and antidrug law enforcers mutually reinforce one another, since prohibition creates a market for illegal drugs, and drug-warrior bureaucrats justify their existence and budget increases by their successes or failures in the drug war. However, it should be noted that American law-enforcement officers in the DWZ are both enactors and agents of the U.S. state, as well as individuals whose private interests are not necessarily coterminous with official ideology.

The consciousness and customs of border law-enforcement officials emerge in relation to the real and hidden agendas of the bureaucracies to which they belong, and to the shifting tactics and maneuvers of drug-trafficking organizations. Although both agents and traffickers engage in deception and selective exposure, they operate under different logics of social action: bureaucratic in the case of the former, and entrepreneurial in the case of the latter. The corruption of border agents by traffickers periodically blurs the boundaries between these two modes (Campbell and Heyman 2007). Likewise, within the minds of border law-enforcement officials, the contradictions between official and hidden ideologies, and between bureaucratic goals and individual self-interest, may not be completely reconciled. The most effective agents may be those that bend or break rules and laws, even if they violate the ethic of control that is the modus vivendi of state bureaucracies.

As Heyman has shown in a series of books and articles (Heyman 1995, 2001, 2002, 2004; also see Maril 2004), border law enforcement places individuals—most acutely in the case of Hispanic officers, who have become the majority ethnic group in the Border Patrol—in acutely contradictory and ambiguous moral terrain. Literally on the border between two states and cultural configurations, the agents are also ensnared in the often conflicting pressures of national policies, local priorities, divergent cultural understandings, and community and family ethoses. DEA agents, for example, may conduct operations effectively in Mexico and thus satisfy their superiors, yet anger Mexican authorities, who feel their sovereignty is being trampled (Toro 1995). Likewise, border law-enforcement bureaucracies are torn between the goals of total confiscation—an unachievable, utopian goal that would ultimately lead to their obsolescence—and the need to justify continued funding of their agencies. Hence, a fine line must be walked between claims of effective deterrence (which might draw political praise but lead to lessened funding) and claims of how gigantic and dangerous border drug traffickers have become (which might generate political criticism but encourage increased funding).

The particular "thought work" of antidrug agents is in some sense more complex than that of immigration and Border Patrol agents, who are concerned primarily with the apprehension of undocumented migrants (Heyman 1995). Undercover narcs, for example, must pose as fellow traffickers while collecting information to build legal cases against traffickers. In anthropological terms, they must "go native" as traffickers while retaining their disciplinary objectivity and ethical framework. Ultimately, border antidrug law-enforcement agents function within a challenging sociocultural world entailing great risk, regardless of what one may think about the war on drugs as social policy. Thus, an ethnographic treatment of such a group requires the same degree of subtlety with which we treat any other cultural group.

For insights into the culture of law-enforcement agents on the ground of the drug war, we must look primarily to journalistic accounts, memoirs, and ethnographies. The works of Mills (1986), Bowden (2005), Kuykendall (2005), Strong (1990), Eddy, Sabogal, and Walden (1988),

Levine (2000), Heyman (1995, 2002), and Maril (2004) demonstrate that there are a wide range of personalities involved in antidrug work: valiant, dedicated officers deeply committed to fighting crime as well as cynical, double-dealing cops on the take; sophisticated, wine-savoring intellectuals as well as street-fighting tough guys; and mysterious undercover agents as well as articulate government spokespeople.[1]

The chapters that follow illustrate that diversity and the human dimension of antidrug efforts in the DWZ. This section explores the following issues: What kinds of people engage in anti-drug-trafficking activity? Why do they choose this kind of work, and how does the work affect their lives? What risks do they confront? How do they attempt to catch drug traffickers? What are their feelings about the politics and practices of the drug war? Additional research questions include the following: What are some of the internal cultural dynamics of border antidrug agencies? What are the cultural impacts of border antidrug law-enforcement efforts? How do the various law-enforcement agencies differ in their strategies for combating drug trafficking?

Part II presents the lives of a range of U.S. law-enforcement agents (and one Mexican policeman) in the DWZ. These include the views and experiences of a ground-level narc ("Undercover Agent on the Border: Cultural Disguises"), a Juárez policeman who was shot and nearly killed by drug traffickers ("A Juárez Policeman Fighting Drug Traffickers"), a Border Patrol agent ("Patrolling the Drug War Zone: A Border Patrol Agent in the War on Drugs"), the former leader of an antidrug task force ("Intelligence and the Drug War: Commander of an Antidrug Task Force on the Border"), and a retired customs agent who fought drug traffickers for many years but who now opposes the war on drugs ("Agent against Prohibition"). This section also includes several accounts that do not come from antidrug officials, but that offer unique perspectives on the difficulties law-enforcement agents face in the fight against drug traffickers. These include the stories of a journalist who specializes in reports on drug traffickers and who was kidnapped by corrupt Juárez policemen ("Journalism and Drug Trafficking: Covering the Narco Beat on the Border"), the story of a drug trafficker turned police informant who was murdered by the Juárez cartel ("The Death of Francisco"), and a firsthand description of a border drug bust (an excerpt from *Weed: Adventures of a Dope Smuggler,* by Jerry Kamstra).

Undercover Agent on the Border: Cultural Disguises

The war on drugs employs law-enforcement officers in numerous capacities, one of the most dangerous being as undercover agents, aka narcs. Narcs, by necessity, live double lives. The rugged U.S.-Mexico border landscape and the transnational culture within which one can quickly and easily move from one country to the other facilitate the narcs' (and drug traffickers') work of passing, concealment, and treachery. U.S. undercover agents seeking to undermine drug cartels are the ultimate anthropologists; as students and researchers of the underworld drug culture, they not only must understand it, but also be able to successfully blend into it. The work requires cleverness, flexibility, strong nerves, and excellent mimetic skills, since a bad acting performance may result in death for the agent.

The account that follows illustrates some of the tricks of the narc's trade: the use of informants, who must be treated with as much respect and care as a mechanic's tool; subtle linguistic maneuvers; the manipulation of clothing styles; the invocation of local knowledge; and playing the role of an eager drug buyer. This is a dangerous game, since informants may be violent and duplicitous criminals, as in the notorious case of "Lalo." Lalo was part of the Juárez cartel cell that tortured, killed, and buried twelve people at the so-called "House of Death" in 2003 and 2004, and he continued to engage in drug deals and dubious transactions that resulted in the death of at least one person in El Paso while he was an ICE informant (for details see http://www.guardian.co.uk/world/2006/dec/03/usa.davidrose).

Perhaps not surprisingly, successful undercover agents, such as the one whose story is presented here, often come from the same socioeconomic background as that of the traffickers they pursue. On the border, agents also may share a common cultural and linguistic heritage with the *narcotraficantes*, though their political interests are radically opposed. Good narcs are well prepared, but ultimately their success or failure depends on their poise in crucial moments of tension and danger.

The drama of narcs and *narcos* is played out every day on the border, and the outcome is prison for some, death for others, and a promotion or raise for still others. Yet the temporary successes or failures of anti-drug operations and local trafficking schemes seem to have little impact on the overall flow of drugs from Mexico into the United States.

The Undercover Agent

Everyone is affected by drugs in the El Paso–Ciudad Juárez region. If it's not the person himself or herself that's directly involved, then it's a friend or a relative. In El Paso, everyone knows someone, or is related to someone, who is a drug trafficker or a consumer. Often, we don't want to discuss it or throw some light on this situation, but it's all around us. And I think that that's something that not everybody understands in other parts of the United States. A lot of times, people wonder why in other places the drug traffickers will get all sorts of punishment for the drugs that authorities find in their possession, and yet in El Paso you can bust someone with a thousand pounds of marijuana and they'll only get probation. The people in the interior of the U.S. will think, "How can that happen?"

In some East Coast towns, they'll bust someone with half a pound, and they'll sentence them to twenty years. That's because in El Paso, when they go to a jury, you know, because there's so much drugs here, the people on that jury will think, "Oh, maybe it's not really that bad. My family has a cousin that's been living off of it [narco-trafficking], together with his family members, you know, most of their lives, and they're nice people. They're very respectful, and they're very nice people." But they're drug dealers! But here in El Paso, people don't want to face the situation, and so, very often *quieren tapar el sol con un dedo* [they cover it up; literally, "they want to block out the sun with a finger"], and so they try to say, "Oh, it's no big deal. Nothing's happening, at least not in my neighborhood. I don't see anything." And so often, it's right under our noses. The neighbor's houses are being rented as stash houses. The apartment upstairs is being used as a stash house. They're borrowing our cars to go cross drug loads from Juárez to the United States.

I was born in the Lower Valley of El Paso; my parents and grand-parents were from a village on the Mexican side, in the Lower Valley of Juárez, or El Valle de Juárez, where there's a lot of little towns. Right across from Ysleta, Texas, on the Mexican side you find Zaragoza, and as you keep going east, there's El Sauzal, there's Loma Blanca, there's San Isidro, San Agustín, then there's a little town called Jesús Carranza, but everybody knows it as La Jorobada, then there's Tres Jacales, and then there's El Millón, Reforma, Caseta, then Guadalupe, and El Porvenir.

As a kid I used to spend most of my summers in one of those towns, with my grandparents at their home. So I grew up, you might say, on both sides of the border. I also had some uncles in other little towns on the Mexican side, where my grandparents lived in an area that was formerly an island in the middle of the Rio Grande. After the river shifted, this land ended up on the U.S. side. As a matter of fact, on my dad's side, our family had some land in La Isla. We've always lived by the river, and so we know what goes on in the area. I've always considered myself more of a small-town guy than a city guy, because growing up, we always lived down in the valley. A lot of the stuff that I know about I learned by living and growing up down on the ranches of El Paso's Lower Valley and El Valle de Juárez. As a kid growing up on the Mexican side, we used to kid about the fact that there were two things you had to like: you had to like baseball, because everyone down there plays baseball; and you had to like *jaripeos* [one of several versions of Mexican rodeo]. Back then, one of the differences between a *jaripeo* and an American rodeo was that anyone could participate in a *jaripeo*. All you had to do was ask someone to let you borrow their *espuelas* [spurs], and just like that, there you were, trying to mount a bronco or ride a bull. [One day] my dad said, "Let me buy you your *espuelas*."

My family is an old family in the region. My grandparents migrated from Mexico right after the [Mexican] Revolution. My grandparents would cross the border into the U.S. to work at the ranches. At that time there were some big ranches on the American side, like the Rancho de Las Flores. My grandparents worked there, but sooner or later they would always go back to their own little plot of land in Mexico. They would cross to work on the American side to supplement their income, and then go back to the Mexican side to work their own land. On the Mexican side, they had a little parcel allotted to them by the Mexican government. But then they started having a bunch of kids, and a tiny piece of land can only support so many people. That's when my parents also started crossing to the U.S. side to work in order to help out with their families' domestic economy. I guess my grandparents foresaw what was happening and what was in store for them and their offspring in the future, because both of my parents were actually born on the American side, the U.S. side of the border, and so my parents were U.S. citizens. Back then, it was fairly easy for people in Mexico to come over to the U.S. and register their kids here.

I was born in El Paso County and went through the local school system, from kindergarten and elementary all the way through high school. My grandfather was the *comisario* of an *ejido* on the Mexican side. [The *comisario ejidal* is a local civic or community leader who represents the inhabitants of *ejidos* before the state and federal governments. *Ejidos* were plots of land, divided equally among the whole community, and given to peasants after the Mexican Revolution.]

Ever since I can remember, I always thought law enforcement was interesting and wanted to get into it. After coming across to live permanently on the U.S. side, my dad got a job at ASARCO, but we never lived in Smeltertown. Instead, my dad commuted daily from El Paso's Lower Valley to ASARCO. He left home every day at five thirty in the morning, or six at the latest, even though his shift didn't start until eight. I would always kid him about it, asking him why he had to leave so early, when it was obvious that he could leave at six thirty or seven and still make it in time to start working at eight. He would always say, "Nunca sabes si se te va a ponchar una llanta" [You never know whether you're going to get a flat tire]. I would counter by telling him, "Dad, you leave so early that you could change the whole motor and still make it to work on time."

He wanted me to go to school so I could find a good-paying job where I wouldn't have to work doing hard labor, like he had to. Later, I also worked at ASARCO for a while, and that's when we started leaving for work together, and I kept kidding him about leaving too early. He would get mad and tell me, "Pues si no quieres ir tan temprano, no te vayas conmigo" [If you don't want to leave early, then don't ride with me]. We used to leave so early that we even had time to stop at the Second Ward *panadería* [bakery; presumably, Bowie Bakery] and get some sweet bread and milk, and eat it there, before going in to work.

So after I graduated from high school, I worked all over El Paso. I worked at the Billy the Kid denim jeans company, then at the Tony Lama boot company, and then I went to work at ASARCO, but the company had some problems, and I got laid off. During the whole time that I was working at these various jobs, I was also going to school at UTEP. When I got laid off from ASARCO, I applied at the Border Patrol, the El

Paso County Sheriff's Department, and the Texas Department of Public Safety. I got hired by the sheriff's department. I took the job because it was the first offer I got. The police department works the municipality, that is to say, within the city limits, while the sheriff's department works the county, but can work in the city as well.

With the Sheriff's Department

I am also on the multicounty drug task force. I started in the detention facility. I worked for a period of two years in detention with the county. The county jail is a problem area for drugs. Prisoners use what they call a fishing line. They drill a small hole by the windows and bring in drugs that way. They throw a little thread all the way down to the ground and grab a bag, and then bring it up by the window. The window frame is weak. There's just putty holding it up, so they can easily make a hole there to bring in the bag.

The authorities of the jail system allow magazines into the facility. Cocaine is melted down and put in the perfume scratch-offs in the magazines. Those people have nothing to do all day but think of how to get drugs in. A local politician and lawyer was honored as best ex-student at my high school, but he was accused of bringing marijuana in during a visitation at the jail. He brought it into the jail in his briefcase. Visitation is another favorite. Prisoners dig under wood panels and receive drugs passed from visitors through there. Also, the attorneys' booths—they're not checked as often, and so holes are drilled in them [and drugs are hidden there]. Female prisoners would use nail files to dig holes in the booths. Some officers are "dirty"—they pass drugs. A lot of it is, in my opinion, the thrill of getting away with stuff. The motive for doing these things is people get an adrenaline rush—they get a hard-on.

I tested out of detention after two years and went to patrol. That is to say, I became a deputy patrolman covering the Lower Valley and the Upper Valley. We learned that so-and-so was moving stuff. So we stopped a car to identify the driver. The driver claimed he had no driver's license or ID. We inventoried the car and found a load of pot in the trunk. He had thrown his driver's license under the seat. I guess he thought he could get away by not giving us his name. The ironic thing is that if he had shown us his license, we would have let him go on his way.

You know, what I've been wanting to do is get out of this business for a while. My wife worked at an immigration detention facility. She worked there as a guard. One of her coworkers was stopped by police at a traffic stop. It turned out the guy had dope in the car. When I was a patrolman, I would go to Juárez's Lower Valley. I would go to this dance club, and one time me and my wife went, and this guy and his wife showed up and had nowhere to sit, so I let this guy and his wife sit at our table. He was a guy from a small village, a guy involved in drug trafficking. He drove an old truck. One time his truck broke down on the way to Juárez, so I gave him a ride. We went to Joe's Place. The guy said to me, "Drink whatever you want, go with whichever girl you want, I'll pay." So I said to him, "Why are you driving that piece of shit?" It was to hide his drug wealth. He had a bad-looking house, too. He said to me, "I have to hide my wealth, because if I don't, the *judiciales* will come down hard on me. They will come to my house and kick my ass, and then take everything I have. But because I hide my wealth very well, if they pass by and see how broken down my house is, they'll just say to each other, 'Ese no trae nada' [He doesn't have anything]."

One time at a car wash in a small town in the El Paso Lower Valley, this same guy was acting suspiciously, hanging around there. I pulled up in my patrol car and said hi, and he acted surprised and scared. I asked him what he was doing, and he told me he was there to get his car washed. I didn't believe him. A friend of mine in the Border Patrol ended up busting him with an eight ball of cocaine in his wallet. He was sentenced to six months in jail.

The reason he was washing his car, it turned out, was because he had just crossed a load of drugs. The whole thing was suspicious because he could have washed it on the Caseta, Mexico, side of the border, since it is cheaper there. Later, when the guy got out, I bumped into him at a bar in the Juárez valley. The guy told me he had been busted and spent some time in jail, and I responded: "I would have busted you too if I had known you had drugs; after all, it is my job, you know. And if I had known you had an eight ball, I would have busted you myself and taken the credit for it. You can be sure I wouldn't have let someone else get the credit."

A lot of people know I work in law enforcement, but I've never admitted that I'm a narcotics officer. All my life I had gone to *jaripeos* on the sixteenth of September, Mexican Independence Day, in El Valle de Juárez. But about three or four years ago, at one of these *jaripeos*, I was with my son and one of my nephews, and some guys saw me and said, "Hey, mi sherifillo" [my little sheriff]. That's when I said to my son and my nephew, "I think now we better leave." And of course we did.

With me it has been, more than anything else, my stubbornness which has pushed me on to bust drug traffickers. It's like I tell myself: who are these guys who are selling drugs to tell me I can't go to my little town? Last year [2006], for the first time since I can remember, I didn't go home on the sixteenth of September. For thirty or forty consecutive years I had been going to the jaripeo held there on that date, but not last year.

I was a patrolman for six years, and then I became a detective. First I worked crimes against property, then I worked sex crimes, then I worked internal affairs. Then I became a narcotics detective. I had heard it was one of the best places to work. The one good thing about internal affairs is that after your two-year tour there is over, you can choose where you want to work. I was hesitant because of all the people I know.

In internal-affairs work, you get ostracized by your coworkers. That's because in internal affairs, you do investigate a lot of your fellow officers. That in itself is stressful. When you walk into a room where there are several officers talking, and as soon as they see you, the conversation dies down. And maybe it's just human nature, you know. For example, this officer who I was investigating as a witness came in and told me, "I don't understand how you became an internal-affairs officer. Word on the street is that you're a real nice guy." So being an internal affairs officer automatically makes me an asshole. I guess one is viewed as a traitor. And he was serious, too. He had actually talked to a lot of officers and asked them about me. And they had told him I was a nice guy. So he just couldn't understand how a nice guy like me ended up in internal affairs.

The Care and Feeding of Informants

I was a little too old for narcotics work, a little overweight, a little out of shape. But I soon learned that the best narcs are the ones who can talk and bullshit the best. I mostly do higher-level deals, you know, deals in kilograms and pounds. I've come to think that the old families in the valley of Juárez are not the ones selling drugs. It's the more recent arrivals that are dealing drugs, individuals or families coming from Torreón or other places from the interior of México. It probably sounds bad, you know, like, "Oh, yeah, yeah, the old families are not involved in drugs, sure. Yeah, right! Whatever you say." But I've been doing this, you know, being a narc, for over five years now, and I've never busted anyone that I knew from the small villages.

When you become a narcotics officer, you're required to attend some courses of specialized training. I guess you could call it a school for narc training. But I was also very lucky, because my first partner had been doing this kind of work for a while, and he sort of took me under his wing and, in fact, continued training me, on the job, so to speak. He was one of the best narcotics officers I've ever known. He threw me into the water right away. But he knew what he was doing, because he was a real pro. The lifeline of a narcotics officer is having good confidential informants. You're only as good as the informants you have, the informants you work with. The type of instructions my first partner gave me, for example, were concepts like this: An informant is a crook. You never trust an informant. If you ever turn your back on him, he's going to stab you in the back. But an informant is also a tool that belongs to you. It's like owning a Craftsman tool. When you have Craftsman-brand tools, you've got some of the best tools around. So what do you do when you've got good tools? Easy: you use them, then you clean them, and then you hang them up so you can use them again. But you don't throw them on the ground, leaving them hanging around under an old tire, because if you do, then pretty soon those tools aren't going to be any good. So you've got to take good care of them. Craftsman tools have a lifetime warranty because they're good. The same thing with an informant: you get a good informant, you take care of that informant, you clean him off so he won't get any heat, and that way you can use him another day. Of course, we pay our informants, but so does every other law enforcement agency. DEA pays them, FBI pays them, and we pay them. So yes, law-enforcement agencies do pay informants; but the reason they come to us is because we protect them. As a narc, I'll tell a potential informant, "If you come and work with me, not only will you get paid, but I'll do whatever I can to try to make sure that no heat comes down on you. And if worse comes to worse, I'd rather drop a case or lose a case than reveal my informants."

Most federal agencies use their informants as witnesses. Now I ask you: how long are you going to last as an informant if you testify against them [your former drug-dealing associates]? Not very long, because as soon as they see you testifying, you've become known—in other words, you've blown your cover—and they will come after you and try to kill you. At the sheriff's department, we're proud to say that of the informants that have worked for us, if any have been killed, it's because they went to work for someone else, for the feds or somebody else. We, in local law enforcement, are a hit-and-run organization. We take drugs off the streets and arrest as many people as we can. We can't do long-term investigations; we just don't have the technology to do that, which involves stuff like phone tapping and other high-tech devices. With most of our investigations, we start them and get them over with as soon as possible.

The first informants I had I got from my partner. Eventually, when he got transferred out, he left me all his informants. Then, later, I started getting my own informants by giving them the little speech about how, if they wanted to help themselves, they were better off working with me. For example, when an individual would get busted by us, I would tell him, "If you work with us, and eventually we bust three times the amount you were busted with, we'll help you get only probation, or if you're lucky, then the charges against you will be completely dropped." Of course, we always try to follow through on these kinds of promises, since we get credibility with our informants that way. A lot of times, after an informant trusts you, he'll bring over one or two of his friends, who will also become informants. You'd be surprised how many informants come to us this way.

After only two or three months working as a narc, my partner told me, "I want you to go meet with this informant at the Ysleta International Bridge. When you go meet with him, he's gonna tell you about this other guy that wants to buy twenty-eight kilos of cocaine." According to the confidential informant, although this guy was from out of town, he, the informant, claimed that this guy was good for the money, that the guy had the money. He even claimed that he had seen the money. Now, one thing I should explain at this point is that, in this type of work, you learn very quickly that most confidential informants are liars. And in this particular case, there was no way the informant could've already seen the money, since that was coming from Mexico. Anyway, I went over and briefed my supervisor and the rest of the crew. So I made a phone call, and I say to the guy, "Hey, I heard you were looking for merchandise. Well, I've got it." So we agree to talk business. So I go to meet this guy. As soon as I start talking to him, I'm doing my little "I'm from Mexico" skit. So I tell him in Spanish, "I'm from Mexico and I don't speak English, but I can help you out," and more stuff like that. When I met with him, I was wearing my gold necklace and other pieces of gold jewelry. I was also wearing my shirt unbuttoned to my navel, like a Mexican drug dealer, like I've seen in Caseta and Guadalupe.

Immediately upon meeting him, I said to him: "Yo soy tal y tal. Yo tengo esa mercancía que tú necesitas. Así que vamos a ponernos de acuerdo" [I am so and so. I have this merchandise that you need. So let's make a deal]. Then we start discussing the price of the merchandise. Previously, over the phone, he had told me that he wanted to see the merchandise, so when I went to meet him, I showed up with the drugs. I remember that after that initial phone call, my supervisor had asked me, "Are you sure you want to go there alone?" I said yeah, because I told him I work alone, so if I show up with someone else, he's gonna get suspicious.

So anyway, when I met him, I showed him some of the "merchandise" that I've got, and he liked it. He shows me a big laundry-soap box full of money. Then he says to me, "I'm really sorry, you're going to have to excuse me, but I only have enough money to buy nine kilos." And then he added, "But bring the rest of the [nineteen] kilos and I'll get you a buyer for them." At the time, since I was very inexperienced, I thought he actually had enough for twenty-eight kilos. I mean, since I was inexperienced, I didn't know the difference. I just saw a lot of money, and I thought that he had enough for the twenty-eight kilos he had ordered.

But anyway, when he told me he only had enough money to buy nine kilos, I told him, "¿Pos qué estás pendejo, o qué? [Are you an asshole or what?] You've got me driving around with all this merchandise in my vehicle. Don't you realize that my life is in jeopardy? If I lose this merchandise, me and my family can get messed up bad." And, of course, I acted like I was really mad at him, because he made me bring all these extra kilos. I told him, "I show up with the amount you want, only with the exact amount you ordered, and then we make the exchange, and that's that." And then he said, "Well, okay, I understand." So to drive the point home, I told him, "Dando y dando, pajarito volando" [We give and take and then fly away]. When the narco-traffickers talk, they like to use codes. And I like to use what I would hear my dad say when I was growing up, or things my grandparents in the village in Mexico would say. That makes it more credible that I'm from over there, Mexico.

The Language of Drugs

Other ways of saying in Spanish street code that the money and the merchandise should be exchanged at the same time are, for example, the following expressions: "Cayendo el muerto y soltando el llanto" [As soon as I show up with the coke, you give me the money; literally, "When he dies, you cry"]. So yeah, these guys like to use *dichos* or *refranes* [popular sayings] to emphasize or drive a point home or express that it's the right thing to do, that it's just common sense.

Another way of saying "I've got the stuff, here it is, ready to go; now do your part and show me the money" is "Yo aquí tengo la novia lista, nomás estoy esperando que traigas a los mariachis" [I have the bride ready, I'm just waiting for you to bring the musicians]. And of course "the bride" means "the white stuff" [cocaine], because wedding dresses are white. Now if I was "selling" some marijuana, I would say, "Ya están las muchachas listas" [The girls are ready now] or "Ya están las muchachas listas para el baile" [The girls are ready for the dance]. "Ahora ya nomás falta la música" [Now the only thing missing is the music]. "Usted téngame la música lista y yo le llevo las muchachas al baile" [You get the music ready and I will take the girls to the dance]. Often, for reasons of security—in other words, so people passing by or listening in won't know what they're talking about—drug dealers talk in code when discussing a deal. And sometimes, drug sellers are just plain dumb, and they'll use silly, stupid sayings or lingo. Like one guy will say, "Quiero comprar calcetines" [I want to buy some socks]. And the other guy will ask, "¿Verdes o blancos?" [Green or white?]. I mean, it's quite obvious what they're talking about. When it comes to socks, who, I ask you, has a taste for white or green ones? And another thing: why are those two colors the only possible options?

Nashville and Chicago

I did a case in which the drug loads were being transported from El Paso to Nashville, Tennessee, where they were sold. The authorities there had a Spanish-speaking officer who was Cuban. He had come from Florida. But the drug dealers were Mexican—a Mexican group selling the pot to another group of Mexican nationals that lived there—and they were saying stuff on the phone, using Mexican street lingo, and the Cuban officer just wasn't picking it up, because it was a totally different slang than what he was used to in Cuba, you know; it was just a totally different code from the one he knew. So he just didn't understand what they were talking about. So the Cuban said to me, "Oh yeah, from what I've figured out so far, these guys like horse racing. They're saying that the horse is coming in this weekend and that the horse weighs 750 pounds." So I said to him, "No, *pendejo*, what they mean is that 750 pounds of marijuana are coming in this weekend."

This kind of bust, or case, is what we call a controlled delivery. To begin with, we had information that these guys wanted to take fifty kilos of cocaine and five hundred pounds of marijuana from El Paso to Nashville and to Chicago. We went back and forth with the middleman, the *contacto*, as they say. In fact, the middleman was our informant, but the narco-traffickers didn't know this, of course. The middleman, in turn, talked to a truck driver. The driver didn't know who the owners of the drug loads were, nor did he know the identities of the guys he was going to deliver the stuff to, and that's exactly the way the narco-traffickers wanted it.

So we started following the truck driver to the point where he was supposed to go to pick up the drugs. He parked for two to three days with his trailer backed up against a fence at a truck stop. He already had the cocaine loaded into his truck, but was waiting for the marijuana load. It was a case of the driver being greedy, since he wanted to kill two birds with one stone, as it were, by transporting both the coke and the weed, since that way he would make more money, and since that was his scheduled itinerary that he was supposed to follow in order to transport and deliver his regular, legal commercial-merchandise loads.

In fact, the coke was from one narco-trafficker and the weed was from another, and the driver was the only one who knew he was transporting both. The thing is, those two days he had parked his trailer backed up against that fence, he called his contact in Chicago several times, and each time told him he was already on his way to Nashville, and that from there he would go on to Chicago. His plan was to deliver the marijuana load to Nashville and get paid there for his services from one group of narco-traffickers, and then from there go on to Chicago, where he was scheduled to deliver the cocaine and get paid by the other group of drug dealers.

When the driver finally got on the road with both loads aboard, we ended up following and busting him, and then "flipped" him [got him to cooperate with us]. We had busted him with a lot of drugs in his possession, and he knew it. So I told him, "Look, you've got fifty pounds of cocaine and five hundred pounds of marijuana on you, and you know you're going to jail for a long, long time." So eventually I persuaded him to make it easy on himself by working for us as an informant. In order to accomplish this, at first I told him, "Look, I don't know how you feel right now, but I think you have to think about yourself right now, and not about your friends. You know, like that old Mexican saying goes:

'Primero mis dientes que mis parientes'" [literally, "First my teeth, then my relatives," that is, I first take care of myself, and then worry about the others]. And then I told him, "If you work for us, you'll get a lighter sentence. Instead of doing fifty years or more in prison, if you work for us, you'll only end up doing ten years." And so he finally agreed. Now since there were FBI agents in on the bust, I told the driver to tell them, "I will cooperate and work for the law, but only with the man I trust," that is to say, me, of course. The feds agreed, and so I became a co–case agent, and got to go to Nashville and Chicago.

And so now, with the driver working with us, we proceeded to do it. We ended up taking the drug load in a plane to Nashville. The driver told the guys that his truck had broken down, and so he had to rent a van, and put the load in there. When we were in Nashville, the cops there helped us out. So we delivered the five hundred pounds and got to meet the guys who were buying it. I loved the way the cops in Nashville work. They pulled up in some big trucks and not only busted the guys that were there to receive the drugs, but ended up taking everything in that stash house. They confiscated everything. They took furniture, a big-screen TV, computers, all the vehicles in the garage. They also seized some boats that these guys owned—I mean, everything. I thought that was great, because that way you hit them where it hurts them the most: in their pocket.

And then we went to deliver the cocaine to Chicago. The drug dealers were supposed to pay the driver when he delivered the cocaine. I wanted to wait until he got the money to bust them, but the feds wanted to bust them immediately; they did so, and thus the money was not confiscated. The driver was going to get paid forty thousand to fifty thousand dollars, but we never got to see that money. All in all, though, it worked out okay, since the drug dealers in Chicago had some properties, and all those were seized.

Another difference between us and the feds is that the feds get bonuses for busting a case like this, but we in local law enforcement don't. We just get our regular paycheck, and that's it. Now, when I'm working a case, my work hours are flexible, since I have to be out in the field a great deal. I only have to go to the office when I have paperwork to turn in. Recently, I worked out in the field from six in the morning to twelve midnight on surveillance. I was watching an [approximately] 1,800-pound marijuana load that eventually we ended up busting. On that occasion, I got relieved at twelve midnight, and then another couple of officers took over for me and my partner, from twelve midnight to eight, and then we came in again. We used to keep all of our busts out of the newspapers so the crooks wouldn't know what happened. If it's not in the paper, you can take down more people, since they're not aware that we're on to them. For example, if it's not in the media, the traffickers in Juárez don't know what happened in El Paso, and so they start suspecting their own people.

The Death of Francisco

The previous interview discusses how drug traffickers are investigated and arrested. But many traffickers suffer a worse fate, including some who cooperate with U.S. law-enforcement agencies. The poignant account of Francisco's death, narrated by his brother, illustrates the devastating human toll taken by the drug war. In border communities like El Paso, the seductive allure and enticing financial appeal of a drug-trafficking life are hard to overestimate. Quick and easy drug money attracts thousands of people, especially the poor, but also members of working-class, middle-class, and well-to-do sectors. Francisco came from a solid Mexican immigrant family in El Paso that had achieved a version of the American Dream. Yet Francisco was a black sheep, and he lived for trouble and the pursuit of fast-money schemes.

Francisco initially made good profits in the drug business, which allowed him to significantly improve his family's standard of living. Yet, as often happens, this prosperity did not endure. Francisco evidently began providing information to law-enforcement officials in exchange for money. Suddenly, what had appeared to be a cushy life turned into a nightmare. The Juaréz cartel suspected him of snitching—the punishment for which is death, according to the unwritten rules of the narco-trafficking business. The cartel lured Francisco to Juaréz and brutally murdered him.

In the course of this research, I have read accounts of thousands of drug killings in the Mexican press. That such cases occur regularly and have led to a desensitization of the public to drug atrocities, however, does nothing to lessen the trauma experienced by the victims and their loved ones and relatives. Francisco, like many government drug informants, was not well protected by the law-enforcement agency that benefited from his information. Nor did his family members feel that the U.S. government really cared about him. Drug investigators simply pumped him for information, took what they could, and provided little to Francisco in return, other than to vigorously search for him when he was kidnapped by the Juaréz cartel. The antidrug agency did not suffer when Francisco died, but his death tore his family apart. Nonetheless, much antidrug law enforcement work relies almost exclusively on informants like Francisco.

Above all, Francisco's life demonstrates how easily people succumb to the temptation of drug money and how quickly the fortunes of drug traffickers can change. It also exemplifies the inequities and injustices associated with the use of confidential informants by drug warriors.

The following account is presented from the standpoint of Francisco's brother.

Francisco

In 1996, Francisco's cousin went to Juárez and was kidnapped. The kidnappers called Francisco, and he said, "I'll make a deal with you: I'll come over and [you] let my cousin go and I'll stay." The kidnappers—narco-traffickers—knew Francisco was an informant who was working with the FBI. The FBI was involved. This was to be Francisco's last drug transaction, and then he was going to quit trafficking. His son-in-law said Francisco's wife gave him an ultimatum—to get out of the business or she would leave him. Some of the family wondered what Francisco was up to and asked what he was doing. He said he was taking care of the family.

I am for legalizing pot. I think the government cut their own head off by making drugs illegal and then having lots of crime. The FBI was using Francisco. They wanted informants and leads. As far as they are concerned, if an informant gets killed by traffickers, *ni modo* [tough luck].

Family Background

The family farm was in the Lower Valley of El Paso. My dad and mom lived there for twenty years. When Dad got old and depressed, they put him in a behavioral center. My father was macho, a worker. He had big hands and dressed like a cowboy. When he was sent to the behavioral center, he was told by the staff, "If you don't make your bed, you won't get breakfast." Dad thought, "I've never made a bed in my life." The staff said, "Today we'll go to the zoo." "I don't want to do that," father said. To him, life was working on machines—work, work, work. He was a very successful man.

Dad recounted, "In 1944–1945, I crossed the bridge with five pesos in my pocket." He was from Chihuahua City. He was a self-taught mechanic. My mother died at the age of ninety. *Nos dio mucha lata* [She gave us a lot of trouble] when she was very old. She smoked for seventy-five years, started at fourteen, never quit until three months before she died. We're all from Chihuahua City. I came to El Paso when I was four years old. Chihuahua was small. There were only two car agencies, or car-repair shops. Dad was working in one. They decided to strike. He was the leader of the strike, and so was blackballed. Then he was doing carpentry and adobe work that brought him to El Paso.

Dad had a friend from International Harvester. He was offered a job at International Harvester and accepted it at the end of World War II. International Harvester was located on Montana Street, but burned down, and then was located on Cotton Street. Dad came first; then Mom came. She was pregnant with my brother. We all looked like dad. My brothers and I are bald now like dad. Mom said, "I'm not moving until I give birth." I have a passport picture of her holding a baby. We came to Juárez and got papers. We had lived in a decent three-bedroom house in Chihuahua that had four and a half acres of land. In El Paso, we had to live all together in one room in the Hollywood Hotel for six months. It was Mom, Dad, and the two children. There were no apartments available in all El Paso. There was a building freeze at that time due to World War II. We went to a little school called Dios Proveerá [God Will Provide] that was run by nuns. We went to that school and learned to read and write Spanish first.

From the hotel we moved to Third Street and Oregon, 208 East Third Street. We attended Sacred Heart School, three blocks from home. We lived in a three-room tenement for six months. Mom gave three hundred dollars to the landlord for an old stove and sofa—really a *mordida* [bribe] to get preference, since so few apartments were available. We moved to the northeast edge of El Paso in Chivas Town, [named thus because] everyone had goats. It was a little community. We lived outside of town and had a big barn. Later, this barn became a house, and my mom lived there. After her death, we sold that house.

Chivas Town was like a colonia. Alabama Street [now in central El

Paso] was still a rough road and not paved yet. We came from Mexico right into the community of other Mexican people. There was no school then. My uncle had many goats—he was a shepherd—and never learned English. We walked to town.

We were a well-known family, but not famous. Altogether my parents had five boys and one adopted boy—Mom's sister's son; she died and we raised him. The adopted brother was the oldest brother, José, and the youngest was Francisco. José was a mechanic. Dad took him to work with him. They worked together for forty years. Dad worked at International Harvester. He made sixty to eighty dollars per week. We had money, and we didn't know how to spend it. It was during World War II, and there was rationing. We used rations and stamps. There was nothing to buy in the stores. Francisco was born in the Segundo Barrio ten years after me. International Harvester was a diesel shop. Dad worked for various agencies, including International Harvester, Riegel Motors, Rudolph Chevrolet, and he retired at International Harvester. When he first got to International Harvester, in 1944, he was asked, "When do you want to start?" "Right now," he answered, and took off his white shirt and went to work.

Dad's dream was to have a farm. Dad started the farm in Guadalupe in the Valle de Juárez. Dad and his three brothers bought the farm and then later sold it. In Guadalupe, they called my dad *el Americano* because he lived in the U.S. and *porque era de ojos azules, güero, alto* [because he was blue eyed, blond, and tall]. He was macho in the sense of being proud and providing for his family. A very handsome man. He was offered welfare benefits, but rejected them, saying, "Thank you very much, I don't need anyone's help." When his wife got some kind of charity once, he said, "Don't tell the boys what happened." He never accepted a handout. He put us through private school at Cathedral [a Catholic parochial school].

The second-oldest boy was Adolfo, who became a real estate broker and took care of our parents when they were old and ill. My father was a man who has worked all his life in physical work. When he couldn't work and his son Francisco died, he became very depressed. Mom received all the pain and distress when Francisco disappeared. It was her birthday, and we were all there for the birthday party. He never arrived. I said angrily, "Where's Pancho [nickname for Francisco]? He knows it's Mom's birthday."

The third boy, Raúl, works for the Texas Highway Department as a civil engineer. Those that wanted to study in college did so. I am the fourth boy. I am a retired schoolteacher. I taught science for thirty-eight years at a school in northeast El Paso. All the brothers went to Cathedral High School except for the oldest, José, who went to Lydia Patterson. Jesús is a pharmacist at Walgreens. José was fired right before he retired from Rudolph Chevrolet, because the company wanted to avoid paying benefits. He was fifty-seven then and tried to get a GED [general equivalency diploma] after that.

Francisco's Life

Francisco was born in 1950. *El empezó a dar lata, era muy raro, tenía mucha personalidad, pero era irresponsable* [He started causing trouble from an early age, he was strange, he had a lot of personality but he was very irresponsible]. It took him three high schools to graduate. First he went to Cathedral, and then to Jesuit High School. He was spoiled, *el consentido*, and he had an inferiority-superiority complex. He graduated from Austin High School. He went to school when he felt like it. He was not into drugs or alcohol. He liked nature; he caught catfish from the Rio Grande. He was also a deer and elk hunter. One time he got a job, he had been there one month. It was hunting season, and he asked if he could take off a week to go hunting. The boss said no, so he quit, *con niños y todo* [with children and everything]. For a living he did *un poquito de todo* [a little bit of everything]. Eventually, he opened a mechanic shop. He was a good mechanic, a self-taught individual. Beto Rocha, who had a mechanic shop on Piedras Street, said Francisco was so accomplished that he taught him to be a mechanic.

Francisco was a *transero*, that is, he was good at manipulating people. He began passing out rubber checks. The judge said, "I am going to teach you a lesson," and sentenced him to Huntsville state prison. The judge said my brother had been in front of him several times. Francisco was married to a woman who was similar to him. She divorced him. They engaged in *puras transas* [purely fraudulent actions]. They bought things with rubber checks. They passed *un chequecito* [a little check] for thousands of dollars, and it bounced. He rented a place to do mechanic work, but the government closed and confiscated it because he did not pay the rent. He was always like that. His kindergarten teacher said, "He is so intelligent that he can avoid doing any work." Something happened, and he had to stay a year in Huntsville prison. He came out a master criminal. He learned from the people in prison and made the connections. He was about thirty years old when he was at Huntsville.

He had four kids when he went to prison. He was a very loving person. He would scold his kids, but he would take them fishing. He never went to prison after that.

When he got out of prison, he fixed cars at his house. He didn't have a formal job. A lot of time lapsed between the time he was in prison and when he disappeared. Pushing drugs, that is what he was doing. The only lead I got was [when] he asked if I could buy him a cell phone and put it in my name. He didn't have any credit, of course. He needed the cell phone to talk to the FBI. He would organize drug loads, and then inform the FBI about them.

[He set up one last drug deal and informed the FBI about it.] He said to the FBI, "Let the shit go through, and let it go all the way to its destination. They are waiting for it in Phoenix." The guy made it all the way to Phoenix. He parked in a vacant lot; the driver left. A security guard came out and found the car. It had a million-dollar load of coke, which was busted, but not by the FBI. The Phoenix cops busted it. The shipment was busted, but not intentionally by Francisco's actions. It was bad luck. [Francisco had intended for the load to go through so that the FBI could trace all the people involved in the deal and so that his drug-trafficking associates would not know that he had informed on them.]

At the time, Francisco lived in the Lower Valley of El Paso on a one-to-two-acre place. Then he bought a trailer home with five to six acres. He was divorced. I remember [that] when they took him to Huntsville, his first wife went bananas. She went to a psych ward, and I had to take care of Francisco's kids. I took care of Francisco's four kids along with my own three. Francisco was not an easy person to live with. He was a kind of person who was not predictable, but the kind who started wobbling, zigzagging. He was not a big womanizer, just a little bit. *El estaba bajito, lleno, una cara muy bonita. Se vestía de cowboy, usaba sombreros* [He was short, stocky and he had a pretty face. He dressed like a cowboy, he wore cowboy hats].

In my last conversation with Francisco, he said, "I am very worried. I fly from New York to California." I said, "¡Qué vida!" [What a life!]. He replied, "¡*Uf!* Most of the time I don't even get out of the plane." He was probably making contacts with drug people. I'm sure he was making money from both sides and getting money from both sides—doing good work for the drug traffickers and the FBI. But you couldn't tell that he was making money. He liked the countryside. He wasn't the type to show off his wealth. He was so disorganized that he didn't know where his money went. His house was very nice, however. He had fixed it up with drug money.

Francisco's Death

When Francisco was killed, Amado Carrillo Fuentes was in charge of the Juárez cartel. Carrillo's men killed Francisco [*Era Carrillo el que tenía el dominio, los que estaban alrededor de Carrillo mataron a Francisco*]. The cartel was angry at Francisco because they blamed him for the loss of the load in Phoenix. First, Francisco's cousin was kidnapped at a store in Juárez and taken to a narco-house and blindfolded. Francisco's cousin was held at the house in Juárez while the traffickers contacted Francisco. They moved him around to several safe houses before they got ahold of Francisco. The cousin said they referred to the person in charge as El Señor [a reference to Amado Carrillo Fuentes].

Carrillo arrived and the traffickers called Francisco. The traffickers told Francisco they would kill his cousin unless he went to Juárez to replace him. The FBI told Francisco not to go to Juárez, but he went anyway. Francisco replaced his cousin in Juárez. The FBI went looking for Francisco. They had leads that he was in a certain house, but when they got there, the drug people had already taken him somewhere else. The FBI went looking for Francisco *a la brava, ni qué permiso, ni nada* [aggressively, without permission from the Mexican government or anything]. But the FBI didn't find him, and he was murdered. His body was later found along with many others in a narco-cemetery that was discovered in Juárez.

I graduated from Sacred Heart elementary school in 1957. At the school's fifty-year anniversary, it was like a big family. One of the girls there, my classmate, also lost a relative, her husband, because of the drug war. He was disappeared in Juárez too. The family was doing fine until then, but now she has to work as a clerk at Wal-Mart.

Francisco's cousin survived, and is a medical doctor now. The killing of Francisco happened thirteen years ago. My family is very large, so I am worried about further reprisals from the Juárez cartel.

A Juárez Policeman Fighting Drug Traffickers

The interview that follows illuminates the difficulties of engaging in police work on the border, where law-enforcement officers are often outgunned by drug traffickers. The story of the Ciudad Juárez municipal policeman also provides valuable information on the inner workings of the corruption network that links law-enforcement agencies, drug dealers, and other criminals in Mexico, and particularly in downtown Juárez. The intimate relationship between police agencies, politicians, and narco-traffickers is a primary feature of the complex social-political-geographic entity known as *la plaza*.

The cops take money from the narcos in exchange for protecting drug loads and killing or kidnapping enemies of the drug-dealing group in control of the *plaza* or territory. They also pass on valuable information and government secrets to cartel members, and warn them of impending crackdowns, raids, and potential apprehension. When one cartel attempts to take over a drug *plaza* from another cartel—as is occurring now in Ciudad Juárez—one of their first actions is to assassinate cops on the payroll of the rival cartel and replace them with their own people. Alternatively, rival cops are confronted by cartel hit men with the dilemma of *plata o plomo* [literally, "silver or lead," that is, accept a bribe to join the new cartel or else be murdered]. Once the police force and other relevant police, military, or political entities have been purged of the enemy cartel's loyalists, the new cartel has free rein over the *plaza*.

Beyond the policeman's claim of having been an honest cop, and the discussion of police corruption, the larger story of this interview is that Mexican antidrug cops and soldiers die or are seriously injured in large numbers while U.S. law enforcement suffers relatively few casualties in the war on drugs. As of December 2008, more than forty Juárez cops have been murdered this year by *narcotraficantes*. Nevertheless, the U.S. government is quick to blame Mexico for the problems created by drugs, even though the number one factor in generating the Mexican drug business is the huge demand for illicit drugs in the United States. This massive demand for narcotics fuels organized crime across Latin America. Moreover, the weapons used by Mexican narcos to commit violent crimes come almost exclusively from the United States.

As a policeman in Ciudad Juárez, this interviewee became acquainted with various players in the drug-dealing and street-crime underworld, especially in the downtown area. In the central district near the international border, bars and brothels outnumber other businesses, and provide fertile ground for the cocaine and heroin trade and other crimes, such as theft and assault. His detailed descriptions of the various types of pickpockets, their often violent methods, and their hangouts give the reader a feel for the dangerous streets of Juárez. This account, then, indicates just how normal and commonplace drug selling, violent crime, and corruption have become on the border.

Another valuable insight provided by the former policeman is how local, state, and federal cops in Mexico obstruct one another's efforts instead of cooperating. He describes a Wild West shootout between the municipal police and the federal police in downtown Juárez in the late 1990s that left three federal police officers dead. This event demonstrated the extreme divisions among Mexican police agencies. They are, in effect, often working against one another. The conflicts between different Mexican agencies have less to do with ideological differences or jurisdictional squabbles than with their alliances with specific drug-trafficking organizations.

Finally, the policeman's story is a classic example of the dilemma faced by all Mexican policemen: accept bribes and become corrupt (thus playing a double game that almost always ends badly), or refuse to take bribes and risk facing the narco-traffickers' wrath. Either way, Mexican policemen are caught in the old maxim known as "La Ley de Herodes," which states: "O te chingas o te jodes." [Herod's Law: You either get fucked or you get screwed].

The Policeman

As a child, I suffered quite a bit. Life was hard. I lived in the Monterrey neighborhood, halfway between downtown and the mountains on the west side of Juárez, near the area where the inscription "La Biblia es la

Verdad, Leela" [The Bible is the Truth, Read It] can be seen on the hillside. By the time I was eight or nine years old, I was already working as a shoeshine boy. I charged a dollar for every pair of shoes I shined. That was a lot of money for me at the time. I gave most of the money to my family, and I only kept five or six pesos for myself. When I was ten or twelve, I started selling *curiosidades* [souvenirs for tourists] to the shopkeepers at the Juárez Market area.

My father sold secondhand clothes in the market located near the Revolución school. My mother worked as a maid in El Paso. She made more money than my father. I would finish my school day and immediately walk over to join my father at his market stall. My father died when he was in his fifties. I had six siblings: three sisters and three brothers. As a kid, I was very active, and already knew my way around the streets of Juárez. Then I started working as a messenger for a studio photographer, delivering photos, and continued going to school. For a while, I worked as a waiter at the Casino Alianza, a big dance hall. By then, I was around eighteen years old. Because of all my jobs and my wandering nature, I got to know the city well from an early age.

When I was a teenager, I met some Jehovah's Witnesses. They wanted to take me with them to work in New Mexico, and then another religious group wanted to take me to Canada. I never accepted those offers, because I didn't know what would happen to me if I went with them. Eventually, I was able to finish a vocational degree and become a computer and electronic technician. Immediately after I graduated as a computer technician, I wanted to further my studies, and perhaps complete a college career, but I was just too busy working at various minor jobs to continue going to school. I remember that while I was still in grade school, and then later during the years I spent studying my vocational career, I kept hearing that fixing computers was "the career of the future." But there was very little work in maquiladora plants at that time. Upon graduating, the only decent jobs available to me were as a cop or as a soldier. I wanted to have medical insurance, and I can now say that was one of the main reasons, besides money, that I became a policeman.

During this time, I completed my [mandatory] military service, which consisted of one year of reporting to the local army outpost for training, once a week, just on Saturdays. I was offered jobs as a *mojado* [wetback] in the U.S., but I wasn't interested in leaving Mexico. Then one day I saw that fateful recruiting ad for the local police force that said: "You, young Juarense, can help your community." So I weighed my two options, becoming a professional soldier or a policeman, and decided to join the police force. Finally, at eighteen, I signed up to be a cop.

At the police academy, cadets were taught personal defense, finger-printing, and first aid, and we also received training in pistol shooting and learned about the penal code and penal law. I was at the police academy for six months. I liked the police academy very much. In those days [1980], compared to now, being a cop was a much more honorable job. So there I was: I finally had a job with a good salary and, above all, medical insurance, and on top of all that, I got to serve my community. I can truly say that it gave me a lot of personal satisfaction to serve people as a policeman.

Fighting Pickpockets

So I became a member of the Ciudad Juárez Police Department. I was eighteen years old and rarin' to go. I really believed in those police recruiting ads. My motto at the time was "To help my fellow man," and I really wanted, with all my heart, to do social labor. There was a lot of corruption back then in the police force, and many cops felt that if they worked honestly, they would be crushed [*si trabajo derecho, me tumban*]. There was a saying among Juárez cops: If you want to be an old cop, you've got to learn to play dumb and just look the other way [*Si quieres llegar a policía viejo, hazte pendejo*].

When I first joined the police force, I worked the downtown beat, mainly combating pickpockets and other common criminals. Back then, pickpockets targeted mainly elderly people as their victims. We would put the thieves in jail whenever we caught them, but just as fast, the judges would let them go free. Boy, did this make me mad! Once freed, a day or two after I had arrested them, the pickpockets would see me on the street and tease me by saying, "As you can see, they let me out of jail, ha ha ha!" So I started inventing names and addresses of people the pickpockets had supposedly robbed, in order to put them in jail, at least for a while.

When I started out as a cop, I was part of the *boinas negras* [black berets], urban policemen. We were the ones in charge of walking around and keeping order in the downtown area, especially in and around Juárez Avenue. We also broke up fights in bars. People came from El Paso to Juárez to party, and there were a lot of brawls. The corner of Mina and Velarde streets was a hot spot back then, since there were a lot of thieves and pickpockets that used to hang around there by the street market, where there are a lot of stalls, especially at night. The pickpockets are just waiting until the cantinas close to grab the drunk people and then ¡*pas*! [they would rob them].

Basically, there were two types of pickpockets:

1. The ones that worked during the day used mostly the *dos de bastos* method [the "two of clubs" technique, in which the index and middle finger are inserted into a pants or suit pocket in pliers-like fashion, smoothly pulling out the wallet without the victim even noticing]. These guys have *manos de seda* [silky-smooth hands]; the victims don't even realize they are being robbed. A lot of these guys used a casually folded jacket or coat over their hands to cover up their moves. Many of them would also bump their victims to distract their attention and thus prevent them further from feeling the extraction of their wallets from their pockets. And then when the victims were walking away, they would think, "Where is my wallet?"
2. The ones that plied their trade during the night used knives, and if the person resisted, they would stab them.

At night, one had to be very careful in the area around 16 de Septiembre, Mariscal, and Segunda de Ugarte streets. They were chock full of pickpockets, as was the area around Ignacio Mejía Street, and also around the downtown gymnasium. I worked with the black berets from 1980 to 1983, and did stints working all three shifts: the morning shift, the afternoon shift, and the night shift. Back then, the night shift was from twelve midnight to six. It was the hardest. From time to time, we would conduct raids on the pickpockets, since we already knew them by sight and by name. However, they would just laugh and say, "That's okay. They'll let me out right away anyway." My job was to watch the downtown area carefully by constantly walking up, down, through, and around it, together with a partner. One person by himself couldn't handle the work.

The Varieties of Police Corruption

When I began as a cop, I was only allowed to use a nightstick [*tolete*] and tear gas. Then, later, I got a pistol. Being a cop was the best-paid job available to me at the time. It was better paid than maquiladora plant work. One couldn't survive on the salary they paid. I was single, so I gave half of my salary to my family and kept the other half for myself.

Back then, the most prevalent form of police corruption consisted of giving bribes to the captains in order to stay in the downtown area, where the action was, instead of being shifted to the police stations, which was boring work, just writing up reports of citizen complaints and listening to the police radio. You just gave the captain a few bills, and you wouldn't be switched. It wasn't serious corruption, such as that involving working for the drug traffickers, as happens today.

I knew two captains of the Juárez police who were corrupt. They showed us big wads of bills that they couldn't have obtained from their salary. They must have been involved in something. Later, they were both forcibly disappeared and never heard from again. One was Captain ——, and the other was Captain —— ["disappeared" in 2001]. Another common form of police corruption in the downtown area was that, for example, in exchange for not taking an individual to jail for urinating in public, the individual would offer us a 50-peso bribe, and thus he would avoid paying the 100- or 200-peso fine. This was just common corruption by the rank-and-file. Now, the top authorities [*los meros, meros*] don't even show their faces. A new police chief arrives, and in order to let the cops work, the prospective policemen must send him a briefcase full of money.

One thing I forgot to mention about pickpockets: not all the ones we caught were allowed to pay us bribes, since this would have caused me and other cops to become compromised. I mean, after all, I joined the police force out of true conviction. No one gave me the job because I paid them. Now, the bosses of the drug trafficking, in order to have people inside the police department, tell their men to go to the police authorities and tell them that they must be allowed to work as cops. This is the real serious corruption. And now people from the drug business go to a cop and say, "Take this money," and if the cop doesn't take it, the next day he or one of his relatives ends up dead. The public used to have more respect for and fear of the cops. Not now.

The police hierarchy consists of the police chief, or *el director*, then the *comandantes*, then the *tenientes*, the *sargentos*, and, at the bottom rung, the regular policemen. The *sargento* extracts money from the regular policemen and passes the money up the chain of command. I left the police force for a year in 1983. I had a problem with one of my immediate superiors, who was pressuring me, and I didn't like it, so I quit. I came back to the force in 1984 and started working with the Policía Especial, guarding banks, dances, and 7–11-type convenience stores. At times, I guarded the Madererías del Norte [a local chain of hardware stores].

During the period that I worked with the Policía Especial [1984–1987], I caught a lot of thieves and many times had to physically fight with them in order to subdue them. During this period, I got an award and a check from Madererías del Norte for my work there. The check was paid to me through the police system. I didn't accept it directly from the business, because that would have been illegal. Then, in 1985, I also got an award from the city government of Juárez.

These awards made me feel good, because one of the police captains didn't like me and used to make fun of me and call me just half a cop because of my slight stature. People thought they could beat up on me because I was short and skinny, but they were wrong. Once I got into a fight with a guy. I turned him in for illegally wearing a police beret when he was just a regular citizen. He was a huge guy who thought that he could easily beat me up. He said to me, "So you think you can take me in?" ¡Pas, pas, pas! I hit him and hit him until I subdued him, and then I dragged him by the belt all the way back to the station. My fellow cops were amazed that I could do it.

After being in the Policía Especial, I worked with the Policía Urbana from 1987 to 1990. I liked being active, and I didn't like to stay in one place, so in 1990, I started working at the patrol division. I liked being a patrolman because I got to see a lot more of the city and its many different kinds of people. They sent me to patrol the area in east Juárez where the rich people live. In one incident that occurred in the Los Nogales residential district, a wealthy neighborhood, a *junior* [young man with rich parents] was making a lot of noise in public at three in the morning. Then my partner and I heard someone whistling. The young guy was with a girl, and he had a half-empty bottle of liquor after hours. When I approached them, the guy insulted us: "¿Y qué, cabrones?" [What's up, assholes?]. He was showing off in front of his girlfriend. He felt like he was Juan Camaney [a supermacho character played by Luis de Alba in 1980s–1990s Mexican B movies]. Then he said, "Vamos a la chingada!" [Let's get it on, suckers!]. So my partner replied, "¿Te sientes muy salsa?" [So you feel like a big man, huh?]. My partner and I ended up beating the living daylights out of him [le pusimos una zapatiza]. Then, once he was in the patrol car, he began fighting again, and we had to hit him some more. Once we got him in front of the judge, we learned this young man was none other than the son of the Juárez mayor, and instantly both my partner and I knew that spelled trouble for us.

Upon finding out who he was dealing with, the police chief immediately ripped up our uniforms to make it look like the young guy had attacked us, two innocent policemen on patrol. No matter. We were arrested anyway, on charges of beating up the mayor's son, and ended up spending forty-eight hours in jail. Then a journalist, a friend of mine, came into the fray. He defended us. "You can't fire them for this," he said to the police officials. They finally agreed. So they let us go free, but only with the condition that the journalist keep the story out of the papers. But it came out in the newspaper anyway. "El que es buen juez por su casa empieza" [The good judge starts by cleaning up his own house] was the headline of the story. I was steadfast. I was only doing my job, following the letter of the law.

Back then, I had a police partner who was abusive and quite corrupt. He detested having to take people to the station, and would rather try to extort a bribe from such individuals. He constantly used cocaine. He would always hang around with *madrinas* [unofficial police "helpers" dedicated to corruption] and other types of lowlifes. I told him not to be like that, but he didn't pay attention. He also played both sides of the fence, first getting bribes from drug sellers, and then extorting bribes from drug buyers. He was warned to stop this type of thing by the narco-traffickers, but he said that he was independent and could do as he pleased. So the leader of the drug business said, "All right then, have it your way!" And then they set him up. He found out about a dope deal that was supposedly going down on a side street, and went to bust it. But it was actually an ambush. When he got there, the drug dealers were already waiting for him. They shot him, and he died on the spot. He ended up being killed with his own pistol.

The Geography of Crime in Juárez

I must confess: I always liked the danger of being a policeman, the action. Back then, drug sellers were more mobile or were better hidden, compared to today's open *picaderos.* They mainly sold coke and heroin, not pot. In those days, drug pushers walked around to sell their merchandise. When they saw cops, they would run away. So-called *tienditas* developed later, with protection from the police. The police protected the *tienditas,* and the *tienditas* made the money. It was during Jesús Macías's tenure as Juárez mayor [1989–1992] that the *tienditas* emerged and became strong. Before then, drugs were sold mostly in bars, especially in the joints located on and around the corner of Mariscal Street and Segunda de Ugarte Street, such as the Club Paraíso and Pepe's and La Fiesta. Of course, there were a lot of other bars on Mariscal that sold drugs, probably all the ones located on that street between the international bridge and 16 de Septiembre Street. And also in the bars located on La Paz Street, frequented by people who worked in the maquiladora plants.

Today, the *tiendita* system is dominant. There are perhaps more than 500 *tienditas*. If the police functioned the way they were supposed to, the *tienditas* would be wiped out. Because the cops have locations, addresses, streets, they have everything they need to get there. Why don't they show up? Why don't they bust them? Because the cash they are given prevents them from seeing them. Everyone else sees the *tienditas* but them.

In the area by the Green Lantern bar, there was—and still is—a lot of drug dealing and homosexual prostitution. I also remember that in the 6-5-4 Dance Hall, located near Francisco Villa Street [also popularly known as Ferrocarril Street], there were a lot of drugs. The owner of that place also owned La Fiesta and Pepe's. There were also drugs available at La Casa Colorada [a well-known brothel] and all along Mariscal Street. This area is infested with dives [*tugurios de mala muerte*]. Be careful there, and also in Carreño Alley. Don't even think about going down there after midnight! Even if you feel *machín*, like Juan Camaney, don't go! It is very heavy down there. If they know you are not from the area, four or five guys will jump on you.

There is also a similar scene around the bars on La Paz Street, although there are a lot more families in this area and fewer street criminals. A lot of older men go to drink and dance in this area. They pay younger girls to dance with them and let them touch them in the dance halls. This is the girls' business in that area. The girls may also go with the men to the cheap rooms nearby for sex. There are also thieves around there. The whores often work together with the thieves to rip off the old guys at the dance halls and brothels. That's how it works on La Paz Street. It's the old *ley del talón—gana el más fuerte* [law of the boot heel—the strongest one wins].

Interagency Conflicts

I liked to drink when I was a cop, and one of the things I remember is that in those days soldiers and cops would often fight over the same women at La Fiesta. Some of the girls would go with cops, and soldiers got mad at this. The cops fought the soldiers, and then would make their getaway when other cops showed up to deal with the disturbance.

Another thing you often saw back then was criminals and cops drinking close to each other in the same bar—for example, in La Fiesta, in Pepe's, and others in that vicinity. They would buy drinks for us. I used to love to drink. Nowadays, I don't go to cantinas anymore, because in a cantina one of two things is going to happen: either someone is going to hit me, or I'm going to hit someone. Something will happen, there will be problems, and the thing will end in the hospital or in jail.

I was arrested only once for police brutality. I had been assigned to guard a dance at a hall located at the corner of Paseo Triunfo de la República and Lago de Pátzcuaro Street. Everything was going fine until five drunks tried to force their way into the dance, uninvited. When I tried to stop them, they attacked me, five on one. So I pulled out my gun and shot one of them in the leg. That stopped them cold in their tracks. I was subsequently arrested for "injuries and abuse of authority." The kid I shot in the leg ended up lame, but if I hadn't done what I did, the injured party would have been me. I was acquitted by the judge, who treated the incident as a case of self-defense, because I was in the right according to the law. That was fortunate, because the police chief was very corrupt. He was happy if you gave him money, but when I needed his help, he did nothing to defend me. This really angered me, and so I told him the truth: that he was corrupt. I didn't hold back. The press didn't attack me much, because I explained to them what happened.

Back then there were also conflicts between different police jurisdictions. Elías Ramírez [who was accused of acts of corruption and torture] was the *comandante* of the federal judicial police [from 1986–1992]. The office of the federales was located in a house that had been confiscated from criminals near the intersection of Hermanos Escobar Street and Avenida de las Américas, and Tomás Alva Edison Street, behind Bancomer, near a dance hall. During this time, the *madrina* system flourished. The *madrinas* were informal "helpers" who hung around federal policemen and did the dirty work for them. At that time, the federal police did not wear uniforms, so it was often easy for a *madrina* to claim he was, in fact, a bona fide federal cop. However, whenever there was a problem with *madrinas*, the PGR [Procuraduría General de la República; Attorney General's Office], would say, "No, they don't work for us." They would wash their hands of them. Many of these *madrinas* have turned up dead.

At one point, some federal policemen from Mexico City came to Juárez and were acting bossy, throwing their weight around all over the place. The federales were creating a public disturbance, so the Policía

Preventiva came and took away the unruly *federales* to the stone jail [*cárcel de piedra*] in downtown Juárez. So the *federales* sent men with *cuernos de chivo* [literally, "goat horns"; AK-47 machine guns] from their headquarters to free their fellow federal policemen. So we municipal policemen got all of our men together at the jail, and a wild gunfight broke out. You could hear gunshots all over the place. I was there in the thick of the fight. Thank God, none of our men fell, but three *federales* died in the shootout.

Another time, a soldier attempted to kill a secret policeman, but the bullet misfired in his gun. Back then, relations between the *federales* and the city cops were often tense. The municipal police, also called the Preventive Police [Policía Preventiva] was supposed to collaborate with the *federales*, but it didn't always pan out that way. The *federales* in Juárez were, almost to a man, all *chilangos* [from Mexico City] or from outside the region. They thought they were the best and that they could do whatever they wanted. But whenever things got hot for them [that is, when there were allegations of corruption], their superiors would simply send them to another place or region. [This contributed to the tensions between *federales* and local cops, since the locals felt the *federales* enjoyed complete immunity when it came to engaging in criminal acts, including kidnapping, and even murder.]

Rafael Aguilar Guajardo, the head of the Juárez cartel in the mid-eighties and early nineties [before Amado Carrillo Fuentes took over by having him killed in 1993 in Cancún], came out of the Mexican Federal Police, where he was first an agent and then a commander before "retiring" to lead the cartel. Back then, the PGR handled the big cartel drug issues in Juárez. Municipal policemen, like myself, were not concerned with the cartel. In my era, about 50 percent of municipal cops were honest, unlike today. In those days [1986–1992], Fernando Baeza was governor of Chihuahua, and it was the *federales* who were protecting all the drug loads crossing through the state of Chihuahua. The *federales* didn't drive those trucks full of drugs—they just "escorted" them through to make sure no one bothered those drivers and their precious loads.

Whenever a driver of a drug truck was busted by the Juárez municipal police, the federales would intervene to release him from jail. The head of the federal cops would say to the local officials, "You know what? There goes a truck, but I want you to leave it alone" [¿Sabes qué? ahí va un camión y quiéro que no me lo molestes]. If I or another cop stopped a vehicle filled with drugs, our superiors would call us and tell us not to get involved in problems, but to just release it. If I would have disobeyed, then I would have been fired or killed the next day. They wouldn't let you do your job in an honest way.

I couldn't arrest the big drug dealers, because they had their stuff in warehouses and if you stopped them on the street, they would have nothing on them. The closest I ever got to them was when I was ordered to guard the mansion of Rafael Muñoz Talavera [a local founder of the Juárez cartel] when he was under investigation. The cops that knew the top drug lords got involved with them, and almost all of them eventually ended up dead. The only reason I'm alive today is because I didn't mix with the narcos and I wasn't obsessed with money. The drug dealers tried to bribe me, and after I retired from the police, they asked me to drive loaded drug cars across the bridge for three thousand dollars a car, but I refused. I said to them, "It's a good offer but I prefer to eat *frijolitos*." If you get involved in the drug world, you can never get out. For a while, a person can enjoy the high life of *billetes* [large amounts of cash], cars, and women, but these pleasures have their price. There comes a time when it all ends.

During the midnineties, Juárez mayor Ramón Galindo named-_____ as Ciudad Juarez's chief of police. In my opinion, this chief was very corrupt, and so things remained the same: the *federales* were almost openly giving protection to the narco-traffickers and their drug-load drivers, and everyone knew it. I also believe that rich families are responsible for the killings of women in Juárez [that began during this time]. But even so, two people I have to admit I did like, during their tenures as mayors of Juárez, were Francisco Barrio [1980–1986] and Francisco Villarreal [1992–1995]. We policemen received a lot of benefits because of Barrio.

Throughout my career as a cop, I fought with criminals many times, but was never seriously hurt. When I worked as a Policía Especial, we, the cops, had to buy the best assignments, such as guarding the American consulate, since the best bribes were always there. As the saying goes, "He who has the most saliva swallows the most *pinole*" [a traditional food made of ground, toasted corn]. But since I didn't pay bribes to my superiors, I was sent all over the place, all over the city. "No me voy a quemar por 50 pesos" [I won't ruin my reputation for a mere fifty pesos]. That's the reason I didn't accept bribes. And since I didn't sell myself for money, I never had any problems.

Whenever I busted criminals connected to cops in corruption networks, other cops always told me: don't get involved in this area, you'll end up having problems. But I never listened to them. So I always ended up being switched around. The authorities would try to keep me away from areas where major drug rings operated, because my investigations would have gotten to the bottom of the matter. They told me, "Your job is to catch the common criminals, not narcotics."

Something else that went on that I disapproved of was the use of clandestine cells where prisoners were tortured. This was when Refugio ("Cuco") Ruvalcaba was a commander of the state judicial police. [Ultimately, he and his sons were brutally murdered by the Juárez cartel.] Municipal cops dressed in civilian clothes engaged in investigations. They had no scruples; they were sadists. When they caught people suspected of crimes—or political dissidents—they threw them in a *calabozo* [a dungeon-like cell that was little more than a hole in the ground with a ladder going down into it] located in a house on Coyoacán Street in the Colonia Hidalgo. There were also other, similar clandestine jails in other parts of the city. The prisoners were tortured using the *chicharra* [bare electrical wires attached to the skin] and the *tehuacanazo* [forcing carbonated water into the nose and lungs], among other methods. They were horribly tortured, and then they would admit to anything, screaming, "It was, it was me, it was me." You would see their faces, the faces of these *compas* [guys] in agony—wow! Francisco Barrio did away with these practices.

Getting Shot

When I was shot in November of 1990, my partner and I had been following a drug trafficker's car from the San Lorenzo curve westward. Initially, we had spotted him at the Motel Las Fuentes. When he saw us, he immediately took off very fast in his car. We suspected he was up to something, so we went after him. The guy claimed he was a *madrina*, but he was actually connected with El Greñas [Gilbero Ontiveros, a well-known Juárez drug lord, recently released from prison]. We chased the trafficker onto Paseo Triunfo de la República and then from 16 de Septiembre Street to Lerdo Street [in downtown Juárez], and from there to the Soriana Sanders area. When we caught up to him, he tried to hit us with his car. He was running stoplights, and it became a wild chase, as in a movie. I had taken several courses in urban policing, so I knew what I was doing.

Then the tires of the narco-trafficker's truck were blown out by the train tracks. When we engaged in a direct confrontation with the narco, I was in the patrol car with my partner, Pedro Cobos Escobedo, who was driving. I was trying to avoid a dangerous encounter, so I told my partner, "Let's let him go for now, and we'll catch up to him later." But my partner said, "No way!" [¡Ni madres!] and kept chasing him. My partner was only about twenty years old.

When we caught up to him, the bad guy surrendered, putting his hands up, but then he suddenly pulled out a pistol and shot us at point-blank range. My partner was killed instantly, and I ended up in the hospital with nine bullet holes in me. The shooter didn't even give us a chance to talk to him and come to some kind of agreement. Who knows if we would have accepted his offer anyway, if he had offered us a bribe to let him go? Afterward, I received threats from the narcos.

After I was shot, I was taken to the hospital in a patrol car. It took ten minutes to get to the hospital. I was treated at the Centro Médico de Especialidades. The shooting had occurred at three A.M., and I felt like all the events after the shooting were happening in slow motion. The narco had emptied his pistol in me, and I was in bad shape. I had very little blood left in my body. It was like in the cartoons where someone is given a glass of water and he has so many bullet holes in him that the water leaks right out. That was the condition I was in. I was in a coma for three days, but to me it felt like it had only been three hours. When I woke up, I immediately asked for my partner. But my partner was dead.

Later, it seemed to me quite ironic that he had died, precisely, on his birthday. We had been very good friends, my partner and I. It had always been as if we were one person. He watched out for me, and I watched out for him. But he was very aggressive. I remember being calmer than my partner on the day of the shooting. He insisted on chasing the narco.

After the shooting, I was in the hospital from November of 1990 to January of 1991. When the doctors first saw me, they said, "Only a miracle will save you." When I was in the hospital, my intestines were sticking out of my abdomen and draining large quantities of infected fluids for a very long time. Also, my liver and lungs had been punctured. My hospitalization incurred a total bill of 500,000 pesos. The recuperation was a lengthy process. I was in a wheelchair for a while.

At the time of the shooting, Jesús Macías was the Juárez mayor, and Carlos Ponce was the Mayor pro tem. They were anxious to get me out of the hospital because my treatment was expensive. Guards were posted outside my hospital room to protect me from possible retaliation by the drug traffickers. The guy who shot me was interned at the Juárez General Hospital because of the injuries he suffered during the shooting. I had grazed him twice. The brother of the shooter tried to kill me while

I was hospitalized at the Centro Médico de Especialidades. He came to the hospital with some men holding *cuernos de chivo* [AK-47s], but the guards wouldn't let them in, and they called in reinforcements.

All the Juárez TV stations, Channels 44, 56, and 5, did stories on the shooting. Later, a *corrido* about the shooting and me was composed by a group of cops who also happened to be musicians. The *corrido* tells the whole story of how and why the shooting took place. The captain who had saved my life after the shooting was the one who wrote the lyrics of that *corrido*. Then, several months later, the shooter's brothers were caught for kidnapping. They claimed, falsely, that they were federal judicial police. Incidentally, the shooter, who is originally from Juárez, is now a free man. Several weeks after the shooting, when the narcos offered me money to keep quiet about what happened to us and why, I simply said, "There's no need for that. Let's just leave it alone and forget about it. As far as I'm concerned, it's water under the bridge. It's something in the past, buried and forgotten."

Even the mayors of Juárez and the chiefs of the city police were in cahoots with the narcos, so what was the point in fighting it? The killers offered me 12,000 pesos, about $1,200, to keep quiet, but I declined to accept the money [and I did not pursue the issue]. My life was more important than accepting the money. In my view, life goes on, and life is beautiful [*la vida sigue y la vida es bonita*].

In total, at the end of my career, I had eighteen years of police experience. If I hadn't been shot, I'd probably still be a cop. Actually, after the shooting, I worked for four or five more years as a cop until I retired in 1998. The police administration had been pressuring me. They have been kicking out all the older policemen in order to avoid having to pay them large pensions. Today, there are mostly young cops. Most of them are fairly new to the force. Because I was honest during my police career, corrupt cops constantly tried to catch me accepting bribes. They even tried to set me up so that they could catch me in the act of taking bribes, but I never accepted them, so they were never able to pin this on me. In the end, I can honestly say that I never got involved in corruption—that's why I'm poor and still alive.

Journalism and Drug Trafficking:
Covering the Narco Beat on the Border

In addition to policemen, Mexican reporters have been especially hard hit by drug violence, to the point that Mexico has become one of the most dangerous countries in the world for journalists. Since 2000, around fifty journalists have been assassinated, and hundreds threatened or assaulted, mostly in drug-related incidents.[1] Journalists from Ciudad Juárez's two main newspapers, *El Diario de Juárez* and *Norte*, fearing reprisals for their reporting on drug trafficking and drug violence, have requested asylum in El Paso. Both papers have minimized their coverage of drug stories.

Rafael Nuñez's story typifies the various ways in which drug traffickers and their accomplices attempt to intimidate reporters into silence. Mexican journalists are notoriously poorly paid, although some supplement their paltry earnings by blackmailing politicians or accepting bribes in exchange for writing stories that favor particular politicians or traffickers. So it is important to note that drug-trafficking organizations not only squelch unfavorable news reports, but also attempt to manipulate or extort media coverage favorable to a particular cartel's perspective or interests. Given how underpaid Mexican journalists are for doing such dangerous work, it is remarkable how many are still willing to risk their lives by publishing stories that incriminate drug-trafficking organizations or high-ranking government officials.

Journalists, in fact, have been the greatest source of inside information about Mexican drug trafficking, since law-enforcement authorities, in addition to having been infiltrated by cartel members, have also been reluctant to publicly divulge details about the drug underworld. Manuel Buendía, the first major print journalist murdered (in 1984) by drug interests, filled his weekly newspaper column, "Red Privada" (Private Network), and several books with reports on government corruption, the emerging drug cartels, and CIA meddling in Mexican affairs. But the greatest Mexican drug reporter was Jesús Blancornelas, who became the editor of the muckraking weekly *Zeta* after its talented editor, Héctor "El Gato" Félix, was murdered by the bodyguards of Jorge Hank Rhon, a wealthy, notoriously corrupt former mayor of Tijuana, in 1988.

Blancornelas himself was nearly murdered by a squad of Tijuana cartel hit men in 1997, and another editor of *Zeta*, Francisco Ortiz Franco, was killed by traffickers in 2004. Blancornelas narrowly survived the bloody assassination attempt, which claimed the life of his driver. Despite his injuries and the need to be protected by government bodyguards for the rest of his life, Blancornelas continued to publish stunningly detailed exposés of the drug trade and government complicity in his weekly column until his death, in 2006. Blancornelas also published half a dozen long books with intimate information about various cartels, but especially the Tijuana cartel.

Ricardo Ravelo is the current star reporter covering the Mexican drug beat for *Proceso*, although recently this key newsweekly has chosen not to put bylines on drug stories in order to protect the safety of its reporters and correspondents. Another newspaper, *El Mañana de Nuevo Laredo*, simply ceased publishing drug stories after several local reporters were murdered and the paper's office was bombed by members of the Gulf cartel. A U.S. journalist, Alfredo Corchado, also received death threats after publishing major stories on the drug violence in Laredo and the brutal atrocities of the Zetas.

We owe a great debt to the often thankless and valiant efforts of these journalists, including photographers and TV cameramen, to disseminate information about the staggering geographical scope, carnage, and broad social, political, and economic impact of the drug trade. In addition to the many lives lost, one of the great tragedies of the drug war has been the drying up of the flow of information as drug-trafficking organizations grow more powerful and more embedded in webs of government corruption. The ability of traffickers to stifle the press and attack or corrupt public institutions has damaged civil society and raised cartels' influence to unprecedented levels. The drug war is thus fought on multiple levels, including military confrontations and the struggle to shape and control ideas and information.

Rafael Nuñez

I am a bilingual investigative journalist, and my name is Rafael Nuñez, but all my colleagues call me Rafa. My good friends in Juárez call me El Despistado [the Clueless One]. I got the nickname because of the way I interviewed people when I arrived to the Ciudad Juárez–El Paso area in the 1990s and worked for the Juárez newspaper *Norte*.

I've been many things in my life: football player, professional soccer player, teacher, television program director, seeker of mystical experiences, translator, and journalist. Yet sometimes I compare my life to that of the main character in the classic Mexican novel *La Vida Inútil de Pito Pérez* [The Useless Life of Pito Pérez], by José Rubén Romero. And my life has indeed been useless if you follow that utilitarian, philistine philosophy that values material things over everything else. I happen to think there is more to life than just accumulating money and material wealth.

I was born in Manteca, California. My parents, both born in Mexico, were very nationalistic. They considered themselves inheritors of the Villista revolutionary tradition, and made sure I had Mexican citizenship papers as well as American ones. From an early age, my family and I shuttled back and forth between Mexico and the U.S. My parents, though humble farmworkers, insisted I become fully literate in both English and Spanish. "Manteca," the name of the small city I was born in, means "lard" in Spanish, but the Anglo Americans and Portuguese residents of the town, ashamed of the connotation, said it meant "butter." I, on the other hand, have always felt that we should call things by their real names. Sometimes I like to joke that I was "born in lard."

A Reporter's Life

I am best known in the El Paso–Juárez area as a journalist. In 1999, while writing for *Norte*, I won the José Vasconcelos Award from the Journalists Forum of the state of Chihuahua. I was also the main informant for Sam Dillon's investigative journalism on drug trafficking in Juárez. Dillon, of the *New York Times*, received a Pulitzer Prize. I, on the other hand, only received heartfelt thanks. My own stories about drug trafficking on the border have sometimes brought me death threats. A story I wrote about a powerful local individual led to a lawsuit. *Ni modo* [So be it]. In my worldview, you take your licks, since integrity is what matters most of all.

When *Norte* fell into a deep financial crisis in 2003, I was laid off. *No hay pedo* [No problem]. I had known hard times before, and I will probably know them a few more times in my life. As a reporter, I once pretended to be a homeless drunk in order to investigate the San José jail. For lack of money, I have lived under bridges or on the floor in a backroom of an accountant's office. My grandfather once told me, "You're not born with a round head; it comes from all the blows you receive in life." *Así es la vida* [Such is life].

One day, about a month after I had been hired by *Norte* [November 1995], a photographer at the paper, who sometimes accompanied me on news assignments, commented in Spanish after one of these interviews, half in jest and smiling broadly, that I always acted *muy despistado* [very clueless] when I asked questions, and that because of this, the interviewee would, more times than not, end up feeling sorry for me, and then would eventually "help me out" by furnishing much more information than what I had originally asked for. I told him that I asked a lot of questions and looked clueless because, in fact, I truly felt clueless, since I had only been residing in the Juárez–El Paso area a very short time. He laughed loudly, and said, "Yeah, sure, you're as clueless as a coyote, that's what you are." I guess the equivalent phrase in English would be "you're as crazy as a fox." I answered by laughing nervously and saying nothing. But inside, I knew I had been found out, and that if the photographer could see through my interviewing technique, then so too, eventually, would the interviewees.

And that wouldn't be a good thing if I wanted to continue being a reporter in the Juárez–El Paso area, since I had already surmised that almost everyone in the media loop, including journalists, politicians, spokespersons, government officials, activists, etc., in El Paso and Juárez knew each other. In this respect, El Paso and Juárez are like one big *rancho* [village, farm]—at least socially, anyway—where almost everyone knows someone related in some way to any given individual being alluded to in conversation. And once these people—that is, your sources—can spot your technique, they immediately become wary of it, guarded and reticent to talk. So I immediately stopped using this technique. Needless to say, though, the nickname stuck.

The Narco Beat

At the time [late 1994], I was covering the El Paso beat and the "border narco-trafficking" beat full-time for *Norte* in Juárez. For two and a half years, I spent every working day (Monday through Saturday) literally straddling the border: in the morning, receiving my assignments in Juárez, then crossing the border to El Paso by bus and on foot, gathering the information needed, and then going back to Juárez around two or three P.M. so that I could sit down at my computer terminal and write my articles—usually between four and six a day, every day. All the reporters' leads were due by 3:30, so almost every day I was in a big rush; but even so, I was almost always late, barely finishing my leads by about four or later, to the daily chagrin of proofreaders, editors, layout people, and everyone else in the newsroom who had to wait for those leads, and my stories, to be turned in. I think the only reason they didn't fire me was because I was one of the very few truly bilingual reporters in Juárez.

I know there are many bilingual people in Juárez and El Paso. But sadly, almost all of them are proficient in only one of the languages (usually English in El Paso, or Spanish in Juárez) and very deficient in the other. In fact, I've met more than a few El Paso journalists who unabashedly claim to be bilingual in their résumés, but in the real world can barely—and only—say "Quan-tou cuay-stah eh-stou, pour fah-vour" whenever they go to Juárez. Others can speak both languages fairly well at the street level, but they can only read or write in one language or the other. Bilingual? Maybe. Bilingual journalists? *Nunca* [Never].

I first arrived in the Ciudad Juárez–El Paso area in the autumn of 1994. I thought I was only stopping by for a week or two to visit a childhood friend who was living in Juárez at the time, but life is full of twists and turns. Little did I know at the time that I would end up spending fourteen continuous years here—and still counting. At the time, I thought I was on my way back to Northern California after a stint of several years working as a print journalist in Spanish in the interior of Mexico.

I had undertaken that adventure to round out my résumé, since before going to Mexico in the early nineties, I had only worked as a journalist, both print and TV broadcast, mostly in English, in Northern California—specifically, the Stockton-Sacramento area corridor. So at the time, I thought, "What a wonderful adventure it would be to go to the interior of Mexico and work as a journalist, in Spanish, to complete my bilingual apprenticeship." I was naïve, since I didn't think of all the hardships that would be involved. But, with my concept of "life as an adventure," I plunged in and didn't look back. Foolhardy? Yes. But it was well worth it in the end: I came out relatively unscathed, and with a whole lot of knowledge and practical know-how I didn't have before and something I could've never acquired if I hadn't taken that life-changing journey.

Being a print journalist on the El Paso–Juárez border is by no means easy. At least, it hasn't been easy for me. For nine years, until the autumn of 2003, I worked as a reporter covering drug trafficking in El Paso–Juárez. Because of this long-term work experience, I can personally attest to the fact that it is indeed very, very dangerous to cover drug smuggling in the Mexican press. To put this in some kind of context, let me give some facts: every year since the mid-1990s, there have been between 100 and 300 murders in Juárez, and, at the very least, half of those are directly related to drug smuggling.

The danger that Mexican journalists covering these events are in has finally gotten, in the last year or so, some much needed attention in the American press, and I am happy for that. But for me, it's really nothing new. The dangerous atmosphere for reporters covering drug smuggling on the Mexican side of the border is something that I have personally experienced since I first started working for *Norte*. In a city like Juárez, which was, all through the 1990s—and to this day remains—a wide-open, Wild West, shoot-'em-up town, where murders are a dime a dozen, this was my daily, albeit grisly, bread and butter. Every day, I would research and tie in any stories about murders in Juárez that were related to my narco-trafficking beat, then write all these stories at the newspaper's headquarters.

One of the by-products of this type of reporting is that, after a while, one begins to decipher certain code words that are widely used in the drug-smuggling world. For example, when a narco-trafficker appears shot to death by the side of a peripheral road, and no one, not even his relatives, seems able to tell you how he earned his living, one of his friends, acquaintances, or family members will ultimately say that he "sold and bought used cars" for a living. This usually means that he was a mid-level drug dealer, whereas [at] the bottom of the narco-trafficking ladder, the street-level dealers are referred to as burrito sellers [*burreros*]. Even when one of these guys is arrested, they themselves will tell the police and the press that they "buy and sell used cars." On the other hand, when a high-ranking drug dealer is shot to death or arrested in Juárez, the police are told that the individual in question was a *ganadero* [cattleman]. This means he had some sizeable amount of capital or power in the drug-smuggling world.

An example of this is that even a guy arrested in the interior of the warehouse of a plastics-recycling business in central El Paso—where the authorities discovered a four-ton load of marijuana—told the arresting DEA agents he was a cattleman from Arrumarrullo, Jalisco. The other two men arrested, the foreman and an employee of the business, later identified him as the owner of the drug load, who had crossed over from Juárez to El Paso in order to be personally present at the warehouse, and thus make sure the load was really delivered to the people who were going to transport it to several cities in the interior of the U.S.

For two and a half years—from November 1994 to May 1997—I lived continuously in Juárez, but I finally had to move to El Paso due to the unusual "pressures" that came with the job. These pressures included receiving, several times over the course of those years, death threats over the phone from unknown parties. I would answer the phone at *Norte*, and a voice that I did not recognize would start shouting, "¡Chinga a tu madre, güey, te vamos a matar!" [Fuck your mother, we are going to kill you!] and other threats and vulgar expressions.

I was also kidnapped for several hours, locked inside a room, and tied up with my head covered with a blindfold by a crew of supposedly Mexican federal policemen. I met the men at a bar, and we had a few drinks and good times together, but when they found out I was a journalist, they imprisoned me in a safe house until they verified my identity and determined I was no threat to them. The whole time I was held, I thought they were going to kill me. Additionally, I was shot at, several rounds, by someone in a passing car, and narrowly avoided being hit by one of the bullets. I was followed at least four times, and then later found bullets or empty bullet cartridges inside my car or inside my apartment, which, in both cases, were hand delivered via broken windows.

As one might imagine, I rapidly started to unravel emotionally. My nerves were shattered, and I became very paranoid. But I kept working, since I felt that my work, that is, journalism, was my only hope for staying somewhat sane. The more I unraveled, the more I had a hard time getting to sleep. Whenever I wrote a particular drug-smuggling news piece that I knew was going to make some bigger-than-normal waves— about once or twice a month, on average—in the drug-smuggling world, I literally had to drink myself to sleep, finally passing out in the wee hours of the morning while sitting at the kitchen table or reclining on the living room couch. But I really felt like I had no other choice, since in Mexico, it's either you work or you starve. And in a city, Juárez, where I had no relatives and no built-in support system of old friends or mentors, and since I knew no other line of work other than journalism, I was, quite literally, stuck. Therefore, I just kept plugging away, despite the obvious damage to my psychic and emotional well-being.

In recent years, some people who knew me through this two-and-a-half-year period have asked me, "If you were going through all that at the time, how come you never told me about it?" I usually just smile and shake my head at this question, as if to say, "You've got to be kidding me!" Because, believe me, when you're going through a situation like that, the last thing you want to do is tell people about it. For one thing, your paranoia, plus the all-too-real, all-too-insidious, and all-too-prevalent nature of the extended narco-trafficking networks on both sides of the border, makes you believe that you're never really sure exactly who you can trust and who you can't with this information. You end up telling people nothing. Most of your acquaintances don't even know where you live, your schedule, or how to reach you, except at the newspaper.

In retrospect, I think I made the right choice by continuing to work at that newspaper in Juárez for those years, because during that time I gained an enormous amount of knowledge of how the drug-trafficking world works on the border. But at the time, it was very difficult to continue. Nevertheless, I must also admit I have always really enjoyed—even during those horrific two and a half years—being a journalist: the adrenaline rush you get from working with a daily deadline; the never-ending stream of interesting new people you meet through your work; the variety of your assignments; and being outdoors every day—instead of cooped up in an office—for several hours in order to gather your daily dose of information.

But as time went by, things were obviously going from bad to worse for me in Juárez, and since I very quickly got pigeonholed into covering the bloody, ghastly, monstrous acts of violence associated with narco-trafficking, I really could see no end in sight—no light at the end of the tunnel. Well into my second year of this daily routine, things were getting so hairy that at one point I had to have friends register their names instead of mine for apartment leases, residential phone service contracts, public utility service contracts, etc., so that my name would not appear on any of these transactions or the paper trail they generated.

At this point, the reader might ask why I didn't just go back to Northern California? The truth is, I couldn't because, to put it bluntly, I just didn't have enough money. During those nine years, the most I ever earned for a full-time, six-days-a-week work schedule was a paltry two hundred dollars a week. Thus, I was truly living paycheck to paycheck. In fact, it was less than paycheck to paycheck, since most of my colleagues who were working for the Mexican press at the time, myself included, had to hold at least one other job besides their newspaper employment in order to make ends meet.

Perennially penniless, in order to get to Juárez to cover stories or meet with my editor, I had to hitch a ride from the El Paso accountant's office where I slept on the floor of a back storage room to the Cordova International Bridge. I customarily took the Cordova, or Free, Bridge to avoid paying the toll charged at the other three main bridges to Mexico. Even at those bridges, I avoided the crossing charge by walking into the U.S. immigration office on the El Paso side and then exiting onto the Juárez pedestrian-crossing area, then jumping a metal fence and cutting through the lines of cars idling on the bridge and sprinting to the pedestrian walkway that led into Mexico. Thus, I bypassed the tollbooth on the U.S. side and saved a quarter. I used a similar maneuver when crossing back into El Paso. I have neither a U.S. nor Mexican passport nor any other kind of legal document.

Life after Journalism

Despite all of these negatives and complications, journalism holds a great allure for those involved in it, as anyone who has ever had the fortune of being a journalist can readily tell you. And so it was—and is—for me. There is something very exhilarating about uncovering a truth and then sharing it with the whole world that is just incomparable to any other job. For me, it's that feeling you get of being in the middle of things, involved in what's happening now: to be present, witnessing, front-row center, and in real time, history in the making. And on top of all that, you get to record it. Nothing quite compares to that, or the feeling one gets of somehow making a difference, be it by informing people of some important piece of news or, even better, by helping change some things that are wrong.

During those nine years at *Norte*, I covered, in depth, many truly gruesome news stories, such as the so-called serial murders of women in Juárez; the late-1999 unearthing of several sites around Juárez containing human remains of male victims tortured, killed, and then buried clandestinely, by Cártel de Juárez narco-traffickers and their associates, which often included police officers; the forced disappearances of over two hundred men in Juárez over a ten-year period [1993–2003], most of whom invariably had some type of tie to drug smuggling and whose bodies, to this day, have never been found. Yet in most of these cases, eyewitnesses have stated, in official documents, that they saw federal or Mexican state police officers taking these individuals by force into vehicles—some marked, some not—never to be seen again, dead or alive.

I could tell many more true horror stories similar to these that happened in Juárez and El Paso during those nine years, but the picture is clear. Suffice it to say that in the three cases mentioned above, as in many others like them, I was at the forefront of the coverage or the discovery of these crimes, since at the time no other media outlet in Juárez or El Paso even believed that these events were actually occurring, and therefore didn't bother to investigate or cover them.

In 1997–1998, U.S. government sources which I am not at liberty to name, as well as agents of the Mexican Federal Police, asked me if I could furnish them copies of all the news stories I'd written on the forced-disappearance cases of men in Juárez. Of course I did so, and one of the results was that a year and some months later, authorities from both the U.S. and Mexico, working together, began unearthing the first of nine bodies of men killed and buried in several ranches (La Campana, Santa Rosalía, etc.) in and around Juárez.[2]

Such happy, cheerful times! Such joy to discover humankind's unparalleled kindness to his fellow man! When asked by friends how I like living in the El Paso–Juárez area, I have more than once remarked that I love living here, since I get to use the full extent of my writing capacities—in English and Spanish. I tell them that whenever I've lived and worked in the interior of the U.S., I always end up missing Mexico, and that when I've worked in the interior of Mexico, I invariably end up missing the U.S. But here, on the border, I don't miss anything, since both countries and cultures are readily available to me. Trouble is, I also know, more than most, the dark side of the border region, which makes me feel sometimes as though living here is like watching a horror movie. The only difference is that when you go see a horror movie at the theater, after two hours or so, you get up and leave, go home, and forget about it. But living here on the border, oftentimes when I wake up in the morning, I wake up screaming, since I know the horror movie is about to start all over again.

I now live in El Paso, and barely eke out a living by doing some freelance reporting work and some academic translations, and also by working part-time writing "soft news" pieces—mostly business and entertainment stories—for a local magazine, as well as doing menial tasks of all kinds or manual labor of any type that comes my way. In fact, I like to joke to my friends that I'm thinking of changing my name to "Manuel Labor," since that's what my main occupation seems to be nowadays.

When people ask me, "Was it all worth it?" I invariably say, "Yes, it was." I guess what helped me survive that scary period of my life was, undoubtedly, a lot of dumb luck and the unwavering sense that my life is, and always will be, an adventure. Today I have no steady job or income. I devote my time to coaching kids' soccer teams, working out, and cultivating my mind. But I have not a care in the world, and only a few cents in my pocket. My irreverence has cost me many professional opportunities, but I don't care too much, since my peace of mind is many times more valuable than mere ephemeral prestige.

A few years ago, then-governor Bush came to Socorro, Texas, to meet with local residents; I, out of common courtesy, conducted simultaneous Spanish-English translations for him. Then Bush returned to El Paso while on the presidential campaign trail. He made a political stop in El Paso at the Texas Workforce Commission office on Brookhollow Street. Laid-off garment workers crowded near the front of the TWC building to protest the limited benefits provided by the NAFTA program for the victims of free trade. Bush entered the building from the rear in order to avoid the protesters. Bush's advisors tried to limit questions from the media to the actual details of the program. I happened to be covering the story for the Mexican newspaper *Norte* and ended up infuriating the Bush advisors by asking why the candidate would not meet with the protesters who, after all, just wanted to shake his hand and give him a protest letter. Bush agreed to my suggestion and met with the protest group. Subsequently, while shaking my hand, Bush invited me to Austin, where he said he could give a job to a talented bilingual person like me. But to be honest, and no offense to President Bush, I simply had no interest in becoming a political hack. And I still don't.

Addendum

Samira Izaguirre
Radio journalist and commentator

There is a female radio journalist and commentator by the name of Samira Izaguirre, who received death threats, then was jailed for about a year in the Juárez Cereso prison, accused of drug smuggling—all because of her criticizing, and uncovering corruption in, the Juarez and Chihuahua State police forces. After being banned from radio by the governor of Chihuahua, Patricio Martínez, and threatened again, she was finally forced to ask the U.S. government for political asylum, and now lives in El Paso, from where she continues to do a radio news-talk show. This all happened in the late 1990s–early 2000s.

Patrolling the Drug War Zone: A Border Patrol Agent in the War on Drugs

On January 21, 2008, a Border Patrol agent from El Paso named Luis Aguilar Jr. was run over and killed near Yuma, Arizona, allegedly by a drug smuggler driving a Hummer vehicle. Aguilar was apparently the first agent murdered by smugglers in recent years. Other agents who died in the line of duty perished by drowning or in vehicle accidents (Sanchez 2008).

In 2006, a military Humvee loaded with marijuana and driven by a large group of heavily armed men with mounted machine guns and dressed in Mexican army uniforms crossed the Rio Grande near Ft. Hancock, Texas. The drug traffickers behaved menacingly toward Border Patrol officers. In another incident, in 2002, seventeen bandits robbed a U.S. train in the Sunland Park, New Mexico, border area. This led to a brawl involving the train robbers and members of a multiagency task force including Border Patrol agents; several FBI agents were severely beaten on Mexican soil in Anapra, an outlying barrio of Ciudad Juárez (Valdez 2002).

There have also been many rumors about Mexican drug cartels offering rewards to those who kill Border Patrol agents, though to date there have been no proven cases of such killings. However, such threats do psychological harm. In addition to the many physical risks confronted by Border Patrol agents—which are amply discussed in this account—they live in a constant state of low-level fear from having to work in hazardous rural settings (for example, canyons, rivers, and mountains) as well as in dangerous urban settings (train trestles, international bridges, river beds, urban barrios, etc.). Additionally, Border Patrol agents face unpredictable attacks by often well-armed immigrant smugglers, common criminals, and drug traffickers, although drug smugglers make up only a small percentage of the people whom agents regularly encounter; most of their work is with undocumented immigrants.

Although the life of a Border Patrol agent may be dangerous and stressful, according to a leading scholar of border law enforcement (Joe Heyman, personal communication, January 25, 2008), city police, who repeatedly respond to crisis situations involving domestic disputes, all manner of criminal behavior, armed individuals, etc., generally perform more dangerous jobs. This is the case because Border Patrol agents detain immigrants, who tend to be more compliant and more vulnerable than many of the people encountered by urban policemen. Likewise, U.S. Marshals, who execute arrest warrants on armed and dangerous persons, may regularly face more perilous threats. The same can be said of ICE antidrug investigators, who are continually confronting known and threatening criminals. Furthermore, if the United States and Mexico adopt the "security cooperation" agreement known as Plan México or the Mérida Initiative, more DEA agents will be sent to do inherently risky undercover work in Mexico. These comments are in no way intended to diminish the problems faced by the Border Patrol, but simply to put them in the larger context of border law-enforcement activities.

The Border Patrol's internal ideology, training, and folklore promote the image that working for the patrol is a highly dangerous job. The U.S. public also generally holds a notion of Border Patrol agents as the sort of swashbuckling adventurers depicted in movies like *The Border*, starring Jack Nicholson. In spite of this image, the daily work life of many Border Patrol agents is boring. The job often consists of sitting in parked trucks in the middle of nowhere for long hours while little happens, and they generally have lower salaries and social status than FBI, DEA, or ICE investigators. Compared to Border Patrol assignments, FBI and DEA work often involves more training or education, the application of intellectual skills, the wearing of three-piece suits, the use of well-appointed offices, etc. In that sense, Border Patrol agents and ICE agents who work at ports of entry are the blue-collar workers in border law enforcement.

As noted, Border Patrol agents belong to just one of the multiple federal, state, and local agencies fighting the war on drugs. Drug interdiction is not the main priority of the Border Patrol, although agents inevitably encounter drug smuggling in the course of their work. In the desert areas near El Paso, this often entails tracking down young men hefting homemade burlap backpacks filled with one hundred to one hundred fifty pounds of marijuana. In other cases, it may consist of coming face-to-face with heavily armed smugglers driving SUVs loaded with cocaine across low spots in the Rio Grande. Confronting narcotics trafficking is an especially onerous task for Border Patrol agents because, despite the danger, they receive little reward for stopping drug smugglers. At most, they get a commendation; in many cases, not even that. Hispanic officers face especially acute contradictions on the border because Mexican smugglers may view them as potentially sympathetic coethnics and attempt to influence them through bribery or other means.

Whatever their ethnic identity, Border Patrol agents in border cities are potentially exposed to bribery attempts by traffickers who live on both sides of the border. In the densely connected binational social webs of the El Paso–Ciudad Juárez area, agents and smugglers inevitably cross paths, whether in stores, schools, parties, bars, or other social venues. Border Patrol agents originally from U.S. border cities or the Mexican side of the border may have relatives, childhood friends, or neighbors who are involved in the drug trade. This makes them particularly vulnerable to pressure to accept bribes, to pass drug loads themselves, or simply to extend favors or convey information that may facilitate smuggling. Border Patrol agents are also subject to criticism from immigration-rights activists on both sides of the border, who may be unaware of or unsympathetic to the Border Patrol's role on the frontlines of the drug war. Moreover, agents also face the moral bind of being charged with enforcing drug-war laws that they, in many cases, neither agree with nor consider effective.

The sometimes boring, at other times highly risky and morally challenging, and often underappreciated or even heavily criticized, job and life of a Border Patrol agent is well illustrated in the account that follows.

The Border Patrol Agent

I was born in South Texas in the 1950s. My mom was a Mexican schoolteacher from Morelos, Coahuila. My dad is a Mexican American born in Laredo, Texas. My parents met at the air force base in Del Rio while my father was stationed there as an air force surface gunner. After my mother died, my father remarried and we went our separate ways. My father now lives in Del Rio, but we don't get along. I lived with my father when I was young and as a teenager. I grew up speaking Spanish and English. I've lived in Mexico (Ciudad Acuña and Torreón) on summer vacations or for short periods, such as when I left the military and we stayed with my mother-in-law. My mother-in-law thought we should be more independent, so we only stayed with her for two months.

I am fluent in Spanish, even though I was educated in the United States. My mom taught me to consider myself a Mexican American, not a Chicano. To her, Chicanos were thieves, low-riders, and bikers that dressed in zoot suits. A professor at Florida International University told me there were two kinds of Mexicans: the type who associates with life in Mexico—Mexican American—and the type who associates with the U.S.—Chicano. I consider myself one who associates with Mexicans, and I married a Mexican. As a child, I would constantly cross the border. My dad was stationed at Laughlin Air Force Base in Del Rio when I was a kid, so I lived near the border.

Since my dad was in the military, I was always exposed to military life. I had traveled with family as a military dependent. I thought twice about whether to be in the military or live the Mexican American civilian way. After high school, I worked at an electronics shop as a handyman, and I would also clean up the shop. In college, I worked at a Church's Fried Chicken and went to Texas A&I, in Kingsville (now Texas A&M at Kingsville), where I studied electronic processing. I chose an electronics major because I thought it was the path to making a lot of money fast. But I found history more interesting, and changed to a history major. My parents divorced and my mother passed away. My source of income got cut off, and I wasn't able to finish at Kingsville.

Eventually, I joined the military and was in the service for eight years. I wanted to be an officer, but was not accepted to officer candidate school. My father was reluctant to be sent to Vietnam. I wanted to show him how a military service member should be. I wanted to go to Vietnam. When I joined the army, I went to Fort Hood, Texas, for the first four years. Next I was at Camp Darby in Italy for four years, fixing equipment in the telephone office. Military life was not what I thought it would be, and I left the army when I was not accepted into officer's training. Back then, around 1988–1989, there was a surplus of officers. I went back to school and got a history degree from the University of Maryland. Then I found out that history majors are a dime a dozen. I tried to get a job teaching in Del Rio, but could not. So I worked at Kmart and in the jail at Del Rio.

As a kid, I knew about smuggling across the U.S.-Mexico border. I also had a negative image of the Border Patrol growing up. I was scared of getting arrested by the Border Patrol. My dad was a little bit darker than me. My mother was light skinned with reddish brown hair. I was viewed as a *güero* [white]. This was a positive in my community.

Working for the INS in Miami

I took a job as a county jailer, which was a stepping-stone to a job at the Krome detention facility in Miami, Florida. From 1990 to 1991, Krome was an INS detention facility for immigrant detainees from Caribbean and South American countries, including Haiti, Cuba, Jamaica, Venezuela, Colombia, and other places. As a guard, I participated in several police actions against protests at the Krome facility. Prisoners rioted, and the guards would be holding shields and batons. The prisoners or detainees had shanks that they made from pieces of metal off bunk beds and used as weapons. The Haitians engaged in voodoo and directed it at the guards. I would be hoping that the voodoo chants would not go through my shield and harm me. The detainees rioted on the inside, and there were 10,000 protesters on the outside of the fence, trying to break it down. If we weren't there, they would have knocked down the fence.

The first year at Krome was okay, but the bad thing is that you are locked up with the detainees. As a guard, I got into a few fistfights to defend myself. I felt that what I was doing was a positive thing. Plus, I was making a little bit more money. Some Marielitos [Cubans from Mariel] were there, but more came a little later. There always was a small contingency of Cubans at the facility.

Next, I became an INS inspector at the Miami airport from 1991 to 1994. I inspected cruise and cargo ships with the marine unit for three years. It was very satisfying work, but I felt like a toll taker. I worked in a gigantic room, stamping passports. I got tired of seeing the long lines.

There were people from South America, Europe, everywhere from all over the world. I tried diligently, but didn't feel like a law-enforcement officer. In Miami, I would go to supermarkets in my uniform, and people thought I was a security guard. In El Paso, everyone knows I am a Border Patrol officer when they see me. I left the INS inspector job in December 1994 and became a Border Patrol agent. I wanted to come back to Texas somehow. I couldn't think of my kids marrying a Jamaican with dreadlocks in Miami. My positions as a detention officer, inspector, and Border Patrol officer were all part of the INS.

With the Border Patrol in El Paso

I attended the Border Patrol Academy in Artesia, New Mexico, for four and a half to five months. It is a long time there away from family, especially when it is Christmas and New Year's. The academy is still there, and has been there forever. Artesia is a no-man's-land with only two bars and a Wal-Mart. There is nothing really out there. When I was there, the most exciting thing was a titty bar. At the academy, you learn some Spanish, just barely enough to get you through. It is a lot of discipline training and weeding out. You get training about the history of smuggling. It is a pretty good preparation. They explain why people smuggle or try to cross the border illegally. They teach you about cultural issues and to have a little compassion.

At the end of Border Patrol Academy training there is a kind of ritual boxing event. They have a boxing ring at the Border Patrol Academy as part of the training to see if you can take a punch. They try to simulate real-life situations. Your opponent is a fellow student who could be a male or female. It is a one-round fight in which you are supposed to try and knock the other person out. The students want to make an impression that they can take and give a punch. They hit you and you hit back. You get pissed when you get hit. But it is not a real thing. Drug smugglers will hit with everything they have. It's not going to be a boxing match.

I graduated from the academy, and have been a Border Patrol officer for many years. December 2008 will make it fourteen years. As a border patrolman, I have worked at the Ysleta station [in the Lower Valley of El Paso] temporarily, and the Mount Cristo Rey to Fonseca Street area, plus the downtown El Paso area. When I first got to the El Paso station, Operation Hold the Line was in full swing. Initially, an officer had to stay in one place right on the border for ten-hour shifts. Your area of responsibility changed from day to day. You worked fifty hours a week with time and a half for extra hours. We were understaffed, and could not manage otherwise. Now, for one to two hours of your shift, you can roam in a territory one to two miles long.

Sometimes it is boring; you are allowed to have reading material or schoolwork. No TVs or DVDs are tolerated—no movies. Downtown along the dead areas of the levee, TVs are allowed. Cell phones are allowed; they encourage cell phones so they can get hold of you if your radio isn't working.

Some of my experiences with drug smuggling were especially distinctive and memorable. The one that really stands out to me was a time when another Border Patrol officer and I encountered a drug smuggler's vehicle going up Trans-Mountain road from the west side of El Paso to the northeast side [headed northeast from Interstate 10]. There are a lot of stash houses and gangs in northeast El Paso. There were three *cholo* types in the passenger part of the vehicle who appeared to duck down as the vehicle passed us. We stopped the vehicle. My partner went to the driver's side of the vehicle, and I was on the passenger's side. I saw a pistol grip in the "canoe area," shoved in between the front seats. I yelled, "Gun, gun, he's got a gun." I'm considered one of the fastest draws at the station, but it seemed like slow motion. Even though I practiced a thousand times, it is different when it really is happening. I pulled my gun out. I told him [the passenger-side guy] if he went for the gun, I was going to blow him away. He obeyed our orders and raised his hands. As I held the gun, I thought, "This asshole is not going to prevent me from watching my girls walk across the stage to graduate at UTEP."

The guy that was on the passenger's side had just gotten out of prison. He claimed he had the weapon to protect him from other *cholos* or rival gang members who would want to kill him or take away the drugs. I was six feet away from him. We pulled them out of the vehicle, put them on their knees, put handcuffs on them, and waited for the sheriff's department. The trunk of the vehicle was loaded with drugs. They had two hundred to three hundred pounds of pot in black duffel bags.

The packages were bricks wrapped in brown packing tape. You could smell the pot strongly. They might have just crossed the border and headed to a stash house in northeast El Paso. From there, the drugs could go to the interior: Dallas, Chicago, I don't know. All three in the car were busted. The guy on parole was sent back to prison for being a felon in possession of drugs and for distribution, plus the weapon possession. It took me a while to get over it. I don't ever remember being that excited. I received no hazard pay, just an attaboy, a pat on the back, and no citation. Once in a blue moon, for a big bust, you might get a Border Patrol Agent of the Year award, but that is very rare. After that bust, I went home, drank a few beers to relax, and told war stories to my wife and kid.

Another memorable occasion occurred at [Border] Monument Number 1 [a boundary marker commemorating the Gadsden Purchase] by the American brick plant on the Mexican side of the river, but still U.S. land. There are some big boulders spaced apart that form a row. Anybody from Juárez can walk over there. Bandits can rob you. There is a little park where the boundary marker is located. Nearby there is the American brick plant with piles of old, discarded bricks and new bricks for sale stacked around it. Mount Cristo Rey is in the background. The Rio Grande runs along Paisano Avenue, and the border boundary runs parallel to it. The New Mexico border and Sunland Park, New Mexico, are to the west. Traffickers try to run from the park area by the boundary marker across a road and up the hill in the direction of Cristo Rey and into the U.S. In this area, the big rows of boulders are the clear boundary between the U.S. and Mexico. Up in the mountains or hills, the boundaries between the two countries are more ambiguous.

On this occasion, the Juárez police were sitting there under the trees at the little park. Not all, but some, Juárez policemen are corrupt. Some are nice guys. These police allowed drug smugglers, laden with drugs in black duffel bags made out of nylon, to walk right across the border. There were two or three Juárez cops sitting in a pickup truck. Two smugglers on foot walked over a little hill, past the cops, through a space in the boulders, across the river to a little dirt road. My partner and I saw the mules, and stumbled across these bags they had left behind. They ran off when they saw us. They dropped the drugs and ran back to Mexico. The Juárez cops did nothing. Those cops probably transported the smugglers to the spot. They watched the whole thing, including the smugglers running back into Mexico. I told my Border Patrol partner, "Don't go talk to the Mexican cops." They might have shot at us for messing up the drug operation, or they might try to arrest us for crossing into Mexico. It was nine A.M. We were just about to go home from the night shift.

There are cameras on high steel poles with zoom lenses or infrared that see everything in this area. We have the choice with the cameras of making human figures look white on black or black on white. Some smugglers know about the cameras, and some don't. We packed up the duffel bags, weighed them (around a hundred pounds) and took photos of the marijuana. Some of these guys are small and skinny and cannot carry a lot of drugs. Typically, marijuana—tens of thousands of dollars worth—is busted on the line, because it is bulky. Once in a while, it is cocaine, because it is smaller-size packages—hundreds of thousands of dollars.

In this area, traffickers often stash drugs and come back at night, when we are not watching, to get the drugs, and then try to cross the wooden bridge over the Rio Grande, and then get a ride on Paisano Drive. They also try to cross the railroad trestle on foot to get to Executive Center Drive. Many times in ambiguous areas such as this one where I confiscated drugs from these foot couriers, I have chased illegals until I thought, "Wait a minute. I'm on the wrong side of the fence. The barbed wire is over there." I've walked past the barbed wire with apprehended illegals in the area around Mount Cristo Rey, where there was an incident involving train robbers from Mexico dragging two FBI agents back into Mexico.

Getting Shot At

I've been involved in five shooting incidents. When you get shot at, you are not always cognizant of it. On one shooting incident, I was at ASARCO, listening and dancing to music to stay awake on the night shift. I heard something like an air-conditioner popping sound inside the truck. When the sun came up, I saw a bullet hole in the windshield. It must have gone out the side window I had open. I thought, "Oh my God, I've been shot at."

I don't know how it happened. The shooters are not always trying to kill you, but to scare you—to annoy or get you to move out of the way so smugglers can cross through. They throw a rock or take a shot to get you to move. Sometimes it is done in general anger toward the Border Patrol. It is so close to the border that anyone can shoot at you with a rifle or handgun. There have been lots of threats made on Border Patrol agents. Supposedly a ten-thousand-dollar bounty by the Arellano Félix cartel was put out on Border Patrol agents. But I don't think any threats have been followed through.

Twice, my rear windshield has been shot out. One time was when I was stationed on the border in the downtown area of El Paso near 6th Street, by Segundo Barrio. Suddenly, I heard a shot and the rear window imploding. The shot came from Juárez, or from on top of the fence, or through an open hole in the fence. It is a little safer to have the rear window shot at than the front one because the bullet has to go through the rear window, middle cage behind the seat, and the seat to get you. I got out of the area and called a supervisor, and they tried to contact the Juárez Police Department. It takes a long time for the Juárez police to get there, even though we have numbered the fence posts to make it easier to locate the trouble spot and shooters. Gun violations are serious in Mexico, and those convicted go to prison for a long time, but they normally get away with it.

In the third shooting I was involved in, my rear window was shot out while I was driving in the area of Fonseca Street where it meets up with the Border Highway. It was daytime, and I was on the line.

The fourth shooting involved multiple shots fired, and occurred during a midnight shift at the ASARCO plant entrance, before the fence was constructed, when you could still run right across the borderline. I was responding to another agent being shot at. His truck was parallel to Paisano and the border when his vehicle took multiple shots. He called me. I rushed over there in my vehicle. Another agent responded too. I used my truck to protect him and myself by forming a half-moon with our trucks. Bullets were whizzing and zinging by. I could hear them and see the dust flying up from impacts on the ground. We pulled out our guns but could not see the shooters, and we can't shoot randomly into Mexico. When shots are fired, some react differently. I took cover this time, but sometimes you are pissed and stand up to the challenge. *Me da coraje* [It makes me mad]. After this shooting, my truck had bullet holes. There may have been just one shooter or maybe more.

These shootings happen all the time. There are constantly incidents of conflict during times we ruin their plans to smuggle people or drugs across. They get upset and try to scare you. Not all of these shootings make the paper. Some years are high in the number of shootings, and some are low. Before the fence, the area by ASARCO was very hot. When the border fence was being built, even some construction workers were shot at. The workers were pointing the shooters out.

The fifth shooting I had was in the area near where I once fell in the river with my Border Patrol truck. It is a hot spot between Mount Cristo Rey and downtown. It is the hottest spot on the line, with a dense population. It is along the "Tortilla Curtain," which refers to the fence separating the two downtowns [El Paso and Juárez] from the Puente Negro [Black Bridge] to Concepción Street, past the Delta Street water-treatment plant. The fence is on the U.S. side of the Rio Grande on top of the cement apron by the irrigation canal. The end of Concepción Street almost touches Border Highway. There is a rock wall at the end of the street to protect the community. Our Lady of the Light Church is near there.

The Tortilla Curtain is a slang nickname the Border Patrol and others use. The fence is chain link and sheet metal. Illegal border crossers cut the fence with bolt cutters or a portable torch. The fence by ASARCO is only chain link; the Tortilla Curtain fence is a little thicker. I was stationary, and heard the bullet blasts like a high-caliber handgun, a pistol. I called the office, and they called the Juárez Police Department. All other Border Patrol Agents know when you call gunshots in, so they can stay alert, be careful, stay away, or respond.

A Fortuitous Drug Bust

On another occasion, that took place in winter 2006, I didn't catch a person, but caught the drugs in a backpack they threw off a bridge. Smugglers throw drugs off the Stanton Street Bridge or other bridges over to the U.S. side just before they cross the bridge to the U.S. side while coming in legally. They might have somebody below waiting to pick the dope up. Or they may fear getting caught, fear apprehension with drugs, so they dump it and run back to Mexico. They would rather take the risk of throwing the drugs. We have cameras and agents that don't always spot the backpacks being thrown. They always seem to use a black backpack.

I just happened to be going by Border Highway on this occasion, and saw the bag fall from the Stanton Street Bridge. This was during the daytime, about two. The camera did not pick it up. I just happened onto it. Otherwise, someone with a car, or walking, would have just run by and got the bag. They do it all the time. Other people on the bridge may see the smugglers throw the drugs off the bridge, but they don't want trouble or to get involved. The pack I saw fell on the gravel sidewalk on the west side under the bridge. I went there and opened it up. Wrapped in brown post-office tape were fifty to sixty-five pounds of marijuana in ten-to-twelve-pound bricks. I took it to the Border Patrol Office first, weighed it, and then waited to see who would take it. Usually, the sheriff's office will come for it. It smelled very strong. I don't like the smell of marijuana and don't like to drive around with it, because it is suspicious.

I have been around half a warehouse of pot in El Paso. The DEA took it to their facility on Mesa Hills. We unloaded it. I went there to provide support and security. It took several hours to weigh. It was enough to fill an entire eighteen-wheel truck and trailer. It was incredibly intense. They were putting it in packing boxes the size of TV boxes and weighing it in their warehouse. I thought I might be able to test positive for drugs just from the smell. That bothered me. I wrote a memo to the agent in charge, for them not to hold me responsible for a negative urine test. Customs usually takes it to Arizona to their certified burn facility. Customs has one of their people drive a truck, with a car following behind. They carry Steyr AUG Austrian machine guns as special protection.

The Border Patrol is the redheaded stepchild of INS. We don't get enough recognition. The only recognition you get is from your colleagues. My agency has a lot of intrinsic hardships; we drive rickety old vehicles, have very difficult work circuits, but have to make do with what we have. There is lots of racism, good-old-boy attitudes, and a lack of incentive to do a good job, which leads to corruption.

I will serve twenty years in the Border Patrol, and I feel I have made no impact on the flow of drugs or undocumented people into the U.S. I have locked up many people, but it makes no difference. I get the feeling that people look at me like I am a criminal and think, "He offends me." Some Border Patrol bosses do give a damn and some don't. Some are corrupt in the higher echelon. They engage in misdeeds. The government just sends them elsewhere. But 75–85 percent are good officers. Some do nothing. You can just tell that some are corrupt or lazy. It will be a problem after I am gone, but it will be somebody else's baby then.

There is constantly low-level suspicion in the Border Patrol. Just like at the military academies: if you find out about cheating, you have to turn them in. I can get in trouble if I don't. There is an EEOO [Equal Employment Opportunity Office] system. But there is constantly low-level gossip about corruption. Morale in the Border Patrol is currently low to medium. There are salary increases every January, plus step increases. There are also merit raises—a cash award, $500 after taxes. I only had one.

Intelligence and the Drug War: Commander of an Antidrug Task Force on the Border

Whereas the Border Patrol does a lot of the dirty frontline work in the drug war, intelligence operatives handle the more cerebral dimensions. Handling the intelligence side of antidrug law enforcement is not as risky as being a Border Patrol agent, nor as glamorous as undercover work, but it is equally important to antidrug policy. Such work, by its very nature, also attracts a different sort or person, often better educated and white collar. Intelligence analysts and directors of task forces must be adept at processing diverse types of "intel" (statistics, reports, informant testimonies, etc.). Task force leaders also must be capable of organizing and managing people within dense thickets of interagency rivalry and conflict. These are some of the key issues that emerge from the account that follows.

Another major point emphasized in this interview is the importance for law enforcement of tracking not just large loads of drugs, but also the huge volume of money generated by the drug trade. This requires skills and tactics that are related but not identical to those involved in antinarcotics operations. Both, however, rely on the expertise of confidential informants and entail hazards for the agent. As noted in his testimony, the commander knew without a doubt that he was confronting the Juárez cartel of Amado Carrillo Fuentes and that this was a dangerous pursuit.

The account is also valuable for the insight it provides into the functioning of stash houses, money-laundering operations at used-car lots, and other tactics and operational strategies of traffickers. Additionally, it sheds light on the different agendas and ways of operating of various U.S. law enforcements agencies, local and federal, concerned with drugs, as well as the functioning of a multiagency task force. The task force commander is proud of his accomplishments in the war on drugs, even though he is well aware of the limitations of such a policy.

The Commander

My father was in the military, so I was born in Germany, in an American hospital. I first came here, to El Paso, when I was two years old. I grew up off and on in El Paso, but moved around a lot because of my father's military career. My first job out of high school was as a translator of German for the military. That was a pretty good job for an eighteen-year-old. As a translator, I would go out with the MPs [military police officers] on police investigations in Germany. That job opened my eyes to a lot of things, since I got to see firsthand and up close some very interesting cases that the MPs were investigating. I remember one case in particular, in which a guy committed a bank robbery using an M-16 rifle. I recall another one in which the lieutenant that was in charge of the drug rehabilitation program at the U.S. military base was actually selling heroin and hashish to the troops.

Then we came back to the U.S. and lived in New York for a while. Back then, I thought I was going to go to law school, but I also liked police work. I studied political science at State University of New York at New Paltz and graduated from SUNY-Albany. I should mention that I speak German. And I also speak a little bit of Spanish. During his military career, my father attained the rank of command sergeant major. My mother is German. While I was growing up, she was a full-time housewife. I have one older brother, who was also in the military. He is currently unemployed. I worked as an aide for a New York state senator and was taking political science classes at the university. Eventually, I moved to El Paso.

Back then, I remember that my intent was to become a paralegal. Of course, back then I didn't speak as much Spanish as I do now. I went to work for the El Paso County Sheriff's Department, and liked it quite a bit. I worked for one year at the El Paso County Jail. When I attended the sheriff's department regional training academy, I actually graduated first in my class. That's when I figured law enforcement was something at which I could really succeed. The sheriff's department covers the Lower Valley and the Upper Valley, but is also authorized to operate in the metropolitan area of El Paso. I guess you could say the whole county is the sheriff's department's jurisdiction. But of course, the main focus is the areas outside the city limits.

The Task Force

The antidrug task force I became a member of covered everything—in other words, we covered the city and the county. This task force is part of the Special Operations Bureau of the sheriff's department. The metro narcotics task force, on my end, was called the West Texas HIDTA [High-Intensity Drug Trafficking Area] Financial Disruption Task Force. The focus was on money laundering, specifically, discovering and then confiscating financial instruments or assets and real estate acquired with money generated by the profits resulting from drug trafficking. HIDTA was the means by which the U.S. federal government funded and supported local law-enforcement agencies to bolster their combat against drug trafficking.

Eventually, I became the commander of the West Texas Financial Disruption Task Force, funded through HIDTA, which in turn was funded through the White House's Office of National Drug Control Policy. The task force had assigned to it agents from U.S. Customs and also agents from the FBI, the IRS's Criminal Investigation Division, and the Texas attorney general's office. This task force had as its members agents from U.S. Customs, the FBI, metro [the El Paso Police Department], the IRS, and Criminal Investigations. Basically, it was a multiagency taskforce. One of our focuses was targeting the Alameda Avenue used-car lots and finding out, through covert investigations, which ones were involved in drug trafficking or laundering money for drug traffickers.

Eventually, we came up with a list of used-car lots on Alameda that we suspected of engaging in drug trafficking. One of the FBI agents assigned to the task force went back to his agency and shared this information with some of his fellow FBI agents. Well, as it turned out, a couple of weeks later I attended a multiagency meeting, and in that meeting, an FBI agent suddenly produced a list of used-car lots on Alameda that were suspected of drug trafficking or money laundering. Of course, we, the task force, unwittingly, through that FBI agent assigned to us, had given them that list. And now they were claiming it, as if they themselves had done all the intelligence work necessary to come up with such a list.

I distinctly remember the FBI guy even said to me, in a low voice: "Man, have I got some really great intel for you." And then he handed me the list. So I just kind of laughed, and started naming the car lots before even looking at the list. The FBI guy looked very surprised, and he asked me: "How is it that you already know the names of the businesses on this list?" And I replied: "Because we produced that list two weeks ago, and then the FBI agent in our task force gave it to you. I personally handed out that list to all the members of our task force, including him."

I could tell he was rather embarrassed by the whole thing. His face started turning red immediately after he heard my answer. This is just the way things work with these multiagency groups. Sometimes we come up with the intel and share it, and then another agency will take credit for the whole thing. Other times, two or more agencies will come up with the same intel on certain organized-crime groups, even though their investigations were totally independent of one another and there was no intel sharing. It's no surprise, since many of these agencies investigate the same organized-crime groups. In either case, it's no big deal. It happens all the time. It's just the nature of the beast, so to speak.

It was in July of 1995 when I first got involved full-time in the investigating and taking down of drug dealers. But prior to that in the sheriff's department, I had already worked for a time in the internal-affairs section and also on patrol. So I guess you could say my experience was pretty well rounded and I had worked in, and seen, many different aspects of law-enforcement work. When I worked patrol, I had some contact with drugs. But at that time, I just made small arrests on patrol. Mostly, I saw small amounts of cocaine and marijuana. Of course, all this was prior to my joining the metro narcotics task force. Once there, we were focused on major arrests involving large amounts of drugs. The minimum amounts we dealt with in the metro narcotics task force were, for example, one kilogram of cocaine or approximately fifty pounds of marijuana. Those amounts are more or less the federal guidelines for prosecution. When a case involved less than the minimum amounts at the state level, they would generally turn those types of cases over to our local division.

So like I said, I became a lieutenant, and then was put in charge of the task force as its commander. Our main objective was to follow the money trails left by businesses involved in money laundering. That's why we had in the task force the expertise of the agents assigned to us by the attorney general's office, the IRS, and Customs. The main objective was to disrupt their operations by seizing their assets. You start out by identifying stash houses. You know, in the buy-bust operations, many times we were able to ascertain where they were going to deliver the drugs. Then we would determine if the house was seizable. Also, we would determine if seizing the vehicle was worth it, and, of course, we would seize the cash. We also followed their bank transactions. Any suspicious activity we would try to follow up on. Any time you deposit any amount over $10,000, the transaction has to be reported in writing to the government. Of course, the drug traffickers also know this, and so they engage in what we call smurfing: making a lot of small deposits of slightly less than $10,000 into a bank account. So when we would see that, we could keep tabs on that individual, and eventually track down where the money was coming from.

In antinarcotics-type law enforcement, the use of confidential informants is invaluable. In order to begin an investigation on an organized, large-scale drug-trafficking organization, the use of informants almost always accounts for the first step, that is to say, the initial tips or clues. That's the first step in developing an investigation that will then evolve with other techniques and tools, such as surveillance, buy-busts, etc. But the crucial first step is the use of informants, especially individuals who are caught trafficking with drugs, and then interrogated in order to work up the food chain.

I was fully aware that by engaging in this line of work, in essence, I was fighting the Cártel de Juárez and its leader at that time, Amado Carrillo Fuentes. Since many of the investigations started by the task force I was commanding are still open, I really can't speak about specific cases. The only thing I can say is that we were involved in combating organized crime and, more specifically, drug-trafficking organizations that operated in and around the Greater El Paso area, including the Juárez cartel. One of the biggest cases we worked and successfully completed was the arrest of a former comandante of the Mexican Federal Police. We worked that case together with the DEA. We had photos of him. The day of his arrest, we had the use of four or five helicopters provided by the U.S. government. The case involved several tons of marijuana. We made several arrests throughout the country on that one. The year was 1996. Of course, we arrested him in the U.S.

Stash Houses

The east side of El Paso, especially the newer residential neighborhoods, is one of the key areas for stash houses in El Paso. Large-scale drug-trafficking organizations seem to prefer areas like that, where most of the neighbors don't really know each other. In older, more established residential areas or communities, such as central or west-side El Paso, the neighbors all know each other, so it's easier to spot someone new. As far as spotting a potential stash house, there are some well-known indicators, such as the yard is unkempt, with the appearance that no one really lives there on a full-time basis, and the air conditioner is kept running all the time to keep the odor of drugs down. The garage hasn't been converted into another use. The smell of water and detergent is notable. Individuals are spotted bringing in big rolls of plastic. You see a lot of duct tape in the trash. You see cars coming and going all the time. Or short periods of intense vehicle activity, and then long periods of no cars there at all. When the front door is opened, you see little or no furniture. Also, the doors to the house are rarely kept open, as if they don't want anyone looking in. I guess it has to do with not wanting to be spotted. The rare times that you can see into the house, you may see plastic furniture, such as a few chairs, and perhaps the mattress is on the floor. Also, they hardly ever talk to the neighbors—in some cases, never.

There is a HIDTA Stash House Unit here in El Paso, and they are dedicated almost exclusively to the detection and taking down of stash houses. The feds like these types of local law-enforcement outfits dedicated to combating narcotics, because they get a lot of information from local units. We also did a good number of buy-bust operations, where the narcos thought they were going to buy large amounts of drugs from our undercover agents posing as sellers. In many of these cases, the drug traffickers were going to buy the drugs from us and then stash the load in a house or a warehouse or other type of establishment, right here in El Paso. They already had a site set aside specifically for that, and eventually, through our investigations, we were able to detect that site.

In general, they are just moving the drug loads to El Paso, and then using a site to repack it in smaller amounts, and then transporting it to other parts of the country. They need to repack the drugs because when they get here, the substance is usually in large bricks, and they need to break down these bricks into smaller packages or units that they can hide more easily in hidden compartments in vehicles. The bricks they get are generally about one kilogram in weight. The marijuana can be in bricks of one kilo or one pound, depending on how they packaged it to come into the country. Sometimes marijuana is initially packaged into fifty-pound bales.

Many times, the cartels will put decals on the bricks to show where it came from. These decals are in code, but in general what they signify is something along the lines of "this is our dope." Sometimes these decals will consist of cartoon characters from Mexico, again, as an identifier. Some drug traffickers will also use sports characters on their decals. [Others actually use their own names as labels, such as "Chapo Guzmán" or "Mayo Zambada."] Marijuana is usually packaged in darker-colored plastic or other materials, generally sturdier, since it's harder to cover up the odor of marijuana. Sometimes they'll wrap it in plastic and then pour transmission fluid around the package to cover up the odor. Other times, they'll use duct tape, again, to cover up the odor and thus throw off the drug-sniffing dogs on the border. With cocaine, they usually use thicker plastic.

Many drug traffickers will engage in both cocaine and marijuana trafficking, and although some people think why mess around with pot when cocaine profits are higher, the reality is that in some areas, marijuana is in higher demand. College students and other young people in many areas, like New York, for example, end up paying a lot more money for marijuana than what it's worth here on the border. Then again, with some high-grade marijuana, the profit margins are pretty high, even comparable to cocaine's profit margins.

We also had some major heroin busts—black-tar heroin, mostly. With heroin, there is smaller packaging, in little balloons. We busted one case where the individual had twenty-eight ounces of heroin. They hadn't even packaged it yet; it was all in one big lump. We had set up a sting in that case. The heroin was going to be delivered to a stash house. We actually audiotaped and videotaped the whole thing. Immediately after they had completed the deal and were exchanging the dope for the money, we busted them.

But generally speaking, when it comes to heroin, it's more of a street-level thing, in small quantities. That twenty-eight-ounce case was a rarity. When it comes to heroin, they only sell to people that are users. It's a more high-risk endeavor for undercover officers, since if you're an undercover agent and you set up a deal where you're going to buy heroin, the drug traffickers will want to see you use it right there and then. I remember that back when I was in charge of the task force, the round numbers we heard were something like for every drug load that was intercepted and confiscated by the authorities, ten to twelve other loads made it through. Sometimes the drug traffickers do have their sacrificial lambs. You know, they get some poor kid to drive a load across the border in a vehicle for a hundred or two hundred bucks, all the while knowing beforehand that that vehicle is going to be stopped and searched, and of course busted, while the other vehicles behind him are going to get through.

Smuggling with Used Cars

We made a major bust of money going southbound across the border in a big commercial truck. Back in those days [the mid to late 1990s], we were able to uncover a lot of the used-car dealerships here in town that were involved in taking drug loads up into the interior of the U.S. and then bringing the money back to the border. In many cases, they had plausible deniability. They could allege that they went to Colorado to buy a car at the big car auctions held there, and that they brought it back to sell here, and that they didn't know what was hidden in the car—large amounts of money. They could also allege more or less the same with a vehicle going north: that they bought the car at an auction and that they didn't know it was full of drugs in hidden compartments. Another thing they were doing was buying cars at sheriff's-department auctions, and then if the car was found to be loaded with drugs in hidden compartments, they would say: "Well, I bought that car at a sheriff's auction, and I guess the sheriffs didn't check that car before selling it. So how was I supposed to know it had drugs hidden in it?" Plausible deniability—that's what it's all about.

Nowadays they're also using the bus lines—you know, the bus transport system. They throw the bag on the bus, and if that load gets intercepted and confiscated somewhere along the route to its destination, they just consider it a loss; but at least the authorities cannot pinpoint who it was going to. They chalk up a loss like that as part of the cost of doing business. I don't think they would risk transporting money that way, because it's high risk. But with drugs, occasional losses are considered a standard part of doing business. One of the preferred modes of taking drugs from one place to another is in duffel bags. They're portable and lightweight.

We took apart many cars loaded with money and drugs. There are some makes and models that lend themselves more to be used as a vehicle to transport drug loads in. This is because of the way the body is built on certain vehicles, providing more room and a larger number of spaces where secret, hidden compartments can be built. For example, one type of car drug traffickers were using a lot was Lincoln Town Cars. We also saw a good number of Chevy Corsicas and Honda Accords. The drug traffickers knew how to "wire" them, that is to say, alter them in such a way that they could build a secret compartment in them.

Others use Bondo brand adhesives. They also use the beds of trucks. They'll put a bed liner in, and if you look very carefully, you'll notice a little irregularity. Nowadays they're also using the compartments where the airbags are stored. They take out the airbag and fill that empty space with drugs. If you take the airbag out, it's a ready-made secret compartment, straight from the factory. They'll also use the door panels or the space under the dashboard. A kilo fits nicely inside the door panels or under the dash. In fact, we once had an incident with a vehicle we had just driven to a law-enforcement auction on the far east side of El Paso. We had previously seized that car with a big load of pot hidden in it. Anyway, when we got to the auction, one of the front doors of the car suddenly caught on fire. We quickly squelched the fire, and then, when looking for the cause of the fire, we were able to surmise that the officers that had searched that vehicle after seizing it had missed a big bag of drugs hidden underneath the dashboard, and that's what had caught on fire. Drug traffickers will often use the space under the spare tire, located inside the trunk.

We saw some cases where the building of the compartment was quite ingenious, inside the motor itself. I mean, you look under the hood, at the engine, and it looks like it is solid metal, but there's a compartment hidden there, under the solenoid. There were a couple of guys from U.S. Customs who were good at spotting when something didn't look right with an engine. They would see something that doesn't look like it belongs there, or a part that looks too big or too bulky. They could also look under a backseat, and it would seem like it was solid metal, welded. But you would hit a button or hit a switch to turn on an inside light, and bam! it would pop open a hidden compartment under the seat. Obviously, there was some thought put into the construction of that compartment.

When we seize one of these vehicles and then later sell it at an auto auction, we notify the buyer that it has a secret compartment, so that the buyer can seal it off before using the vehicle for general transportation purposes. We do dismantle or break those compartments, so they do need fixing. Of course, sometimes the individuals who buy those vehicles leave the hidden compartments in there so that they can use that vehicle again as a drug-load car. And then if they get caught, they can argue that they didn't know the compartment or the drugs were in there, since they bought the vehicle at a law-enforcement auction. Drug traffickers would rather buy a car at an auction to transport drug loads than use a stolen vehicle. They figure it's too risky to use stolen cars, since they know that we know where the secret VINs (vehicle identification numbers) are on vehicles, and that if they get stopped for a traffic violation, through a fairly quick computer check of those numbers we can determine if that vehicle is stolen. Locally, the used-vehicle market is plagued by this type of buying vehicles for drug-transporting purposes. At one point, we did actually take photos and videos of used-car lots to record what vehicles were there. And then you'd see the same vehicles there for three or four months. In other words, there was absolutely no movement of those vehicles, no purchases, and they'd be reporting expenses. That's another method of money laundering.

The used-car lots wouldn't sell any cars, but at night they had other vehicles coming in there, and then they would be put in the back, as if they were being fixed. But you wouldn't see them in the lot. That's because these cars were being used for drug-transportation purposes. Most of the time, they wouldn't be there the next day. So we would sit on them to get the vehicle descriptions, and then we would report them for interception-interdiction purposes.

Intelligence Sharing

Since 9/11, the emphasis has been on fighting terrorism, not on fighting drugs. So nowadays we don't have the resources we had before. I know that the FBI has changed their emphasis almost entirely to counterterrorism type of investigations and operations. I also know that at the local level, law enforcement just doesn't have the amount of resources we had for fighting drug trafficking prior to 9/11. And that's a big difference, if you ask me. Back then, we had federal funding, and that could pay for overtime, for assigning a certain amount of sheriff's deputies to work antidrug operations, and also to pay for more patrol officers working against drug-trafficking activities. Back then we could do more in-depth, long-term investigations. Nowadays we can't.

The DEA depends exclusively on informants. In fact, sometimes we'd develop an investigation and a case, and then we would take it to them and they'd do it. The DEA just doesn't have enough agents to develop all the investigations they could in this region. That's where they depend on us, the local law-enforcement agencies. They also don't have control personnel. That's one of the benefits or advantages of being a sheriff's department officer, because you can go into the jail and you know who the players are in the jail, because they're the same ones out on the street. So when you meet them on the street, you know you're on the right track and that you're going to develop and investigate the case.

As sheriff's department officers, we worked with the criminal element in the jail, in a closed environment. In fact, that's one of the things the sheriff's department requires of all its beginning officers. And that's a good thing, because I think if you can deal with that type of person in a confinement environment, then it'll be easier to deal with them on the street. In that sense, the sheriff's department is the most effective in training its officers to deal with various types of criminal elements. I think that type of training is unique to El Paso County. Because we would hear the feedback from some of the other law-enforcement jurisdictions in Texas, and we would notice that they would be high-fiving each other over busting someone for a couple of eight balls of cocaine [an eight ball is about three and a half grams], whereas here in El Paso, the amounts are much bigger, and a couple of eight balls is no big thing, taking into account the sheer volume of the stuff that comes through this region. Of course, once the loads are on the road, the state police do a lot of interception-interdiction work.

The weakest link in the chain of law-enforcement work against drug-trafficking activities is, hands down, the sharing of intelligence. Plodding federal investigations take too long. We would identify somebody locally and be ready to make an arrest, but the feds, usually the FBI, would ask us to wait, since they were working something bigger, because they knew the drugs were going to Washington state or North Carolina. So they would ask us to lie low here in El Paso while they developed the investigation at the other end, whether that meant North Carolina or somewhere else. By the time they get up here, because they're going elsewhere, all the assets we had identified had been disposed of. But that's the nature of the beast.

Our mission was to disrupt and dismantle. From my perspective, there's no doubt that we could have made a lot more seizures, but you need to do a long-term investigation for that, and we didn't always have the time or the money to do that. We didn't advertise a lot of the seizures that we made, because the drug dealers would find out about it and immediately thereafter move their operations. For us, the decision to disclose publicly a big seizure of drugs would depend on whether this was going to lead to a multistate investigation or just a local case. If you want to publicize a bust, you call the media and schedule a press conference. At that press conference, you give the media a photo opportunity showing them all those bricks of cocaine or bales of marijuana, and you explain all the details of the case. But again, some cases don't get publicized, since the investigation of that case is leading elsewhere and so it's ongoing, and probably eventually leads to a bigger case. Another instance where the case isn't publicized is when we make a major money seizure and the guy who we confiscated that money from doesn't want to cooperate. Of course if we don't publicize it, and then the guy is set free and goes back to his bosses, the drug traffickers, and tells them that law enforcement took the money; they're not going to believe him, and he'll have to pay hell for the loss of that money. So not publicizing the case is a way of applying pressure on this guy so that he'll cooperate.

One thing I should mention is that at the sheriff's department, we had no incentive to make a drug bust other than a pat on the back and getting congratulated for doing our job well. Other than that, if we did a seizure at the local level and there was asset sharing, the district attorney's office would get 30 percent and we would get 70 percent. With the feds, there was a similar arrangement when we would work cases together with them. The money from the selling of these assets would usually go to educational programs within the sheriff's department or for the purchase of vehicles or law enforcement equipment; also, drug-education programs are funded through those assets. The percentage of the seized assets that each agency ends up with depends on the participation level. To give you an example, there was a major multistate case we worked, and when all was said and done, we ended up with 40 percent of the money that came from the seized assets, whereas other jurisdictions, with a smaller number of arrests, ended up with only 10 percent, and so forth.

The Wrong Time at the Right Place

Back then, I was divorced, so I had the time to do a lot of the paperwork necessary to obtain grants. I also had the time to put in a lot of overtime. Sometimes when you're working a major case, you're literally at the job almost twenty-four hours a day. And, of course, you're on call around the clock whenever a major seizure is made or a major bust is about to come down. I remember one case that involved two Nicaraguan guys from New York who flew to El Paso to buy some drugs at the downtown international bridge [the Paso del Norte port of entry]. They had $105,000 in a briefcase that U.S. Customs had found. We went over to the Paso del Norte Bridge to interview them, and they finally admitted that they were there to buy heroin. They said that they had walked over to the top of the bridge, where the sellers were supposed to meet them at three P.M., but they never showed up. It was on their way back to the U.S., through the pedestrian lanes at the bridge, that the U.S. Customs agents had checked that briefcase and found all that money.

When they were walking back across the bridge into the U.S. through the pedestrian lanes, a money-sniffing dog hit on their briefcase. Their plan had been to go to the top of the bridge to meet their connection. Agents from INS and Customs saw them going to the top of the bridge and then pacing back and forth and looking at their watches. Then, when they came back to the U.S. side of the bridge, the agents decided to check them out. Then the money-sniffing dogs hit on their briefcase. That's when they called us, and after interrogating them, we were able to get a full confession from them. They were busted for having the money to invest specifically in the buying of drugs.

When we were interviewing them, it was only two fifteen, so I asked them, "Well, what time do you think it is right now?" One of them looked at his watch and answered that it was four fifteen. But, of course, his watch was still on New York time, or Eastern Time, whereas here in El Paso and Juárez, we're on Mountain Time. So in essence, these guys got busted with all that money because they had forgotten to set their watches back two hours after landing at the El Paso airport. We waited at the top of the bridge to see if someone would show up at the appointed time, but no one did. I'm sure the sellers had spotted all the activity going on at the bridge and figured something was wrong.

Following the Money Trail

I also remember a major case involving a student from Iowa who came down to El Paso to buy a huge quantity of steroids in Juárez. After he was busted trying to cross the bridge into the U.S. with this load of steroids in his possession, we called the authorities in Iowa to see if they knew anything about it. The Iowa authorities told us that up there a couple of individuals had recently died as a result of overdosing on steroids. He was busted at the international bridge by Customs. The fellow told the authorities that he could buy steroids in Mexico at incredibly reduced prices, and without a prescription, and that he would then turn a very handsome profit by selling them up there in Iowa. He was driving his dad's truck, a nice, brand-new pickup.

I recall another case where one of our patrol officers trained in interdiction stopped a guy with $267,000 in a bag. It turned out the detained individual was a runner for an outlaw biker gang from Arizona. We called the authorities in Arizona, and they were very familiar with him. We provided them with enough information to get a search warrant, and they were able to seize some drugs over there.

When I was in charge of this task force, I had sixteen to eighteen agents working under me. I also had a couple of analysts, who would input all the information into our system and keep track of all the stuff that had to do with statistics, projections, etc. Analysts organize, weed out, and sort out all the information we got during our interviews: addresses, phone numbers, bank account numbers. They would make elaborate spreadsheets for us, showing where the money of the individuals investigated was going. So the task force had agents, analysts, and detectives. The detectives are local sheriff's deputies. The detectives are the ones that were developing the informants, working with the information, and doing the surveillance. The agents were federal agents, essentially FBI special agents, but we also had two IRS-CID [Internal Revenue Service Criminal Investigation Division] agents and, at different times, between one and four Customs agents.

I had operational authority. So I could detail some of these agents to ride along with a search-warrant unit to see if they could find financial documents or bank records. Or if we would hear that a sheriff's department patrol unit was doing an interdiction at that moment, I could detail some of my people to go and interrogate the suspects. A lot of the cases the patrol division was working were the same ones we were working, so it wasn't totally out of the blue. There are essentially two units in the same facility: a metro narcotics task force and a financial-disruption unit. The metro unit would target the drugs, while we, the financial-disruption unit, would look into the financial records and follow the money trail. So I had working for me eight detectives—local sheriff's deputies—whose job it was to develop informants and do surveillance. They would also ride with the El Paso metro guys when they would execute a search warrant on a property. The metro guys were looking for drugs, while my guys were looking for financial documents or records, and assets that were presumably bought with drug proceeds.

To work jointly with other law enforcement agencies, there is a sort of master agreement. The HIDTA funding agreements are essentially geared in a way that two or more agencies can decide to work together on certain initiatives, and they're different initiatives, like one would be a stash-house initiative; financial disruption—us—would be another initiative; the Border Patrol may have another initiative at the time, having to do with drug interdiction. And, of course, the participants in this initiative come into these joint operations with the mindset that we all have to cooperate in order to make this operation a success. So, depending on a particular operation, we had some agents assigned to us who weren't with us full-time, but were essentially there if we needed them. But the eight detectives under me did report directly to me. We might share information with other agencies, but it was all done according to the assistance we needed in each particular case.

Truthfully speaking, a lot of the agents from other law-enforcement agencies—like, for example the FBI—do not have a lot of training in undercover operations, whereas our detectives do. So they may ask our detectives to go out and do the undercover work necessary to develop a particular case, such as setting up drug buys, etc. Especially in cases where they would be bringing in agents who are Anglo, who wouldn't fit in with our population here locally. FBI agents don't make as many arrests as our sheriff's deputies, or our undercover detectives, do. I mean, an FBI agent can work all year and maybe make one or two arrests during that time. Generally, FBI agents and other federal agents have more high-tech resources with databases to do federal prosecutions. Whereas we focus on our local area, the feds have a more global perspective.

We also, from time to time, developed intelligence or confidential information for EPIC [El Paso Intelligence Center]. EPIC is a multi-agency task force that tracks all drug-trafficking movements on a global basis, including the shipping of drug loads from the producing countries, the receiving of these loads in other countries, and finally the delivery of these loads into the U.S. and other consumer countries. EPIC supposedly handles and processes the highest-level intelligence on drug trafficking in the whole country. EPIC is located in Biggs Army [Air] Field, inside Fort Bliss grounds. They're concerned with the big picture when it comes to drug trafficking. Various law-enforcement agencies share their info with EPIC. All the HIDTA-funded agencies would share their info with EPIC too. I guess you could say that EPIC puts a global perspective on the info that we get locally. We had one case where a drug dealer was using the Internet for drug trafficking. We found a notebook that had all these codes written in it. After our analysts looked at this info with the aid of our computers, they were able to determine that what this guy was doing was actually selling marijuana over the Internet. The codes were his record of transactions with others. The codes referred specifically to how much dope each customer wanted. The price was another code.

Even though the sharing of information between us and the feds was pretty good, there were still some instances, though, where the FBI, for example, would never tell us who their informants were, and we would do the same thing. We do know that sometimes our informants overlap. The one central authority agency that makes all the decisions concerning anti-drug efforts is supposed to be the ONDCP [Office of National Drug Control Policy], which is in Washington, D.C., and is run by the drug czar. All in all, I think we were very effective at the local level, particularly when it came to interdiction and following up on the drug traffickers. Since EPIC is dealing with drug trafficking on a national level, it is not obsessed with El Paso, even though it is one of the major drug-smuggling areas in the country, together with the San Diego area and the Miami area.

A case that sticks out in my mind is one involving interdiction on the highway. It all started when a patrol officer did a routine traffic stop. What the officer noticed right away is that this guy was basically living out of his vehicle. He also noticed that the guy was sweating profusely, even though it was October and therefore not that hot. So the officer started asking the guy where he was going and where he was coming from, and the guy was volunteering the information. But then he asked the officer if there was a point to his interrogation, because he wanted to be on his way. So the officer told him that he suspected that he was transporting drugs. So the officer called a unit with a currency-sniffing dog aboard rather than a drug-sniffing dog.

The dog hit on the guy's leg, and when the officers pulled up his pants, they found $50,000 dollars strapped to that leg. And then they found a drug stash in the trunk of the vehicle. So they called us in, and together with our Customs and IRS agents, we started following a trail based on his vehicle registration. We contacted regional law-enforcement agencies as well as out of state agencies, and it turned out that law enforcement in Arizona knew this guy. He was involved with an outlaw biker gang whose home base was in the Arizona area. The Arizona authorities were able to get a search warrant for his house over there. Besides the money we had found on him, the authorities in Arizona, through the intelligence we shared with them, were able to make a major amphetamine seizure in his house. So what had started as a routine traffic stop turned out to be a major bust. We had found out where he came from and where he lived. And through that, and our contacting and sharing information with the authorities in Arizona, we were able to put together the pieces of the puzzle—and wham! We kept the confiscated cash here locally, while the authorities in Arizona confiscated the drugs, the property, and the vehicles.

We've had some interdictions at the international bridges where the guy we busted will actually start to cooperate with us and agree to tell us to which stash house he was going to take the drug load we had just seized at the bridge. So we go there and arrest the owner or the occupant of the house. That individual will then tell us how much money they were paying him to stash the drugs for a day or two, until it's eventually transported out of El Paso. So then we set up surveillance on that house, and follow the drug load to its final destination somewhere in the interior of the U.S., and working with the local and federal authorities in that city, we execute a search warrant and start following the paper trail. All that work results in a bust and many seizable assets. Sometimes the narcos will use rental vehicles or vehicles that are not worth any money, but then again, sometimes you'll get a guy driving a Porsche Boxster.

Money Laundering and Stash Houses in El Paso

We, of course, were always concentrating on the money-laundering aspects and finding the illegal proceeds from drug trafficking. As far as the money-laundering aspects, and how to specifically uncover these types of activities, I can give you an example. In one case we worked, we found that this guy had filed taxes for the last few years indicating that he made less than $15,000 a year. But he lived in a house that was worth half a million dollars. We were also able to prove that every day he was making deposits of $9,999, that is to say, just under the $10,000 figure that the law requires a person to report. Of course the banking officials had reported that, and they had been tracking those transactions all along. So we started connecting all the dots, and were eventually able to determine that this guy was a moneyman for the buying of drug loads and then laundering the profits. So after you tie everything in and show in court that the proof is all there, you start getting to the seizable assets, and that's what it's all about. You get money-laundering types all over El Paso, but one area where you see the upper echelon of money launderers is in the Saul Kleinfeld area, on the east side of El Paso, where all these big houses are. We suspected a lot of this type of activity was going on there.

When it comes to these high-end stash houses, there are some signs to look for, such as huge steel doors and windows blockaded. From the outside, from the street, you can't see inside the property. This is done so in case of a raid, the authorities would have to consider a high-risk entry. Generally, you can say that the money people are on the west side, or in the Upper Valley of El Paso, and in the high-dollar, or rich, areas on the east side. In the Lower Valley, you find the lower-level stash houses and traffickers. There is thinner police coverage in the county, and there are areas where Operation Hold the Line is dwindling, and that is where you'll see the people crossing the river with backpacks full of drugs. Back in my day, there were some cases of this out of San Elizario, Texas. When it comes to big stash houses and money laundering, there is not as much going on in the northeast side of El Paso. Back in my day, there were mostly just gangs, bad urban-blight-type areas like the so-called Devil's Triangle, maybe a few stash houses, but not much.

Excerpt from *Weed: Adventures of a Dope Smuggler,* by Jerry Kamstra

There's a pattern customs inspectors look for when rigs drive into the inspection stalls. A good inspector can sniff out a smuggling operation, picking up the little telltale signs some smugglers inevitably give off. It might be a look in the eye, it might be a too cool indifference on the part of the driver, it might be a jittery dance the smuggler goes through to keep his butterflies down. Experienced inspectors look for any action that is abnormal. In my case it was getting out of my car and raising the hood.

The irony was that I had a legitimate mechanical problem, and in the helter-skelter last-minute adjustments one makes when approaching a customs checkpoint with $40,000 worth of weed, my two-bit brain figured that the inspectors would be just as interested in the problem as I was. I was right with inspector numero uno, but numero dos had too many years on the job; he looked out of his window and smelled something fishy. When he started walking across the tarmac toward my rig I was already figuring distance and windage to the Mexican border. The approaching moment was one every smuggler imagines but there is really no adequate way to describe the feeling that goes through your body. Every nerve is exposed and tense, like a wire, and at the same time a weird floating unreality seems to seep under your skin; you see it happening but reality refuses to register. You don't believe it.

As inspector number two approached I opened the driver's door and sat down in the front seat. I suddenly remembered all the incriminating evidence I had in the car: photographs and notebooks, paraphernalia and accouterments you never think about until The Man's about to come down on your ass. What I especially wanted to get was a photograph of Jesse [Kamstra's drug-smuggling partner] and me that we'd had taken a couple of weeks before in a Mexico City nightclub. The photograph was stashed behind the sun visor. If the heat got the photograph and checked it out I was finished, because Jesse was one big hombre as far as they were concerned, wanted on both sides of the border.

While the inspector opened the rear door of my wagon and started prodding the upholstery, I quietly slipped the photo out from behind the visor and put it under my shirt. Number two was a dogged son of a bitch, and after rifling my furniture he pulled out a little light on the end of a long flexible cable and tried to stick it down inside the doors. Fortunately all the kilos were wrapped in black plastic and he couldn't see anything, but for good measure he tapped the side of the Ford, running his knuckles along the rear quarter-panel like a piano tuner tuning a piano. His thin, smirky lips got thinner as he worked his way along the side of the car, then he turned to me and said, "I think I'll go get a screwdriver and take off this panel." I stood beside the car while he walked over to the office and returned with the screwdriver. He reached inside and started taking out the screws on a small rear panel and I gingerly patted my pockets to make sure I was ready. The photograph was safe, so was a bag of amphetamine pills I'd snatched, and as the panel came off revealing a dozen beautifully wrapped kilos, I took off too, making like Speedy Gonzalez for the Mexican side of the border.

Jerry Kamstra, author of Weed *and several published and yet to be published novels, was a contemporary of Jack Kerouac, Allen Ginsberg, and others in the San Francisco bohemian scene. He still resides in northern California.*

Agent against Prohibition

Terry Nelson's story is a vivid example of how a true-blue "drug warrior" could lose faith in governmental policy. Although he was a very effective Border Patrol and Customs agent—one year he busted 118,000 pounds of marijuana—eventually Nelson realized that not only was the U.S. not winning the drug war, but also that the policy itself was wasteful and harmful to the country. Nelson attempted to reform the government agencies he worked for, but found that to be an impossible mission. Since his retirement, Nelson has dedicated his efforts to raising consciousness about the futility and counterproductive effects of the war on drugs.

As an ancestral Texan steeped in the culture and traditions of the Southwest, as well as a dyed-in-the-wool Republican, Nelson could hardly be branded unpatriotic. Yet through painful experience, he came to the conclusion that the war on drugs needed to be replaced with a more realistic, more practical, and more effective approach to the perennial issues of drug use, abuse, and trafficking. He is not alone in this regard. In fact, many of the people I interviewed in U.S. law enforcement expressed skepticism about the reality of the nation's drug policies. Like many police officers, these drug agents harbor a "contradictory consciousness," on the one hand believing in their mandate as agents of the state, and on the other mistrusting and questioning the very policies they carry out daily.

Nelson should be commended for his courage in laying on the table the problematic nature of the war on drugs and in calling for a new, more sensible strategy. His account also provides a rich inside look at the cultures of border drug trafficking and law enforcement.

Terry Nelson

I was born in London, Texas, in 1948. London is in Kimball County by Junction, Texas. It is a little hole-in-the-wall town. My family moved to a ranch near Brackettville when I was nine. My dad was ranch manager for an 88,000-acre ranch. The ranch had cattle, sheep, goats, pigs, etc. I learned Spanish from the *braceros* who worked on the ranch, and learned more Spanish in the Border Patrol. My favorite years were spent on the ranch. I pretty much know everything there is to know about ranching.

I am from a poor family with deep Texas roots, from the other side of the tracks. My ethnic background is Heinz 57. Mom was a homemaker, part French and part Comanche. I'm one-sixteenth Comanche. My dad is Scotch-Irish or possibly Scandinavian ("Nelson" may have come from "Nielsen," hence possible Scandinavian background). My grandfather was a Texas Ranger who lived to be 103. My grandmother lived to 104.

After I finished high school, in 1966, I went to work as a telegrapher on the railroad out in Marathon, Texas. I volunteered for Vietnam [because] "Nelsons don't get drafted." Dad was in the navy. One uncle received a silver star in World War II. Another uncle was also in World War II. For me not to join was unthinkable. I was a communications specialist in Vietnam. The army was filled with people like me from small towns. Going overseas gave me a different perspective and broadened my horizons. I was stationed in Thailand. I was the only trained radio man in Southeast Asia. I was with the coast guard for a year and two months in Southeast Asia. I love people. I lived in Thailand, the Philippines, and many other places. People are all the same around the world. Everyone in the world wants a house, food in their belly, and food for their children.

I came back to the States in 1972 and went to work for the railroad. In 1974, I joined the Border Patrol. I was sent to El Paso–Juárez. Drugs weren't bad in 1974; mostly we caught immigrants. On Easter Sunday in 1977, I shot an escaped convict after he shot me. He tried to run the Carlsbad [New Mexico] checkpoint. We tried to surround him, and he shot at us. I shot him in the back of the head—that slowed him down. I was involved in one other shoot-out, with a drug boat in the Florida Keys.

From 1974 to 1982, I did mostly immigration work for the Border Patrol in the El Paso area. I never busted cocaine; it was all marijuana at that time. Coke got big in the 1990s. There were some big busts, but mostly small ones, from eight ounces to a hundred pounds to four hundred pounds of marijuana, mainly trunk loads. From 1982 to 1985,

I was involved in drug interdiction with the U.S. Customs Tactical Enforcement in the Florida Keys. I did antidrug work as a customs marine patrolman. I busted 118,000 pounds of marijuana in one year, and was commended for this. In 1986, I was a customs inspector in Dallas–Fort Worth, at the airport. It was boring. I was supposed to bust someone for marijuana residue. I've swept more dope over the side of a boat in Florida than we busted there.

Once, U.S. officers busted a big load of pot in a dry lakebed twenty miles south of Juárez. The traffickers used to land lots of drug planes in these lakebeds south of Juárez. The officers busted the dope, then put it underneath a culvert. [In order to impress their superiors] the officers broke the load into smaller amounts of about three hundred pounds each and then busted the dope little by little; but they were caught and arrested.

We used to make this joke, "Who do you work for and never get any arrests? Customs!" One time under the overpass close to the Hacienda Restaurant in El Paso, I ran face to face into a white guy—an officer who went over to the dark side, selling drugs—but I couldn't catch him. Smugglers used to smuggle lots of dope in the drain [arroyo] that ran by UTEP (see map in the photo section). I was not involved in it, but there was a 10,000-pound load busted in the desert by Gate 4 near Columbus, New Mexico. The traffickers would drive across the desert, until the sensors were put in. They were ground sensors, like the ones used in Vietnam. There were mostly small busts and not on a regular basis. The Border Patrol didn't have DEA authority; we just used federal law at the time to bust traffickers. It was cowboy time back then. When the sun went down, the respect went up. We didn't take the bullshit the people in the Border Patrol take these days. We started a baseball league with the Juárez police to try to improve relations. We even caught a Juárez murderer. Border Patrol chief Silvestre Reyes [now a congressman], Chihuahua state policemen, the Juárez cops, and I found him in El Paso.

The job was firm. I felt sorry for the people, but it was good money. We didn't have much corruption in the force then. I didn't work drugs full-time until the 1980s. One guy tried to bribe me; however, we busted him. [Name withheld], a Cherokee Indian, offered me $15,000 [to let drugs through El Paso]. He had originally offered me 3.5 to 4 cents per each pound. I said, "Do you think I'm stupid or what? I want $15,000 per load—paid each time." He agreed and he was busted, but he only served 2 years. I'd have gone to jail for ten years [if I had accepted the bribe].

Juárez cops then were paid thirty dollars a month and all they could steal, but they had to pay a *mordida* to their commander, who gave it to his commander, and on up the line. Mexican cops were not deeply involved in trafficking at that time. There wasn't the money in it. But Mexican cops have always protected the drug lords. Six federal officers were killed by the army in Veracruz; I've got the photos of this incident. I was flying a plane above the incident, and we took the pictures, we caught them in the act. Some of the feds had gunpowder stains on their teeth from being shot at point blank range.

I was single then and did a lot of nightclubbing. I knew a lot of drug traffickers and criminals from the bars. One time a trafficker named "Danny Joe," or "D.J.," said, "What's it worth for you to let dope through?" I replied, "You can't afford it." He was a smuggler who turned in the competition. We met at the Cockpit Restaurant on Montana Street in El Paso. He gave me a map with names and times that led to the bust of four corrupt agents and an inspector. Dopers take out other dopers to eliminate competition. Or people are mad at someone else and they turn them in. Informants are always how you do it in law-enforcement drug work. When I wasn't working, I was partying with the traffickers and criminals in their places. But they respected me because I didn't burn people. If I got information, I turned it over to the authorities.

I used to eat at a restaurant downtown which had a mob connection. There was a big mob presence in El Paso in the 1980s for stolen goods. Anything that was moved was handled by the Mafia. There was a transition from control of El Paso by the Italian Mafia to the emergence of large Mexican drug cartels in the 1990s. This was an example of unintended consequences. You cut the head off this snake, and another one grows somewhere else.

Initially, the Colombian cartel commissioned drug shipments to Mexicans. Sinaloa is the state where smuggling started. Mexicans got one-fourth of the shipment to sell for themselves. Eventually, the Mexican traffickers became so big they bought all the drugs from the Colombians and sold them themselves. I was on a bust in Chihuahua City in the mid-nineties. I was in a Cessna Citation airplane, a twin-engine plane with two jets on the back. Colombians off-loaded ten thousand pounds of cocaine. The Mexicans paid the Colombians $30 million for the cocaine. A fourteen-foot Bobtail [air-cargo tractor] held the money. Eight vehicles took the cocaine away. It went to the Amado Carrillo Fuentes organization. In Colombia, a bank truck came and took the $30 million to the bank.

A gun was pulled on me once in the middle of the night in Villa-hermosa, Tabasco. The gun was stuck in my face by a sixteen-year-old soldier. He stuck a rifle in my face and held me for an hour until his supervisor came and let us go. The kid was just doing his job. A bunch of gringos flew in in the middle of the night. Our Mexican colleagues didn't call in to tell them we were coming.

White boys were selling a lot of the drugs in the early days. A white boy who lived off Alameda Street in El Paso would smuggle planes of marijuana and take loads anywhere. He would also smuggle transistor radios to Mexico. White guys knew how to fly the planes. Every dirt road in El Paso had airplanes land on it with dope back in those days. Even airports were used. You squeeze the balloon here, and it comes out somewhere else.

Mexico is a wonderful country, but a country of haves and have-nots. A rich country, Mexico's problem is its centralized government. I know those people [Mexicans], have been around them all my life. I worked in the embassy in Mexico City from 1996 to 1998. I worked in an office run by the military and staffed by Customs. My job was to facilitate antidrug efforts. I dealt with Mexican police who used airplanes to stop smug-glers. I told them where the target was, where you could find a bunch of drug smugglers. We caught a lot of loads of cocaine. We were fighting three cartels: the Sinaloa, Juárez, and Gulf (García Abrego) cartels.

I am more afraid now than when I was in Mexico City; that is why I carry a gun. The dopers are afraid I will put them out of business [because I want to stop drug prohibition]. I wasn't afraid in Mexico be-cause you don't kill U.S. federal officers and get away with it. When I was there, the Mexicans tolerated us because we were just the price of doing business. The Mexican agents would sometimes bust drugs, even though they were in cahoots with traffickers. Sometimes you make it so apparent that there is drug activity going on that they have to bust them. It would be embarrassing not to.

I am now retired and work for LEAP [Law Enforcement Against Prohibition] because I think we are losing the war on drugs. My transi-tion was a long one. After I started working in drug law enforcement in Mexico and South America, I began to see the immensity of the situa-tion and knew that the approach we were taking would not work. I tried to discuss my views at several planning meetings, and was either ignored or informed that I did not make policy, only enforced it. Such arrogance and the insistence on continuing a failed or flawed policy did not sit well with me.

I had put way too much effort into the drug war to not win it, and it was too dangerous for the enforcers and the people of the source countries to just continue doing what we were doing because that was the way it was. To put a common expression on it, many of the cops did not know what it was like before the war on drugs was institutionalized. They did not know what it was like to sit around a party and have people using these now-prohibited drugs recreationally and causing no harm to themselves or others. I had seen enough drug use to know that it was not the huge evil that the government was portraying it as. That is not to say that it cannot be dangerous if you abuse drugs or use them irresponsibly.

Once retired, I read about LEAP while on a college visit with my daughter, and then contacted them. Once I had a chance to meet the directors, I knew they were not a bunch of "drug-smoking wackos" and that they truly wanted to help by reducing crime and violence as well as by treating users that become addicted with medical care instead of incarceration.

We base our work at LEAP on Vietnam Veterans against [the] War. What we say is based on our knowledge of having been there [fighting the war on drugs].

Terry Nelson is an active member of LEAP. What follows is LEAP'S mission statement. Also see www.leap.cc.

MISSION STATEMENT

The mission of LEAP is to reduce the multitude of unintended harmful consequences resulting from fighting the war on drugs and to lessen the incidence of death, disease, crime, and addiction by ultimately ending drug prohibition.

Founded on March 16, 2002, LEAP is made up of current and former members of law enforcement who believe the existing drug policies have failed in their intended goals of addressing the problems of crime, drug abuse, addiction, juvenile drug use, stopping the flow of illegal drugs into this country and the internal sale and use of illegal drugs. By fighting a war on drugs the government has increased the problems of society and made them far worse. A system of regulation rather than prohibition is a less harmful, more ethical and a more effective public policy.

LEAP does not condone nor encourage the use of any illegal substance.

Epilogue and Conclusion

As the agent hauled the heavy steel door open and the overwhelming smell of marijuana enveloped us, we stepped inside. About sixty feet long and thirty feet wide, the room is stuffed with hundreds of bags, packets, suitcases and bricks of marijuana; black tar heroin; cocaine; pills; and hallucinogens. The parcels were stacked helter-skelter, one on top of the other almost to the ceiling. The four chain-link cages on one side of the room are not sufficient to hold the hundreds of packages, so the room is almost inaccessible because the entryway is also stacked almost 10 feet high with caramel-colored taped bundles. The smell permeates our clothes, and the federal agent jokes that U.S. Customs might detain us for the intense smell wafting out of the car. We ask the street value of the drugs in the storage room and the agents speculate it to be in the millions of dollars.

LEELA LANDRESS, *EL PASO TIMES*, JUNE 1, 2008, DESCRIBING THE
STORAGE FACILITY CONTAINING ILLEGAL DRUGS CONFISCATED BY THE
MEXICAN ATTORNEY GENERAL'S OFFICE IN CIUDAD JUÁREZ

Juárez Drug War, 2008

As of December 2008, Ciudad Juárez remains a drug war zone. In January, the DEA arrested the second-in-command of the Juárez police force as he made arrangements for a drug deal with an undercover narc in an El Paso parking lot, and a series of startling revelations and violent reprisals followed. In early spring, Juárez investigators unearthed forty-six cadavers buried under the patios of two Juárez cartel safe houses.[1] Bloody shoot-outs and vicious executions occur daily as the Chapo Guzmán cartel of Sinaloa attempts to usurp the *plaza* of the Carrillo

Fuentes family, the youngest of whom, Rodolfo (aka "el Niño de Oro," "the Golden Boy") died at the hands of rival hit men in the parking lot of an upscale Culiacán shopping mall.[2] Using an intimidation strategy employed successfully in Nuevo Laredo, the Sinaloan "invaders" destabilized the Juárez *plaza* through a coordinated plan of targeted assassinations, arson attacks, kidnappings, or extortions directed at policemen, businessmen, street dealers, and foot soldiers of the Juárez cartel.

Policemen tuned to their restricted radio frequencies heard an anonymous voice identified with the Chapo Guzmán cartel announce that a "cleansing" (*la limpia*) of the police force had begun.[3] Local people interpreted this as an attempt by the Guzmán cartel to install loyal policemen in the place of those affiliated with the Carrillo Fuentes cartel, which had controlled the Juárez *plaza* for fifteen years. Every day during 2008, the Juárez newspapers, radio, and television reported the grisly body counts: some days eleven people died, other days eight or nine, and still others as few as three.[4] In one instance, drug killers dumped three decapitated bodies near the small town of El Sauzal in the Juárez Valley. The heads were left in black plastic bags nearby, one of which was found by a stray dog and dragged into town, leading to the discovery of the bodies. In several cases, gunmen murdered police officers in the presence of their small children.

The bullet-riddled bodies discarded in the streets of Juárez—many bearing signs of brutal torture, and some burned or decapitated—appeared wrapped in tape and blankets and frequently bore written signs or statements containing direct threats against the Juárez cartel (which issues counterthreats). The attackers also scrawled threatening messages and slogans on walls and buildings in Juárez and other cities of Chihuahua, and posted lists or banners on bridges and monuments—as well as on YouTube videos—naming policemen subject to execution if they did not join the new dominant cartel or leave their posts.[5] One sign threatened the governor of Chihuahua if he did not fire a specific police commander. Seven policemen on one list indeed were murdered soon thereafter; others were attacked but managed to survive, then quit or disappeared promptly. Anonymous individuals, presumably cartel members, even threatened emergency medical workers, who were told that if they rendered aid to shooting victims, they would also be killed. Several drug murders actually took place within hospitals or in emergency facilities.[6]

In response to these attacks, the Juárez cartel, apparently now allied with the Zetas and the Beltrán trafficking organization, massacred

Sinaloa cartel members, and the bloody war spread all over the state of Chihuahua, including the capital city (Chihuahua, Chihuahua), the Juárez Valley, Palomas, Parral, and inside the notorious Cereso prison of Juárez.[7] In Villa Ahumada, Chihuahua, the entire police force resigned or disappeared after the murder of several cops by armed commandos. In Sinaloa, a parallel war developed as the Juárez drug-trafficking organization took the war to its opponents' home turf by gunning down the son of drug lord Chapo Guzmán and killing many others.[8] Throughout Mexico, but especially in Mexico City (where cartel members murder top antidrug officials), Durango (where six heads in beer coolers turned up on the streets), Yucatán (where twelve decapitated bodies were found in a pile), Michoacán, Guerrero, Tijuana, Nuevo Laredo, the state of Mexico (twenty-four bodies were dumped in a wooded area), and Tamaulipas, the Juárez cartel and its allies fought the Chapo Guzmán group, or factions within the Chapo Guzmán–Sinaloa cartel squared off against each other or battled the emergent Zetas for control of key smuggling routes and *plazas*.

The Calderón administration sent thirty thousand soldiers to drug hot spots, including Juárez, Nuevo Laredo, Tijuana, Culiacán, and the state of Michoacán; but these forces did little to quell the violence.[9] In fact, they resulted in higher levels of casualties from battles between soldiers and cartel members, while the intercartel war continued unabated. Juárez citizens also accused the army of committing arbitrary detentions and human rights abuses. Thousands of residents of Juárez, especially nightclub owners and other business people, horrified by the violence and threats, fled to the United States. Dozens requested asylum.

The cartel violence, the collapse of the outgunned and corrupt Juárez police force, and the exclusive focus of local, state, and federal police forces and the military on antidrug efforts produced a security vacuum in Juárez. Cartel criminals and other organized-crime groups immediately took advantage of the breakdown in law enforcement. Car theft, bank and store robberies, kidnapping for ransom, extortion (especially by telephone), and other crimes skyrocketed in Juárez, creating a kind of "failed city" government.[10] Those committing the crimes frequently identified themselves as Zetas, whether truthfully or not, in order to scare their victims and the general public. The Juárez mayor fired 400 corrupt cops and attempted to replace them with soldiers from other parts of Mexico. (In addition, 112 Juárez cops resigned and nearly one-third left the force during 2008.) Yet few local people felt this would make any difference, and they complained that the police and military simply stood by at the scenes of numerous murders in broad daylight. The soldiers and policemen rightly feared that if they intervened or confiscated drug loads, they would be executed. The Juárez police fortified their stations with sandbags and snipers, but this made it only more evident that the drug-trafficking organizations were the most powerful forces in town.

The local consensus was that the Mexican government's war on the drug cartels was a failure. Thousands of businesses in the state of Chihuahua closed their doors. Tourists ceased going to Juárez. Foreign investors avoided the city after seeing news reports about a decapitated body hung from a bridge, severed heads left on sidewalks and in plazas, commando invasion robberies of maquiladoras, dead bodies propped against walls, teachers threatened with violence against schoolchildren if they did not hand over their Christmas bonuses, and the firebombing of numerous businesses that refused to pay protection money.

At the national level, the Calderón administration seemed bewildered and in disarray amid narco attacks on military convoys, the bombing of a crowd attending a Mexican independence day celebration in Calderón's home state of Michoacán, the murder of high-ranking police authorities, corruption cases involving top antidrug officials, and violent threats and political attacks directed at the federal government by drug-cartel members. Some analysts even discussed whether Mexico had become a failed state, while right-wing Americans began to call for a U.S. invasion to stop the drug violence.

As an anthropologist, I struggled to decipher the conflicting signs of the often confusing and labyrinthine DWZ. In addition to conducting my border research, I traveled to Culiacán, Sinaloa (the historical heartland of Mexican drug cartels), and observed the deep community roots of narco-culture, including whole neighborhoods, rich and poor, devoted to drug trafficking; churches and chapels built by narcos and devoted to narco-saints; and the huge, sumptuous section of the main cemetery that celebrated the short, violent lives of young men who died pursuing their fortunes in the drug trade. The young narcos' comfortable mausoleums sport images of Cessna drug planes, marijuana leaves, bottles of Buchanan's whiskey, and photos of the deceased in their prime, decked out in expensive leather boots, *norteño* cowboy hats, and *cintos piteados* while holding pistols or AK-47s.

Rather than hide their trafficking lifestyle, the families of the deceased brazenly celebrate the narco-culture. I interviewed prominent narco-novelists and other knowledgeable insiders, who made references to phenomenal fortunes, exotic narco-mansions, and horrific massacres, but, as they repeatedly said, *sin dar nombres, porque nos mete en cuestiones* [without giving names, because it gets us in trouble]. Many Sinaloenses complained that the narcos of the past obeyed gentlemanly codes of honor, whereas the new breed of drug traffickers kills women, children, and innocent bystanders indiscriminately. Like Studs Terkel, I record the voices of common workers, but I am also aware of the selectiveness of self-representations in the DWZ.

An observer of the immediate aftermath of the murder of the "Golden Boy," Rodolfo Carrillo Fuentes, showed me where seven or eight *sicarios* ambushed him, his wife, and several bodyguards in the parking lot of a fancy Culiacán shopping mall. My guide even showed me bullet holes in palm trees and buildings. The observer noted that he picked up a shell casing from the shooting as a souvenir, as well as a fragment of the Golden Boy's mutilated brain in case a DNA test proving his identity became necessary. This macabre and surreal field datum added to the inside information I acquired from sources as diverse as the former maid of an arrested Juárez policeman; a cousin of the former occupant of a Juárez safe house where dozens of bodies were uncovered; and close associates of a well-known Juárez–El Paso businessman who died outside of one of the gaudy nightclubs he ran in addition to (allegedly) working directly with the Cártel de Juárez.[11]

Days after his death, several of his Juárez nightclubs burned to the ground. These same nightclubs were mentioned in chain-letter-like Internet messages, e-mails, and cell-phone text messages in which alleged cartel members warned Juárez residents to stay home on the weekend of May 23–25, a weekend that would prove to be the bloodiest on record, as twenty-five died in drug violence.[12] Subsequently, a number of powerful Juárez families—listed by name—received notice that they would have to pay "war taxes" to the Juárez cartel or be decapitated.[13] In an especially ugly incident, eight men were murdered during a religious service at a drug rehabilitation clinic.

During the spring and summer of 2008, pro-Chapo *narcocorridos* played on police radio frequencies, supposedly broadcast by the Sinaloa cartel to intimidate Juárez policemen allied with Carrillo Fuentes. Moreover, folklore spread that Chapo himself walked into a Juárez restaurant (El Aroma) and ordered everyone present to turn off their cell phones and put them on the tables and to neither visit the bathroom nor try to leave the restaurant. While his bodyguards surrounded him, Chapo reportedly ate his meal calmly, paid the tab for all of the diners with hundred dollar bills, and then strolled out.

This same story has been reported in other drug hot spots, such as Nuevo Laredo and Torreón, and has become an urban legend. As Sanders (2008) observes about similar accounts concerned with devils or the occult in Tanzania and other poor countries hard-hit by neoliberal economic policies, such folklore represents the contradictory, ambivalent feelings of common people, who view rapid socioeconomic changes with hope and trepidation. The Chapo stories simultaneously express the average Mexican's anxiety about the vicious narco-violence and the arbitrary power of *narcotraficantes*, their dissatisfaction with the state's inability to protect them from drug violence and economic recession, and their morbid fascination with the power and ostentatious wealth of drug lords. These stories convey an image of Chapo appearing suddenly from nowhere to shower wealth and abundance on some while thumbing his nose at the government and dealing harshly with his rivals. Yet they also manifest Mexican citizens' fear that neither the neoliberal state nor the nouveau riche drug traffickers can provide safety and prosperity.

The everyday scenes of violence, emerging urban folklore, and *narco-mensajes* (narco-messages; primitive political manifestos displayed in public places) produce a collective hysteria in the Juárez population.[14] Panic-stricken people avoid their typical weekend shopping and night-life activities, and the insurgent Sinaloan narcos prove their point: that the police, military, elected government officials, and Juárez cartel are unable to guarantee the security of the population. The implied message is that only the new, Chapo Guzmán cartel can restore order and that it is a legitimate political and social entity. The Juárez cartel counters with its own narco-propaganda, arguing that only it has the best interests of Juárez in mind.

Whether or not the Sinaloa cartel is ultimately able to take over the Juárez *plaza*, it is clear that the top Mexican cartels have become masters at manipulating public opinion through the selective release of symbolically coded messages and images, and violent narco-spectacles.[15] One morning, eight *narco-mantas* [placards with messages espousing cartel perspectives] appeared, hanging from bridges in strategic locations throughout Juárez.[16] This media-savvy propaganda campaign has taken on the ideological dimensions of urban guerrilla warfare. Previous Mexican drug-trafficking organizations preferred clandestinity and focused strictly on the smuggling business. They were highly skilled at the arts of occultation and dissimulation. Today, cartels struggle to control territory and shape public opinion as well as to reap lucrative profits from drug sales.

The Mexican government sent 3,000 soldiers and hundreds of federal policemen to "restore order" to Chihuahua in Operación Conjunta Chihuahua [roughly, Operation Chihuahua United]. Despite announced results of the confiscation of 50 tons of marijuana and 900 guns, and the arrests of 1,200 suspected drug traffickers, the military and police presence has to date been a pronounced failure. Violence and criminality in Juárez continue unabated. The constant flow of drugs from Mexico to the United States seems barely affected. Drug traffickers grow more powerful by the day and begin adopting the weapons (such as car bombs made of butane gas cylinders with remote detonators) and tactics of Middle Eastern terrorist groups.

Overall, *narcotraficantes* and narco-culture have become the most significant current challenge to the Mexican state and status quo—economically, culturally, militarily, and politically—given the weakness and internal disintegration of the organized left (that is, the PRD [Partido de la Revolución Democrática, or Party of the Democratic Revolution]) and the incorporation of the traditionally right-wing PAN (Partido Acción Nacional, or National Action Party) into the system.[17] During the PRI's seventy-one-year reign, Mexico suffered from endemic corruption and drug trafficking flourished, but at least there was a type of stability, since a small group of powerful traffickers and PRI government officials maintained relatively predictable relationships. The democratization of Mexico, coupled with the decentralization and expansion of drug cartels, has produced a more fluid and more volatile sociopolitical environment.[18]

Final Observations about the Border DWZ

Ethnographically, I am able to get close to the Juárez drug war by walking through the city and talking to knowledgeable informants in El Paso and Juárez, but the morass of grisly details and the veracity of numerous emerging conspiracy theories are not transparent, obvious, or self-explanatory. Moreover, the nightmarish atmosphere of street homicides and firebombing terrorizes the local population and leads to a climate of fear that limits ethnographic research. Nonetheless, as outlined in the introduction to this book and fleshed out in the interviews, a number of patterns have emerged.[19] The Juárez violence and propaganda war illustrate key elements of the DWZ. Most significantly, these events show that the border DWZ is a space of unequal power, extreme brutality, anarchy, mystery, and flux. Drug cartels—understood as shifting alliances of drug traffickers loosely connected in efficient but illegal military-like, corporate businesses—in collusion with politicians, policemen, and government functionaries, exploit this chaotic situation to control *plazas* and transit routes for both local sales and the contraband shipment of drugs into the United States. Cartels capitalize on the murky yet economically fluid binational border environment to acquire high-tech weapons, stolen cars, radio and telecommunication equipment, and other technologies, and to bribe public officials in Mexico and the United States. They also constantly invent new ways to transport, hide, smuggle, and sell drugs, and come up with new tactics to fight their enemies. These tactics include novel forms of torture, kidnapping, and murder as well as creative modes of intimidating and terrorizing their enemies, politicians, neutral policemen, and society in general. This takes places amidst schisms within and between cartels, as well as between cartels and various groups within the police, military, government, and society at large.

Recent events demonstrate several emerging trends in narco-culture and narco-strategy.[20] These include the increasingly greater use of high-tech weapons and military equipment, such as bazookas, bulletproof vehicles, grenades and grenade launchers, body armor, armor-piercing bullets, car bombs, etc. Several cartels now maintain small armies, complete with their own distinctive uniforms. La Familia cartel even has its own bible, which specifies the duties of loyal Familia soldiers.

Cartels also adopt sophisticated espionage and computer technology to intercept telephone, especially cell-phone, conversations, to encrypt and transmit e-mail messages, and to diffuse propaganda through the Internet (such as the Chapo Guzmán cartel's video in which captured Zetas confess to murders and corrupt actions before being shot in the head). For modern cartels, it is not sufficient to establish business connections with Colombian cocaine brokers, bribe government officials, and creatively transport drugs across Latin America and the U.S.-Mexico border and into U.S. cities. It is also necessary to engage in ongoing urban guerrilla wars to maintain *plazas* and shipment routes; devise elaborate, high-finance money-laundering schemes; spy on rival cartels and the Mexican government; and fight a symbolic, ideological battle through blogs, Web sites, videos, e-mails, songs, public placards, paid advertisements in newspapers, and television and radio broadcasts.

Perhaps not consciously or deliberately, the strategies of modern drug cartels, though directed toward different ends, closely parallel those of Middle Eastern terrorist groups such as al Qaeda. Both are mobile, international, rapidly changing, and technologically savvy. They are also quite willing to use violent force and actions designed to kill—but just as importantly, to terrorize and traumatize. Last, both types of organizations recognize the importance of the Internet, television coverage, and the mass media generally for the promotion and diffusion of their causes: for recruiting, putting a particular spin on events and actions, creating an identity and mythos, and attacking their rivals.

The interviews and oral histories presented in this book illuminate various facets of the border DWZ. The stories of La Nacha, Fred Morales, and David the heroin trafficker demonstrate the deep roots of contraband smuggling in border economic, social, and cultural life. They show how the urban geography and transnational dimensions of the El Paso–Juárez community make drug trafficking a logical, even predictable, response to poverty and social inequality. Over time, smuggling techniques and tactics disseminate within families and neighborhoods, and are creatively elaborated on by resourceful entrepreneurs such as Cristal, Juan, Jorge, the "Chicano smuggler," the young smuggler, and the Anarchist. As noted earlier, the DWZ is not separate from the larger society but interpenetrated within it, especially in border areas.

Historically, DEA success against Colombian cartels in south Florida in the 1980s shifted the flow of cocaine from the Caribbean to the U.S.-Mexico border. New, Mexican drug-trafficking organizations, including the Aguilar-Muñoz Talavera cartel and eventually the Juárez cartel of the Carrillo Fuentes brothers replaced the smaller, more grassroots-oriented operations of La Nacha and others. Larger-scale cartels began to fight over the billions of dollars generated by the coke trade; this degenerated into the horrific violence that has wracked Juárez since 1993. The case of Francisco's brother illustrates the dire impact of drug killings on individuals and families. The stories of the businessman-scuba-diving instructor and the witness to a Juárez shooting exemplify the tragic effects on innocent bystanders and the community at large. Few people on either side of the El Paso–Juárez border have been unaffected by the drug war.

Law-enforcement efforts to combat the border drug trade have grown in rough proportion to the expanding cartels. Main U.S. government antidrug efforts include an extended wall, new surveillance systems, and the placement of more agents on the border—all part of a growing militarization of the international boundary with Mexico. The complexities of the expanding law-enforcement culture in the DWZ, and the diverse experiences of social actors within it, are illustrated by the oral histories of the Border Patrol agent, the undercover agent, and the intelligence officer. Antidrug agents, journalists, and other border-community residents have been hit hard by the bloody and divisive drug wars, as shown by the cases of the Juárez cop and the border reporter.

U.S. claims to victory in the drug war are clearly belied by the stories presented in this book. At present, there seems to be no immediate resolution to the problems and paradoxes provoked by the "war on drugs" policy, the seemingly bottomless U.S. demand for illegal drugs, and the feisty adaptability of transnational drug cartels. The multiple millions (probably billions) of dollars that the U.S. government intends to grant Mexico to fight drug trafficking as part of the Mérida Initiative cannot fix a broken policy. Though no quick solutions are possible, the words of Terry Nelson and the other voices presented here all point toward the need for revised practices, innovative strategies, and new ways of thinking about the DWZ.

Notes

Introduction

1. Estimates of the revenues obtained by Mexican drug traffickers vary widely. A U.S. Government Accountability Office report from 2007 estimated Mexican drug-trafficking revenue at $23 billion (for details, see Manuel Roig-Franzia, "Mexican Drug Cartels Move North; U.S. Effort to Battle Groups Is Flawed, GAO Report Says," *Washington Post*, September 20, 2007; http://www.washingtonpost.com/wp-dyn/content/article/2007/09/19/AR2007091902442.html (accessed July 18, 2008). Many estimates of the value of Mexican illegal-drug revenue exceed the estimated $30 billion budget of combined U.S. anti-drug forces (for the $30 billion figure, see Decker and Chapman 2008, 2).

2. My approach differs from Terkel's primarily in the degree to which I insert my own story into the mix and attempt to analyze and theorize my data. Terkel mainly provided a forum for the voices of his interviewees, without evaluating or commenting on them. The multiple voices presented in this book illustrate the complexity of perspectives and "truths" in the border drug war zone (DWZ).

3. Much of what is publicly known about Mexican drug trafficking is made available in the Mexican newsweekly *Proceso*.

4. The Juárez cartel is also known as the Carrillo Fuentes cartel. Corrupt policemen associated with this cartel are sometime referred to as *La Línea* (the Line). The Sinaloa cartel is also known as the Chapo Guzmán cartel or, in some cases, as *Gente Nueva* (the New People).

5. On the ubiquity of drug trafficking and folklore about the drug trade on the U.S.-Mexico border, see the article by Campbell (2005).

6. The drug trade is so widespread in Juárez that the discovery of a thirty-one-acre field of marijuana in the Teófilo Borunda irrigation canal, which cuts through the populous commercial heart of the city, had little local impact (Dávila 2007a, 17).

7. On the thankless, often violent, but seldom lucrative jobs performed by the mostly unskilled common workers in the drug trade, see the article by Tobar

and Sánchez (2007). The seminal work of Sullivan (1990) deals with limitations of petty crime as a subsistence strategy. Kopinak (1996) discusses the dead-end aspect of maquiladora jobs, which are similar in some respects to those at the lower rungs of the drug trade (i.e., they are poorly paid, sometimes dangerous, short term, and provide little chance for social mobility).

8. Even if marijuana is a relatively innocuous substance, its large-scale trafficking by criminal organizations produces violence. In that sense, even pot smuggling is not strictly victimless.

9. Substances such as those referred to here as "drugs" are not inherently good or bad, healthy or unhealthy. Such classifications can be understood only within culturally constructed notions of morality, medicine, and consumer behavior, as well as within social, economic, and political hierarchies.

10. It should also be noted, however, that large-scale underground drug commerce cannot function effectively without numerous aboveground elements, such as bankers, lawyers, real estate agents, etc.

Another relevant concept is "state criminalization" (Geffray 2002), which refers to systematic corruption that links members of organized crime, such as drug traffickers, with representatives of the state. I also find persuasive Scott's notion of a "deep politics"—a hidden interface between criminals and politicians—although my usage differs from his because in the Mexican case examined here, the involvement of the state in illegal activity is much more apparent and well known than in the Kennedy murder conspiracy he studied.

11. According to Mexican governmental sources, at least eighty *municipios* (similar to counties) are controlled by drug traffickers. For details, see the article " . . . Y controla 80 alcaldías, dice la PGR," http://www.diario.com.mx/nota.php?notaid=ad5c4b1bd47299c080d1fd4398012ac6 (accessed July 15, 2008). An expert on Latin American drug trafficking claims that at least that many municipalities are controlled by traffickers in Michoacán state alone and that 8 percent of Mexican territory is controlled by narcos (Ravelo 2008).

12. Benavides (2008, 120) considers narco-dramas and *narcocorridos* as forms of popular resistance to inequality in the postcolonial, globalized, neoliberal Americas. His analysis shows how narco-melodrama expresses popular frustration with the status quo, but it neglects the extent to which drug cartels and their narco-cultural expressions become new forms of oppressive power in places like Juárez.

13. Mexico has produced many complex, ambiguous, or contradictory movements (the Pancho Villa rebels, Zapatistas, Cardenismo, etc.) as well as the emblematic leaders of such groups. For other world areas, we have the example of Khun Sa in Burma (McCoy 1999) or Italian organized-crime groups (Schneider and Schneider 2005).

14. There are other forms of illicit drug use that we might prefer to call "abuse" or to label as either "recreational" or "artistic"—my point is to emphasize the self-administered dimension of much of what we call drug use.

15. The free trade facilitated by NAFTA actually streamlined Mexican drug-cartel operations by improving transportation systems, communications equipment, infrastructure facilities, and technological wherewithal, including weaponry. Yet I argue that, in a kind of feedback loop, illegal-drug commerce ends

up stimulating the larger economic system in which the United States is a superordinate, and Mexico a subordinate, power.

16. The U.S. government has only recently begun constructing a solid wall along its southern border, and already there are reports of Mexican smugglers scaling it with ladders or using high-tech blowtorches to cut holes in it.

17. Ostensibly, the steel mesh was built to provide shade to pedestrians, but it was probably mainly meant to stop people from climbing over the fence.

18. Although exact figures are not available, even border law-enforcement officials admit that they catch only a small amount of the drugs smuggled from Mexico into the United States; some of my informants estimated that the figure may be as low as 10 percent. The U.S. government hopes to achieve a 25 percent drug interdiction rate in 2008, an indication that the actual rate is lower than that. For details, see U.S. Office of National Drug Control Policy, *National Drug Control Strategy: 2008 Annual Report* (especially page 48), available at http://www.ondcp.gov/publications/policy/ndcs08/2008ndcs.pdf. On the general failures of the Mexican judicial and police systems, see the studies edited by Bailey and Goodson (2001). A specific example of impunity in Ciudad Juárez: In March 2008 there were 117 murders in Juárez, none of which had been solved by May 2008; see "Menos asesinatos, pero cero arestos," *El Diario*, May 3, 2008. Many soldiers and police officers are among the victims of drug violence. When government officials or politicians are murdered by traffickers, explanations of the killings often do not claim that the victims were innocent, but that they were cartel employees who had been killed for disobedience.

19. Drug smugglers in the El Paso–Juárez area also place classified advertisements in newspapers to recruit unsuspecting drivers to take loads of drugs (hidden in vehicles) across the border. Potential smugglers seeking work in the drug trade also may place "job wanted" pleas on so-called narco-blogs (Sas 2007). Other places where contraband drugs have been hidden by Mexican traffickers include "in boxes of cookies, under frozen fish, among beer cans, in hermetically-sealed in loads of frozen chicken or among boxes of soap . . . in the mail, in boxes of French fries, in cans of chiles in vinegar, or in bags of marshmallows" (Jiménez 2008).

20. Robert Chessey, personal communication, April 2008.

21. Many critics of the war on drugs suggest that it is not meant to be won, but to be used to justify a series of political interventions, bureaucratic prerogatives, and cultural positions (on these issues, see the Terry Nelson interview in this volume and the study by Valentine [2006]).

22. This is now a common element of drug folklore, but may be derived from a cassette tape that Caro Quintero supposedly distributed after he was captured and incarcerated in the 1980s.

23. A more specific use of the phrase "the Federation" (i.e., *La Federación*) used to refer specifically to Sinaloa-rooted traffickers, including the Carrillo Fuentes family, Chapo Guzmán, "El Azul," "El Mayo" Zambada, members of the Beltrán family, et al. But this loose alliance disintegrated. Today the Carrillo Fuentes group, allied with the Beltrán faction, is at war with Chapo Guzmán.

24. Here is novelist Homero Aridjis (2003, 67) describing the (fictional) top narco-architect in Mexico: "This man had constructed in the country mansions

of many styles: narco-baroque, narco-colonial, art-narco, narco-Californian, and narco end of the millennium" (free translation by author). Gulf cartel members who control the Nuevo Laredo *plaza* are devoted to La Santa Muerte (the Grim Reaper), to whom they reportedly dedicate "narco-satanic" rituals (Alfredo Corchado, personal communication, March 2008). Another dimension of narco-culture and use of the "narco-" prefix is seen in narco-dramas, popular films about drug traffickers (Benavides 2008).

25. In the case of the Tijuana cartel, Blancornelas (2003, 397–407) calls this a move from a "cartel" to a "corporate" form of business organization.

26. I use the term *plaza* in a broader sense than do many journalists and analysts such as Lupsha (1991), for whom *plazas* are primarily local drug-trafficking arrangements. I conceive of the *plazas* as wide matrices of political, economic, and logistical connections through which international drug-trafficking networks operate. I do concur, however, with Lupsha's interpretation of the dynamic nature of *plazas* (44). Like the term "cartel," *la plaza* is often used in imprecise or misleading ways by commentators on drug-trafficking issues.

27. Traffickers and law-enforcement officials may modify the physical landscape with tunnels or walls or employ new technologies or transportation systems to overcome geographical barriers and great distances. Nonetheless, geographical obstacles that either separate drug crops in the field from their ultimate consumers in American and Mexican cities or, conversely, protect drug traffickers from the reach of law enforcement are more constant and predictable than are the changing social networks of drug traffickers.

28. However, drug-shipment routes, especially on airlines and boats, can change, though less so along highways and smaller roads. Moreover, political circumstances also change, most notably by the growing power of the Partido Acción Nacional (National Action Party, or PAN) nationally and of the Partido de la Revolución Democrática (Party of the Democratic Revolution, or PRD) in Mexico City and some states.

29. Although it should be noted that in parts of Tamaulipas, Michoacán, Sinaloa, and Durango, the Mexican state has ceded some power to drug organizations, and the relative power of cartel groups vis-à-vis state actors is increasing.

30. The Arellano Félix cartel, which was founded by a well-to-do family and later joined by middle- to upper-class youths, known as *los narcojuniors*, represents an exception to the generally lower-class origins of Mexican drug lords. Enedina Arellano Félix, who now heads the Arellano Félix cartel, is a female exception to the general male domination of cartels. On the specificities of women's lives in the drug-trafficking milieu, see Campbell (2008).

31. In 2006 there were approximately 2,000 drug executions in Mexico. During 2007, this total increased to 2,500 (Grillo 2007). In 2008 there were at least 5,300 drug murders in the country.

32. The Zetas are highly trained Mexican soldiers and antidrug operatives who deserted the government and joined the Gulf cartel before gaining independence and possibly forming their own separate trafficking organization and challenging the Chapo Guzmán cartel for supremacy (Corchado 2007; Ravelo 2007c). They are known for their sophisticated knowledge of military weapons and tactics, their extreme brutality, and their expansion from drug trafficking

into other sources of organized crime, including kidnapping, extortion, and armed robbery.

33. I have very little information on the methamphetamine business, which is also handled by Mexican cartels. The focus of this book is on heroin, cocaine, and marijuana trafficking.

34. Although Benavides (2008, 128) rightfully points out that the main enemy in Mexican narco-dramas is the Mexican state, the actual functioning of drug cartels is such that drug traffickers and agents of the state are often either one and the same or entangled in tight bonds of collusion, i.e., the relationship that allows the drug *plaza* to function. In that sense, the narco-culture expressed in movies, songs, and novels is not necessarily a true reflection of "narco-reality."

35. For a remarkable list of Mexican police on the payroll of drug organizations in 1993, see Blancornelas (2002, 104–107). Space limitations prevent me from discussing Mexican antidrug law-enforcement activities to the extent they deserve. The best book on this subject is by Toro (1995).

36. Small-scale sellers of drugs, often independent operators separate from cartels, are known as *poquiteros* (from *poco*, a small amount) or *burreros* (literally, burrito vendors).

37. Gertz served as secretary of public security from 2000 to 2004, during the Fox administration.

38. The "Barbie" is Edgar Valdez Villareal, the lead hit man for the Chapo (short for Archibaldo) Guzmán cartel; "Chacky" is Arturo Hernández, lead enforcer for Amado Carrillo Fuentes, deceased leader of the Juárez cartel; the "Lord of the Skies" was Amado Carrillo Fuentes; "Blondie" is Héctor Palma, a top capo from Sinaloa; the "Wild Pig" is Manuel Salcido Uzeta, sanguinary Sinaloa cartel leader and hit man; and the "Little Tiger" is Francisco Javier Arellano Félix, imprisoned leader of the Arellano Félix cartel.

39. Sinaloa, the historical home of Mexican drug trafficking, has the largest regional influence on the general narco-cultural style. It should also be noted that many accomplices of the drug cartels, such as money launderers, politicians, bankers, and others, deliberately avoid the narco style, although, ironically, many federal policemen, who are supposed to be the opponents of organized crime, also adopt a narco look.

40. *Narco-fiestas* are memorably evoked and stylized in Aridjis's *La Santa Muerte* (2003).

41. Recently, because of the aggressive use of stash-house prevention units by the El Paso police, some traffickers have chosen to avoid repeatedly using a single location for drug storage. Instead, they use a different house for drug storage each trip, creating a kind of mobile stash house in order to avoid detection.

42. The most insightful information available about the activities of cartel hit men is the extensive account of the life of Michael Decker, a gringo hit man for the Sicilia Falcón cartel (Mills 1986, 281–316, 815–855). Often, shootings culminate in the *tiro de gracia*, the coup de grâce shot to the head or face at close range.

43. Messages may be as simple as thinly veiled threats, like "For those who don't believe" or "Respect your promises," or more elaborate taunts addressed

to specific individuals or specific actions by rival cartel members, police, or politicians (Gilot 2007).

44. Particular *narcocorridos* may be played on the radio, on police radios, at concerts, or in bars and other venues as a way to announce that a certain cartel is in charge of a region or is attempting to take control of it.

The most famous narco-video to date is one sent to *Dallas Morning News* reporter Alfredo Corchado (a clip from which is presented in this volume) in which government agents allied with the Sinaloa cartel appear to interrogate, torture, and murder members of the Zetas (Corchado and Samuels 2005).

45. These violent "action sets" both partake of existing idioms or objects within Mexican popular culture and appropriate techniques seen in drug movies like *Scarface*. They also represent the anarchic, destructive "creativity" of marginal but upwardly mobile men in Mexican society, who blaze independent paths through the suffocating, caste-like hierarchies of the mainstream Mexican class system. For an analysis of the emergence of new marginal men in the Mexican social structure, see the studies by Wolf (1966) and Friedrich (1987).

46. The law-enforcement half of the book, which contains interviews with antidrug agents of various types, represents in some sense a critical ethnography of the state, although its primary purpose is to shed light on the issue of drug trafficking.

Part I: Smuggling in the Drug War Zone

Introduction

1. In addition to the fieldwork on which this book is based, my knowledge of the Mexican drug trade is informed by nearly twenty years' residence on the border, near the activities of one of the major cartels, and by a careful reading of almost every issue of *Proceso* since its inception, in 1976. Since the early 1980s, most issues have contained important information about the drug trade.

2. There are also several minor genres of narco-art, including paintings, installations, *narco-novelas* (soap operas with a drug theme), the narco-dramas discussed by Benavides (2008), narco-blogs, and *narcocorridos*.

3. Taussig's brilliant ethnographic diary of everyday violence in Colombia (Taussig 2003) is closer in spirit to the present book than are his more philosophical discussions in *My Cocaine Museum* (2004). Many of the points made by Taussig (2003) regarding the social and cultural dimensions and impacts of Colombian paramilitary violence are relevant to the U.S.-Mexico border DWZ.

4. This book was completed before the advent of the drug violence that wracked Juárez during 2008. In general, my interviews focused on earlier periods in border history, since discussing current events was often prohibitively dangerous.

La Nacha

1. Exceptions to Sinaloan dominance of large-scale drug trafficking historically have consisted of the Gulf cartel (along the Tamaulipas and Nuevo León

borders with Texas), founded in the 1930s by Juan N. Guerra and eventually controlled by Juan García Ábrego and later by Osiel Cárdenas; the Sicilia Falcón group in Tijuana; Pablo Acosta in Ojinaga, Chihuahua (Sicilia Falcón and Acosta were prominent in the 1970s, and the latter continued into the 1980s); La Familia in Michoacán, the Herreras of Durango, and the Díaz Parada organization in Oaxaca.

Selling Drugs in Downtown Juárez

1. According to the National Drug Intelligence Center, 380 tons of South American cocaine passed through Mexico into the United States in 2006 (editorial, *New York Times*, November 19, 2007, available at www.nytimes.com/2007/11/19/opinion/19mon2.html). That same year, Mexico produced between 9 and 19 tons of heroin for the U.S. market. Given that Ciudad Juárez (along with the Nuevo Laredo and Tijuana areas) is one of the three main gateways for drug importation from Mexico into the United States, it is safe to assume that many tons of illegal drugs passed through Chihuahua (and specifically Juárez), either undetected by Mexican police and military authorities or with their consent.

Witness to a Juárez Drug Killing

1. The information from this section comes from numerous discussions I have held with Jaime Hervella since 1994, from countless news stories in the *El Paso Times*, *El Diario de Juárez*, and *Norte* newspapers, and from accounts by dozens of residents of Juárez.

Part 2: Law Enforcement in the Drug War Zone

Introduction

1. The ideas I presented here were heavily influenced by the publications of Joe Heyman, many of whose works are cited above, and by countless conversations we have engaged in over a five-year period. As discussed in the introduction and throughout Part II, "law enforcement" refers to U.S. law enforcement unless otherwise specified.

Journalism and Drug Trafficking

1. For information on human rights violations committed against Mexican journalists, see PEN's "2005 Resolution on Mexico," which is available at www.pen.org/page.php/prmID/1008. In November 2008, veteran Juárez crime reporter Armando Rodríguez was murdered in front of his home, allegedly by drug traffickers.
2. Francisco, the subject of the chapter "The Death of Francisco," was buried in one of these mass graves.

Epilogue and Conclusion

1. Some of the bodies were dismembered, so further investigation may change the exact total number of victims. In the first six months of 2008, more than 400 people had been murdered in Juárez, compared to only 4 in El Paso, a shocking example of the inequities of the DWZ.

Vast numbers of Mexicans suffer in the drug war, but very few Americans, the ultimate recipients of most of the drugs, are affected. Generally, the weapons used to commit the murders in Mexico were purchased in the United States, particularly in El Paso, and then smuggled across the border. Lax U.S. gun controls and lax monitoring of smuggling from the United States into Mexico is another profound inequality of the DWZ.

2. The murder of Rodolfo Carrillo Fuentes was widely viewed as a signal that the Chapo Guzmán cartel had declared war on the Carrillo Fuentes cartel. The bloody conflict, which intensified in Juárez in 2008 and has claimed unprecedented numbers of victims, is the main front in the war between the two cartels, which is waged throughout Mexico. A previous war for control of the Juárez *plaza* occurred in 1997 and 1998, after the death of Amado Carrillo Fuentes. That war pitted Rafael Muñoz Talavera against Vicente Carrillo Fuentes, the brother of Amado and Rodolfo, and claimed hundreds of lives—far fewer that the number of victims in the current conflict. The Vicente Carrillo Fuentes faction, which currently runs the Juárez cartel, was the clear victor in the first Juárez drug war.

3. Cartel members also commandeered the emergency broadcasting system in Juárez and used it to spread pro-cartel propaganda and messages. A typical narco-message, presumably written by the Juárez cartel to attack the Chapo Guzmán cartel, consisted of the following words left on a sign that was hung from a bridge in Ciudad Juárez in June 2008: "Welcome goddamn assholes, dogfuckers, people that don't give a damn and only scare fools, killers of innocent people. Even if you hide, you are going to have to fuck your mothers, come on out so that we can face each other. Chapo . . . " [a list of names of members of the Chapo Guzmán cartel follows]. For details, see *El Diario*, June 11, 2008. The Chapo Guzmán cartel often refers to members of the Juárez cartel as *puercos* (pigs), in reference to their supposedly greedy control of the Juárez *plaza* drug profits. In pro–Chapo Guzmán propaganda, Chapo is called the *quitapuercos*, the one who rids the *plaza* of greedy pigs.

4. Juárez morgues had a hard time coping with the high volume of corpses. In Culiacán, which has experienced horrendous levels of drug violence for at least thirty years, the funerary business expanded from a mere two in the 1980s to 22 by 2008 (Juan Carlos Ayala Barrón, personal communication, March 2008).

5. Many of the YouTube videos are carefully crafted, and present the names, nicknames, phone numbers, and other personal details of supposed members of the Juárez or Chapo Guzmán cartels, or of corrupt policemen and politicians. At the time of this writing, more than forty Juárez policemen have died in drug violence in 2008. According to several of my sources, segments of the Chihuahua state police owe allegiance to the Vicente Carrillo Fuentes car-

tel, whereas federal agents in Chihuahua are more likely to be allied with the Chapo Guzmán cartel.

Drug cartel members have also sent YouTube videos and e-mails to prominent Juárez entrepreneurs, as well as residents of El Paso and New Mexico, threatening them with death or the destruction of their businesses. In some cases, cartel hit men threaten their victims by phone before killing them. Stories and folklore related to these events heighten the terror felt by the community. On "mythological warfare" and the power of death lists to function as a kind of "wall-poster journalism," see the study by Taussig (2003, 11, 67–68).

6. Full details of these events are available in issues of the Juárez newspapers *El Diario* and *Norte* and the *El Paso Times* from 2008.

7. The Beltrán and Guzmán families had been the keystones of the Sinaloa cartel, but this alliance broke down after Chapo Guzmán allegedly provided information to the Mexican government that allowed it to capture one of the most powerful Beltrán brothers.

8. Like Chapo Guzmán, the leaders of the Juárez cartel are originally from Sinaloa, but they have less power there than does Chapo.

9. The Mexican military presence may have increased rather than lessened the violence in Juárez. The military arrested some low-level cartel workers, but only one high-level cartel member, Pedro Sánchez. The military is also alleged to have protected a load of cartel cocaine in a Hummer that got stuck in the Rio Grande near Neely's Crossing, Texas, in 2006. A Mexican government crackdown on traffickers in the 1970s, Operation Condor, was temporarily successful in slowing the flow of drugs to the United States, but had little long-term impact. Sinaloan narcos simply regrouped in Guadalajara, and eventually fortified their operations on the border and returned to Sinaloa, the mecca of Mexican drug trafficking. The government's confiscation of two hundred million dollars from a Mexico City stash house and a load of twenty tons of cocaine in a boat off the coast of Michoacán in recent years barely affected cartel operations.

10. There were eighty-six bank robberies in Juárez in 2008, three times the former highest figure, and business fires increased dramatically. Juárez has become so dangerous that even the mayor resides in El Paso.

11. I had also arranged to interview a top drug lord in a key border town in Coahuila. When I learned that the drug boss was a member of the Zetas, however, I canceled the interview.

12. Subsequently, drug-cartel commandos burned numerous Juárez bars controlled by their adversaries or by vulnerable businessmen. This is an example of how drug-trafficking organizations have expanded into other forms of crime, including kidnapping for ransom and the extortion of business owners, to compensate for declining revenues caused by the violence and disorganization that have resulted from the intercartel wars and the presence of thousands of Mexican soldiers and police agents in border cities. In the case of the twelve bars torched as of June 16, 2008, observers speculate that in several cases the bar owners refused to pay extortion demands made by cartel members. Many business people, such as a group of more than 300 owners of auto-related sales outlets (junkyards, used-car lots, car parts stores, etc.), simply closed their doors, perhaps permanently.

13. The mayors of small Mexican towns are also frequent victims of extortion by drug-trafficking groups like the Zetas. In March 2008, I spoke with the mayor of the second-largest town in the state of Aguascalientes. He told me that during his first day in office, he received a phone call from the Zetas, demanding that he work for them and pay protection money. The mayor refused to comply. It is not always clear which cartel or faction is responsible for the killings, extortions, threats, kidnappings, etc. The main cartels use roughly the same weaponry or tactics, although the Zeta group is notorious for quickly moving into a city or region and then intimidating the population, extorting money from businesses, and kidnapping prominent people and holding them for ransom (Ravelo 2007c).

14. According to another piece of urban folklore that I collected, a woman in a Juárez hair salon began criticizing *sicarios* for committing brutal acts of violence. Unbeknownst to her, a *sicario* was actually getting a haircut in the same salon while the woman was talking. When the woman sat down in the salon chair to have her hair cut, the *sicario* approached the hairstylist with a loaded gun and ordered her to shave the woman's head. Such folklore, recounted to me with trepidation by a local woman, has spread rapidly in conjunction with the expansion of violence in Juárez.

15. In Sinaloa, the Chapo Guzmán cartel has even organized protest marches against the Mexican government's policy of sending the military to the state to fight drug traffickers.

16. The same day, a YouTube video appeared, purportedly presented by Juárez businessmen, in which a self-proclaimed businessmen's "death squad" announced it would take revenge against those who were burning and destroying local businesses. The video stated that revenge would take the form of "an eye for an eye and a tooth for a tooth."

17. Moreover, American authorities have begun to consider Mexican cartels a major threat to the national security of the United States. Mexican cartels now supply drugs to all the major U.S. cities and hundreds of smaller communities. Locally, the drug violence has spilled over into El Paso. About fifty people wounded in the Juárez drug war sought treatment at El Paso's Thomason Hospital in 2008. Some of them required El Paso police protection because of fears that hit squads from Mexico would attempt to finish off the wounded. Additionally, according to credible sources, more than a dozen people have been kidnapped in El Paso and taken to Juárez by drug-cartel members.

18. In spring 2009, as this book was going to press, the Mexican government sent an additional 5,000 soldiers and about 1,000 police agents to Juárez. The Mexican military took control of the municipal police department. This "surge" strategy led to a decline in homicides and an apparent lull in the local drug war for one month, but the violence worsened thereafter.

19. Here my interpretation differs from that of Bowden (2008), who views the current wave of violence in Juárez as a kind of chaotic, patternless Armageddon, a mindless bloodbath without rhyme or reason. Regrettably, Bowden has misread the situation. He claims that recent homicide victims have not been cartel members and that the war in Juárez is not between cartels, because it is a fight to control street drug sales. He fails to realize, as discussed in this book,

that organized-crime groups, that is, Mexican cartels, in fact dominate local street cocaine sales in cities like Juárez, Culiacán, Nuevo Laredo, Tijuana, and elsewhere. His theory of wild, uncontrolled violence is wrongheaded.

In fact, many local observers are able to clearly identify which faction has committed specific murders—identifications that are made much easier by notes or signs left on or near the victims' bodies by cartel members. These notes or signs, typically, taunt or attack a rival cartel or explain why an individual was killed. Such messages are not always transparent and may, in some instances, be deliberately misleading, but they are often quite revealing. The homicide victims have not always been high-level cartel members, but the affiliation of many of the victims with one cartel, faction, or gang (or the fact that they were viewed as a threat to the interests of a cartel or faction) has been generally apparent. The existence of an ongoing cartel war for control of the Juárez *plaza* is undeniable. We should naturally be skeptical of an observer, such as Bowden, who characterizes Mexico as "a country where the weak are always prey, where the favorite verb is *chingar*, to fuck over" (2008, 103).

20. One trend noted by some observers was the development of a "Juárez style" of committing drug murders, which consists of the occupants of several vehicles blocking the path of another vehicle and then spraying the driver of the blocked vehicle with bullets (Borunda 2008c). Perhaps this tactic could be more accurately described as "Sinaloa style," since both the Juárez and Sinaloa cartels are run by Sinaloa natives. I experienced this maneuver sans bullets in March 2008 while conducting research in the Jardines del Humaya narco-cemetery in Culiacán, Sinaloa, with journalist Alfredo Corchado. As we prepared to leave the cemetery after photographing the crypts of top Mexican drug lords, our car was quickly surrounded by two late-model pickups belonging to the Culiacán municipal police. Each pickup contained six or seven gunmen clutching high-powered automatic rifles. We were at the mercy of the policemen, who, according to our local guide, were on the payroll of "El Mayo" Zambada, a top member of the Sinaloa cartel. Fortunately, we were quickly released once the police commander determined that we were unarmed. Throughout our visits to Culiacán churches, neighborhoods, and other public places controlled by traffickers, our movements were observed and reported to cartel superiors by spotters known as *balcones* (literally, "balconies").

References

Adler, Patricia. 1993. *Wheeling and dealing: An ethnography of an upper-level drug dealing and smuggling community.* New York: Columbia Univ. Press.

Agamben, Giorgio. 1998. *Homo sacer: Sovereign power and bare life.* Stanford, Calif.: Stanford Univ. Press.

Agar, Michael. 2006. *Dope double agent: The naked emperor on drugs.* Lulubooks [online publisher].

Alfaro, Leónidas. 2005. *Tierra blanca.* Córdoba, Spain: Editorial Almuzara.

Andrade Bojorges, José Alfredo. 1999. *La historia secreta del narco: Desde navolato vengo.* Mexico City: Oceano.

Andreas, Peter. 2000. *Border games: Policing the U.S.-Mexico divide.* Ithaca, N.Y.: Cornell Univ. Press.

Andreas, Peter, and Ethan Nadelmann. 2006. *Policing the globe: Criminalization and crime control in international relations.* New York: Oxford Univ. Press.

Appadurai, Arjun. 1996. *Modernity at large: Cultural dimensions of globalization.* Minneapolis: Univ. of Minnesota Press.

Aridjis, Homero. 2003. *La santa muerte: Sexteto del amor, las mujeres, los perros y la muerte.* Mexico City: Alfaguara.

Astorga, Luis. 2005. *El siglo de las drogas: El narcotráfico, del porfiriato al nuevo milenio.* Mexico City: Plaza y Janés.

Bailey, John, and Roy Goodson, eds. 2001. *Organized crime and democratic governability in Mexico and the U.S. borderlands.* Pittsburgh: Univ. of Pittsburgh Press.

Bagley, Bruce, and William Walker, eds. 1994. *Drug trafficking in the Americas.* Coral Gables, Fla.: Univ. of Miami, North-South Center Press.

Baum, Dan. 1996. *Smoke and mirrors: The war on drugs and the politics of failure.* Boston: Little, Brown.

Benavides, O. Hugo. 2008. *Drugs, thugs, and divas: Telenovelas and narco-dramas in Latin America.* Austin: Univ. of Texas Press.

Bertram, Eva, Morris Blachman, Kenneth Sharpe, and Peter Andreas. 1996. *Drug war politics: The price of denial.* Berkeley and Los Angeles: Univ. of California Press.

Blancornelas, Jesús. 2002. *El cártel: Los Arellano Félix; La mafia más poderosa en la historia de América Latina*. Mexico City: Plaza y Janés.

———. 2003. *Horas extra: Los nuevos tiempos del narcotráfico*. Mexico City: Plaza y Janés.

———. 2005. *En estado de alerta: Los periodistas y el gobierno frente al narcotráfico*. Mexico City: Plaza y Janés.

Borunda, Daniel. 2008a. Arrests expected to put dent in Barrio Azteca leadership. *El Paso Times*, January 11.

———. 2008b. Activities of gang detailed at hearing. *El Paso Times*, January 17.

———. 2008c. Drug cartels possess more fire power, technology. *El Paso Times*, June 2.

Bourgois, Philippe. 1995. *In search of respect: Selling crack in el barrio*. New York: Cambridge Univ. Press.

Bowden, Charles. 2002. *Down by the river: Drugs, money, murder, and family*. New York: Simon and Schuster.

———. 2005. *A shadow in the city: Confessions of an undercover drug warrior*. Orlando, Fla.: Harcourt.

———. 2008. Mexico's red days. *GQ*, August 2008.

Burnett, John. 2007. The forgotten war on drugs; War on drugs hasn't stemmed flow into U.S. http://www.npr.org/templates/story/story.php?storyId=9213877 (accessed October 24, 2007).

Burroughs, William. 1989. *Interzone*. New York: Viking.

Campbell, Howard. 2004. Foreword to *El narcotraficante: Narcocorridos and the construction of a cultural persona on the U.S.-Mexico border*, by Mark Edberg, ix–xi. Austin: Univ. of Texas Press.

———. 2005. Drug trafficking stories: Everyday forms of narco-folklore on the U.S.-Mexico border. *International Journal of Drug Policy* 16, no. 5: 326–333.

———. 2006. ¿El soma de un mundo infeliz? Una mirada sobre el narcotráfico desde la antropología. [Extended interview of the author by Lucy Leyva.] *Akademia* 6, no. 4: 4–15.

———. 2008. Female drug smugglers on the U.S.–Mexico border: Gender, crime, and empowerment. *Anthropological Quarterly* 81, no. 1: 233–268.

Campbell, Howard, and Josiah Heyman. 2007. Slantwise: Beyond domination and resistance on the border. *Journal of Contemporary Ethnography* 36, no. 1: 3–30.

Caporal, José Antonio. 2003. *Cárteles protegidos: Droga y sangre en México*. Bogotá: Ediciones Gato Azul.

Cartwright, Gary. 1998. *Dirty dealing: Drug smuggling on the Mexican border and the assassination of a federal judge; An American parable*. El Paso: Cinco Puntos.

Central Intelligence Agency. 1995. *International Narcotics Review* (June–July 1995). http://www.foia.cia.gov/ (search under "International Narcotics Review"; accessed February 11, 2008).

Certeau, Michel de. 2002. *The practice of everyday life*. Translated by Steven Rendall. Berkeley and Los Angeles: Univ. of California Press.

Corchado, Alfredo. 2007. Cartel's enforcers outpower their boss. *Dallas Morning News,* June 11, 2007. http://www.dallasnews.com/sharedcontent/dws/news/world/stories/061107dnintzetas.3a6238.html (accessed February 6, 2008).

Corchado, Alfredo, and Lennox Samuels. 2005. Video from Mexico shows drug brutality. *Dallas Morning News,* December 1, 2005. http://www.streetgangs.com/billboard/viewtopic.php?t=10461&sid=c8ce480348f8f1055eed4e294baef981 (accessed February 6, 2008).

Courtwright, David T. 2001. *Forces of habit: Drugs and the making of the modern world.* Cambridge, Mass.: Harvard Univ. Press.

Daudistel, Howard. 2007. Substance abuse: A public health and security problem. Unpublished MS in possession of author.

Dávila, Patricia. 2007a. La tierra de los narcos. *Proceso* 1597 (June 10, 2007), 14–17.

———. 2007b. Y el capo mayor se casó con Emma I. *Proceso* 1609 (September 2, 2007), 6–11.

Davis, Wade. 1997. *One river: Explorations and discoveries in the Amazon rain forest.* New York: Simon and Schuster.

Debord, Guy. 2006. *Society of the spectacle.* Oakland, Calif.: AK Press.

Decker, Scott, and Margaret Chapman. 2008. *Drug smugglers on drug smuggling: Lessons from the inside.* Philadelphia: Temple Univ. Press.

Deleuze, Gilles, and Felix Guattari. 1983. *Anti-Oedipus: Capitalism and schizophrenia.* Minneapolis: Univ. of Minnesota Press.

Dennis, Phillip. 2003. Cocaine in Miskitu villages. *Ethnology* 42, no. 2: 161–172.

Diario, El. 2008. Decomisan al narcomenudeo solo medio kilo de cocaína. January 17. http://www.diario.com.mx/templates/nota_servicios/print.php?notaid (accessed January 17, 2008).

Díaz-Cotto, Juanita. 2006. *Chicana lives and criminal justice: Voices from el barrio.* Austin: Univ. of Texas Press.

Dick, Philip K. 1991 [1977]. *A scanner darkly.* New York: Vintage.

Dobkin de Rios, Marlene. 1984. *Visionary vine: Hallucinogenic healing in the Peruvian Amazon.* Prospect Heights, Ill.: Waveland.

Douglas, Mary. 1978. *Purity and danger: An analysis of concepts of pollution and taboo.* London: Routledge.

Dugan, Richard. 1997. Benefit of location: The national rationing system and El Paso, Texas, 1942–1945. MA thesis, University of Texas–El Paso.

Dunn, Timothy. 1996. *The militarization of the U.S.–Mexico border, 1978–1992.* Austin: Univ. of Texas, Center for Mexican American Studies, CMAS Books.

Edberg, Mark. 2004. *El narcotraficante: Narcocorridos and the construction of a cultural persona on the U.S.–Mexico border.* Austin: Univ. of Texas Press.

Eddy, Paul, Hugo Sabogal, and Sara Walden. 1988. *The cocaine wars: Murder, money, corruption, and the world's most valuable commodity.* New York: Norton.

Ferguson, James. 2006. *Global shadows: Africa in the neoliberal world order.* Durham, N.C.: Duke Univ. Press.

Flores, Paul. 2001. *Along the border lies.* Berkeley, Calif.: Creative Arts.

Ford, Don Henry, Jr. 2005. *Contrabando: Confessions of a drug-smuggling Texas cowboy*. El Paso: Cinco Puntos.

Foucault, Michel. 1967. Of other spaces (1967): Heterotopias. http://foucault .info/documents/heteroTopia/foucault.heteroTopia.en.html (accessed January 31, 2008).

Friedrich, Paul. 1987. *The princes of Naranja: An essay in anthrohistorical method*. Austin: Univ. of Texas Press.

Furst, Peter, ed. 1972. *Flesh of the gods: The ritual use of hallucinogens*. Prospect Heights, Ill.: Waveland.

Geffray, Christian. 2002. Introduction: Drug trafficking and the state. In *Globalisation, drugs and criminalisation*, edited by Christian Geffray, Guilhem Fabre, and Michel Schiray, 1–5. Paris: UNESCO. CD-ROM.

Gilot, Louie. 2007. Message on cardboard left on slain man's body. *El Paso Times*, August 3.

Glendinning, Chellis. 2005. *A village takes on the heroin trade*. Gabriola Island, Canada: New Society.

Gómez, María Idalia, and Darío Fritz. 2005. *Con la muerte en el bolsillo: Seis desaforadas historias del narcotráfico en México*. Mexico City: Planeta.

Gootenberg, Paul, ed. 1999. *Cocaine: Global histories*. New York: Routledge.

Grillo, Ioan. 2007. Who is killing Mexico's musicians? *Time*, December 24. http://205.188.238.109/time/world/article/0,8599,1698119,00.html (accessed February 7, 2008).

Gupta, Akhil, and James Ferguson, eds. 1997. *Culture, power, place: Explorations in critical anthropology*. Durham, N.C.: Duke Univ. Press.

Habermas, Jürgen. 1991. *The structural transformation of the public sphere: An inquiry into a category of bourgeois society*. Translated by Thomas Burger. Cambridge, Mass.: MIT Press.

Hansen, Thomas, and Finn Stepputat. 2005. Introduction to *Sovereign bodies: Citizens, migrants and states in the postcolonial world*, edited by Thomas Hansen and Finn Stepputat, 1–26. Princeton, N.J.: Princeton Univ. Press.

Hardt, Michael, and Antonio Negri. 2001. *Empire*. Cambridge, Mass.: Harvard Univ. Press.

Heyman, Josiah. 1995. Putting power in the anthropology of bureaucracy. *Current Anthropology* 36, no. 2: 261–287.

———. 2001. Class and classification at the U.S.–Mexico border. *Human Organization* 60, no. 2: 128–139.

———. 2002. U.S. immigration officers of Mexican ancestry as Mexican Americans, citizens, and immigration police. *Current Anthropology* 43, no. 3: 479–507.

———. 2004. Ports of entry as nodes in the world system. *Identities* 11:303–327.

Heyman, Josiah, and Howard Campbell. 2007. Corruption in the U.S. borderlands with Mexico: The "purity" of society and the "perversity" of borders. In *Corruption and the secret of the law: A legal anthropological perspective*, edited by Monique Nuijten and Gerhard Anders, 191–217. Aldershot, UK: Ashgate.

Heyman, Josiah, and Alan Smart. 1999. States and illegal practices: An overview. In *States and illegal practices*, edited by Josiah Heyman, 1–24. Oxford: Berg.

Hoffer, Lee. 2006. *Junkie business: The evolution and operation of a heroin dealing network.* Belmont, Calif.: Thomson Wadsworth.

Jiménez, Benito. 2008. Emplea el narco nuevos "trucos" en sus entregas. *El Diario,* March 2.

Kafka, Franz. 2003. *The castle.* Adapted by David Fishelson and Aaron Leichter from a dramatization by Max Brod. New York: Dramatist's Play Service.

Kamstra, Jerry. 1974. *Weed: Adventures of a dope smuggler.* New York: Harper and Row.

Katz, Friedrich. 1998. *The life and times of Pancho Villa.* Stanford, Calif.: Stanford Univ. Press.

Katz, Jack. 1988. *Seductions of crime: Moral and sensual attractions in doing evil.* New York: Basic Books.

Knauft, Bruce. 2007. Provincializing America: Imperialism, capitalism, and counterhegemony in the twenty-first century. *Current Anthropology* 48, no. 6: 781–805.

Kopinak, Kathryn. 1996. *Desert capitalism: Maquiladoras in North America's western industrial corridor.* Tucson: Univ. of Arizona Press.

Kuykendall, James. 2005. *¿O plata o plomo? Silver or lead? The abduction and murder of DEA agent Kiki Camarena.* Xlibris [online publisher].

Levine, Michael. 2000. *Deep cover: The inside story of how DEA infighting, incompetence, and subterfuge lost us the biggest battle of the drug war.* iUniverse [online publisher].

Lupsha, Peter. 1991. Drug lords and narco-corruption: The players change but the game continues. *Crime, Law and Social Control* 16:41–58.

Lupsha, Peter, and Kip Schlegel. 1980. *The political economy of drug trafficking: The Herrera organization.* Working Paper 2. Albuquerque: Univ. of New Mexico, Latin American Institute.

Lugo, Alejandro. 2000. Theorizing border inspections. *Cultural Dynamics* 12, no. 3: 353–373.

Lutz, Catherine. 2006. Empire is in the details. *American Ethnologist* 33:593–611.

Macdonald, David. 2007. *Drugs in Afghanistan: Opium, outlaws, and scorpion tales.* London and Ann Arbor: Pluto Press.

Malkin, Victoria. 2001. Narcotrafficking, migration, and modernity in rural Mexico. *Latin American Perspectives* 28:101–128.

Marez, Curtis. 2004. *Drug wars: The political economy of narcotics.* Minneapolis: Univ. of Minnesota Press.

Maril, Robert Lee. 2004. *Patrolling chaos: The U.S. Border Patrol in deep South Texas.* Lubbock: Texas Tech Univ. Press.

Marks, Howard. 1998. *Mr. Nice.* London: Vintage.

Martínez, Oscar. 1978. *Border boom town: Ciudad Juárez since 1848.* Austin: Univ. of Texas Press.

McCoy, Alfred. 1999. Requiem for a drug lord: State and commodity in the career of Khun Sa. In *States and illegal practices,* edited by Josiah Heyman, 129–167. Oxford: Berg.

McDonald, James. 2005. The narcoeconomy and small-town, rural Mexico. *Human Organization* 64, no. 2: 115–125.

Mendoza, Elmer. 2001. *Un asesino solitario.* Barcelona: Tusquets.

Miller, Joel. 2004. Why drug cops can't win. *WorldNet Daily,* June 18. http://www.worldnetdaily.com/news/article.asp?ARTICLE_ID=39026 (accessed February 1, 2008).

Mills, James. 1986. *The underground empire: Where crime and governments embrace.* New York: Dell.

Mintz, Sidney. 1986. *Sweetness and power: The place of sugar in modern history.* New York: Penguin.

Molano, Alfredo. 2004. *Loyal soldiers in the cocaine kingdom: Tales of drugs, mules, and gunmen.* New York: Columbia Univ. Press.

Morales, Edmundo. 1990. *Cocaine: White gold rush in Peru.* Tucson: Univ. of Arizona Press.

Naim, Moises. 2006. *Illicit: How smugglers, traffickers and copycats are hijacking the global economy.* New York: Anchor.

Nevins, Joseph. 2002. *Operation Gatekeeper: The rise of the "illegal alien" and the making of the U.S.-Mexico boundary.* New York: Routledge.

Nordstrom, Carolyn. 2007. *Global outlaws: Crime, money, and power in the contemporary world.* Berkeley and Los Angeles: Univ. of California Press.

Nuijten, Monique, and Gerhard Anders, eds. 2007. *Corruption and the secret of the law: A legal anthropological perspective.* Aldershot, UK: Ashgate.

Ong, Aihwa. 1999. *Flexible citizenship: The cultural logics of transnationality.* Durham, N.C.: Duke Univ. Press.

———. 2006. Experiments with freedom: Milieus of the human. *American Literary History* 18:229–244.

Ovalle, Lilián Paola. 2007. Las fronteras de la "narcocultura." *@Juárez,* August 24. http://www.arrobajuarez.com/news/imprime.php?IDNOTA=3943 (accessed December 26, 2007).

Packer, George. 2006. Knowing the enemy: Can social scientists redefine the "war on terror"? *New Yorker,* December 18. http://www.newyorker.com/archive/2006/12/18/061218fa_fact2 (accessed February 7, 2008).

Páez Varela, Alejandro. 2007. Historias del narcotráfico. *Letras Libres,* November. http://www.letraslibres.com/index.php?art=12456 (accessed November 5, 2007).

Pape, Robert. 2005. *Dying to win: The strategic logic of suicide terrorism.* New York: Random House.

Payán, Tony. 2006. The drug war and the U.S.-Mexico border: What does not kill you, makes you stronger. *South Atlantic Quarterly* 105, no. 4: 863–880.

Pérez-Reverte, Arturo. 2004. *The queen of the south.* New York: Putnam.

Poppa, Terrence. 1998. *Drug lord: The life and death of a Mexican kingpin.* Seattle: Demand Publications.

Quiñones, Sam. 2007. *Antonio's gun and Delfino's dream: True tales of Mexican migration.* Albuquerque: Univ. of New Mexico Press.

Ravelo, Ricardo. 2005. *Los capos: Las narco-rutas de México.* Mexico City: Plaza y Janés.

———. 2006. *Los Narcoabogados.* Mexico City: Grijalbo.

———. 2007a. Bajo la amenaza del pacto. *Proceso* 1606 (August 12, 2007): 6–9.

———. 2007b. Los capos se reparten territorios. *Proceso* 1600 (July 1, 2007): 6–12.

———. 2007c. *Crónicas de sangre: Cinco historias de los Zetas.* Mexico City: Random House Mondadori.

———. 2007d. *Herencia maldita: El reto de Calderón y el nuevo mapa del narcotráfico.* Mexico City: Grijalbo.

———. 2007e. Policías al servicio del narco. *Proceso* 1600 (July 1, 2007): 8–9.

———. 2008. El narco es ya una estructura nacional. *Proceso* 1664 (September 21, 2008): 6–11.

Recio, Gabriela. 2002. Drugs and alcohol: U.S. prohibition and the origins of the drug trade in Mexico, 1910–1930. *Journal of Latin American Studies* 34:21–42.

Reinarman, Craig, and Harry Levine. 2004. Crack in the rearview mirror: Deconstructing drug war mythology. *Social Justice* 31, nos. 1–2: 182–199.

Richardson, Chad, and Rosalva Resendiz. 2006. *On the edge of the law: Culture, labor, and deviance on the South Texas border.* Austin: Univ. of Texas Press.

Roig-Franzia, Manuel. 2007. Mexican drug cartels move north; U.S. effort to battle groups is flawed, GAO report says. *Washington Post,* September 20. http://www.washingtonpost.com/wp-dyn/content/article/2007/09/19/AR2007091902442.html (accessed July 18, 2008).

Ronquillo, Víctor. 2006. *Un corresponsal en la guerra del narco.* Mexico City: Ediciones B.

Roseberry, William. 1989. *Anthropologies and histories: Essays in culture, history, and political economy.* New Brunswick, N.J.: Rutgers Univ. Press.

Sabbag, Robert. 1998 [1976]. *Snow blind: A brief career in the cocaine trade.* Edinburgh: Canongate.

———. 2002. *Loaded: A misadventure on the marijuana trail.* Boston: Little, Brown.

Sanabria, Harry. 1993. *The coca boom and rural social change in Bolivia.* Ann Arbor: Univ. of Michigan Press.

Sanchez, Stephanie. 2008. Agent's death "devastating." *El Paso Times,* January 22.

Sanders, Todd. 2008. Buses in Bongoland: Seductive analytics and the occult. *Anthropological Theory* 8, no. 2: 107–132.

Sas, Luis Ángel. 2007. Yo quiero ser narco. *El Periodico de Guatemala,* September 28. http://www.elperiodico.com.gt/es/20070929/14/44155 (accessed October 1, 2007).

Schaefer, Stacy, and Peter Furst, eds. 1997. *People of the peyote: Huichol Indian history, religion, and survival.* Albuquerque: Univ. of New Mexico Press.

Schlosser, Eric. 2003. *Reefer madness: Sex, drugs, and the American black market.* Boston: Houghton Mifflin.

Schneider, Jane, and Peter Schneider. 2005. Mafia, antimafia, and the plural cultures of Sicily. *Current Anthropology* 46, no. 4: 501–520.

Scott, James. 1999. *Seeing like a state: How certain schemes to improve the human condition have failed.* New Haven, Conn.: Yale Univ. Press.

Scott, Peter Dale. 1996. *Deep politics and the death of JFK.* Berkeley and Los Angeles: Univ. of California Press.

Shannon, Elaine. 1988. *Desperados: Latin drug lords, U.S. lawmen, and the war America can't win.* New York: Viking.

Singer, Merrill. 2006. *Something dangerous: Emergent and changing illicit drug use and community health.* Long Grove, Ill.: Waveland.

Staudt, Kathy. 1998. *Free trade? Informal economies at the U.S.–Mexico border.* Philadelphia: Temple Univ. Press.

Strong, Arturo Carrillo. 1990. *Corrido de cocaine: Inside stories of hard drugs, big money, and short lives.* Tucson, Ariz.: Harbinger House.

Sullivan, Mercer. 1990. *"Getting paid": Youth crime and work in the inner city.* Ithaca, N.Y.: Cornell Univ. Press.

Taussig, Michael. 1992a. *The nervous system.* New York: Routledge.

———. 1992b. *Mimesis and alterity: A particular history of the senses.* New York: Routledge.

———. 2003. *Law in a lawless land: Diary of a limpieza in Colombia.* New York: New Press.

———. 2004. *My cocaine museum.* Chicago: Univ. of Chicago Press.

Terkel, Studs. 1974. *Working: People talk about what they do all day and how they feel about what they do.* New York: Pantheon. Reprint, New York: Free Press, 2004.

Tobar, Héctor, and Cecilia Sánchez. 2007. In Mexico's drug trade, no glitter for grunts. *Los Angeles Times,* December 6. http://www.latimes.com/news/nationworld/columnone/la-fg-hitmen6dec06,1,5696247.story (accessed February 7, 2008).

Toro, María Celia. 1995. *Mexico's "war" on drugs: Causes and consequences.* Boulder, Colo.: Rienner.

U.S. Office of National Drug Control Policy. 2008. *National Drug Control Strategy: 2008 Annual Report.* http://www.ondcp.gov/publications/policy/ndcs08/2008ndcs.pdf (accessed November 24, 2008).

Valdez, Diana Washington. 2002. Officials link 2 charged in FBI beating with gang. *El Paso Times,* September 18.

———. 2005. *La cosecha de mujeres: El safari mexicano.* Mexico City: Oceano.

Valentine, Douglas. 2006. *The strength of the wolf: The secret history of America's war on drugs.* London: Verso.

Valenzuela, José Manuel. 2002. *Jefe de jefes: Corridos y narcocultura en México.* Mexico City: Plaza y Janés.

Van Schendel, Willem, and Itty Abraham. 2005. *Illicit flows and criminal things: States, borders, and the other side of globalization.* Bloomington: Indiana Univ. Press.

Wald, Elijah. 2001. *Narcocorrido: A journey into the music of drugs, guns, and guerrillas.* New York: HarperCollins.

Walker, William. 1996. *Drugs in the Western Hemisphere: An odyssey of cultures in conflict.* Wilmington, Del.: Scholarly Resources.

Wallerstein, Immanuel. 2003. *The decline of American power: The U.S. in a chaotic world.* New York: Norton.

Webb, Gary. 1998. *Dark alliance: The CIA, the Contras, and the crack cocaine explosion.* New York: Seven Stories Press.

Weimann, Gabriel. 2008. The psychology of mass-mediated terrorism. *American Behavioral Scientist* 52, no. 1: 69–86.

West, Harry, and Todd Sanders, eds. 2003. *Transparency and conspiracy: Ethnographies of suspicion in the new world order.* Durham, N.C.: Duke Univ. Press.

Whiteford, Michael. 2002. Business as usual or unusual business: Accommodation and adjustment to drug dealers, guerrilla movements, and paramilitary terrorism in Colombia. *Human Organization* 61, no. 2: 107–112.

Wilson, James. 2001. Against the legalization of drugs. In *The American drug scene: An anthology,* edited by James Inciardi and Karen McElrath, 440–449. Los Angeles: Roxbury.

Wolf, Eric. 1966. *Sons of the shaking earth: The people of Mexico and Guatemala; Their land, history, and culture.* Chicago: Univ. of Chicago Press.

———. 1982. *Europe and the people without history.* Berkeley and Los Angeles: Univ. of California Press.

Index